MARY McCARTHY

GARLAND REFERENCE LIBRARY
OF THE HUMANITIES
(VOL. 1251)

Mary McCarthy: Going to Vassar as a Freshman, 1929.
Photo credit: Henri Jacobs. Courtesy, Vassar College
Library.

MARY McCARTHY
An Annotated Bibliography

Joy Bennett
Gabriella Hochmann

GARLAND PUBLISHING, INC. • NEW YORK & LONDON
1992

Library of Congress Cataloging-in-Publication Data

Bennett, Joy, 1946–
    Mary McCarthy : an annotated bibliography / Joy Bennett, Gabriella
Hochmann.
        p.   cm. — (Garland reference library of the humanities ; vol.
1251)
    Includes index.
    ISBN 0–8240–7028–3
    1. McCarthy, Mary, 1912–   —Bibliography. I. Hochmann,
Gabriella, 1946–   . II. Title. III. Series.
Z8531.8.B46   1992
[PS3525.A1435]
016.8185′209—dc20   91–47702
                                                              CIP

Printed on acid-free, 250-year-life paper
Manufactured in the United States of America

Dedication

This book is dedicated to the three children who came into our lives during the writing of this book--Joy Bennett's daughter, Marian Caroline, and Gabriella Hochmann's niece and nephew, Michelle Karpman and Simon Elijah Hochmann. We hope that Mary McCarthy's wit and intelligence will be a source of inspiration to them all.

Contents

Book Reviews cont'd

Acknowledgments

A project of this magnitude would not be such a pleasure to undertake if it were not for the research assistants who have been with us over the years and through various undertakings, and who have once again contributed their enthusiasm and expertise. We are indebted to both Anne Wade Stephen and Elyse Greenberg for the exceptionally precise, intelligent, and above all good-natured manner in which they approached and completed this project. Under our very loose direction, Anne and Elyse organized the masses of citations and created an ordered, clean database from which to work. They assisted with the writing of the annotations and input most of the material. As one of the staff members in the Concordia University Libraries Interlibrary Loans Department, Elyse is to be credited with tracking down many of the more elusive articles and books, leaving no source untapped. She also did the copy editing with a sense of care and responsibility that are rare. Anne was responsible for the formatting of the book. Her attention to detail and patience with checking and rechecking the individual entries have much to do with the quality of our final product. They both have our heartfelt appreciation.

We would like to express our gratitude for the experience and encouragement of Jacqueline Dealy who was responsible for much of the initial online and manual searching. Thanks are also due to Irene Fernandez who wrote the English annotations for the Italian articles and to John Kipphoff for the German.

Some of the articles about McCarthy were made available to us by her American and British publishers. In many cases we were familiar with these citations but incomplete references had made locating them impossible. We are grateful to the publishers for helping us piece together the jig-saw puzzle and produce a more complete bibliography. In particular we would like to acknowledge Simon Cobley of Weidenfeld and Nicolson and Jean Rose of the Octopus Publishing Group.

The frontispiece photograph of McCarthy was generously made available to us by Nancy McKechine of Vassar College Library.

This research was made possible by a strategic grant from the Social Science and Humanities Research Council of Canada and supported by the Concordia University Libraries.

Introduction

We had no sooner completed the final manuscript for SIMONE
DE BEAUVOIR: AN ANNOTATED BIBLIOGRAPHY (Garland,
1988) than we began to look about for a suitable candidate for our next
project. As academic librarians, we read the book reviewing journals
on a regular basis. Call it serendipity, but featured on the front page of
THE NEW YORK TIMES BOOK REVIEW of May 8, 1988 was a
review of Carol Gelderman's MARY MCCARTHY: A LIFE. Our
search ended then and there; Mary McCarthy was an obvious choice.

McCarthy was an outspoken, intelligent woman who wrote about
topical and controversial issues, in many ways an American counterpart
of De Beauvoir. Although McCarthy was most assuredly not a fan of
De Beauvoir and did in fact dislike the inevitable comparisons, it is
clear that these two formidable women, coming from similar socio-
economic circumstances, albeit a continent apart, were both brilliant,
gifted writers who attempted to unflinchingly expose the truth.

McCarthy's political views were an integral part of her life and
her work. Her conversion to the political left began with her
association with THE PARTISAN REVIEW. At the onset of World
War II she showed no support for the war, either theoretically or
practically, believing it to be a rivalry of imperialists, and maintained
that the United States ought not to be drawn in. Later she spoke out
vociferously against U.S. involvement in Vietnam, and on her "fact-
finding" trip to Vietnam admitted that she had gone with the
preconceived notion of American guilt.

McCarthy wrote nine books of fiction and fifteen books of
nonfiction as well as numerous reviews, essays and short stories all in a

xi

style distinctively her own--sharp, biting and witty. It is however as a novelist that she is best known. Throughout her career, neither academics nor intellectuals, progressives nor terrorists have escaped her penetrating gaze. Passionately engaged with questions of truth and social conscience, her work consistently reflected her own life and concerns. She viewed the relationship between life and literature as one of "mutual plagiarism," and used friends and colleagues as real-life models for many of the characters in her books, often with devastating effect. The publication of THE GROUP in 1963 put her on the international literary map. A "cause celebre," its seduction scene was considered shocking, both in its explicit detail and,more importantly, in that it was written from a woman's point of view. Critical response to her work has always been varied, from the lyrically positive to the hostile negative. Nonetheless, nothing dissuaded her from continuing to write, to explore and probe the delicate and difficult issues of the times.

Mary Therese McCarthy was born in Seattle, Washington on June 21, 1912 into an upper middle class American family. When she was six years old the influenza epidemic, which killed half a million Americans, took the lives of both her parents.The change in her life was overwhelming. One moment Mary and her three brothers were cherished children of loving parents; the next, orphans packed off to live with an elderly aunt and uncle, seemingly selected as guardians on the basis of "availability." Margaret and Myers Shriver were fixated on rules and discipline; Margaret supervised every detail of Mary's life, while Myers once beat her with a razor strap after she won a city and state-wide essay contest to make sure she didn't become "stuck-up." Stifled by this cold and austere environment, she turned to the Catholic Church as the only permissible outlet for her aesthetic sensibilities.

When she was eleven years old Mary was "rescued" by her maternal grandparents. They provided a nice home, fashionable clothes, good schools, books, and most important, affection and encouragement. She was permitted to read, study and learn, and managed to manoeuvre sufficient freedom to lose both her faith and her virginity by age fourteen.

McCarthy attended Vassar College, graduating in 1933. Like Kay Strong in THE GROUP, McCarthy was the "first to run around the table" at the graduation dinner, a ritual indicating that she was engaged to be married. The story of Kay and Harald Peterson's wedding and short-lived marriage was an almost exact rendering of

McCarthy's own marriage to Harold Johnsrud. Subsequent marriages to critic Edmund Wilson, with whom she had a son, and to Bowden Broadwater, ended unhappily. Only with her marriage to James West, a career diplomat, did she find lasting joy and contentment.

Throughout her career McCarthy was the consummate writer; scrupulous in her use of language, she had an intense belief in the power of the pen. She wrote almost constantly from the early 1930s until her death in 1989. Her own output was prodigious and the criticism about her kept pace. She has been acclaimed as a master of the English sentence and critics have agreed that her prose style was exceptional. This style, coupled with her innate intelligence, and sharp and ready wit made her truly an American woman of letters, with few, if any, equals. Yet, in the words of Gretchen Munroe, it may well be the "brutal honesty of her confrontations" that is ultimately responsible for McCarthy's place in the "mainstream of modern American writing." She was a perfectionist, setting exceedingly high standards, for herself no less than for the world around her. Shortly after the publication of HOW I GREW, she was asked for a self-assessment-- "not favourable," she replied. Would she have agreed with Robert Browning's view that "man's reach should exceed his grasp or what's a heaven for?"

As bibliographers we feel privileged to have discovered this remarkable woman. We hope this work will assist other researchers and scholars in their explorations of the life and work of Mary McCarthy.

Joy Bennett
Gabriella Hochmann
Montreal, Canada
December 1991

Notes

Envisioned primarily for the use of McCarthy scholars, this
bibliography of works by and about Mary McCarthy, a woman whose
aim was, in her own words, to make "a contribution to the sanity of
our times," may in addition prove a valuable source for an exploration
of contemporary American social and political history.

Our intention was to make the bibliography as comprehensive in
scope as possible. To this end we searched all major national and
international indices, for the years 1935 to 1991, print format and online. We also relied on: Goldman, Sherli Evans. MARY MCCARTHY:
A BIBLIOGRAPHY. N.Y.: Harcourt Brace, 1968; Schweyer, Janet.
"L'Oeuvre de Mary McCarthy devant la critique: première
bibliographie des livres, articles et recensions parus jusqu'en 1970."
RECHERCHES ANGLAISES ET AMERICAINES 4 (1971); clipping
files from McCarthy's British publisher, William Heinemann; and
George Weidenfeld & Nicolson for the reviews of HOW I GREW.
Several of the citations from Heinemann could not be confirmed in a
second source and as such have been noted with "Citation not verified."

The bibliography is predominantly comprised of English
language material, with some French, German and Italian.

The bibliography has been arranged in two major sections--
Works By McCarthy in section one; and **Works About McCarthy** in
section two. All items have been numbered sequentially. The first
section, **Works By McCarthy**, includes Books, Essays, Short Stories,
Book Reviews, Theater and Film Reviews, Translations, Letters to the
Editor, Miscellanea and Interviews. Because we set up a classification
of her work by either fiction or nonfiction, we decided to put the short

stories which later appeared in her autobiographical works, in the nonfiction section as essays. The original publication is the main entry for all items. Subsequent publications have been listed with the note "also published in." Any revisions to the original have been noted. We have attempted to list all editions of the books, including foreign editions. A contents note with article titles and dates of original publication has been appended for all McCarthy's books. All essays, book/theater reviews have been indexed by name and title to provide additional information about their content. Translations of individual essays have been noted.

The second section, **Works About McCarthy**, includes General Criticism, Book Reviews, Theses, Biographies and Obituaries. We have also included the Goldman Bibliography with its reviews in this section because we felt it provided a different perspective of McCarthy's career. General Criticism covers major studies of McCarthy or background studies that include substantial reference to her work. Letters to the Editor dealing with various reviews of her books, or providing general comments have been placed in this chapter. All named persons/titles have been indexed. Book Reviews have been restricted to articles that discuss one or two of her books. Articles discussing three or more of her books have been placed in the General Criticism chapter with the book titles indexed. In the case of reviews that discuss two books, an entry appears for each book, but the annotation appears only with the book that was published first. A "see" reference has been provided with the second entry. The items have all been arranged chronologically within each chapter. The Theses chapter includes both Master's and Ph.D. dissertations written at North American institutions. The chapter on Biographies was divided into a section on book length biographies complete with reviews of those biographies, and a second section devoted to articles appearing in biographical sources. The latter have not been annotated. All annotations were intended to be objective rather than evaluative and were meant to provide an idea of the scope and content of the article or book. In cases where one article refers to, or is in response to another, a note to that effect has been added.

We have provided two indexes--Author and Named Person/Title. The Author Index includes the names of all authors, editors, compilers and translators of all cited works. The Named Person/Title Index includes major references to individuals, books, journal titles, films and plays. It should be noted that it is the actual article that has been indexed and not the abstract; therefore names and titles listed in the index, although an indicator of significance in the original article, do not necessarily appear in the abstract. Short stories have not been indexed. Bold faced item numbers in the index indicate that the item appears in the first section--**Works By McCarthy**.

SECTION I - WORKS BY McCARTHY

Books

1. THE COMPANY SHE KEEPS. New York: Simon & Schuster; Harcourt, Brace & Co., 1942, 304p.

   Contents:
   "Cruel and Barbarous Treatment" originally published in SOUTHERN REVIEW (Spring 1939); "The Man in the Brooks Brothers Shirt" in PARTISAN REVIEW (July-August 1941); "The Genial Host" in SOUTHERN REVIEW (Autumn 1941); and "Ghostly Father, I Confess" in HARPER'S BAZAAR (April 1942).

   "Portrait of the Intellectual as a Yale Man" and "Rogue's Gallery" were not previously published. "Portrait of the Intellectual as a Yale Man" was also published in THE ROOSEVELT ERA, edited by Crane Milton. 253-298. New York: Boni & Gaer, 1947.

   a) **British edition:** THE COMPANY SHE KEEPS. London: Weidenfeld & Nicolson, 1943.

   b) **Paperback edition:** THE COMPANY SHE KEEPS. New York: Dell Pub., 1955, 223p.

   c) **Second British edition:** THE COMPANY SHE KEEPS. 2d ed. London: Weidenfeld & Nicolson, 1957, 246p.

d) **Hebrew edition**: Deror, Z. and Etan Korngold, trans. HA-HEVRA VAH HI MEVALAH, OMANUT HA-NISSUIN HA-MEUSSARIM. Tel Aviv: Ziw, 1962, 374p. (Translation of THE COMPANY SHE KEEPS and COURS DE BONHEUR CONJUGAL by André Maurois.)

e) **Second American edition**: THE COMPANY SHE KEEPS. New York: Harcourt, Brace & Co., c1960, 304p.

f) **Italian edition**: Daré, Augusta, trans. GLI UOMINI DELLA SUA VITA. Milan: Giangiacomo Feltrinelli Editore, 1962, 312p.

g) **French edition**: Lévi, Angélique, trans. DIS-MOI QUI TU HANTES. Série Domaine étranger. Paris: Editions Stock, 1963, 231p.

h) **British paperback edition**: Harmondsworth: Penguin Books, 1965, 224p.

i) **German edition**: Soellner, Hedda and Rolf Soellner, trans. SIE UND DIE ANDEREN. Munich: Droemer-Knaur, c1965, 317p.

j) **Dutch edition**: Ferguson, Margaretha, trans. EERSTE PERSOON MEERVOUD. Amsterdam: Polak & Van Gennep Uitgeversmaatschappij N.V., 1966, 276p.

k) **Second German edition**: Soellner, Hedda and Rolf Soellner, trans. SIE UND DIE ANDEREN. Vienna: Buchgeneinschoft Donauland, 1967.

l) **German paperback edition**: Soellner, Hedda and Rolf Soellner, trans. SIE UND DIE ANDEREN. Munich: Droemer-Knaur, 1968, 200p.

m) **Romanian edition**: Stanescu, Sarina, trans. MARGARET SARGENT SI LUMEA EI. Bucharest: Editura Pentru Literatura Universala, 1969.

n) **Yugoslavian edition**: Crnkovic, Zlatko, trans. ONA I NJEZINO DRUSTVO. Rijeka: Otokar Kersovani, 1971.

o) **Second British paperback edition**: THE COMPANY SHE KEEPS. Harmondsworth: Penguin, 1975, 224p.

p) **Second French edition**: Lévi, Angélique, trans. DIS-MOI QUI TU HANTES. Paris: Union Générale d'éditions, 1986.

2. THE OASIS. New York: Random House, 1949, 181p.

Originally published as "The Oasis" in HORIZON (February 1949). Also published in: CAST A COLD EYE. 131-212. New York: Harcourt, Brace & World, 1950.

a) **British edition**: A SOURCE OF EMBARRASSMENT. London: Heinemann, 1950, 152p.

b) **British paperback edition**: A SOURCE OF EMBARRASSMENT. London: Panther Books, 1964.

c) **German edition**: Zedlitz, Ursula, trans. DIE OASE. Munich: Droemer-Knaur, c1965, 132p.

d) **Dutch edition**: Koning, Dolf, trans. DE OASE. Amsterdam: Meulenhoff, 1973, 158p.

e) **French edition**: Hechter, Michèle, trans. L'OASIS ET AUTRES RECITS. Paris: Fayard, 1988, 244p. (Includes two essays from HOUNDS OF SUMMER AND OTHER STORIES. New York: Avon Books, 1981.)

3. CAST A COLD EYE. New York: Harcourt, Brace & World, 1950, 212p.

Contents:
"The Blackguard" was originally published in NEW YORKER

(October 12, 1946); "C.Y.E." in MADEMOISELLE (April 1944); "The Cicerone" in PARTISAN REVIEW (February 1948); "Friend of the Family" in TOWN & COUNTRY (January 1947); "The Old Men" in NEW YORKER (May 20, 1950); "The Weeds" in NEW YORKER (September 16, 1944); and "Yonder Peasant, Who Is He?" in NEW YORKER (December 4, 1948).

a) **British edition**: CAST A COLD EYE. London: William Heinemann, 1952, 169p.

b) **Spanish edition**: Grau, Maria Angélica, trans. MIRALO FRIAMENTE. Santiago: Zig-Zag, [1968]. (Not seen)

c) **Russian edition**: Radman, Ju, trans. OKIN' HOLODNYM VZGLJADOM. Moscow: Gvardiia, 1970.

d) **Paperback edition**: CAST A COLD EYE. New York: New American Library, 1972, 212p.

4. A SOURCE OF EMBARRASSMENT. London: Heinemann, 1950, 193p.

Originally published as THE OASIS. New York: Random House, 1949.

Also published: A SOURCE OF EMBARRASSMENT. London: Panther Books, c1964, 127p.

5. THE GROVES OF ACADEME. New York: Harcourt, Brace & Co., 1952, 302p.

Chapter one was originally published in somewhat different form as "The Groves of Academe" in NEW YORKER (February 3, 1951).

Pages 63-67 were also published as "Life at Jocelyn College" in
EDUCATION IN SOCIETY: READINGS, edited by Bernard N.
Meltzer, Harry R. Doby, and Philip H. Smith. 74-76. New
York: Thomas Y. Crowell Co., 1958 and as "Jocelyn College"
in AMERICAN SATIRE IN PROSE AND VERSE, edited by
Henry C. Carlisle. 248-253. New York: Random House, 1962.

a) **British edition**: THE GROVES OF ACADEME. London:
William Heinemann, 1953, 272p.

b) **Paperback edition**: THE GROVES OF ACADEME. New
York: New American Library, 1963, 255p.

c) **British paperback edition**: THE GROVES OF ACADEME.
London: Panther Books, 1964, 223p.

d) **Spanish edition**: Varela, Mireya, trans. ARBOLEDAS
UNIVERSITARIAS. Santiago, Chile: Zig-Zag, 1968, 251p.

e) **Dutch edition**: Metsalaar, D., trans. DE ACADEMISCHE
VELDEN. Amsterdam: Meulenhoff, 1978, 261p.

6. A CHARMED LIFE. New York: Harcourt, Brace & Co., 1955,
    313p.

    Chapter one was originally published in somewhat different form
    as "A Charmed Life" in NEW YORKER (October 9, 1954).

    a) **British edition**: A CHARMED LIFE. London: Weidenfeld
    & Nicolson, 1956, 335p.

    b) **French edition**: Meunier, Denyse, trans. LA VIE
    D'ARTISTE. Paris: Librairie Plon, 1957.

    c) **Paperback edition**: A CHARMED LIFE. New York: Dell
    Pub., 1958.

d) **Dutch edition**: Lanson, H.S., trans. BOHEMIENS ZIJN OOK MENSEN. Laren: A.G. Schoonderbeek, 1961, 234p.

e) **Second paperback edition**: A CHARMED LIFE. New York: New American Library, 1964, 223p.

f) **British paperback edition**: A CHARMED LIFE. Harmondsworth: Penguin Books, 1964, 262p.

g) **Finnish edition**: Pennanen, Eilal and Aale Tynni, trans. LUMOTTU ELÄMÄ. Helsinki: Weilin & Göös, 1965, 316p.

h) **Italian edition**: Fantonetti, Carlo Rossi, trans. VITA STREGATA. Milan: Aldo Garzanti Editore, c1966, 287p.

i) **German edition**: Carlsson, Maria, trans. DER ZAUBERKREIS. Munich: Droemer-Knaur, 1967, 352p. (Originally published in DIE WELT (February 1966): all issues.)

j) **Revised French edition**: Lévi, Angélique, trans. LA VIE D'ARTISTE. Paris: Livres de Poche, c1967.

k) **Japanese edition**: Mariko, Fukamachi, trans. HYOHAKU NO TAMASHII. Tokyo: Kadokawa shoten, 1969, 420p.

l) **Spanish edition**: Ferrater, Gabriel, trans. UNA VIDA ENCANTADA. Barcelona: Editorial Lumen, 1971, 342p.

m) **Swedish edition**: Alfons, Harriet and Jadwiga P. Westrup, trans. LIVETS TROLLMAKT. Stockholm: Trevi, c1974.

7.   SIGHTS AND SPECTACLES 1937-1956. New York: Farrar, Straus & Cudahy, 1956, 183p.

Contents:
"Two Bad Cases of Social Conscience" originally published in a somewhat different form as "Theatre Chronicle" in PARTISAN REVIEW (December 1937); "Odets Deplored" as "Theatre

Chronicle" in PARTISAN REVIEW (January 1938);
"Elizabethan Revivals" as "Versions of Shakespeare" in
PARTISAN REVIEW (February 1938); "Class Angles and a
Wilder Classic" as "Class Angles and Classless Curves" in
PARTISAN REVIEW (April 1938); "The Federal Theatre" as
"The Federal Theatre Settles Down" in PARTISAN REVIEW
(May 1938); "Shaw and Chekhov" as "New Sets for the Old
House" in PARTISAN REVIEW (June 1938); "Saroyan, an
Innocent on Broadway" as "An Innocent on Broadway" in
PARTISAN REVIEW (March-April 1940); "THE SKIN OF
OUR TEETH" as "Chaos Is Come Again" in PARTISAN
REVIEW (January-February 1943); "The Russian Soul in
Wartime" as "The Russian Soul" in PARTISAN REVIEW
(March-April 1943); "Broadway's Spring Offensive" in
PARTISAN REVIEW (May-June 1943); "Wartime Omnibus" as
"Winter in the Theatre" in PARTISAN REVIEW (Spring 1944);
"We Must Have Faith" in PARTISAN REVIEW (Winter 1945);
"Eugene O'Neill--Dry Ice" as "Dry Ice" in PARTISAN
REVIEW (November-December 1946); "Five Curios" as
"Gerontion" in PARTISAN REVIEW (January-February 1947);
"George Kelly" as "Something About the Weather" in
PARTISAN REVIEW (March-April 1947); "The Unimportance
of Being Oscar" in PARTISAN REVIEW (May-June 1947);
"What a Piece of Work Is Man!" in PARTISAN REVIEW
(July-August 1947); "Four 'Well-Made' Plays" as "Props and
Property" in PARTISAN REVIEW (January 1948); "A Streetcar
Called Success" as "Oh, Sweet Mystery of Life" in PARTISAN
REVIEW (March 1948); "Little Theatre" as "Modest Proposals"
in PARTISAN REVIEW (April 1948); "A Prince of Shreds and
Patches" in PARTISAN REVIEW (January 1949); "The Little
Gate" as "Bard with Blood: Some Reflections on a Rare
Presentation Opening the City Center Season" in NEW YORK
TIMES (February 1, 1953); "Shaw Off Broadway" as "Shaw at
the Phoenix" in PARTISAN REVIEW (Spring 1955); "The
Family Tea Party" OBSERVER (July 24, 1955); and "The Will
and Testament of Ibsen" in PARTISAN REVIEW (Winter 1956).

"Three Plays with Music" (written June 1947) was not
previously published.

a) **Second edition**: SIGHTS AND SPECTACLES: THEATRE
CHRONICLES 1937-1956. New York: Meridian Books, 1957,
183p.

b) **British edition**: SIGHTS AND SPECTACLES: THEATRE
CHRONICLES 1937-1956. London: Heinemann, 1959, 202p.

c) **Augmented edition**: MARY McCARTHY'S THEATRE
CHRONICLES 1937-62. New York: Farrar, Straus & Co.,
1963, 248p.

8. VENICE OBSERVED: COMMENTS ON VENETIAN
CIVILIZATION. New York: Reynal & Co.; Paris: G. & R.
Bernier, 1956, 199p.

Originally published in different form as "Profiles: The Revel of
the Earth: Part I and II" in NEW YORKER (July 7; July 14,
1956).

a) **British edition**: VENICE OBSERVED: COMMENTS ON
VENETIAN CIVILIZATION. London: A. Zwemmer, 1956,
199p.

b) **French edition**: Sibon, Marcelle, trans. VENISE CONNUE
ET INCONNUE. Lausanne, Switzerland: Editions de l'Oeil,
1956, 223p.

c) **Second edition**: VENICE OBSERVED: COMMENTS ON
VENETIAN CIVILIZATION. New York: Reynal & Co.; Paris:
G. & R. Bernier, 1957, 199p.

d) **Second British edition**: VENICE OBSERVED:
COMMENTS ON VENETIAN CIVILIZATION. London:
Heinemann, 1961, 158p.

e) **Paperback edition**: VENICE OBSERVED: COMMENTS
ON VENETIAN CIVILIZATION. Harvest Book ed. New York:
Harcourt, Brace & World, 1963, 158p.

f) **German edition:** Zedlitz, Ursula, trans. VENEDIG. Munich: Droemer-Knaur, 1968, 154p.

g) **Augmented edition:** THE STONES OF FLORENCE AND VENICE OBSERVED. Harmondsworth: Penguin Books, c1972, 280p.

h) **Second German edition:** Zedlitz, Ursula, trans. VENEDIG. Munich: Kiepenheuer & Witsch, 1984, 154p.

i) **Third German edition:** Bethke, Ursula and Ursula Zedlitz, trans. FLORENZ. VENEDIG. Munich: Droemer-Knaur, 1973, 286p. (Includes translation of THE STONES OF FLORENCE.)

9. MEMORIES OF A CATHOLIC GIRLHOOD. New York: Harcourt, Brace & Co., 1957, 245p.

Contents:
"Yonder Peasant, Who Is He?" was originally published in somewhat different form in NEW YORKER (December 4, 1948); "A Tin Butterfly" in NEW YORKER (December 15, 1951); "The Blackguard" in NEW YORKER (October 12, 1946); "C'est le Premier Pas Qui Coûte" in NEW YORKER (July 12, 1952); "The Figures in the Clock" in NEW YORKER (February 28, 1953); "Yellowstone Park" in HARPER'S BAZAAR (November 1955); and "Ask Me No Questions" in NEW YORKER (March 23, 1957). "Names" was not previously published.

Pages 148-153 were published as "Miss Gowrie" in THE ACT OF WRITING AND READING: A COMBINED TEXT, edited by Alan Casty. 181-182. Englewood Cliffs, N.J.: Prentice-Hall, 1966.

a) **British edition:** MEMORIES OF A CATHOLIC GIRLHOOD. London: Heinemann, 1957, 226p.

b) **French edition:** Meunier, Denyse, trans. UNE JEUNE
FILLE SAGE. Paris: Librairie Plon, 1959, 245p.

c) **Paperback edition:** MEMORIES OF A CATHOLIC
GIRLHOOD. New York: Berkley Medallion Books, 1963, 224p.

d) **British paperback edition:** MEMORIES OF A CATHOLIC
GIRLHOOD. Harmondsworth: Penguin Books, 1963, 208p.

e) **Italian edition:** Mattioli, Augusta, trans. RICORDI DI UN'
EDUCAZIONE CATTOLICA. Milan: Arnoldo Mondadori
Editoire, c1963, 443p.

f) **Dutch edition:** Brunt, N., trans. HERINNERINGEN AAN
MIJN ROOMSE JEUGD. Amsterdam: N.V. De Arbeiderspers,
1966, 243p.

g) **German edition:** Dessauer, Maria, trans. EINE
KATHOLISCHE KINDHEIT. Munich: Droemer-Knaur, 1966,
264p.

h) **Revised French edition:** Meunier, Denyse, trans.
MEMOIRES D'UNE JEUNE CATHOLIQUE. Collection
femme. Paris: Denoël-Gonthier, c1966.

i) **Polish edition:** Wojewoda, Cecylia, trans. WSPOMNIENIA
Z LAT KATOLICKIEJ MLODOSCI. Warsaw: Czytelnik, 1968.

j) **Hungarian edition:** Zilahi, Judith, trans. EGY KATOLIKUS
LEANY EMLÉKEZÉSEI. Budapest: Európa Kiadó, 1968.

k) **Spanish edition:** Camarasa, Ramón Folchi, trans.
APARADORS PER A UNA DONA. Barcelona: Edicions,
[1969]. (Not verified)

l) **Second Italian edition:** Mattioli, Augusta, trans. RICORDI
DI UN' EDUCAZIONE CATTOLICA. Milan: Il Saggiatore,
1972, 287p.

m) **Swedish edition:** Alfons, Harriet and Jadwiga P. Westrup, trans. EN KATOLSK FLICKAS MINNEN. Stockholm: Trevi, 1973.

n) **Second German edition:** Dessauer, Maria, trans. EINE KATHOLISCHE KINDHEIT. Darmstadt, Neuweid: Luchterhand, 1981, 252p.

10. THE STONES OF FLORENCE. New York: Harcourt, Brace & Co., 1959, 228p.

Originally published in different form as a three-part series entitled "Profiles: A City of Stone, Parts I-III" in NEW YORKER (August 8-22, 1959).

Various excerpts were also published as "The Stones of Florence" in: THE HUMAN TRADITION, edited by Sarah Herndon and others. 324-334. New York: Holt, Rinehart & Winston, 1964.

a) **British edition:** THE STONES OF FLORENCE. London: William Heinemann, 1959, 129p.

b) **French edition:** Houbart, Jacques, trans. PIERRES DE FLORENCE. Paris: Editions Sequois, 1960, 130p.

c) **German edition:** Bethke, Ursula, trans. FLORENZ. Gütersloh: C. Bertelsmann Verlag, 1960, 128p.

d) **Unillustrated American edition:** THE STONES OF FLORENCE. New York: Harcourt, Brace & World, 1963, 230p.

e) **Paperback edition:** THE STONES OF FLORENCE. Harvest Book ed. New York: Harcourt, Brace & World, 1963, 230p.

f) **Second German edition**: Bethke, Ursula, trans. FLORENZ. Munich: Droemer-Knaur, 1967.

g) **Augmented edition**: THE STONES OF FLORENCE AND VENICE OBSERVED. Harmondsworth: Penguin Books, c1972, 280p.

h) **Third German edition**: Bethke, Ursula and Ursula Zedlitz, trans. FLORENZ. VENEDIG. Munich: Droemer-Knaur, 1973, 286p. (Includes translation of VENICE OBSERVED.)

i) **Fourth German edition**: Bethke, Ursula, trans. FLORENZ. Cologne: Kiepenheuer & Witsch, 1983, 207p.

11. ON THE CONTRARY: ARTICLES OF BELIEF 1946-1961. New York: Farrar, Straus & Cudahy, 1961, 312p.

Contents:
"A Letter to the Editor of POLITICS" was originally published as "The Hiroshima NEW YORKER" [Letter to the Editor] in POLITICS (November 1946); "America the Beautiful: The Humanist in the Bathtub" in COMMENTARY (September 1947); "Gandhi" in POLITICS (Winter 1948); "Mlle. Gulliver en Amérique" in REPORTER (January 22, 1952); "No News, or, What Killed the Dog" in REPORTER (July 1952); "Artists in Uniform" in HARPER'S MAGAZINE (March 1953); "My Confession" in REPORTER (December 22, 1953 & January 5, 1954); "Letter from Portugal" in NEW YORKER (February 5, 1955); "Mister Rodriguez of Lisbon" in HARPER'S MAGAZINE (August 1955); "Naming Names: The Arthur Miller Case" in ENCOUNTER (May 1957); "The VITA ACTIVA" as "Philosophy at Work" in NEW YORKER (October 1958); "Tyranny of the Orgasm" in NEW LEADER (April 5, 1947); "Up the Ladder from CHARM to VOGUE" in REPORTER (July 18, & August 1, 1950); "The Vassar Girl" in HOLIDAY (May 1951); "Recalled to Life, or Charles Dickens at the Bar" in REPORTER (March 1953); "Settling the Colonel's Hash" in HARPER'S MAGAZINE (February 1954); "An

Academy of Risk" in PARTISAN REVIEW (Summer 1959);
"The Fact in Fiction" in PARTISAN REVIEW (Summer 1960);
"Characters in Fiction" in PARTISAN REVIEW (March-April
1961); and "The American Realist Playwrights" as "Realism in
the American Theatre" in ENCOUNTER (July 1961).

"The Contagion of Ideas" was a speech delivered to a group of
teachers in Summer 1952.

a) **British edition**: ON THE CONTRARY: ARTICLES OF
BELIEF 1946-1961. London: Heinemann, 1962, 312p.

b) **Second American edition**: ON THE CONTRARY:
ARTICLES OF BELIEF 1946-1961. New York: Noonday,
1962, 312p. Reprinted New York: Octagon Books (Div. of
Farrar, Straus & Cudahy), 1975.

c) **French edition**: Lévi, Angélique, trans. A
CONTRE-COURANT. Paris: Editions Stock, 1965, 250p.
(Translation of ON THE CONTRARY and SIGHTS AND
SPECTACLES.)

d) **Danish edition**: Hertel, Hans, trans. TVÆRTIMOD.
Fredensborg, Arena: Forfatternes Forlag A/S, 1966, 245p.

e) **Spanish edition**: Traber, Ebbe, trans. AL CONTRARIO.
Biblioteca Breve, 265 Ensayo. Barcelona: Seix Barral, 1967,
313p.

f) **Second British edition**: ON THE CONTRARY: ARTICLES
OF BELIEF 1946-1961. London: Weidenfeld & Nicolson, 1980,
312p.

12. THE GROUP. New York: Harcourt, Brace & World, 1963,
378p.

Chapter one was originally published in somewhat different form
as "The Group" in: AVON BOOK OF MODERN WRITING,

32-54. New York: Avon Pub., 1954; chapter three as "Dottie Makes an Honest Woman of Herself" in PARTISAN REVIEW (January-February 1954); and chapters eleven and twelve as "Polly Andrews, Class of '33" in NEW YORKER (June 29, 1963).

a) **British edition:** THE GROUP. London: Weidenfeld & Nicolson, 1963, 360p.

b) **Paperback edition:** THE GROUP. New York: New American Library, 1963, 397p.

c) **Swedish edition:** Alfons, Harriet and Jadwiga P. Westrup, trans. GRUPPEN. Stockholm: Albert Bonniers Förlag AB, 1964, 362p.

d) **Italian edition:** DeCristofaro, Magda, trans. IL GRUPPO. Verona: Arnoldo Mondadori Editore, c1964, 584p.

e) **French edition:** Gentien, Antoine, and Jean-René Fenwick, trans. LE GROUPE. Paris: Editions Stock, 1964, 513p.

f) **Finnish edition:** Saloma, Antti, trans. RHYMÄ. Helsinki: Weilin & Göös, 1964, 426p.

g) **Danish edition:** Hertel, Hans, trans. GRUPPEN. Fredensborg, Arena: Forfatternes Forlag A/S, 1964, 461p.

h) **Dutch edition:** Kliphuis, J.F., and R.W. Kliphuis-Vlaskamp, trans. DE GROEP. Leyden: A.W. Sijthoff's Uitgeversmaatschappij N.V., c1964, 367p.

i) **Norwegian edition:** Simonsen, Helge, trans. KLIKKEN. Oslo: Gyldendal Norsk Forlag A/S, 1964, 316p.

j) **German edition:** Zedlitz, Ursula, trans. DIE CLIQUE. Munich: Droemer-Knaur, c1964, 440p.

k) **Portuguese edition**: deCastro, Fernando, trans. O GRUPO. Rio de Janeiro: Editôra Civilização Brasileira S.A., 1965, 379p.

l) **Second Portuguese edition**: Gonçalves, Daniel, trans. O GRUPO. Lisbon: Editôra Ulisseia, 1965, 463p.

m) **British paperback edition**: THE GROUP. Harmondsworth: Penguin, 1966.

n) **Spanish edition**: DeVelasco, Carmen Rodríguez and Jaime Ferrán, trans. EL GRUPO. Mexico City: Editorial Joaquín Mortiz, 1966, 389p.

o) **Second German edition**: Zedlitz, Ursula, trans. DIE CLIQUE. Zurich: Buchclub Ex Libris, 1966, 440p.

p) **Czechoslovakian edition**: Simecková, Eva, trans. SKUPINA. Bratislava: Smena, 1967, 389p.

q) **Third German edition**: Zedlitz, Ursula, trans. DIE CLIQUE. Gütersloh, Germany: Bertelsmann-Lesering, 1967, 440p.

r) **French paperback edition**: Gentien, Antoine, and Jean-René Fenwick, trans. LE GROUPE. Paris: Livres de Poche, 1968.

s) **Fourth German edition**: Zedlitz, Ursula, trans. DIE CLIQUE. Vienna: Buchgemeinschaft Donauland, 1969, 440p.

t) **Second Danish edition**: Hertel, Hans, trans. GRUPPEN. Denmark: Fremads Fakkelboger, 1970, 419p.

u) **Yugoslavian edition**: Bostjancic-Turkova, Vera, trans. SKUPINA. Ljubljana: Presernova Druzba, 1972.

v) **Japanese edition**: Ogasawara, Toyoki, trans. GURUPU. Tokyo: Hayakawa Shobo & Co., 1972, 555p.

w) **Hungarian edition**: Dezsényi, Katalin, trans. A CSOPORT.
Budapest: Európa, 1974, 470p.

x) **Turkish edition**: Yeginobali, Nihal, trans. BIZIM KIZLAR.
Istanbul: Altin Kitaplar Yayinevi, 1974.

y) **Second Swedish edition**: Alfons, Harriet and Jadwiga P.
Westrup, trans. GRUPPEN. Stockholm: Trevi, 1974.

z) **Second Spanish edition**: DeVelasco, Carmen Rodríguez and
Jaime Ferrán, trans. EL GRUPO. Barcelona: Ediciones Grijalbo,
1976.

zz) **Limited edition**: THE GROUP, illustrated by Miki. Limited
ed. Franklin Center, Penn.: Franklin Library, 1978, 419p.

13. MARY McCARTHY'S THEATRE CHRONICLES 1937-1962.
New York: Farrar, Straus & Co., 1963, 248p.

The major part of this book was originally published as SIGHTS
AND SPECTACLES 1937-1958. New York: Farrar, Straus &
Cudahy, 1956. (See item no. 7 for contents note.)

Additional reviews include: "Sheep in Wolves' Clothing" was
originally published in PARTISAN REVIEW (Spring 1957); "A
New Word" in HARPER'S BAZAAR (April 1958); "Odd Man
In" in PARTISAN REVIEW (Winter 1959); "American Realist
Playwrights" as "Realism in the American Theatre" in
HARPER'S MAGAZINE (July 1961); "Drapes" as "Curtains for
Tynan?" in OBSERVER (October 22, 1961); and "General
Macbeth" in HARPER'S MAGAZINE (June 1962).

14. THE HUMANIST IN THE BATHTUB [Selected Essays From MARY McCARTHY'S THEATRE CHRONICLES and ON THE CONTRARY]. New York: New American Library, 1964, 216p.

Contents:
"A New Word," "Odd Man In" and "Drapes" are from MARY McCARTHY'S THEATRE CHRONICLES, all other essays are from ON THE CONTRARY.

"America the Beautiful: The Humanist in the Bathtub" was originally published in COMMENTARY (September 1947); "Mlle. Gulliver en Amérique" in REPORTER (January 22, 1952); "American Realist Playwrights" as "Realism in the American Theatre" in ENCOUNTER (July 1961); "The Vassar Girl" in HOLIDAY (May 1951); "Artists in Uniform" in HARPER'S MAGAZINE (March 1953); "Settling the Colonel's Hash" in HARPER'S MAGAZINE (February 1954); "A New Word" in HARPER'S BAZAAR (April 1958); "Odd Man In" in PARTISAN REVIEW (Winter 1959); "Drapes" as "Curtains for Tynan?" in OBSERVER (October 22, 1961); "My Confession" in REPORTER (December 22, 1953 & January 5, 1954); "Tyranny of the Orgasm" in NEW LEADER (April 5, 1947); "An Academy of Risk" in PARTISAN REVIEW (Summer 1959); and "Characters in Fiction" in PARTISAN REVIEW (March-April 1961).

15. VIETNAM. New York: Harcourt, Brace & World, 1967, 106p.

Originally published in different form as a four-part series as "Report from Vietnam: Part I-III" and "Vietnam: Solutions" in NEW YORK REVIEW OF BOOKS (April 20-November 9, 1967).

a) **British edition**: VIETNAM. London: Weidenfeld & Nicolson, 1967.

b) **Italian edition:** Chiaromonte, Nicola, trans. VIETNAM. Milan: Mondadori, [1967]. (Not seen)

c) **German edition:** Harpprecht, Klaus, trans. VIETNAM-REPORT. Munich: Droemer-Knaur, 1967, 160p.

d) **Spanish edition:** Aguilar, José, trans. VIETNAM. Barcelona: Seix Barral, 1968, 126p.

e) **Burmese edition:** Lwin, Thein Oo and Kan Oo Nyunt, trans. YANE VIETNAM. Rangoon: Alin Yaung Sarpay, 1968. (Not seen)

f) **Portuguese edition:** Mendes, Berta, trans. VIETNAME. Lisbon: Bertrand, [1968]. (Not seen)

g) **French edition:** Paniguian, J., trans. VIETNAM. Paris: Jean-Jacquess Pauvert, 1968, 181p.

h) **Japanese edition:** Tetsuo, Shinjô, trans. VIETNAM HOKOKU. Tokyo: Kawade World Books, 1968, 209p.

i) **Hungarian edition:** Apostol, András, trans. VIETNAMI JALENTÉS. Budapest: Magveto Kiadó, 1969.

j) **Yugoslavian edition:** Sarinic, Hrvoje, trans. VIJETNAM. Zagreb: Znanje, 1969.

k) **Russian edition:** [unknown], trans. OKIN' HOLODNYM VZGLJADOM. Foreword by I. Shchedrov. Moscow: Molodaya Gvardiia, 1970, 239p.

l) **Augmented edition:** THE SEVENTEENTH DEGREE. New York: Harcourt Brace Jovanovich, 1974, 451p. (Includes ""How It Went," HANOI, MEDINA and "Sons of the Morning.").

16. HANOI. New York: Harcourt, Brace & World, 1968, 134p.

Chapters one to four were originally published in somewhat different form as a four-part series entitled "Hanoi" in NEW YORK REVIEW OF BOOKS (May 23-July 11, 1968); and the Foreword entitled "On Withdrawing from Vietnam: An Exchange" was published in NEW YORK REVIEW OF BOOKS (January 18, 1968).

Also published:

a) **British edition**: HANOI. London: Weidenfeld & Nicolson, 1968, 134p.

b) **Italian edition**: Cicogna, Enrico, trans. HANOI. Milan: A. Mondadori, 1968.

c) **Dutch edition**: Kliphuis, J.F., trans. HANOI. Leyden: Sijthoff, 1968.

d) **British paperback edition**: HANOI. Harmondsworth: Penguin, 1969, 159p.

e) **German edition**: Czernicki, Karl-Otto, trans. HANOI. Munich: Droemer-Knaur, 1969.

f) **Japanese edition**: Motohiro, Murakami, trans. KITA VIETNAM TONO KAIWA. Tokyo: Hayakawa Shobo & Co., 1969, 221p.

g) **Augmented edition**: THE SEVENTEENTH DEGREE. New York: Harcourt Brace Jovanovich, 1974, 451p. (Includes "How it Went," VIETNAM, MEDINA and "Sons of the Morning.")

17. WINTER VISITORS. New York: Harcourt Brace Jovanovich, 1970, 57p.

Published as chapter one of BIRDS OF AMERICA. 1-50. New York: Harcourt Brace Jovanovich, 1971.

Note on title page: "This limited edition is published as a New Year's greeting to friends of the author and of the publisher."

18. WRITING ON THE WALL AND OTHER LITERARY ESSAYS. New York: Harcourt, Brace & World, 1970, 213p.

Contents:
"General Macbeth" originally published in HARPER'S MAGAZINE (June 1962); "A Bolt from the Blue" in NEW REPUBLIC (June 4, 1962); "J.D. Salinger's Closed Circuit" in HARPER'S MAGAZINE (October 1962); "Burroughs' NAKED LUNCH" as "Déjeuner sur l'herbe" in NEW YORK REVIEW OF BOOKS (Special issue 1963); "Hue and Cry" in PARTISAN REVIEW (Winter 1964); "On MADAME BOVARY" in PARTISAN REVIEW (Spring 1964); "Crushing a Butterfly" in PREUVES (February 1965); "Everybody's Childhood" in STATESMAN (July 15, 1966); "The Inventions of I. Compton-Burnett" in ENCOUNTER (November 1966); "More on Compton-Burnett" in DER SPIEGEL (February 27, 1967); "Writing on the Wall" as "Appraisal: The Man Who Wanted Out" in NOVA (May-June 1969); "Hanging By a Thread" in NEW YORK REVIEW OF BOOKS (July 31, 1969); and "One Touch of Nature" as "Reflections: One Touch of Nature" in NEW YORKER (January 24, 1970).

a) **British edition:** WRITING ON THE WALL AND OTHER LITERARY ESSAYS. London: Weidenfeld & Nicolson, 1970, 213p.

b) **German edition:** Dessauer, Maria, and Hilde Spiel, trans. EIN BLITZ AUS HEITEREM HIMMEL. Munich: Droemer-Knaur, 1970, 302p. (Not seen)

c) **Spanish edition:** Ferrater, Gabriel, trans. ESCRITO EN LA
PARED Y OTROS ENSAYOS LITERARIOS. Barcelona:
Editorial Lumen, 1972, 248p.

d) **Italian edition:** d'Anna, Andrea, trans. LA SCRITTA SUL
MURO E ALTRI SAGGI LETTERARI. Milan: Mondadori,
1973, 262p.

e) **Dutch edition:** Surendonk, H. and Gerrit Komrji, trans.
HET TEKEN AAN DE WAND EN ANDERE LITERAIRE
ESSAYS. Amsterdam: Meulenhoff, [1973].

f) **French edition:** Lévi, Angélique, trans. SUSPENDU A UN
FIL, ET AUTRES ESSAIS LITTÉRAIRES. Pavillons. Paris:
Robert Laffont; Editions Stock, 1974, 273p.

19. BIRDS OF AMERICA. New York: Harcourt Brace Jovanovich,
1971, 344p.

Chapters one and two were originally published in somewhat
different form as "Birds of America" in SOUTHERN REVIEW
(July 1965); chapter one was also published in book form as
WINTER VISITORS. Limited ed. New York: Harcourt Brace
Jovanovich, c1965; chapter two as "Battle of Rocky Port" in
McCALLS (January 1971): 87-90 and chapter six as
"Thanksgiving in Paris" in ATLANTIC (August 1970): 43-62.

a) **British edition:** BIRDS OF AMERICA. London: Weidenfeld
& Nicolson, 1971, 318p.

b) **German edition:** Stege, Gisela, trans. EIN SOHN DER
NEUEN WELT. Munich: Droemer-Knaur, 1971, 437p.

c) **Swedish edition:** Alfons, Harriet, and Jadwiga P. Westrup,
trans. FÄGLAR. Stockholm: Esselte Tryck, 1971, 280p.

d) **Italian edition:** Diacono, Mario, trans. UCCELLI D'AMERICA. [Milan]: Arnoldo Mondadori Editore, 1972, 374p.

e) **French edition:** Lévi, Angélique, trans. LES OISEAUX D'AMERIQUE. Montreal, Que.: Editions du Jour; Paris: Robert Laffont, 1972, 413p.

f) **British paperback edition:** BIRDS OF AMERICA. Harmondsworth: Penguin Books, 1972, 300p.

g) **Paperback edition:** BIRDS OF AMERICA. New York: New American Library, 1972, 288p.

h) **Portuguese edition:** Pólvora, Hélio, trans. PASSAROS DA AMÉRICA. Rio de Janeiro: Artenova, 1973, 319p.

i) **Japanese edition:** Yajirô, Furusawa, trans. AMERIKA NO WATARIDORI. Tokyo: Hayakawa Shobo & Co., 1974, 380p.

j) **Polish edition:** Wojewoda, Cecylia, trans. PTAKI AMERYKI. Warsaw: Panstwowy Instytut Wydawniczy, 1975, 373p.

k) **French paperback edition:** Lévi, Angélique, trans. LES OISEAUX D'AMERIQUE. Paris: Livres de Poche, 1976.

l) **Second Portuguese edition:** Pólvora, Hélio, trans. PASSAROS DA AMÉRICA. São Paulo: Circulo do Livro, 1976.

20. MEDINA. New York: Harcourt Brace Jovanovich, 1972, 87p.

Originally published as "Reflections: A Transition Figure" in NEW YORKER (June 10, 1972).

a) **Italian edition:** Bianchi, Marina, trans. MEDINA. Milan: Mondadori, 1972.

b) **British edition**: MEDINA. London: Wildwood House, 1973, 92p.

c) **French edition**: Cowen, Claudine, trans. RAPPORT SUR LE PROCES DU CAPITAINE MEDINA. Libertés 2000. Montreal, Que.: Editions du Jour; Paris: Editions Robert Laffont, 1973, 143p.

d) **German edition**: Wölfi, Norbert, trans. MEDINA DIE MY LAI PROZESSE. Zurich: Droemer-Knaur, 1973.

e) **Hungarian edition**: Sziágyi, Tibor, trans. MEDINA. Budapest: Európa, 1974.

f) **Augmented edition**: THE SEVENTEENTH DEGREE. New York: Harcourt Brace Jovanovich, 1974, 451p. (Includes "How It Went," VIETNAM, HANOI, "Sons of the Morning.")

21. CAN THERE BE A GOTHIC LITERATURE? Amsterdam: Uitgeverij De Harmonie, 1973, 33p.

This is the complete text of the Johan Huizinga lecture, delivered by McCarthy in a slightly revised form, on December 7, 1973 at the Pieterskerk at Leyden, Holland.

22. MASK OF STATE: WATERGATE PORTRAITS. New York: Harcourt Brace Jovanovich, 1974, 165p.

Chapters one and three to seven were originally published in somewhat different form as a six-part series entitled "Watergate: Mary McCarthy Reports" in OBSERVER (June 17-August 5, 1973); "Notes of a Watergate Resident" was originally published in NEW YORK REVIEW OF BOOKS (July 19, 1973); "Always That Doubt" in NEW YORK REVIEW OF BOOKS (April 4, 1974); and "Postscript on the Pardon" in NEW YORK REVIEW OF BOOKS (October 17, 1974).

a) **French edition**: Lévi, Angélique, trans. WATERGATE: LA TRAGEDIE DE L'AMERIQUE. Paris: Gallimard, 1974, 200p.

b) **Spanish edition**: Desmonts, Antonio, trans. RETRATOS DE WATERGATE. Barcelona: Anagrama, 1974.

c) **Second American edition**: Harvest paperback ed. New York: Harcourt Brace Jovanovich, 1975, 183p.

23. THE SEVENTEENTH DEGREE. New York: Harcourt Brace Jovanovich, 1974, 451p.

Contents:
"Vietnam" was originally published in somewhat different form as a four-part series entitled "Report from Vietnam: Part I-III" and "Solutions" in NEW YORK REVIEW OF BOOKS (April 20-November 9, 1967); "Hanoi" as a four-part series entitled "Hanoi" in NEW YORK REVIEW OF BOOKS (May 23-July 11, 1968); "Medina" as "Reflections: A Transition Figure" in NEW YORKER (June 10, 1972); and "Sons of the Morning" in NEW YORK REVIEW OF BOOKS (January 25, 1973). "How It Went" was not previously published.

"Vietnam" was also published in book form as VIETNAM. New York: Harcourt, Brace & World, 1967; "Hanoi" as HANOI. New York: Harcourt, Brace & World, 1968; and "Medina" as MEDINA. New York: Harcourt Brace Jovanovich, 1972.

a) **British edition**: THE SEVENTEENTH DEGREE. London: Weidenfeld & Nicolson, 1975, 451p.

24. CANNIBALS AND MISSIONARIES. New York: Harcourt Brace Jovanovich, 1979, 369p.

a) **British edition**: CANNIBALS AND MISSIONARIES. London: Weidenfeld & Nicolson, 1979, 369p.

b) **French edition:** Lévi, Angélique, trans. CANNIBALES ET MISSIONAIRES. Série Domaine étranger. Paris: Arthème Fayard, 1980, 423p.

c) **Portuguese edition:** Wissemberg, Aurea, trans. CANIBAIS E MISSIONARIOS. Rio de Janeiro: Nove Fronteira, 1980, 393p.

d) **Spanish edition:** Silió, Soledad, trans. CANIBALES Y MISIONEROS. Barcelona: Planeta, 1981, 347p.

e) **German edition:** Thaler, Willy, trans. KANNIBALEN UND MISSIONARE. Munich: Droemer-Knaur, c1981, 384p.

f) **Danish edition:** Tvermoes, Rose-Marie, trans. KANNIBALER OG MISSIONÆRER. Copenhagen: Danmarks Bogklub, 1981, 373p.

g) **British paperback edition:** CANNIBALS AND MISSIONARIES. Harmondsworth: Penguin, 1982, 369p.

h) **Talking book edition:** CANNIBALS AND MISSIONARIES [sound recording]. 12 cassettes (16 hours): 1 7/8 ips., 2 tracks, mono. Vancouver, B.C.: Library Services Branch, 1982.

25. IDEAS AND THE NOVEL. Northcliffe Lectures; 1980. New York: Harcourt Brace Jovanovich, 1980, 121p.

Lectures one and four were originally published in somewhat different form in LONDON REVIEW OF BOOKS.

a) **British edition:** IDEAS AND THE NOVEL. London: Weidenfeld & Nicolson, 1981, 121p.

b) **French edition:** Lévi, Angélique, trans. LE ROMAN ET LES IDEES ET AUTRES ESSAIS. Paris: Fayard, 1988, 273p. (Includes nine essays from OCCASIONAL PROSE.)

26. HOUNDS OF SUMMER AND OTHER STORIES: MARY McCARTHY'S SHORT FICTION. New York: Avon Books, 1981, 240p.

Most of the stories in this volume were previously published in McCarthy, Mary. CAST A COLD EYE. New York: Harcourt, Brace & World, 1950. (See item no. 3 for contents note.)

Additional stories include: "The Appalachian Revolution" originally published in NEW YORKER (September 11, 1954); and "The Hounds of Summer" in NEW YORKER (September 14, 1963).

27. OCCASIONAL PROSE. New York: Harcourt Brace Jovanovich, 1985, 341p.

Contents:
"Philip Rahv" originally published in NEW YORK TIMES BOOK REVIEW (February 17, 1974); "The 'Place' of Nicola Chiaromonte" as "Nicola Chiaromonte and the Theatre" in NEW YORK REVIEW OF BOOKS (February 20, 1975); "Saying Good-bye to Hannah" in NEW YORK REVIEW OF BOOKS (January 22, 1976); "F.W. Dupee" in NEW YORK REVIEW OF BOOKS (March 8, 1979); "On the Demo, London" as "Mary McCarthy on the Demo" in TIMES (London, G.B.) (December 8, 1968); "A Guide to Exiles, Expatriates and Internal Emigrés" as "Exiles, Expatriates and Internal Emigrés" in LISTENER (November 25, 1971); "Novel, Tale, and Romance" in NEW YORK REVIEW OF BOOKS (May 12, 1983); "The Tolstoy Connection" in SATURDAY REVIEW (September 16, 1972); "Acts of Love" in NEW YORK REVIEW OF BOOKS (June 25, 1981); "Politics and the Novel" as "Lasting Power of the Political Novel" in NEW YORK TIMES BOOK REVIEW (January 1, 1984); "In the Family Way" in NEW YORK REVIEW OF BOOKS (December 8, 1983); "Democracy" as "Love and Death in the Pacific" in NEW YORK TIMES BOOK REVIEW (April 22, 1984); "American Revolution of Jean-François Revel" in Revel, Jean-François.

WITHOUT MARX OR JESUS, translated by J.F. Bernard.
Afterword by Mary McCarthy. 243-257. Garden City, N.Y.:
Doubleday, 1971; "On F.W. Dupee" in NEW YORK REVIEW
OF BOOKS (October 27, 1983); "Paradox of History" as
"Unresigned Man" in NEW YORK REVIEW OF BOOKS
(February 14, 1985); "LA TRAVIATA Retold" in Verdi,
Giuseppe. LA TRAVIATA. Story adaptation by Mary
McCarthy. Boston: Little, Brown, 1983; "The Rake's Progess"
in NEW YORK REVIEW OF BOOKS (November 5, 1981); and
"The Very Unforgettable Miss Brayton" as "Indomitable Miss
Brayton" in HOUSE AND GARDEN (December 1983).

"On Rereading a Favorite Book" (written March 22, 1981),
"Language and Politics," and "Living with Beautiful Things"
were not previously published.

28. HOW I GREW. San Diego: Harcourt Brace Jovanovich, 1987,
278p.

a) **British edition**: HOW I GREW. London: Weidenfeld &
Nicolson, 1987, 278p.

b) **Paperback edition**: HOW I GREW. New York: Harcourt
Brace Jovanovich, 1988, 272p.

c) **British paperback edition**: HOW I GREW. Harmondsworth:
Penguin, 1989, 278p.

d) **Large print edition**: HOW I GREW. Americana Series.
Thorndike, Maine: Thorndike Press, 1988, 450p.

EDITED BOOKS

29. Arendt, Hannah. THE LIFE OF THE MIND (Vol 1.
     THINKING and Vol 2. WILLING), edited with a Postface by
     Mary McCarthy. New York: Harcourt Brace Jovanovich, 1978,
     258p.

     Delivered in briefer form as the Gifford Lectures at the Univ. of
     Aberdeen in 1974. See also McCarthy's Editor's Note p. xi-xii
     (Vol.1) and ix-x (Vol.2).

     This two volume set was also published in one volume. LIFE OF
     THE MIND. 1st Harvest/Harcourt, Brace & Jovanovich ed. New
     York: Harcourt, Brace & Jovanovich, 1981.

Essays

30. "Contrasts." SAMPLER [Vassar College] 11, no.1 (November 21, 1929): 5.

31. "Old-Town." SAMPLER [Vassar College] 11, no.1 (November 21, 1929): 5.

32. "Touchstone Ambitions." VASSAR JOURNAL OF UNDERGRADUATE STUDIES 7 (1933): 86-101.

33. "In Pace Requiescamus." CON SPIRITO 1, no.2 (April 1933): 1-2.

34. Marshall, Margaret. "Our Critics, Right or Wrong. Part I-V." NATION 141, no.3668-3676 (October 23-December 18, 1935).

"Our Critics, Right or Wrong: Part I." NATION 141, no.3668 (October 23, 1935): 468-472; "Our Critics, Right or Wrong: II. The Anti-Intellectuals." NATION 141, no.3670 (November 6, 1935): 542-544; "Our Critics, Right or Wrong: III." NATION 141, no.3672 (November 20, 1935): 595-596, 598; "IV. The Proletarians." NATION 141, no.3674 (December 4,

1935): 653-655; and "Our Critics, Right or Wrong: V. Literary
Salesmen." NATION 141, no.3676 (December 18, 1935):
717-719.

35. "Murder and Karl Marx." NATION 142, no.3690 (March 25,
1936): 381-383.

36. "Circus Politics in Washington State." NATION 143, no.16
(October 17, 1936): 442-444.

See also Menefee's letter in response to this article (item no.
290) and McCarthy's reply (item no. 255).

37. "Our Actors and the Critics, Part I & II." NATION 144, no.19;
no.20 (May 8; May 15, 1937): 536-537; 566-567.

38. "I Was There But I Didn't See It Happen." NEW REPUBLIC
103, no.19 (November 4, 1940): 633-635.

39. "On the Home Front: Letter from New York." TOWN AND
COUNTRY 98, no.4249 (July 1943): 56, 91.

40. "Graham Greene and the Intelligentsia." PARTISAN REVIEW
11, no.2 (Spring 1944): 228-230.

41. "The Blackguard." NEW YORKER 22, no.35 (October 12,
1946): 31-35.

Also published in:
McCarthy, Mary. CAST A COLD EYE. 112-120. New York:
Harcourt, Brace & World, 1950.

McCarthy, Mary. MEMORIES OF A CATHOLIC GIRLHOOD. 87-101. New York: Harcourt, Brace & Co., 1957.

McCarthy, Mary. HOUNDS OF SUMMER AND OTHER STORIES. 134-143. New York: Avon Books, 1981.

42. "Lausanne." TOWN AND COUNTRY 100, no.4290 (November 1946): 130+.

43. "America the Beautiful: The Humanist in the Bathtub." COMMENTARY 4, no.3 (September 1947): 201-207.

Also published in:
Laughlin, James, ed. NEW DIRECTIONS IN PROSE AND POETRY: AN ANNUAL EXHIBITION GALLERY OF NEW AND DIVERGENT TRENDS IN LITERATURE. 23-33. New York: Blue Ridge Mountain Press, 1948. (Laughlin also refers to McCarthy in "A Few Random Notes from the Publisher," p.20.)

PERSPECTIVES, USA, no.2 (Winter 1953): 11-22.

Fiedler, Leslie A., ed. THE ART OF THE ESSAY. 247-256. New York: Thomas Y. Crowell, 1958 and in 2nd. ed. 184-194. New York: Thomas Y. Crowell, 1969.

McCarthy, Mary. ON THE CONTRARY. 6-19. New York: Farrar, Straus & Cudahy, 1961.

McDonnell, Robert F., and William E. Morris, eds. FORM AND FOCUS. 312-320. New York: Harcourt, Brace & World, 1961.

Gold, Herbert, ed. FIRST PERSON SINGULAR: ESSAYS FOR THE SIXTIES. 160-172. New York: Dial Press, 1963.

44. "Gandhi." POLITICS 5, no.1 (Winter 1948): 1-7.

    Includes notes by McCarthy, Chiaromonte, Agee, Goodman,
    Tucci and Macdonald.

45. "Yonder Peasant, Who Is He?" NEW YORKER 24, no.41
    (December 4, 1948): 33-39.

    Also published in:
    55 SHORT STORIES FROM THE NEW YORKER. 172-184.
    New York: Simon & Schuster, 1949.

    McCarthy, Mary. CAST A COLD EYE. 97-111. New York:
    Harcourt, Brace & World, 1950.

    McCarthy, Mary. MEMORIES OF A CATHOLIC GIRLHOOD.
    29-53. New York: Harcourt, Brace & Co., 1957.

    Somerville, Rose M., ed. INTIMATE RELATIONSHIPS:
    MARRIAGE, FAMILY AND LIFESTYLES THROUGH
    LITERATURE. 357-367. Englewood Cliffs, N.J.: Prentice-Hall,
    1975.

    McCarthy, Mary. HOUNDS OF SUMMER AND OTHER
    STORIES. 116-133. New York: Avon Books, 1981.

46. "Greenwich Village at Night: [Eleven part series]." NEW YORK
    POST (February 20-March 3, 1950).

    "Greenwich Village at Night: Monday." NEW YORK POST.
    (February 20, 1950): 3, 7; "Greenwich Village at Night:
    Tuesday." NEW YORK POST. (February 21, 1950): 5, 20-21;
    "Greenwich Village at Night: Wednesday." NEW YORK POST.
    (February 22, 1950): 35; "Greenwich Village at Night:
    Thursday." NEW YORK POST. (February 23, 1950): 5;
    "Greenwich Village at Night: Friday." NEW YORK POST.
    (February 24, 1950): 67; "Greenwich Village at Night:

Saturday." NEW YORK POST. (February 26, 1950): 5, 20;
"Greenwich Village at Night: Part 7." NEW YORK POST.
(February 27, 1950): 35; "Greenwich Village at Night: Part 8."
NEW YORK POST. (February 28, 1950): 45; "Greenwich
Village at Night: Part 9." NEW YORK POST. (March 1, 1950):
65; "Greenwich Village at Night: Part 10." NEW YORK POST.
(March 2, 1950): 39; and "Greenwich Village at Night: Part
11." NEW YORK POST. (March 3, 1950): 65.

47. "Up the Ladder from Charm to Vogue, Part I & II."
    REPORTER 3, no.2; no.3 (July 18, 1950; August 1, 1950):
    36-40; 32-35.

    Also published in:
    Ascoli, Max, ed. THE REPORTER READER. 152-168. Garden
    City, N.Y.: Doubleday & Co., 1956.

    McCarthy, Mary. ON THE CONTRARY. 174-192. New York:
    Farrar, Straus & Cudahy, 1961.

48. "The Vassar Girl." HOLIDAY 9, no.5 (May 1951): 46-55+.

    Also published in: McCarthy, Mary. ON THE CONTRARY.
    193-214. New York: Farrar, Straus & Cudahy, 1961.

49. "A Tin Butterfly." NEW YORKER 27, no.44 (December 15,
    1951): 28-38.

    Also published in:
    McCarthy, Mary. MEMORIES OF A CATHOLIC GIRLHOOD.
    54-86. New York: Harcourt, Brace & Co., 1957.

    Martin, Harold C. and Richard M. Ohmann, eds. INQUIRY
    AND A COLLEGE READER EXPRESSION. rev. ed. 675-682.
    New York: Holt, Rinehart & Winston, 1963.

as "Uncle Myers" in PROSE MODELS: AN INDUCTIVE
APPROACH TO WRITING, edited by Gerald Levin. 56-58.
New York: Harcourt, Brace & World, 1964 and 2nd ed. 28-30.
New York: Harcourt, Brace & World, 1970.

50. "No News, or, What Killed the Dog." REPORTER 7, no.1 (July
     8, 1952): 30-33.

     Based on a speech given at the American Committee for Cultural
     Freedom Conference in March 1952.

     Also published in: McCarthy, Mary. ON THE CONTRARY.
     32-42. New York: Farrar, Straus & Cudahy, 1961.

51. "C'est le Premier pas qui Coûte." NEW YORKER 28, no.21
     (July 12, 1952): 30-49.

     Also published in:
     McCarthy, Mary. MEMORIES OF A CATHOLIC GIRLHOOD.
     102-126. New York: Harcourt, Brace & Co., 1957.

     as "A Memory of a Catholic Girlhood" in WRITING ABOUT
     ONESELF: SELECTED WRITING, edited by Robert Garis.
     Uses of English: A Series for College Composition. 98-113.
     Boston: D.C. Heath & Co., 1965. (Garis refers to McCarthy in
     the Introduction.)

52. "New Trends in American Education." LISTENER (July 24,
     1952): 136-137.

53. "The Figures in the Clock." NEW YORKER 29, no.2 (February 28, 1953): 24-32.

    Also published in: McCarthy, Mary. MEMORIES OF A CATHOLIC GIRLHOOD. 141-168. New York: Harcourt, Brace & Co., 1957.

54. "The Menace to Free Journalism in America." LISTENER (May 14, 1953): 791-792.

55. "The Revolt of the American Authors." LISTENER (November 26, 1953): 901-902.

56. "My Confession, Part I & II." REPORTER 9, no.11; 10, no.1 (December 22, 1953; January 5, 1954): 28-34; 27-31.

    Also published in:
    ENCOUNTER 2, no.2 (February 1954): 43-56.

    McCarthy, Mary. ON THE CONTRARY. 55-74. New York: Farrar, Straus & Cudahy, 1961.

    Spender, Stephen; Irving Kristol and Melvin J. Lasky, eds. ENCOUNTERS: AN ANTHOLOGY FROM THE FIRST TEN YEARS OF ENCOUNTER MAGAZINE. 34-54. New York: Basic Books; London: Weidenfeld & Nicolson, 1963.

    French translation by Lévi, Angélique, trans. "Ma confession." PREUVES, no.154 (1963): 3-18.

57. "Thoughts of an American in England." LISTENER (June 17, 1954): 1041-1042.

58. "Letter from Portugal." NEW YORKER 30, no.51 (February 5, 1955): 83-102.

    Also published in:
    McCarthy, Mary. ON THE CONTRARY. 106-131. New York: Farrar, Straus & Cudahy, 1961.

    Slavin, Neal. PORTUGAL, afterword by Mary McCarthy. 698-888. New York: Lustrum Press, 1971.

59. "The Family Tea Party." OBSERVER (July 24, 1955): 13.

    Also published in: McCarthy, Mary. SIGHTS AND SPECTACLES 1937-56. 111-115. New York: Farrar, Straus & Cudahy, 1956 and MARY McCARTHY'S THEATRE CHRONICLES. 111-115. New York: Farrar, Straus & Co., 1963.

60. "Mister Rodriguez of Lisbon." HARPER'S MAGAZINE 211, no.1263 (August 1955): 65-70.

    Also published in: McCarthy, Mary. ON THE CONTRARY. 132-146. New York: Farrar, Straus & Cudahy, 1961.

61. "Yellowstone Park." HARPER'S BAZAAR 89, no.2928 (November 1955): 120-121+.

    Also published in:
    McCarthy, Mary. MEMORIES OF A CATHOLIC GIRLHOOD. 169-194. New York: Harcourt, Brace & Co., 1957.

    PRIZE STORIES 1957: THE O. HENRY AWARDS, selected and edited by Paul Engle, assisted by Constance Urdang. 292-309. Garden City, N.Y.: Doubleday & Co., 1957.

    Hondius, Katherine, ed. IDENTITY: STORIES FOR THIS

GENERATION. 200-216. Chicago: Scott, Foresman & Co., 1966.

German translation by Dessauer, Maria, trans. as "Yellowstone Park" in ANNABELLE (March 1966).

62. "Profiles: The Revel of the Earth, Parts I & II." NEW YORKER 32, no.20; no.21 (July 7, 1956; July 14, 1956): 27-62; 29-68.

This two part article was also published in book form with revisions as VENICE OBSERVED. New York: Reynal & Co., 1956, 199p.

63. "Ask Me No Questions." NEW YORKER 33, no.5 (March 23, 1957): 33-95.

Also published in:
McCarthy, Mary. MEMORIES OF A CATHOLIC GIRLHOOD. 195-245. New York: Harcourt, Brace & Co., 1957.

as "Grandmother" in WRITING FROM OBSERVATION, edited by Lester W. Cameron and Samuel A. Golden, 3rd ed. 94-102. New York: Harcourt, Brace & Co., 1959.

STORIES FROM THE NEW YORKER 1950-1960. 353-391. New York: Simon & Schuster, 1960 and in British ed. London: Victor Gollancz, 1961.

READ WITH ME, selected by Thomas B. Costain. 345-381. Garden City, N.Y.: Doubleday & Co., 1965.

64. "Naming Names: The Arthur Miller Case." ENCOUNTER 8, no.5 (May 1957): 23-25.

Also published in: McCarthy, Mary. ON THE CONTRARY. 147-154. New York: Farrar, Straus & Cudahy, 1961.

65. "Profiles: A City of Stone, Parts I - III." NEW YORKER 35, no.25 - 27 (August 8-22, 1959).

   This is a three-part essay: "Profiles: A City of Stone - I." NEW YORKER 25, no.25 (August 8, 1959): 36-75; "Profiles: A City of Stone - II." NEW YORKER 25, no.26 (August 15, 1959): 32-79; and "Profiles: A City of Stone - III." NEW YORKER 25, no.27 (August 22, 1959): 38-94.

   Also published in book form with revisions as THE STONES OF FLORENCE. New York: Harcourt, Brace & Co., 1959, 119p.

66. "Brunelleschi's Dome." HARPER'S BAZAAR 92, no.2974 (September 1959): 206-209+.

67. "The Fact in Fiction." PARTISAN REVIEW 27, no.3 (Summer 1960): 438-458.

   Text of a lecture delivered to several British audiences.

   Also published in: McCarthy, Mary. ON THE CONTRARY. 249-270. New York: Farrar, Straus & Cudahy, 1961.

68. "The Contagion of Ideas." In ON THE CONTRARY, 43-54. New York: Farrar, Straus & Cudahy, 1961.

   Speech delivered to a group of teachers in Summer 1952.

69. "Characters in Fiction." PARTISAN REVIEW 28, no.2 (March-April 1961): 171-191.

   Also published in:
   McCarthy, Mary. ON THE CONTRARY. 271-292. New York: Farrar, Straus & Cudahy, 1961.

Phillips, William, and Philip Rahv, eds. THE PARTISAN
REVIEW ANTHOLOGY. 250-262. New York: Holt, Rinehart
& Winston; London: Macmillan, 1962.

Kumar, Shiv K., and Keith McKean, eds. CRITICAL
APPROACHES TO FICTION. 79-95. New York: McGraw-Hill,
1968.

70. "'Realism' in the American Theatre." HARPER'S MAGAZINE
223, no.1334 (July 1961): 45-52.

See also Gluckman's and Chayefsky's letters in response to this
review (item no. 325).

Also published with revisions:
as "Americans, Realists, Playwrights" in ENCOUNTER 17,
no.1 (July 1961): 24-31.

as "The American Realists Playwrights" in McCarthy, Mary.
ON THE CONTRARY. 293-312. New York: Farrar, Straus &
Cudahy, 1961 and in MARY McCARTHY'S THEATRE
CHRONICLES. 209-229. New York: Farrar, Straus & Co.,
1963.

71. "Cold War and the West." PARTISAN REVIEW 29, no.1
(Winter 1962): 47-50.

72. "The Stones of Florence." In THE HUMANISTIC
TRADITION, edited by Sarah Herndon, Russell J. Reaver,
Robert F. Davidson, William Ruff, and Nathan Comfort Starr.
324-334. New York: Holt, Rinehart & Winston, 1964.

Excerpts and photographs from THE STONES OF FLORENCE.
New York: Harcourt, Brace & Co., 1959.

73. "Prose Literature." In TRADITION AND INNOVATION IN
    CONTEMPORARY LITERATURE/TRADITION ET
    MODERNITÉ DANS LA LITTÉRATURE DE NOTRE
    TEMPE, 81-82, 133, 144+. A round table conference of
    International P.E.N. in Budapest, October 16-17, 1964.
    Budapest: Corvina, 1964.

    McCarthy, Auden, Cooper, Allen and Veres were all
    contributors.

74. Flaubert, Gustave. THE TRIAL OF MADAME BOVARY.
    Translated by Evelyn Gendel, foreword by Mary McCarthy. vii-
    xxiii. New York: New American Library, 1964.

75. "Mary McCarthy Ad-Libs on Shakespeare's Women and Sundry
    Matters: A Show Soliloquy." SHOW 4, no.2 (February 1964):
    93, 101.

76. "La Littérature à la mutualité." PREUVES 15, no.168 (February
    1965): 64-66. French.

    Also published:
    German translation as "Jean-Paul Sartre und die Löwen [Sartre et
    le nouvel roman]" in DER MONAT, no.197 (February 1965):
    92-94.

    English translation as "Crushing a Butterfly" in ENCOUNTER
    24, no.3 (March 1965): 53-55 and in McCarthy, Mary.
    WRITING ON THE WALL. 95-101. New York: Harcourt,
    Brace & Co., 1970.

    Italian translation as "Letteratura a comizio" in TEMPO
    PRESENTE 10, no.1 (1965): 72-74.

77. "The Inventions of I. Compton-Burnett." ENCOUNTER 27, no.5 (November 1966): 19-31, 96.

     Also published:
     German translation as "Der Reigen--en famille anglaise: Über Ivy Compton-Burnett." DER MONAT 19, no.220 (January 1967): 53-61.

     French translation as "Les inventions d'Ivy Compton-Burnett." PREUVES, no.192 (February 1967): 13-30.

     McCarthy, Mary. WRITING ON THE WALL. 112-144. New York: Harcourt, Brace & World, 1970.

78. "Report from Vietnam: Part I-IV." NEW YORK REVIEW OF BOOKS (April 20-November 9, 1967).

     This four-part series published as "Report from Vietnam, Part I: The Home Program." NEW YORK REVIEW OF BOOKS 8, no.7 (April 20, 1967): 5-11; "Report from Vietnam, Part II: The Problems of Success." NEW YORK REVIEW OF BOOKS 8, no.8 (May 4, 1967): 4-9; "Report from Vietnam, Part III: Intellectuals." NEW YORK REVIEW OF BOOKS 8, no.9 (May 18, 1967): 4-11; and "Vietnam: Solutions." NEW YORK REVIEW OF BOOKS 9, no.8 (November 9, 1967): 3-6.

     The first three parts were published as "Mary McCarthy in Vietnam" in OBSERVER (April 30, 1967): 11-12; (May 7, 1967): 11-12; and (May 14, 1967): 21, 32. The fourth part was also published as "Solutions" in MORAL ARGUMENT AND THE WAR IN VIETNAM: A COLLECTION OF ESSAYS, edited by Paul T. Menzel. 129-139. Nashville, Tenn.: Aurora Pub., 1971.

     Also published:
     German translation by Harpprecht, Klaus as "Nichts Wäre Schlimmer Als der Sieg (Part I-IV)" in DER SPIEGEL 21, no.29 (July 10, 1967): 79-92; DER SPIEGEL 21, no.30 (July

17, 1967): 67-81; DER SPIEGEL 21, no.31 (July 24, 1967):
60-72; and DER SPIEGEL 21, no.32 (July 31, 1967): 50-63.

French translation as "Les deux guerres du Vietnam" in
PREUVES, no.197 (July 1967): 8-20; PREUVES, no.198-99
(September 1967): 12-23 and PREUVES, no.200 (July-October
1967): 51-63.

Italian translation as "Rapporto dal Vietnam" in TEMPO
PRESENTE 12, no.6 (1967): 5-41.

Also published in book form with revisions as VIETNAM. New
York: Harcourt, Brace & World, 1967, 106p. and in McCarthy,
Mary. THE SEVENTEENTH DEGREE. 59-166. New York:
Harcourt Brace Jovanovich, 1974.

79.   "Was soll in Vietnam geschehen?" DER MONAT (Berlin) 19,
      no.229 (October 1967): 5-8, 10-14. German.

80.   "On Withdrawing from Vietnam: An Exchange." NEW YORK
      REVIEW OF BOOKS 10, no.1 (January 18, 1968): 5-7.

      See also Trilling's article (item no. 404); her letter in response to
      McCarthy (item no. 407); and other responses to this exchange
      (item nos. 405 and 406).

      Also published in: McCarthy, Mary. HANOI. xii-xxv. New
      York: Harcourt, Brace & World, 1968.

81.   "Hanoi." NEW YORK REVIEW OF BOOKS 10 (May 23 - July
      11, 1968).

      This four-part series was published as "Hanoi--1968." NEW
      YORK REVIEW OF BOOKS 10, no.10 (May 23, 1968): 3-6;
      "Hanoi II." NEW YORK REVIEW OF BOOKS 10, no.11 (June
      6, 1968): 5-8; "North Vietnam: The Countryside." NEW YORK
      REVIEW OF BOOKS 10, no.12 (June 20, 1968): 6, 10-16; and

"North Vietnam: Language." NEW YORK REVIEW OF
BOOKS 11, no.1 (July 11, 1968): 10-15.

"Hanoi-1968" also published as "Waiting for the All Clear" in:
TIMES (London, G.B.) [Sunday Ed.] (May 26, 1968): 49-51
and "North Vietnam: Language" as "The War of Words" in:
TIMES (London, G.B.) [Sunday Ed.] (July 21, 1968): 25-26.

Also published in book form with revisions as HANOI.
Harcourt, Brace & World, 1968, 134p. and in: McCarthy,
Mary. THE SEVENTEENTH DEGREE. 167-322. New York:
Harcourt Brace Jovanovich, 1974.

82. "Notes on the Election." NEW YORK REVIEW OF BOOKS 11,
no.7 (October 24, 1968): 3-4.

83. "Mary McCarthy on the Demo." TIMES. SUNDAY TIMES
MAGAZINE (London, G.B.), no.7593 (December 8, 1968):
26-27+.

Also published as "On the Demo, London 1968" in: McCarthy,
Mary. OCCASIONAL PROSE. 47-68. New York: Harcourt
Brace Jovanovich, 1985.

84. "Appraisal: The Man Who Wanted Out." NOVA (London, G.B.)
(May-June 1969): 28-46.

Also published as "The Writing on the Wall" in: McCarthy,
Mary. WRITING ON THE WALL. 153-171. New York:
Harcourt, Brace & World, 1970.

85. "Reflections: One Touch of Nature." NEW YORKER 45, no.49 (January 24, 1970): 39-40+.

    Also published as "One Touch of Nature" in: WRITING ON THE WALL. 189-213. New York: Harcourt, Brace & World, 1970.

86. Revel, Jean-François. WITHOUT MARX OR JESUS: THE NEW AMERICAN REVOLUTION HAS BEGUN. Translated by J.F. Bernard, afterword by Mary McCarthy. 243-257. Garden City, N.Y.: Doubleday, 1971.

    Also published as "The American Revolution of Jean-François Revel" in: McCarthy, Mary. OCCASIONAL PROSE. 233-247. New York: Harcourt Brace Jovanovich, 1985.

87. "Exiles, Expatriates and Internal Emigrés." LISTENER 86, no.2226 (November 25, 1971): 705-708.

    Also published as "A Guide to Exiles, Expatriates and Internal Emigrés" in: McCarthy, Mary. OCCASIONAL PROSE. 69-82. New York: Harcourt Brace Jovanovich, 1985.

88. "Art, Culture and Conservatism." PARTISAN REVIEW 39, no.3 (1972): 382-453.

89. "Reflections: A Transition Figure." NEW YORKER 48 (June 10, 1972): 38-93.

    Also published in book form with revisions as MEDINA. New York: Harcourt Brace Jovanovich, 1972 and in: THE SEVENTEENTH DEGREE. 323-410. New York: Harcourt Brace Jovanovich, 1974.

90. "Imagination, Anyone?" NEWSWEEK 80, no.2 (July 10, 1972): 23-25.

91. "Watergate: Mary McCarthy Reports." OBSERVER (London, G.B.) (June 17-August 5, 1973).

    This six-part series was published as "The Athlete of Evasion and the Prodigal Son." OBSERVER (London, G.B.) (June 17, 1973): 8; "The Wagons Are Drawn Up Around the White House." OBSERVER (London, G.B.) (July 1, 1973): 9; "A Steady Dose of Lies." OBSERVER (London, G.B.) (July 15, 1973): 25; "A Bomb in the White House." OBSERVER (London, G.B.) (July 22, 1973): 25; "The Moral Certainties of John D. Ehrlichman." OBSERVER (London, G.B.) (July 29, 1973): 25; and "Exit Mutt, Enter Jeff." OBSERVER (London, G.B.) (August 5, 1973): 21.

    Also published as chapters one and three to seven in: McCarthy, Mary. MASK OF STATE: WATERGATE PORTRAITS. New York: Harcourt Brace Jovanovich, 1974.

92. "Watergate Notes." NEW YORK REVIEW OF BOOKS 20, no.12 (July 19, 1973): 5-8.

    Also published as "Notes of a Watergate Resident" in: McCarthy, Mary. MASK OF STATE: WATERGATE PORTRAITS. 17-34. New York: Harcourt Brace Jovanovich, 1974.

93. "Philip Rahv 1908-1973." NEW YORK TIMES BOOK REVIEW (February 17, 1974): 1-2.

    See also letters by Howe et al. (item no. 448).

    Also published in:
    Rahv, Philip. ESSAYS ON LITERATURE AND POLITICS

1932-1972, edited by Arabel Porter & Andrew J. Dvosin, with a memoir by Mary McCarthy. vii-x. Boston: Houghton Mifflin, 1978.

McCarthy, Mary. OCCASIONAL PROSE. 3-8. New York: Harcourt Brace Jovanovich, 1985.

94. "Watergate." NEW YORK REVIEW OF BOOKS 21, no.5 (April 4, 1974): 6-19.

Also published as "Always That Doubt" in: McCarthy, Mary. MASK OF STATE: WATERGATE PORTRAITS. 123-166. New York: Harcourt Brace Jovanovich, 1974.

95. "Postscript to Nixon." NEW YORK REVIEW OF BOOKS 21, no.16 (October 17, 1974): 10-12.

Also published:
as "Postscript on the Pardon" in McCarthy, Mary. MASK OF STATE: WATERGATE PORTRAITS. 167-183. New York: Harcourt Brace Jovanovich, 1974.

French translation as "Pourquoi le président Ford a-t-il gracié Nixon?" HISTORAMA, no.283 (June 1975): 71-78.

96. "Nicola Chiaromonte and the Theatre." NEW YORK REVIEW OF BOOKS (February 20, 1975): 25-30.

Also published as "The 'Place' of Nicola Chiaromonte (1905-1972)" in: McCarthy, Mary. OCCASIONAL PROSE. 9-34. New York: Harcourt Brace Jovanovich, 1985.

97. "Boycott: A Matter of Personal Taste or Public Principle?"
    INDEX ON CENSORSHIP 4, no.2 (Summer 1975): 29-30.

    Replies to a questionnaire on cultural boycotts.

98. Chiaromonte, Nicola. THE WORM OF CONSCIOUSNESS
    AND OTHER ESSAYS, edited by Miriam Chiaromonte, preface
    by Mary McCarthy. xiii-xvi. New York: Harcourt Brace
    Jovanovich, 1976.

99. "Saying Good-bye to Hannah." NEW YORK REVIEW OF
    BOOKS (January 22, 1976): 8-11.

    Also published in: McCarthy, Mary. OCCASIONAL PROSE.
    35-42. New York: Harcourt Brace Jovanovich, 1985.

100. "F.W. Dupee 1904-1979." NEW YORK REVIEW OF BOOKS
     (March 8, 1979): 6.

    Also published in: McCarthy, Mary. OCCASIONAL PROSE.
    43-44. New York: Harcourt Brace Jovanovich, 1985.

101. "'Ideas Were the Generative Force of His Life'." NEW YORK
     TIMES [Sunday Ed.] (May 6, 1979): D12, 30.

    Tribute to Harold Rosenberg delivered by McCarthy at a
    memorial service held on April 25, 1979 at the New York Public
    Library.

102. "For Jim Farrell's Funeral." NEW YORK REVIEW OF BOOKS
     26 (November 8, 1979): 52.

103. "The Novels That Got Away." NEW YORK TIMES BOOK
     REVIEW 84 (November 25, 1979): 9, 100-101.

104. "Hannah Arendt--Inspiration, Provocateur, Respected Foe."
     NEW YORK TIMES (October 11, 1981): E9.

     Excerpts from a conference held at New York University.
     Conference speakers included: McCarthy, Rubinstein, Kateb,
     Wolin, Megged and Wieseitier.

105. "Pearl Harbor: The View from Cape Cod." OBSERVER
     (London, G.B.) (December 6, 1981): 24.

106. "Watergate Over the Dam." NEW YORK REVIEW OF BOOKS
     29, no.12 (July 15, 1982): 44.

     Originally published in NEWSDAY. (Not seen)

107. "Novel, Tale, Romance." NEW YORK REVIEW OF BOOKS
     30 (May 12, 1983): 49-56.

     Also published in: McCarthy, Mary. OCCASIONAL PROSE.
     127-152. New York: Harcourt Brace Jovanovich, 1985.

108. "Pleasures of Rereading." NEW YORK TIMES BOOK
     REVIEW (June 12, 1983): 15.

109. "On F.W. Dupee (1904-1979)." NEW YORK REVIEW OF
     BOOKS 30, no.16 (October 27, 1983): 19-21.

     Also published in:
     Dupee, F.W. THE KING OF CATS, with an introduction by
     Mary McCarthy. 2nd ed. xiii-xxi. Chicago: Univ. of Chicago
     Press, 1984.

     McCarthy, Mary. OCCASIONAL PROSE. 248-256. New York:
     Harcourt Brace Jovanovich, 1985.

110. "Indomitable Miss Brayton." HOUSE AND GARDEN 155
(December 1983): 140-145+.

Also published as "The Very Unforgettable Miss Brayton" in:
McCarthy, Mary. OCCASIONAL PROSE. 326-341. New York:
Harcourt Brace Jovanovich, 1985.

111. "Hannah Arendt and Politics." PARTISAN REVIEW 51, no.4
(1984): 729-738.

This was first presented at a conference sponsored by Bard
College, Empire State College, the New School for Social
Research and New York University in October 1981.

112. "Lasting Power of the Political Novel." NEW YORK TIMES
BOOK REVIEW 89 (January 1, 1984): 1, 27-29.

Also published as "Politics and the Novel" in: McCarthy, Mary.
OCCASIONAL PROSE. 200-209. New York: Harcourt Brace
Jovanovich, 1985.

113. "Language and Politics." In OCCASIONAL PROSE, 83-100.
New York: Harcourt Brace Jovanovich, 1985.

Text of a speech given in Philadelphia and Lawrence, Kansas in
November 1973.

114. "Living with Beautiful Things." In OCCASIONAL PROSE,
101-126. New York: Harcourt Brace Jovanovich, 1985.

Text of a speech given in Aberdeen, Scotland in Spring 1974.

115. "On Rereading a Favorite Book." In OCCASIONAL PROSE.
179-186. New York: Harcourt Brace Jovanovich, 1985.

116. "The Unresigned Man." NEW YORK REVIEW OF BOOKS 32
     (February 14, 1985): 27-28.

     Also published in:
     Chiaromonte, Nicola. THE PARADOX OF HISTORY,
     afterword by Mary McCarthy. Philadelphia: Univ. of
     Pennsylvania Press, 1985.

     as "The Paradox of History" in: McCarthy, Mary.
     OCCASIONAL PROSE. 257-266. New York: Harcourt Brace
     Jovanovich, 1985.

117. "Role-Modeling." PARIS REVIEW 28, no.100 (Summer-Fall
     1986): 339-358.

118. "Personal History: Getting an Education, Parts I & II." NEW
     YORKER 62 (July 7; July 14, 1986): 35-57; 34-53.

119. "Forgotten People." NEW YORK REVIEW OF BOOKS 34
     (February 12, 1987): 32.

     Also published in: Macdonald, Nancy. HOMAGE TO THE
     SPANISH EXILES: VOICES FROM THE SPANISH CIVIL
     WAR, preface by Mary McCarthy. 17-23. New York: Human
     Sciences Press, 1987.

120. "Felipe Alfau's LOCOS." REVIEW OF CONTEMPORARY
     FICTION 8, no.3 (Fall 1988): 145-149.

     Also published in:
     Alfau, Felipe. LOCOS: A COMEDY OF GESTURES,
     afterword by Mary McCarthy. 201-206. Elmwood Park, Ill.:
     Dalkey Archive Pr., 1988.

as "Looking Back on LOCOS" in: NEW YORK REVIEW OF BOOKS 35, no.20 (December 20, 1988): 40-42.

121. "A Memory of James Baldwin." NEW YORK REVIEW OF BOOKS 36, no.7 (April 27, 1989): 48-49.

Includes correspondence with Edmund Wilson.

122. "Edmund Wilson." PARIS REVIEW, no.119 (1991): 11-37.

McCarthy was working on her second volume of her memoirs when she died in October 1989. This chapter which, according to McCarthy, was the most difficult to write, was just completed before her death.

Short Stories

123. "Cruel and Barbarous Treatment." SOUTHERN REVIEW 4,
no.4 (Spring 1939): 713-725.

Also published in:
McCarthy, Mary. THE COMPANY SHE KEEPS. 1-22. New
York: Harcourt, Brace & Co., 1942.

Brooks, Cleanth, and Robert Penn Warren, eds. AN
ANTHOLOGY OF STORIES FROM THE SOUTHERN
REVIEW. 249-261. Baton Rouge, La.: State Univ. Press, 1953.

Warren, Robert Penn, and Albert Erskine, eds. SHORT STORY
MASTERPIECES. New York: Dell Pub., c1954.

Slonim, Marc, and Harvey Breit, eds. THIS THING CALLED
LOVE. 101-112. New York: New American Library, 1955.

Brooks, Cleanth, and Robert Penn Warren, eds.
UNDERSTANDING FICTION. 2nd ed. 251-261. New York:
Appleton-Century-Crofts, 1959; Englewood Cliffs, N.J.: Prentice-
Hall, c1959. (McCarthy is also referred to in the Preface and an
interpretation follows the story, p.261-262.)

Bonazza, Blaze O., and Emil Roy, eds. STUDIES IN FICTION.
177-188. New York: Harper & Row, 1965.

Knickerbocker, K.L., and H.W. Reninger, eds.
INTERPRETING LITERATURE. 3rd ed. 107-115. New York:
Holt, Rinehart & Winston, 1965; 4th ed. 96-102. New York:
Holt, Rinehart & Winston, 1969; and 5th ed. 77-83. New York:
Holt, Rinehart & Winston, 1974.

CONTEMPORARY AMERICAN SHORT STORIES, selected
and intro. by Douglas and Sylvia Angus. 230-244. Greenwich,
Conn.: Fawcett Pub., 1967; and Ballantine Books ed. 223-244.
New York: Random House, 1983.

FitzGerald, Gregory, ed. MODERN SATIRIC STORIES: THE
IMPROPRIETY PRINCIPLE. 327-341. Glenview, Ill.: Scott,
Foresman & Co., 1971. (FitzGerald refers to McCarthy's short
story in the Introduction.)

124. "The Man in the Brooks Brothers Shirt." PARTISAN REVIEW
8, no.4 (July-August 1941): 279-288; 324-343.

Also published in:
McCarthy, Mary. THE COMPANY SHE KEEPS. 79-134. New
York: Harcourt, Brace & Co., 1942.

Phillips, William, and Philip Rahv, eds. PARTISAN READER:
TEN YEARS OF PARTISAN REVIEW 1934-44: AN
ANTHOLOGY, intro. by Lionel Trilling. 110-141. New York:
Dial Press, 1946.

Foff, Arthur, and Daniel Knapp, eds. STORY: AN
INTRODUCTION TO PROSE FICTION. 2nd ed. 206-235. San
Francisco: Wadsworth Pub., 1971. (Foff and Knapp refer to
McCarthy in the Introduction, p.13.)

125. "Genial Host." SOUTHERN REVIEW 7, no.2 (Autumn 1941): 280-297.

     Also published in:
     McCarthy, Mary. THE COMPANY SHE KEEPS. 135-164.
     Harcourt, Brace & Co., 1942.

     Kouwenhoven, John A., and Janice Farrar Thaddeus, eds.
     WHEN WOMEN LOOK AT MEN: AN ANTHOLOGY.
     104-120. New York: Harper & Row, 1963.

126. "Ghostly Father, I Confess." HARPER'S BAZAAR 75, no.2764
     (April 1942): 52-53+.

     Also published in:
     McCarthy, Mary. THE COMPANY SHE KEEPS. 247-304.
     New York: Harcourt, Brace & Co., 1942.

     Aswell, Mary Louise, ed. IT'S A WOMAN'S WORLD: A
     COLLECTION OF STORIES FROM HARPER'S BAZAAR.
     261-300. New York: McGraw-Hill; London: Whittlesey House,
     1944.

127. "C.Y.E." MADEMOISELLE (April 1944): 112-113, 190-194.

     Also published in:
     McCarthy, Mary. CAST A COLD EYE. 121-128. New York:
     Harcourt, Brace & World, 1950.

     McCarthy, Mary. HOUNDS OF SUMMER AND OTHER
     STORIES. 144-155. New York: Avon Books, 1981.

128. "The Company Is Not Responsible." NEW YORKER 20, no.10
     (April 22, 1944): 77-80.

129. "The Weeds." NEW YORKER 20, no.31 (September 16, 1944): 25-43.

    Also published in:

    McCarthy, Mary. CAST A COLD EYE. 9-31. New York: Harcourt, Brace & World, 1950.

    McCarthy, Mary. HOUNDS OF SUMMER AND OTHER STORIES. 10-37. New York: Avon Books, 1981.

130. "The Unspoiled Reaction." ATLANTIC MONTHLY 177, no.3 (March 1946): 98-101.

    Also published in:
    Doremus, Robert B., Edgar W. Lacy, and George B. Rodman, eds. PATTERNS IN WRITING: A BOOK OF READINGS FOR COLLEGE STUDENTS. 675-683. New York: William Sloan Assoc., 1950; rev. ed. 697-705. New York: Dryden Press, 1956 and 3rd ed. 627-635. New York: Holt, Rinehart & Winston, 1963. (Commentary and questions follow story in all editions.)

    Felheim, Marvin, Franklin B. Newman, and William R. Steinhoff, eds. MODERN SHORT STORIES. 232-240. New York: Oxford Univ. Press, 1951.

    Baudin, Maurice, ed. CONTEMPORARY SHORT STORIES: REPRESENTATIVE SELECTIONS. American Heritage Series, Vol.3. 214-224. New York: Bobbs-Merrill, 1965, c1954. (Baudin also refers to this short story in the Introduction, p.ix.)

    McClennen, Joshua, ed. MASTERS AND MASTERPIECES OF THE SHORT STORY. 2nd. series. 425-431. New York: Holt, Rinehart & Winston, 1960. (Not seen)

    Greet, T.Y., C.E. Edge, and J.M. Munro, eds. WORLDS OF FICTION: STORIES IN CONTEXT. 376-389. Boston: Houghton Mifflin Co., 1964.

McKenzie, Barbara, ed. PROCESS OF FICTION: CONTEMPORARY STORIES AND CRITICISM. 86-96. New York: Harcourt, Brace & World, 1969. (McKenzie refers to this short story in the Introduction.)

131. "Portrait of the Intellectual As a Yale Man." In THE ROOSEVELT ERA, edited by Milton Crane, foreword by Jonathan Daniels. 253-298. New York: Boni & Gaer, 1947.

Originally published in: McCarthy, Mary. THE COMPANY SHE KEEPS. 165-246. New York: Simon & Schuster, 1942.

132. "The Friend of the Family." TOWN AND COUNTRY 101, no.4292 (January 1947): 101-105, 136-137.

Also published in:
McCarthy, Mary. CAST A COLD EYE. 32-56. New York: Harcourt, Brace & World, 1950.

Auchincloss, Louis, ed. FABLES OF WIT AND ELEGANCE. 211-234. New York: Charles Scribner's Sons, 1972.

McCarthy, Mary. HOUNDS OF SUMMER AND OTHER STORIES. 38-66. New York: Avon Books, 1981.

133. "The Cicerone." PARTISAN REVIEW 15, no.2 (February 1948): 151-176.

Also published in:
McCarthy, Mary. CAST A COLD EYE. 57-82. New York: Harcourt, Brace & World, 1950.

MORE STORIES IN THE MODERN MANNER FROM PARTISAN REVIEW. 64-90. New York: Avon Pub., 1954.

McKenzie, Barbara, ed. PROCESS OF FICTION: CONTEMPORARY STORIES AND CRITICISM. 53-75. New York: Harcourt, Brace & World, 1969. (McKenzie refers to McCarthy in the Introduction and an in-depth analysis follows story.)

McCarthy, Mary. HOUNDS OF SUMMER AND OTHER STORIES. 67-98. New York: Avon Books, 1981.

134. "The Oasis." HORIZON 19, no.110 (February 1949): 75-152.

135. "The Old Men." NEW YORKER 26, no.13 (May 20, 1950): 28-34.

136. "Groves of Academe." NEW YORKER 26, no.50 (February 3, 1951): 28-32.

Also published with revisions as Chapter one in: McCarthy, Mary. THE GROVES OF ACADEME. 1-19. New York: Harcourt, Brace & Co., 1952.

137. "Artists in Uniform." HARPER'S MAGAZINE 206, no.1234 (March 1953): 41-49.

Also published in:
Knoll, Robert E., ed. CONTRASTS, IDEA & TECHNIQUE. 370-383. New York: Harcourt, Brace & Co., 1955. (Knoll also refers to McCarthy in the Introduction.)

Campbell, Oscar James, Justin Van Gundy, and Caroline Shrodes, eds. PATTERNS FOR LIVING. 606-617. New York: Macmillan, c1955.

McCarthy, Mary. ON THE CONTRARY. 55-74. New York: Farrar, Straus & Cudahy, 1961.

Mizener, Arthur, ed. MODERN SHORT STORIES: THE USES OF IMAGINATION. rev. ed. 128-144. New York: W.W. Norton & Co., 1967; 3rd ed. New York: W.W. Norton & Co., 1971; 4th ed. New York: W.W. Norton, 1979.

HANDBOOK OF ANALYSES, QUESTIONS AND A DISCUSSION OF TECHNIQUES FOR USE WITH MODERN SHORT STORIES. 3rd ed. 19-26. New York: W.W. Norton, 1971 and HANDBOOK FOR MODERN SHORT STORIES: THE USES OF IMAGINATION. 4th ed. 19-26. New York: W.W. Norton, 1979. (Includes an analysis of the story with excerpts from "Settling the Colonel's Hash.")

138. "The Group." In AVON BOOK OF MODERN WRITING, edited by William Phillips and Philip Rahv. 32-54. No. 2. New York: Avon Publications, 1954.

Also published with revisions as Chapter one in: McCarthy, Mary. THE GROUP. 3-29. New York: Harcourt, Brace & World, 1963.

139. "Dottie Makes an Honest Woman of Herself." PARTISAN REVIEW 21, no.1 (January-February 1954): 34-52.

Also published:
Dardis, T.A., comp. DAUGHTERS OF EVE: A COLLECTION OF STORIES. 172-192. Berkeley, Calif.: Berkeley Publishing Co., 1956.

with revisions as Chapter three in McCarthy, Mary. THE GROUP. 47-71. New York: Harcourt, Brace & World, 1963.

140. "Settling the Colonel's Hash." HARPER'S MAGAZINE 208, no. 1245 (February 1954): 68-75.

     Also published in:
     Knoll, Robert E., ed. CONTRASTS, IDEA AND TECHNIQUE. 383-394. New York: Harcourt, Brace & Co., 1955. (Refers to McCarthy in chapter's introductory paragraph, p.351.)

     Ludwig, Richard M., ed. ESSAYS TODAY. 84-94. New York: Harcourt, Brace & Co., 1955.

     Campbell, Oscar James, Justin Van Gundy, and Caroline Shrodes, eds. PATTERNS FOR LIVING. 4th ed. 617-628. New York: Macmillan, 1955.

     Rideout, Walter B., ed. EXPERIENCE OF PROSE. 151-162. New York: Thomas Y. Crowell, 1960.

     Beebe, Maurice, ed. LITERARY SYMBOLISM: AN INTRODUCTION TO THE INTERPRETATION OF LITERATURE. 43-54. Belmont, Calif.: Wadsworth Pub., 1960.

     McCarthy, Mary. ON THE CONTRARY. 225-241. New York: Farrar, Straus & Cudahy, 1961.

141. "Appalachian Revolution." NEW YORKER 30, no.30 (September 11, 1954): 40-74.

     Also published in: McCarthy, Mary. HOUNDS OF SUMMER AND OTHER STORIES. 156-192. New York: Avon Books, 1981.

142. "A Charmed Life." NEW YORKER 30, no.34 (October 9, 1954): 36-44 +.

    Also published with revisions as Chapter one in: McCarthy, Mary. A CHARMED LIFE. 1-29. New York: Harcourt, Brace & Co., 1955.

143. "September Morn." NEW YORKER 31, no.31 (September 17, 1955): 40-48.

144. "Life at Jocelyn College" [Excerpt from GROVES OF ACADEME]. In EDUCATION IN SOCIETY: READINGS, edited by Bernard N. Meltzer, Harry R. Doby, and Philip H. Smith, 74-76. New York: Thomas Y. Crowell Co., 1958.

    Originally published as Chapter four in: McCarthy, Mary. THE GROVES OF ACADEME. 63-67. New York: Harcourt, Brace & Co., 1952.

    Also published as "Jocelyn College" in: AMERICAN SATIRE IN PROSE AND VERSE, edited by Henry C. Carlisle. 248-253. New York: Random House, 1962.

145. "Polly Andrews, Class of '33." NEW YORKER 39, no.19 (June 29, 1963): 23-32 +.

    Also published with revisions as Chapters eleven and twelve in: McCarthy, Mary. THE GROUP. 248-306. New York: Harcourt, Brace & World, 1963.

146. "The Hounds of Summer." NEW YORKER 39, no.30 (September 14, 1963): 47-117.

    Also published in:
    Poirier, Richard, and William Abrahams, eds. PRIZE STORIES 1965: THE O. HENRY AWARDS. 249-285. Garden City,

N.Y.: Doubleday & Co., 1965. (Abrahams refers to McCarthy in the Introduction, p.xii.)

Abrahams, William, ed. FIFTY YEARS OF THE AMERICAN SHORT STORY: FROM THE O. HENRY AWARDS 1919-1970. 450-484. Garden City, N.Y.: Doubleday & Co., 1970.

McCarthy, Mary. HOUNDS OF SUMMER AND OTHER STORIES. 193-240. New York: Avon Books, 1981.

147. "Birds of America." SOUTHERN REVIEW n.s., 1, no.3 (July 1965): 644-683.

An excerpt from the chapter "The Figures in the Clock" in:
Also published with revisions as Chapters one and two in: McCarthy, Mary. BIRDS OF AMERICA. 1-90. New York: Harcourt Brace Jovanovich, 1971.

148. "Miss Gowrie [Excerpt from MEMORIES OF A CATHOLIC GIRLHOOD]." In Casty, Alan. THE ACT OF WRITING AND READING: A COMBINED TEXT. 181-182. Englewood Cliffs, N.J.: Prentice-Hall, 1966.

An excerpt from the chapter "The Figures in the Clock" in:
McCarthy, Mary. MEMORIES OF A CATHOLIC GIRLHOOD. 148-153. New York: Harcourt, Brace & Co., 1957.

149. "Thanksgiving in Paris 1964 [Excerpt from BIRDS OF AMERICA]." ATLANTIC 226, no.2 (August 1970): 43-52.

Also published as "Round Table, with the Damsel Parcenet" in: McCarthy, Mary. BIRDS OF AMERICA. 189-216. New York: Harcourt Brace Jovanovich, 1971.

150. "Battle of Rocky Port." McCALLS 98 (January 1971): 87-90.

    Also published in: McCarthy, Mary. BIRDS OF AMERICA.
51-90. New York: Harcourt Brace Jovanovich, 1971.

Book Reviews

151. "Two Crystal-Gazing Novelists." CON SPIRITO 1, no.1 (February 1933): 1-2.

This is an unsigned article, although identified by McCarthy as hers.

152. "Pudding of Saints." NEW REPUBLIC 125, no.974 (August 2, 1933): 323.

153. "Mr. Belloc's Theory of History." NATION 138, no.3574 (January 3, 1934): 24-25.

154. "A Novel About the 'Trouble'." NATION 138, no.3581 (February 21, 1934): 226.

155. COMMON SENSE 3, no.3 (March 1934): 29.

156. "Coalpit College." NEW REPUBLIC 78, no.1013 (May 2, 1934): 343.

157. "A Novel About Distinction." NATION 138, no.3595 (May 30, 1934): 626.

158. "Larger than Life." NATION 138, no.3596 (June 6, 1934): 655.

159. "Vivified History." NATION 138, no.3597 (June 13, 1934): 679-680.

160. "The Old South." NATION 139, no.3605 (August 8, 1934): 167-168.

161. "Alexander the Eccentric." NATION 139, no.3606 (August 15, 1934): 194-195.

162. "Mr. Burnett's Short Stories." NATION 139, no.3614 (October 10, 1934): 416-417.

163. "Romance of Paris." NATION 139, no.3625 (December 26, 1934): 746-747.

164. "Pass the Salt." NATION 140, no.3630 (January 30, 1935): 137-138.

165. "One Man's Road." NATION 140, no.3635 (March 6, 1935): 282, 284.

166. "Living History." NATION 140, no.3636 (March 13, 1935): 312-313.

167. "Two Novels About Musicians." NATION 140, no.3638 (March 27, 1935): 366-367.

168. "Claudius As Emperor." NATION 140, no.3640 (April 10, 1935): 424.

169. "Miscellany." NATION 140, no.3650 (June 19, 1935): 718, 720.

170. "An Old Battle." NATION 141, no.3654 (July 17, 1935): 82.

171. "Young Gloom." NATION 141, no.3659 (August 21, 1935): 220.

172. "Tall Timber." NATION 141, no.3660 (August 28, 1935): 248-249.

173. "Middle Western Marriage." NATION 141, no.3661 (September 4, 1935): 278-279.

174. "Saint Francesca of the Pacific Northwest." NATION 142, no.3680 (January 15, 1936): 82.

175. "Minority Report." NATION 142, no.3688 (March 11, 1936): 326-327.

176. "Highbrow Shockers." NATION 142, no.3692 (April 8, 1936): 458-459.

177. "Two Discoveries." NATION 142, no.3704 (June 27, 1936): 848.

178. "An Antique Genre." NATION 143, no.2 (July 11, 1936): 52.

179. "Paris, 1848." NATION 143, no.7 (August 15, 1936): 191-192.

180. "Shorter Notices." NATION 143, no.20 (November 14, 1936): 584-585.

181. NATION 143, no.22 (November 28, 1936): 641.

182. "Summer Fiction." NATION 145, no.3 (July 17, 1937): 79-80.

183. "The Latest Shudder." NATION 145, no.12 (September 18, 1937): 296.

184. NATION 145, no.17 (October 23, 1937): 454-455.

185. "The People's Choice." PARTISAN REVIEW 6, no.1 (Fall 1938): 106-110.

186. "Two in Our Time." PARTISAN REVIEW 6, no.4 (Summer 1939): 111-114.

187. "Portrait of a Typical Negro?" NEW LEADER 28, no.25 (June 13, 1945): 10.

188. "Tyranny of the Orgasm." NEW LEADER 30, no.14 (April 5, 1947): 10.

     Also published in: McCarthy, Mary. ON THE CONTRARY. 167-173. New York: Farrar, Straus & Cudahy, 1961.

189. "Mlle. Gulliver en Amérique." REPORTER 6, no.2 (January 22, 1952): 34-37.

     Also published in:
     German as "Mademoiselle Passepartout." DER MONAT 4, no.42 (March 1952): 651-653.

     McCarthy, Mary. ON THE CONTRARY. 24-31. New York: Farrar, Straus & Cudahy, 1961.

     French as "Mademoiselle Gulliver découvre l'Amérique." ARTS (October 14-20, 1964).

     Marks, Elaine, ed. CRITICAL ESSAYS ON SIMONE DE BEAUVOIR. 44-48. Boston: G.K. Hall, 1987.

190. "Recalled to Life, or, Charles Dickens at the Bar." REPORTER 8, no.5 (March 3, 1953): 35-40.

     Also published in: McCarthy, Mary. ON THE CONTRARY. 217-224. New York: Farrar, Straus & Cudahy, 1961.

191. "Philosophy at Work." NEW YORKER 34, no.35 (October 18, 1958): 198-205.

     Also published as "The VITA ACTIVA" in: McCarthy, Mary. ON THE CONTRARY. 155-167. New York: Farrar, Straus & Cudahy, 1961.

192. "An Academy of Risk." PARTISAN REVIEW 26, no.3
     (Summer 1959): 476-480.

     Also published in: McCarthy, Mary. ON THE CONTRARY.
     242-248. New York: Farrar, Straus & Cudahy, 1961.

193. "Exit a Conscience." SUNDAY TELEGRAPH (London, G.B.)
     (February 26, 1961): 6.

194. "A Bolt from the Blue." NEW REPUBLIC 146, no.23 (June 4,
     1962): 21-27.

     See also letters (item no. 332) and McCarthy's response (item
     no. 258); Kermode's article (item no. 335); Field's article (item
     no. 391); and McCarthy's reply to Field (item no. 263).

     Also published with revisions:
     as "Nabokov's PALE FIRE" in ENCOUNTER 19, no.4
     (October 1962): 71-84.

     McCarthy, Mary. WRITING ON THE WALL. 15-34. New
     York: Harcourt, Brace & World, 1970.

195. "J.D. Salinger's Closed Circuit." HARPER'S MAGAZINE 225,
     no.1349 (October 1962): 46-48.

     Originally published in OBSERVER (London, G.B.). (Not seen)

     Also published in: McCarthy, Mary. WRITING ON THE
     WALL. 35-41. New York: Harcourt, Brace & World, 1970.

196. "Déjeuner sur l'herbe." NEW YORK REVIEW OF BOOKS, Special Issue (1963): 4-5.

    Also published with revisions:
    as "Burroughs' NAKED LUNCH" in ENCOUNTER 20, no.4 (April 1963): 92-98.

    McCarthy, Mary. WRITING ON THE WALL. 42-53. New York: Harcourt, Brace & World, 1970.

197. "On MADAME BOVARY." PARTISAN REVIEW 31, no.2 (Spring 1964): 174-188.

    Also published in: McCarthy, Mary. WRITING ON THE WALL. 72-94. New York: Harcourt, Brace & World, 1970.

198. "Hue and Cry." PARTISAN REVIEW 31, no.1 (Winter 1964): 82-94.

    Also published in: McCarthy, Mary. WRITING ON THE WALL. 54-71. New York: Harcourt, Brace & World, 1970.

    See also series of letters in response to this review (item no. 357); McCarthy's reply (item no. 259); Sparrow's unsigned letter (item no. 366); McCarthy's reply (item no. 260); and Maxwell's letter (item no. 372).

199. "Books of the Year: A Personal Choice." OBSERVER (London, G.B.) (December 19, 1965): 22.

200. "Everybody's Childhood." NEW STATESMAN 72, no.1844 (July 15, 1966): 90-94.

    Also published in: McCarthy, Mary. WRITING ON THE WALL. 102-111. New York: Harcourt, Brace & World, 1970.

201. "Books of the Year: Some Personal Choices." OBSERVER (London, G.B.) (December 18, 1966): 23.

202. "Mary McCarthy Über Ivy Compton-Burnett: eine Familie und ein Vermögen." DER SPIEGEL 21, no.10 (February 27, 1967): 131-132. German.

203. "Writing on the Wall." NEW YORK REVIEW OF BOOKS (January 30, 1969): 3-6.

    Also published in: McCarthy, Mary. WRITING ON THE WALL. 153-171. New York: Harcourt, Brace & World, 1970.

204. "Hanging by a Thread." NEW YORK REVIEW OF BOOKS 13, no.2 (July 31, 1969): 4-6.

    Also published in: McCarthy, Mary. WRITING ON THE WALL. 172-188. New York: Harcourt, Brace & World, 1970.

205. "The Tolstoy Connection." SATURDAY REVIEW 55, no.38 (September 16, 1972): 79-96.

    Also published in:
    Dunlop, John B., Richard Haugh, and Alexis Klimoff, eds. ALEKSANDR SOLZHENITSYN: CRITICAL ESSAYS AND DOCUMENTARY MATERIALS. 332-350. Belmont, Mass.: Nordland Pub., 1973; and in 2nd ed. 332-350. New York: Collier Books, 1975.

    McCarthy, Mary. OCCASIONAL PROSE. 155-178. New York: Harcourt Brace Jovanovich, 1985.

206. "Sons of the Morning." NEW YORK REVIEW OF BOOKS 19, no.12 (January 25, 1973): 3-12.

    See also Leonard's response to this review (item no. 444).

    Also published in: McCarthy, Mary. THE SEVENTEENTH DEGREE. 413-435. New York: Harcourt Brace Jovanovich, 1974.

207. "On Colonel Risner." NEW YORK REVIEW OF BOOKS 21, no.3 (March 7, 1974): 10-12.

    See also Fallow's article (item no. 449).

208. "Acts of Love." NEW YORK REVIEW OF BOOKS 28, no.11 (June 25, 1981): 3-6.

    Also published in: McCarthy, Mary. OCCASIONAL PROSE. 187-189. New York: Harcourt Brace Jovanovich, 1985.

209. "The Rake's Progress." NEW YORK REVIEW OF BOOKS 28, no.17 (November 5, 1981): 20, 22.

    Also published in: McCarthy, Mary. OCCASIONAL PROSE. 315-325. New York: Harcourt Brace Jovanovich, 1985.

210. "In the Family Way." NEW YORK REVIEW OF BOOKS 30 (December 8, 1983): 17-18.

    Also published in: McCarthy, Mary. OCCASIONAL PROSE. 210-216. New York: Harcourt Brace Jovanovich, 1985.

211. "Love and Death in the Pacific." NEW YORK TIMES BOOK
REVIEW (April 22, 1984): 1, 18-19.

Also published as "Democracy" in: McCarthy, Mary.
OCCASIONAL PROSE. 217-229. New York: Harcourt Brace
Jovanovich, 1985.

212. "Breeders, Wives and Unwomen." NEW YORK TIMES BOOK
REVIEW (February 9, 1986): 1, 35.

See also Low's letter in response to this review (item no. 534).

Theater and Film Reviews

213. "Theater Chronicle." PARTISAN REVIEW 4, no.1 (December 1937): 54-56.

Also published as "Two Bad Cases of Social Conscience" in: McCarthy, Mary. SIGHTS AND SPECTACLES. 3-8. New York: Farrar, Straus & Cudahy, 1956 and MARY McCARTHY'S THEATRE CHRONICLES. 3-8. New York: Farrar, Straus & Co., 1963.

214. "Theater Chronicle." PARTISAN REVIEW 4, no.2 (January 1938): 48-49.

Also published as "Odets Deplored" in: McCarthy, Mary. SIGHTS AND SPECTACLES. 9-12. New York: Farrar, Straus & Cudahy, 1956 and MARY McCARTHY'S THEATRE CHRONICLES. 9-12. New York: Farrar, Straus & Co., 1963.

215. "Versions of Shakespeare." PARTISAN REVIEW 4, no.3 (February 1938): 34-38.

Also published as "Elizabethan Revivals" in: McCarthy, Mary. SIGHTS AND SPECTACLES. 13-20. New York: Farrar, Straus & Cudahy, 1956 and MARY McCARTHY'S THEATRE CHRONICLES. 13-20. New York: Farrar, Straus & Co., 1963.

216. "Theater Chronicle: Class Angles and Classless Curves."
     PARTISAN REVIEW 4, no.5 (April 1938): 52-56.

     Also published as "Class Angles and a Wilder Classic" in:
     McCarthy, Mary. SIGHTS AND SPECTACLES. 21-29. New
     York: Farrar, Straus & Cudahy, 1956 and MARY
     McCARTHY'S THEATRE CHRONICLES. 21-29. New York:
     Farrar, Straus & Co., 1963.

217. "Theater Chronicle: The Federal Theater Settles Down."
     PARTISAN REVIEW 4, no.6 (May 1938): 43-47.

     Also published as "The Federal Theatre" in: McCarthy, Mary.
     SIGHTS AND SPECTACLES. 30-38. New York: Farrar, Straus
     & Cudahy, 1956 and MARY McCARTHY'S THEATRE
     CHRONICLES. 30-38. New York: Farrar, Straus & Co., 1963.

218. "Theater Chronicle: New Sets for the Old House." PARTISAN
     REVIEW 5, no.1 (June 1938): 41-44.

     Also published as "Shaw and Chekhov" in: McCarthy, Mary.
     SIGHTS AND SPECTACLES. 39-45. New York: Farrar, Straus
     & Cudahy, 1956 and MARY McCARTHY'S THEATRE
     CHRONICLES. 39-45. New York: Farrar, Straus & Co., 1963.

219. "Theatre Chronicle: An Innocent on Broadway." PARTISAN
     REVIEW 7, no.2 (March-April 1940): 135-138.

     Also published as "Saroyan, an Innocent on Broadway" in:
     McCarthy, Mary. SIGHTS AND SPECTACLES. 46-52. New
     York: Farrar, Straus & Cudahy, 1956 and MARY
     McCARTHY'S THEATRE CHRONICLES. 46-52. New York:
     Farrar, Straus & Co., 1963.

220. "Theatre Chronicle: Chaos Is Come Again." PARTISAN
REVIEW 10, no.1 (January-February 1943): 82-83.

   Also published in:
   Phillips, William, and Philip Rahv, eds. PARTISAN READER:
   TEN YEARS OF PARTISAN REVIEW 1934-44, AN
   ANTHOLOGY, intro. by Lionel Trilling. 655-657. New York:
   Dial Press, 1946.

   as "THE SKIN OF OUR TEETH" in: McCarthy, Mary.
   SIGHTS AND SPECTACLES. 53-56. New York: Farrar, Straus
   & Cudahy, 1956 and MARY McCARTHY'S THEATRE
   CHRONICLES. 53-56. New York: Farrar, Straus & Co., 1963.

221. "Theatre Chronicle: The Russian Soul." PARTISAN REVIEW
10, no.2 (March-April 1943): 184-186.

   Also published as "The Russian Soul in Wartime" in: McCarthy,
   Mary. SIGHTS AND SPECTACLES. 57-62. New York: Farrar,
   Straus & Cudahy, 1956 and MARY McCARTHY'S THEATRE
   CHRONICLES. 57-62. New York: Farrar, Straus & Co., 1963.

222. "Theatre Chronicle: Broadway's Spring Offensive." PARTISAN
REVIEW 10, no.3 (May-June 1943): 279-280.

   Also published as "Broadway's Spring Offensive" in: McCarthy,
   Mary. SIGHTS AND SPECTACLES. 63-66. New York: Farrar,
   Straus & Cudahy, 1956 and MARY McCARTHY'S THEATRE
   CHRONICLES. 63-66. New York: Farrar, Straus & Co., 1963.

223. "Theatre Chronicle: Winter in the Theatre." PARTISAN
REVIEW 11, no.2 (Spring 1944): 168-172.

   Also published as "Wartime Omnibus" in: McCarthy, Mary.
   SIGHTS AND SPECTACLES. 67-75. New York: Farrar, Straus

& Cudahy, 1956 and MARY McCARTHY'S THEATRE
CHRONICLES. 67-75. New York: Farrar, Straus & Co., 1963.

224. "A Filmy Vision of the War." TOWN AND COUNTRY 99,
no.4259 (April 1944): 72, 112.

Also published as "Mary McCarthy Goes to the Movies" in:
FILM COMMENT 12, no.1 (January-February 1976): 32-34.

225. "Theatre Chronicle: We Must Have Faith." PARTISAN
REVIEW 12, no.1 (Winter 1945): 90-92.

Also published as "We Must Have Faith" in: McCarthy, Mary.
SIGHTS AND SPECTACLES. 76-80. New York: Farrar, Straus
& Cudahy, 1956 and MARY McCARTHY'S THEATRE
CHRONICLES. 76-80. New York: Farrar, Straus & Co., 1963.

226. "Theater Chronicle: Dry Ice." PARTISAN REVIEW 13, no.5
(November-December 1946): 577-579.

Also published with "The Farmer's Daughter" (published in
NEW YORK TIMES BOOK REVIEW (August 31, 1952): 7) as
"Eugene O'Neill--Dry Ice" in: McCarthy, Mary. SIGHTS AND
SPECTACLES. 81-88. New York: Farrar, Straus & Cudahy,
1956 and MARY McCARTHY'S THEATRE CHRONICLES.
81-88. New York: Farrar, Straus & Co., 1963.

227. "Theater Chronicle: Gerontion." PARTISAN REVIEW 14, no.1
(January-February 1947): 62-66.

Also published as "Five Curios" in: McCarthy, Mary. SIGHTS
AND SPECTACLES. 89-96. New York: Farrar, Straus &
Cudahy, 1956 and MARY McCARTHY'S THEATRE
CHRONICLES. 89-96. New York: Farrar, Straus & Co., 1963.

228. "Theater Chronicle: Something About the Weather." PARTISAN REVIEW 14, no.2 (March-April 1947): 174-179.

    Also published in:
    Phillips, William, and Philip Rahv, eds. NEW PARTISAN READER 1945-1953. 531-536. New York: Harcourt, Brace & Co., 1953.

    as "George Kelly" in McCarthy, Mary. SIGHTS AND SPECTACLES. 97-105. New York: Farrar, Straus & Cudahy, 1956.

    as "George Kelly" in MARY McCARTHY'S THEATRE CHRONICLES. 97-105. New York: Farrar, Straus & Co., 1963.

229. "Theater Chronicle: The Unimportance of Being Oscar." PARTISAN REVIEW 14, no.3 (May-June 1947): 302-304.

    Also published in:
    McCarthy, Mary. SIGHTS AND SPECTACLES. 106-110. New York: Farrar, Straus & Cudahy, 1956.

    MARY McCARTHY'S THEATRE CHRONICLES. 106-110. New York: Farrar, Straus & Co., 1963.

    Corrigan, Robert, ed. LAUREL BRITISH DRAMA: THE NINETEENTH CENTURY. 399-402. New York: Dell Pub., 1967.

230. "Theater Chronicle: What a Piece of Work Is Man!" PARTISAN REVIEW 14, no.4 (July-August 1947): 393-395.

    Also published as "What a Piece of Work Is Man!" in:
    McCarthy, Mary. SIGHTS AND SPECTACLES. 116-120. New York: Farrar, Straus & Cudahy, 1956 and MARY

McCARTHY'S THEATRE CHRONICLES. 116-120. New
York: Farrar, Straus & Co., 1963.

231. "Theater Chronicle: Props and Property." PARTISAN REVIEW
      15, no.1 (January 1948): 74-80.

      Also published as "Four 'Well-Made' Plays" in: McCarthy,
      Mary. SIGHTS AND SPECTACLES. 121-130. New York:
      Farrar, Straus & Cudahy, 1956 and MARY McCARTHY'S
      THEATRE CHRONICLES. 121-130. New York: Farrar, Straus
      & Co., 1963.

232. "Theater Chronicle: Oh, Sweet Mystery of Life." PARTISAN
      REVIEW 15, no.3 (March 1948): 357-360.

      Also published as "A Streetcar Called Success" in: McCarthy,
      Mary. SIGHTS AND SPECTACLES. 131-135. New York:
      Farrar, Straus & Cudahy, 1956 and MARY McCARTHY'S
      THEATRE CHRONICLES. 131-135. New York: Farrar, Straus
      & Co., 1963.

233. "Theater Chronicle: Modest Proposals." PARTISAN REVIEW
      15, no.4 (April 1948): 477-480.

      Also published as "Little Theatre" in: McCarthy, Mary. SIGHTS
      AND SPECTACLES. 136-140. New York: Farrar, Straus &
      Cudahy, 1956 and MARY McCARTHY'S THEATRE
      CHRONICLES. 136-140. New York: Farrar, Straus & Co.,
      1963.

234. "Theater Chronicle: A Prince of Shreds and Patches."
      PARTISAN REVIEW 26, no.1 (January 1949): 82-84.

      Also published in: McCarthy, Mary. SIGHTS AND
      SPECTACLES. 141-145. Farrar, Straus & Cudahy, 1956 and

MARY McCARTHY'S THEATRE CHRONICLES. 141-145.
New York: Farrar, Straus & Co., 1963.

235. "Theatre: Sartre and the McCoy." POLITICS 6, no.1 (Winter
1949): 49-51.

236. "The Farmer's Daughter." NEW YORK TIMES BOOK
REVIEW (August 31, 1952): 7.

See also Krutch's article (item no. 323) and Abel's article (item
no. 310).

Also published with "Theater Chronicle: Dry Ice" (published in
PARTISAN REVIEW 13 (November-December 1946): 577-579)
as "Eugene O'Neill-Dry Ice" in: McCarthy, Mary. SIGHTS
AND SPECTACLES. 81-88. New York: Farrar, Straus &
Cudahy, 1956.

Also published as "A Moon for the Misbegotten" in O'NEILL
AND HIS PLAYS: FOUR DECADES OF CRITICISM, edited
by Oscar Cargill, N.Bryllion Fagin, and William J. Fisher.
209-211. New York: New York Univ. Press, 1961. (Refers to
McCarthy in the Introduction, p.12-14.)

237. "Bard with Blood: Some Reflections on a Rare Presentation
Opening the City Center Season." NEW YORK TIMES
(February 1, 1953): 1, 3.

Also published as "The Little Gate" in: McCarthy, Mary.
SIGHTS AND SPECTACLES. 146-150. New York: Farrar,
Straus & Cudahy, 1956 and in MARY McCARTHY'S
THEATRE CHRONICLES. 146-150. New York: Farrar, Straus
& Co., 1963.

238. "Theater Chronicle: Shaw at the Phoenix." PARTISAN REVIEW 22, no.2 (Spring 1955): 252-259.

     Also published as "Shaw Off Broadway" in: McCarthy, Mary. SIGHTS AND SPECTACLES. 151-162. New York: Farrar, Straus & Cudahy, 1956 and MARY McCARTHY'S THEATRE CHRONICLES. 151-162. New York: Farrar, Straus & Co., 1963.

239. "Three Plays with Music." In SIGHTS AND SPECTACLES 1937-56. 111-115. New York: Farrar, Straus & Cudahy, 1956.

     Also published in: MARY McCARTHY'S THEATRE CHRONICLES 1937-1962. 111-115. New York: Farrar, Straus & Cudahy, 1963.

240. "The Will and Testament of Ibsen." PARTISAN REVIEW 23, no.1 (Winter 1956): 74-80.

     Also published in: McCarthy, Mary. SIGHTS AND SPECTACLES. 168-178. New York: Farrar, Straus & Cudahy, 1956 and MARY McCARTHY'S THEATRE CHRONICLES. 168-178. New York: Farrar, Straus & Co., 1963.

241. "Theater Chronicle: Sheep in Wolves' Clothing." PARTISAN REVIEW 24, no.2 (Spring 1957): 270-274.

     Also published in: MARY McCARTHY'S THEATRE CHRONICLES 1937-1962. 179-185. New York: Farrar, Straus & Co., 1963.

242. "A New Word." HARPER'S BAZAAR 91, no.2957 (April 1958): 176-177, 202, 210.

     Also published in: MARY McCARTHY'S THEATRE CHRONICLES. 186-198. New York: Farrar, Straus & Co., 1963.

243. "Theater Chronicle: Odd Man In." PARTISAN REVIEW 26, no.1 (Winter 1959): 100-106.

     Also published in: MARY McCARTHY'S THEATRE CHRONICLES. 199-208. New York: Farrar, Straus & Co., 1963.

244. "Curtains for Tynan?" OBSERVER (London, G.B.) (October 22, 1961): 28.

     See also Pryce-Jones' response to this review (item no. 326) and Atkinson's article (item no. 327).

     Also published with revisions as "Drapes" in:
     PARTISAN REVIEW 29, no.1 (Winter 1962): 140-142.

     MARY McCARTHY'S THEATRE CHRONICLES 1937-1962. 230-234. New York: Farrar, Straus & Co., 1963.

245. "General Macbeth." HARPER'S MAGAZINE 224, no.1345 (June 1962): 35-39.

     Also published in:
     MARY McCARTHY'S THEATRE CHRONICLES. 235-248. New York: Farrar, Straus & Co., 1963.

     Barnet, Sylvan, ed. WILLIAM SHAKESPEARE: THE TRAGEDY OF MACBETH. 229-247. London: New American Library, 1963. (Not seen)

McCarthy, Mary. WRITING ON THE WALL. 3-14. New York: Harcourt, Brace & World, 1970.

246. "Verdict on Osborne." OBSERVER (London, G.B.) (July 4, 1965): 17.

See also Tynan's response to this review (item no. 283) and McCarthy's reply (item no. 262).

Translations

247. "The 27th of September." PARTISAN REVIEW 3, no.2 (March 1936): 19-21.

   A translation of an article by André Gide.

248. "Second Thoughts on the U.S.S.R." PARTISAN REVIEW 4, no.2 (January 1937): 21-28.

   A translation of an article by André Gide. Although unsigned, this article was identified by McCarthy as her own.

249. "The Iliad or, The Poem of Force." POLITICS 2, no.11 (November 1945): 321-331.

   A translation of an article by Simone Weil.

   Also published in book form: Weil, Simone. THE ILIAD OR THE POEM OF FORCE, translated by Mary McCarthy. A Pendle Hill Pamphlet, no.91. Wallingford, Pa.: Pendle Hill, 1948, 37p.

Also published in:
WIND AND THE RAIN 6, no.4 (Spring 1950): 228-247.
Anderson, Quentin, and J.A. Mazzeo, eds. THE PROPER
STUDY. 4-29. New York: St. Martin's Press, 1962.

CHICAGO REVIEW 18, no.2 (1965): 5-30.

250. ON THE ILIAD. Bollingen Series IX. New York: Pantheon
Books, 1947, 126p.

A translation of a book by Rachel Bespaloff.

251. "Eye for Eye." POLITICS 4, no.4 (July-August 1947): 134-140.

A translation of an article by Simone de Beauvoir.

252. "Sartre and the Prize." ENCOUNTER 24, no.2 (February
1965): 55-57.

A translation of an article by Nicola Chiaromonte.

253. McCarthy, Mary, and Donald Strom, trans. "On Pirandello's
CLOTHING THE NAKED." NEW YORK REVIEW OF
BOOKS (February 20, 1975): 30-31.

A translation of an article by Nicola Chiaromonte.

Letters to the Editor

254. Marshall, Margaret. "Sorry." NATION 142, no.3678 (January 1, 1936): 18.

    A correction to final article of "Critics: Right or Wrong" series which appeared in NATION (December 18, 1935): 717-719.

255. "Mary McCarthy and Her Critics." NATION 143, no.24 (December 12, 1936): 715-716.

    Replies to Menefee's letter which was written in response to McCarthy's article "Circus Politics in Washington State" (item no. 36). See also Menefee's letter (item no. 290).

256. "The Hiroshima NEW YORKER." POLITICS 3, no.10 (November 1946): 367.

    See also Yavenditti's reference to this letter (item no. 452).

    Also published as "A Letter to the Editor of POLITICS" in: McCarthy, Mary. ON THE CONTRARY: ARTICLES OF BELIEF. 3-5. New York: Farrar, Straus & Cudahy, 1961.

257. "Ibsen and Kierkegaard." PARTISAN REVIEW 23, no.2
     (Spring 1956): 287-288.

     Replies to Arnold's letter. See also McCarthy's review entitled
     "The Will and Testament of Ibsen" (item no. 240) and Arnold's
     letter (item no. 301).

258. "Pale Fire." NEW REPUBLIC 147, no.1 (July 2, 1962): 31.

     Replies to letters by Yoder, Osterlag, and Higgins. See also
     McCarthy's review entitled "A Bolt from the Blue" (item no.
     194) and letters (item no. 332).

259. "More On Eichmann." PARTISAN REVIEW 31, no.2 (Spring
     1964): 276-277.

     Replies to critics. See also McCarthy's review entitled "Hue and
     Cry" (item no. 198) and letters (item no. 357).

260. "Judges in Israel." TIMES LITERARY SUPPLEMENT,
     no.3252 (June 25, 1964): 551.

     Replies to Maxwell's letter (item no. 372).

261. "Letter to a Translator: About THE GROUP." ENCOUNTER
     23, no.5 (November 1964): 69-71, 74-76.

     Also published in French as "A Propos du GROUPE: Lettre à
     mon traducteur Danois" in PREUVES 15, no.174 (August 1965):
     69-75.

262. "Patriot or Coward." OBSERVER (London, G.B.) (July 25, 1965): 26.

   Replies to Tynan's letter. See also McCarthy's review "Verdict on Osborne" (item no. 246) and Tynan's letter (item no. 383).

263. "Nabokov." NEW YORK TIMES BOOK REVIEW (July 10, 1966): 50.

   Responds to a comment made by Field in his review of Nabokov's DESPAIR. See also McCarthy's review "A Bolt from the Blue" (item no. 194); Field's review (item no. 391); and his reply to this letter (item no. 393).

264. "Out of Limbo." NEW YORK REVIEW OF BOOKS 8, no.12 (June 29, 1967): 29.

265. "Ideology and Vietnam." NEW YORK REVIEW OF BOOKS 10, no.4 (February 29, 1968): 34.

   See also original exchange between Trilling and McCarthy (item nos. 80 and 404).

266. "Anti-American." LISTENER 80, no.2073 (December 19, 1968): 828.

   Responds to Serpell's review of HANOI. See also Serpell's review (item no. 1310) and his reply to this letter (item no. 415).

267. "Lillian Hellman." TIMES LITERARY SUPPLEMENT, no.4194 (August 19, 1983): 882.

   See also Hitchen's article (item no. 510) and Spender's letter (item no. 511).

268. "Mexico 'Is Being Strangled'." WASHINGTON POST
      (September 9, 1983): A16.

269. "Spender's 'Journals'." TIMES LITERARY SUPPLEMENT,
      no.4324 (February 16, 1986): 165.

Miscellanea

270. Von Kaltenborn, Hans. KALTENBORN EDITS THE NEWS: EUROPE-ASIA-AMERICA. With editorial assistance by Mary McCarthy and Roger Craig. Gold Seal Books, no. 3. New York: Modern Age Books, 1937, 183p.

    Ghost written by McCarthy and Roger Craig, the acknowledgments read: The author's thanks are due to Roger Paul Craig and Mary McCarthy for valuable editorial assistance.

271. "La Traviata." In LA TRAVIATA, edited by Guiseppe Verdi, Libretto by Francesco Maria Piave, story adaptation by Mary McCarthy, intro. by Gary Schmidgall, 43-77. Metropolitan Opera Classics Library. Boston: Little, Brown & Co., 1983.

    Also published in: McCarthy, Mary. OCCASIONAL PROSE. 269-312. New York: Harcourt Brace Jovanovich, 1985.

Interviews

272. Niebuhr (Sifton), Elisabeth. "The Art of Fiction: Mary
   McCarthy." PARIS REVIEW 7, no.27 (Winter-Spring 1962):
   58-94.
      Remarks that her forthcoming book, THE GROUP, is about
   the "idea of progress as seen in the female sphere." Discusses
   several of her stories and confesses they are more or less
   autobiographical. Expresses annoyance that so much attention is
   paid to who is who in her novels, maintaining that it deflects
   from what she is trying to do. Discusses her teaching career,
   early literary career, political opinions and their effect on her
   writing, literary preferences, and literary practices.

   Also published in:
   Plimpton, George, ed. WRITERS AT WORK: THE PARIS
   REVIEW INTERVIEWS, intro. by Van Wyck Brooks. 2nd
   Series. 283-315. New York: Viking Press, c1963; 239-263.
   London: Secker & Warburg, 1963; New York: Viking Compass,
   1965; and 283-315. Harmondsworth: Penguin Books, c1977.

   WRITER'S YEARBOOK 35 (1964): 10-15+.

   Plimpton, George, ed. WOMEN WRITERS AT WORK: THE
   PARIS REVIEW INTERVIEWS, intro. by Margaret Atwood.
   169-199. New York: Viking Penguin, 1989.

273. Smith, Peter Duval. "Mary McCarthy Said." VOGUE 142, no.7 (October 15, 1963): 98-99+.
     Categorizes women novelists as "sense women" or "sensibility women," and discusses Austen in those terms. Examines the creation of male characters by female authors, and the more successful, female characters by male authors. Talks about her forthcoming book THE GROUP, and her clear preference for the mothers over the daughters in the book.

274. Le Clec'h, Guy. "Mary McCarthy--romancière Américaine progressiste--est anti-MacCarthyste." FIGARO LITTÉRAIRE (March 4-10, 1965): 4. French.
     Interviews McCarthy and discusses her recent book and her thoughts on American politics.

275. Jardin, Claudine. "Une Nouvelle vague littéraire: le Mary-McCarthysme." FIGARO (March 24, 1965): 24. French.
     Talks with McCarthy about her book and asks her pointed questions about similarities with De Beauvoir. Quotes McCarthy as saying that De Beauvoir writes badly and the only point of similarity between them is they both wrote books about their Catholic upbringing.

276. Flanner, Janet. "Conversation Piece." NEW YORK TIMES BOOK REVIEW (November 21, 1965): 5, 88-91.
     McCarthy interviews Flanner, author of PARIS NOTEBOOK.

277. Wiggins, John R. "An Interview with Mary McCarthy." ELLSWORTH AMERICAN (Ellsworth, Maine) (August 9, 1967).
     Speaks about growing up in Seattle, her years at Vassar, starting out as a writer, and the writing of THE GROUP, VIETNAM, and BIRDS OF AMERICA. Briefly reflects on poverty, and the youth in America.

278. Mossman, James. "Mary McCarthy Talks to James Mossman about the Vietnam War." LISTENER 79 (January 18, 1968): 78-80.
     Explores McCarthy's purpose and motives for going to

Vietnam and writing about it. Questions her prejudgment of the situation and her determination to find America at fault.

279. Rhode, Eric. "A Discourse on Nature." LISTENER 83, no.2150 (June 11, 1970): 785-786.
     Talks to McCarthy about the role of nature in her work in general, and in BIRDS OF AMERICA in particular. Mentions Compton-Burnett, Nabokov and Orwell and their treatment of nature.

280. Rahv, Philip. "The Editor Interviews Mary McCarthy." MODERN OCCASIONS 1, no.1 (Fall 1970): 14-25.
     Explores McCarthy's views on the Vietnam War and Nixon's role, the political and cultural situation in France, French literature, the youth culture, and the relationship between art and politics.

281. Wade, Valerie. "Chez Elles: The Paris of Lesley Blanch, Nancy Milford and Mary McCarthy." TIMES. SUNDAY TIMES MAGAZINE (London, G.B.) (September 27, 1970): 50-53.
     Visits McCarthy's Paris apartment and describes it for the reader.

282. Revel, Jean-François. "Miss McCarthy Explains." NEW YORK TIMES BOOK REVIEW (May 16, 1971): 2, 24-27.
     Discusses the structure of BIRDS OF AMERICA, and the development of the themes: death of nature, the desire to create balance and equality, and the philosophy of Kant. Talks briefly about living in Paris and her thoughts on the Vietnam War. See also Gross's letter (item no. 432).

     Also published in French as "Mary McCarthy: 'Je ne vois pas comment on en sortira. . . .'" FIGARO (June 3, 1972): 13, 16.

283. Ress, Paul. "Underpinning of BIRDS OF AMERICA: An Interview." HARPER'S BAZAAR 104 (June 1971): 92-93.
     Talks with McCarthy about BIRDS OF AMERICA, her passion for truth and authenticity in fiction, and her models for Peter.

284. Ehrlich, Arnold W. "Authors & Editors." PUBLISHERS
WEEKLY 200, no.4 (July 26, 1971): 19-21.
    Reviews of BIRDS OF AMERICA form the springboard for
this interview with McCarthy. Expresses annoyance with what
she calls the "bitchiness" of the reviews, noting the "sinister case
of standardization of opinion" and the belief in the decline of the
quality of reviewing. Includes one-liners by McCarthy on a
number of writers and concludes with a discussion of her future
writing plans.

    Also published in: Publishers Weekly, eds. THE AUTHOR
SPEAKS: SELECTED PW INTERVIEWS 1967-1976. 107-109.
New York: R.R. Bowker, c1978.

285. Burstall, Christopher. "'The Incident is not Closed': A
Conversation about Jane Austen." LISTENER 94 (December 25,
1975; January 1, 1976): 875.
    Conversation from the program Omnibus (BBC television) in
which Greer, McCarthy and Stassinopoulos talk about Austen's
work.

286. Gross, Miriam. "A World Out of Joint." OBSERVER (October
14, 1979): 35.
    Talks with McCarthy about CANNIBALS AND
MISSIONARIES and the message she was trying to convey in
the discussions on the value of art and human life. Explores
McCarthy's views on Vietnam, women's liberation, marriage,
nature and the sorry state of the American book reading public.

287. McCarthy, Kevin. "A New Kind of McCarthyism: Actor Kevin
Interviews Sister Mary on Her Books, Loves, and Life."
PEOPLE WEEKLY 12 (November 12, 1979): 92 + .
    Interviews his sister about their childhood, the Vietnam War,
and the reasons for her failed marriages.

288. Kufrin, Joan. "The Novelist: Mary McCarthy." In
     UNCOMMON WOMEN, with photographs by George Kufrin,
     72-91. Piscataway, N.J.: New Century Pubs., 1981.
        Talks with McCarthy about her novels and essays, exploring
     her writing techniques and various aspects of her work.

289. Brightman, Carol. "Mary Still Contrary." NATION 238 (May
     19, 1984): 611-619.
        Talks with McCarthy about her attempts to start a magazine,
     Vietnam and her essays against the war, fiction and writing,
     feminism and feminist literature, De Beauvoir, and her
     forthcoming intellectual biography HOW I GREW.

SECTION II - WORKS ABOUT McCARTHY

General Criticism

290. Menefee, Selden C. "Mary McCarthy and Her Critics [Letter to the Editor]." NATION 143, no.24 (December 12, 1936): 715.

    Criticizes the reactionary tone of McCarthy's article "Circus Politics in Washington State," in which she states her thoughts on the progressive movement in Washington. See also McCarthy's article (item no. 36) and her reply to this letter (item no. 255).

291. "Critical Spirit." TIME 31, no.12 (March 21, 1938): 75.

    Notes Wilson's marriage to McCarthy and comments that she refers to him as "the best of American critics."

292. Jones, Frank N. "Well-Intentioned/Well-Equipped." PARTISAN REVIEW 15, no.5 (May 1948): 587-593.

    Finds Bespaloff's ON THE ILIAD inferior to Weil's THE ILIAD: POEM OF FORCE, however, mentions McCarthy translated both superbly.

293. Hook, Sidney. "The Waldorf Conference." POLITICS 6, no.1 (Winter 1949): A32-A36.

    Provides an in-depth account of the Cultural and Scientific Conference for World Peace organized by the Communist front organization, the National Council of the Arts, Sciences and Professions (NCASP). Recounts verbatim various speeches including questions posed by McCarthy, one of the attendees.

294. "Meet Mary McCarthy." NEW YORK POST 149, no.80
     (February 20, 1950): 3.
        Summarizes McCarthy's publications and literary awards to
     date.

295. Isherwood, Christopher. "Young American Writers."
     OBSERVER (London, G.B.) (May 13, 1951).
        Notes that McCarthy and Tennessee Williams are among the
     few writers who present a mature attitude toward sexual love in
     their writing.

296. James, Daniel. "The Debate on Cultural Freedom." NEW
     LEADER 35, no.4 (April 7, 1952): 3-4.
        Provides a summary of the conference "In Defense of Free
     Culture." Reports that the most divisive session was the one
     entitled "Who Threatens Cultural Freedom?" in which three
     schools of thought relating to communism were seen to emerge.
     Contends that the faction to which McCarthy belongs understands
     the need to combat the Soviet threat but also recognizes the
     dangers of [Senator] McCarthyism.

297. Crosby, John. "Mr. Highet Talks on Books." NEW YORK
     HERALD TRIBUNE (May 21, 1952): 25.
        Discusses a series of radio programs about books hosted by
     Gilbert Highet. Quotes from various shows including one which
     mentions that McCarthy is the most effective satirist in America.

298. Sheerin, John B. "What Makes a Communist?" CATHOLIC
     WORLD 178 (February 1954): 321-325.
        Examines what motivated so many to convert to communism
     in the 1940s and 1950s. Traces McCarthy's experience as
     recounted in "My Confession" and suggests it was typical of that
     of thousands of Americans. Questions why she felt she had to
     renounce her involvement but does admit that such a confession
     evinced a refreshing and surprising humility. Suggests that her
     zest for adventure is correlated with the zeal for reform and
     experimentation so prevalent in French Catholic intellectuals.

299. Churchill, Allen. "The Author." SATURDAY REVIEW 38
(November 5, 1955): 17.
     Reports that McCarthy is in Venice gathering material for a
travel book. Notes that her partisans feel that she "has struck her
vein of emotional understanding, and being human, readers of A
CHARMED LIFE are likely to forget the question of Miss
McCarthy's emotional growth in favor of speculation about the
town of New Leeds."

300. "Cye." TIME 66, no.20 (November 14, 1955): 126, 129-130,
132.
     Chronicles McCarthy's personal and professional past.
Remarks that she is a clever writer who chooses to write her
friends and enemies into her books and challenges the experts to
discover who is who. Parallels her heroines to Eliot's, suggesting
that McCarthy's heroines do not merely "smooth their hair . . .
and put a record on the gramophone, they come out of the
clinches . . . to rearrange reality in a more comfortable shape."
Offers brief descriptions of several of McCarthy's books.

301. Arnold, G. L. "Correspondence: Ibsen and Kierkegaard."
PARTISAN REVIEW 23, no.2 (Spring 1956): 287.
     Responds to McCarthy's review of Ibsen's THE WILD
DUCK saying that the British version differs from the New York
production in that in London, Gregers Werle "looks and talks
rather like Soren Kierkegaard." See also McCarthy's review
(item no. 240) and her reply to this letter (item no. 257).

302. Fiedler, Leslie A. "Adolescence and Maturity in the American
Novel." In AN END TO INNOCENCE: ESSAYS ON
CULTURE AND POLITICS, 206. Boston: Beacon Press, 1957.
     Refers briefly to McCarthy in a discussion on THE
PARTISAN REVIEW.

     Also published in: AN END TO INNOCENCE: ESSAYS ON
CULTURE AND POLITICS. 2d ed. New York: Stein & Day,
1972.

303. Alpert, Hollis. "Coterie Tales." SATURDAY REVIEW 40
     (January 19, 1957): 42.
          Briefly examines the short stories awarded prizes by Engle,
     in PRIZE STORIES 1957. Claims "Yellowstone Park" was
     written with badly concealed snobbishness. Suggests that the
     majority of the prize winning stories would not appeal to the
     average reader. Notes that most of the awards were given to
     stories published in magazines with limited circulation.

304. Hoggart, Richard. "A Matter of Rhetoric? American Writers and
     British Readers." NATION (April 27, 1957): 361-364.
          Evaluates the writing styles of various American writers, and
     observes that Trilling and McCarthy are not distinctively
     American novelists. Refers to McCarthy's mode of writing as
     "New York European," a "refined and intellectually
     self-conscious form of Europeanism."

305. "Nineteen Chosen for Art Awards." NEW YORK TIMES (May
     1, 1957): 43.
          Reports that McCarthy is one of a number of artists, authors
     and composers awarded grants by the American Academy of
     Arts and Letters and National Institute of Arts and Letters.

306. "The Elegant Miss McCarthy." TIMES LITERARY
     SUPPLEMENT, no.2889 (July 12, 1957): 426.
          Analyzes McCarthy's work to date, from her PARTISAN
     REVIEW theater reviews, to THE COMPANY SHE KEEPS in
     which her satirical attitude to "the victims pinned as neatly as
     butterflies" is questioned; to her later books in which she is "too
     self-conscious" and conveys only the pain of her own
     experiences. Concludes that she is a writer who has not yet
     realized her abundant talents.

307. Bradford Aresty, Esther. "The Fulfilled Woman [Letter to the
     Editor]." SATURDAY REVIEW (July 13, 1957): 21.
          Responds to McGinley's article, writing that there is nothing
     "trite" about happy wives and mothers; they are also successful
     writers, painters, heads of colleges and businesses. See also
     McGinley's article (item no. 909) and her response to this letter
     (item no. 308).

308. McGinley, Phyllis. "Defendant: Miss McGinley [Letter to the Editor]." SATURDAY REVIEW (July 13, 1957): 21.

    Replies to the omission of the word "little" in the last sentence of her review of MEMORIES OF A CATHOLIC GIRLHOOD. Says that the error cancels the ironic overtone which had been intended, leaving the sentence to read as a declaration that McCarthy could never be pictured as a "happy wife and mother." Begs the editor to come to her defense. See also McGinley's article (item no. 909) and Bradford Aresty's letter (item no. 307).

309. Hungerland, Isabel C. "Symbols in Poetry." In POETIC DISCOURSE, edited by W. R. Dennes, John Myhill, and E. W. Strong, 135-136. Univ. of California Pub. in Philosophy, Vol. 33. Berkeley, Calif.: Univ. of California Press, 1958.

    Quotes from McCarthy's essay "Settling the Colonel's Hash" to illustrate the importance of symbols in modern literary criticism. Uses McCarthy's words to emphasize the fact that critics have become so determined in their search for meaning that they see symbols everywhere.

    Also published: Westport, Conn.: Greenwood Press, 1977.

310. Abel, Lionel. "O'Neill and His Critics." NEW LEADER 41, no.1 (January 6, 1958): 25-26.

    Follows on Krutch's reply to Bentley and McCarthy's criticism of O'Neill. Allows that Bentley has earned the right to his opinions, but does not give the same latitude to McCarthy, whose views Abel declares to be immoderate, violent and feminine. Defends O'Neill's writing, calling him a master of rhetoric and argues that a dramatist's aim is not necessarily elegance, but authenticity. See also McCarthy's review "Farmer's Daughter" (item no. 236) and Krutch's article (item no. 323).

311. Gold, Herbert. "The Writer as Nag." THE NATION 187, no.3 (January 18, 1958): 54-56.

    Challenges contemporary writers whose work builds upon

gossip and moralizing. Uses McCarthy as an example of a
popular practitioner of the art.

312. Antonini, Giacomo. "Mary McCarthy." FIERA LETTERARIA
(Rome, Italy) 13, no.6 (February 9, 1958): 1-2. Italian.
    Commends McCarthy for her spirit, acute intelligence and
surprisingly avid interest in anything Italian. Says she is her own
protagonist, setting an unmistakable personal and characteristic
tone to her writing. Discusses her background and the influences
in her life.

313. Fitch, R. E. "The Cold Eye of Mary McCarthy." NEW
REPUBLIC 138, no.18 (May 5, 1958): 17-19.
    Defines great literature as that which speaks to "the head, the
heart, the guts and the groin." Labels modern literature as
"cerebral-genital" skipping the two intermediate organs. Analyzes
McCarthy's literary style and judges her to be one of the most
skillful practitioners of the cerebro-genital perspective, at one
with her contemporaries in her dualism--between the body and
the mind, the flesh and the spirit, and the cerebral and the
genital. See also Ross's response to this article (item no. 314).

314. Ross, T. J. "Passion, Moral and Otherwise." NEW REPUBLIC
139 (August 18, 1958): 23-26.
    Responds to Fitch's article which states that McCarthy has
no "point of view," defames all values and gains a false sense of
superiority by satirizing ideals including the ones in her own
book. See also Fitch's article (item no. 313).

315. Brustein, Robert. "The Theatre Is Losing Its Minds."
COLUMBIA UNIVERSITY FORUM 2, no.1 (Fall 1958).
    Blames the current low ebb in popularity and standards of
the American theater on critics, such as McCarthy, who delight
in destroying a play and make no effort to offer positive
suggestions.

316. "Mary McCarthy." In A LIBRARY OF LITERARY
     CRITICISM: MODERN AMERICAN LITERATURE, compiled
     and edited by Dorothy Nyren, 303-305. New York: F. Ungar
     Pub., 1960.
         Notes that the book in its entirety is meant to serve as a
     "critical key to twentieth century American writing through the
     1950s." Includes excerpts and citations to ten critical
     commentaries on McCarthy.

     Also published in: A LIBRARY OF LITERARY CRITICISM:
     MODERN AMERICAN LITERATURE. 2nd ed. 303-305. New
     York: F. Ungar Pub., 1961 and 3rd. ed. 303-305. New York: F.
     Ungar Pub., 1964.

317. Rowe, Dilys. "Clarity and Candour." GUARDIAN (Manchester,
     G.B.) (February 22, 1960): 6.
         Describes the British leg of one of McCarthy's European
     literary tours and provides a brief biographical sketch of "this
     beautiful woman."

318. "Institute of Arts Picks 12 Members." NEW YORK TIMES
     (February 24, 1960): 74.
         Notes that McCarthy is one of a dozen new members elected
     to the National Institute of Arts and Letters.

319. "U.S. Arts Institute Elections." TIMES (London, G.B.)
     (February 24, 1960): 11.
         Notes McCarthy's election to the National Institute of Arts
     and Letters.

320. Cloyne, George. "Behind the Times." TIMES (London, G.B.)
     (March 3, 1960): 15.
         Examines McCarthy's comment that the theater lags behind
     the novel by some thirty years and proposes the explanation that
     a novel "surrounds" the reader, requiring total attention and
     focus, while the theater opposes the audience to the action on the
     stage.

321. "2 Art Groups Give $40,000 in Awards." NEW YORK TIMES (May 26, 1960): 38.

      Notes that McCarthy has been inducted into the Department of Literature of the National Institute of Arts and Letters and the American Academy.

322. Robinson, David. "MONITOR in Profile." SIGHT AND SOUND (London, G.B.) 30, no.1 (Winter 1960-1961): 41-43.

      Mentions McCarthy as one of the people interviewed on the television program MONITOR.

323. Krutch, Joseph Wood. "Eugene O'Neill's Claim to Greatness." In O'NEILL AND HIS PLAYS: FOUR DECADES OF CRITICISM, edited by Oscar Cargill, N. Bryllion Fagin, and William J. Fisher, 472-476. New York: New York University Press, 1961.

      Quotes McCarthy in a discussion of O'Neill's works. See also McCarthy's review (item nos. 226 and 236).

324. Poli, Sara. "La Narrativa di Mary McCarthy." STUDI AMERICANI 7 (1961): 215-259. Italian.

      Considers that McCarthy's narrative demonstrates her acute observation, a penetrating and vivacious capacity for psychological introspection and uncommon analytical intelligence. Discusses her work in detail noting that her satire is motivated by personal experience.

325. Gluckman, Ivan B., and Paddy Chayefsky. "Gloomy Playwrights [Letter to the Editor]." HARPER'S MAGAZINE 223, no.1336 (September 1961): 4-5.

      Responses to McCarthy's "interesting" and "provocative" article on realism in contemporary American drama. See also McCarthy's essay (item no. 70).

326. Pryce-Jones, Alan. "Contrary Mary." OBSERVER (London, G.B.) (October 22, 1961): 28.

      Responds to McCarthy's in-depth review of Tynan's CURTAINS. Notes various examples of inconsistencies within McCarthy's piece and accuses her of not knowing Tynan's work well enough. See also McCarthy's review (item no. 244) and Atkinson's response to this article (item no. 327).

327. Atkinson, Brooks. "Critic at Large: Adverse Review of Tynan's Book by Mary McCarthy Created Literary Tempest." NEW YORK TIMES (October 27, 1961): 30.

Refers to the heated debate between McCarthy and Pryce-Jones. Notes McCarthy was in top form in her review of CURTAINS and decides to join in the dispute taking issue with Tynan's comment that "tragedy . . . barely exists in pinchback simulacra." See also McCarthy's review (item no. 244) and Pryce-Jones' response to the review (item no. 326).

328. Hardwick, Elizabeth. "The New Books--Manner and Matter in Non-Fiction." HARPER'S MAGAZINE 224, no.1340 (January 1962): 91-92.

Explores McCarthy's unique style in THE COMPANY SHE KEEPS, A CHARMED LIFE, SIGHTS AND SPECTACLES, and ON THE CONTRARY. Points out that while plot and dramatic sense are weak in her fiction, taste and accuracy are not. Maintains that most of her fiction contains an element of autobiography and this is where McCarthy excels.

Also published in: Hardwick, Elizabeth. A VIEW OF MY OWN: ESSAYS IN LITERATURE AND SOCIETY. 33-40. New York: Farrar, Straus & Cudahy, 1962; New York: Noonday Press, 1963; London: Heinemann, 1964 and New York: Ecco Press, 1982.

329. Balakian, Nona. "The Prophetic Vogue of the Anti-Heroine." SOUTHWEST REVIEW (Tex.) 42, no.2 (Spring 1962): 134-161. (Not seen)

330. Antonini, Giacomo. "Umore della McCarthy." FIERA LETTERARIA (Rome, Italy) 17, no.10 (March 11, 1962): 1-2. Italian.

Comments that McCarthy may not have the strong narrative talent and poetic insight of McCullers or Porter, but her artistic creations are based on experience and autobiographical elements.

Says that although THE STONES OF FLORENCE and VENICE OBSERVED provide a superficial and personal reaction to Italy, producing a "guidebook" impression, McCarthy is worthy of attention.

331. "The Glass Ménage." NEWSWEEK 59, no.25 (June 18, 1962): 50-51.
    Quotes from McCarthy's critical review of Salinger's FRANNY AND ZOOEY.

332. "Conflagration [Letters to the Editor]." NEW REPUBLIC 146, no.26 (June 25, 1962): 31.
    Combines a series of responses by Higgins, Osterlag, Kauffmann, Conner and Yoder, mostly favorable, to McCarthy's review of Nabokov's PALE FIRE. See also McCarthy's review (item no. 194) and her reply to these letters (item no. 258).

333. Brower, Brock. "Mary McCarthyism." ESQUIRE 58, no.1 (July 1962): 62-67, 113.
    Presents a bio-critical analysis focusing on several of McCarthy's long-term relationships. Argues that despite external influences, McCarthy remains her own woman, incredibly honest, forthright and sure of herself.

    Also published in: OTHER LOYALTIES: A POLITICS OF PERSONALITY. 61-77. New York: Atheneum, 1968.

334. Paden, W. D. "U.S. Passport [Letter to the Editor]." SPECTATOR, no.6997 (August 3, 1962): 157.
    Notes two oversights in Moore's review of ON THE CONTRARY: the government's refusal to grant passports to Communists; and the belief that Howard Fast faced jail due to his ideas on communism. See also Moore's review (item no. 1046).

335. Kermode, Frank. "Zemblances." NEW STATESMAN 64 (November 9, 1962): 671-672.
    Refers to McCarthy's review in this discussion of Nabokov's PALE FIRE. States that while reading the book one is reminded

of McCarthy's assertion that it is "one of the very
great works of art of this century." See also McCarthy's review
(item no. 194).

336. Wershba, Joseph. "Lady of Letters." NEW YORK POST
(November 15, 1962): 27.
Comments on McCarthy's scathing review of Salinger's
FRANNY AND ZOOEY, in which she claims that it "isn't a
novel anyway, whatever it is." Notes that in her own writing
McCarthy has always been against "slovenliness, intellectual
flabbiness, moral cowardice and vacuity . . . her purpose is
strictly to educate and elevate." See also McCarthy's review
(item no. 195).

337. Chamberlain, John Rensselaer. "The Novels of Mary
McCarthy." In THE CREATIVE PRESENT: NOTES ON
CONTEMPORARY AMERICAN FICTION, edited by Nona
Balakian and Charles Simmons, 239-255. Garden City, N.Y.:
Doubleday & Co., 1963.
Analyzes McCarthy's novels as satire and compares her
writing to that of Waugh saying that Waugh's chosen enemies
are "more powerful." Goes on to criticize McCarthy for the
somewhat trivial nature of her work and concludes she "has yet
to take on an adversary that is worthy of her scorn." Refers to
McCarthy in the Introduction.

Also published in:
THE CREATIVE PRESENT: NOTES ON CONTEMPORARY
AMERICAN FICTION. 2nd ed. 241-255. New York: Gordian
Press, 1973.

Spanish translation of this book as "Las Novelas de Mary
McCarthy" in LA NARRATIVA ACTUAL EN LOS ESTADOS
UNIDOS. 319-339. Buenos Aires: Editorial Nova, 1963.

338. Eisinger, Chester E. "Mary McCarthy as the Sceptical New Liberal." In FICTION OF THE FORTIES, 128-134. Chicago: Univ. of Chicago Press, 1963.

    Suggests that McCarthy is a "heartless chronicler" who does not become emotionally involved with her characters and concludes that she is "a new liberal by default."

339. Thompson, Barbara. "Katherine Anne Porter: An Interview." PARIS REVIEW 8, no.29 (1963): 87-114.

    Describes McCarthy as one of the wittiest and in some ways the worst-tempered woman in American letters.

    Also published in:
    Plimpton, George, ed. WRITERS AT WORK: PARIS REVIEW INTERVIEWS, intro. by Van Wyck Brooks. 2nd. series. New York: Viking Press, 1963.

    Plimpton, George, ed. WOMEN WRITERS AT WORK: THE PARIS REVIEW INTERVIEWS, intro. by Margaret Atwood. 45-70. New York: Viking Penguin Press, 1989.

340. "Contrary Mary: Vassar '33." NEWSWEEK 62, no.10 (September 2, 1963): 80-83.

    Offers an in-depth essay on McCarthy. Believes that the "insurance" that THE GROUP will be a best seller lies in chapter two, which might end up in a time capsule as a minute description of the sexual activities of Americans of the 1930s. Praises McCarthy who "stands out like the female brainy one for whom the Greeks built the Parthenon." See also letters by Efthimiou and Falcone in response to this article (item no. 341) and (item no. 343).

341. Efthimiou, Cleo Lefouses. "Who's Stupid? [Letter to the Editor]." NEWSWEEK 62, no.12 (September 16, 1963): 11.

    Responds to an article written in NEWSWEEK and says that McCarthy "must indeed have sprung from Zeus's head." See also article "Contrary Mary: Vassar '33" (item no. 340) and letters (item no. 343).

342. Bonfante, Jordan. "Lady with a Switchblade." LIFE 55
(September 20, 1963): 61, 64-65.
     Presents some of McCarthy's controversial and uninhibited
views on a wide variety of topics, including Salinger, radicals
and reactionaries and the narrowing gap between communism
and capitalism.

343. Falcone, Marion, and James L. Roberts. "Contrary Mary [Letter
to the Editor]." NEWSWEEK 62, no.13 (September 23, 1963):
6.
     Offers responses to the original article in NEWSWEEK.
Writes that McCarthy is "more of a common scold than a wit."
See also article "Contrary Mary: Vassar '33" (item no. 340) and
Efthimiou's letter (item no. 341).

344. Prynne, Xavier. "The Gang." NEW YORK REVIEW OF
BOOKS (September 26, 1963): 22.
     Presents a parody of THE GROUP by Elizabeth Hardwick
written under the pseudonym Xavier Prynne.

345. Hartt, Elfreida, and Margaret K. Hunt. "Vassar, Vassar
Everywhere [Letters to the Editor]." REPORTER 29, no.8
(November 7, 1963): 12.
     Responds to Knapp's review of THE GROUP in these two
letters by Vassar graduates. See also Knapp's review (item no.
1127).

346. Gould, Diana. "Mary McCarthy and Her Admirers, Literary
Reunion at 'The Y' - Author Reads from THE GROUP."
COLUMBIA OWL (S.C.) 5, no.8 (November 20, 1963): 1, 6.
     Describes a gathering during which McCarthy read from
THE GROUP and explained her writing technique.

347. "Newsmakers: Mary, Quite Contrary." NEWSWEEK 62, no.22
(November 25, 1963): 64.
     Notes McCarthy's quip that if she had a daughter she would
send her to Radcliffe, "the snob college of today--what Vassar
used to be."

348. Austin, John Evans. "Letters to the Editor." VASSAR
ALUMNAE MAGAZINE (December 1963): 30.
Comes to the defense of Vassar girls and claims that the
novel could be about a group of girls from any college.

349. Trilling, Diana. "Who's Afraid of the Culture Elite?" ESQUIRE
(December 1963): 69-88.
Refers to McCarthy's essay on Salinger and her theory that
both Salinger and Hemingway portray their characters as
members of an exclusive club who live in a "closed circuit"
excluding the rest of humanity. Suggests McCarthy's theory
stops short of recognizing that this game of what's in and what's
out is not merely a pastime of Salinger or Hemingway, but is in
fact the very universal enterprise of contemporary literature and
contemporary life. See also McCarthy's review (item no. 195).

Also published as "The Riddle of Albee's WHO'S AFRAID OF
VIRGINIA WOOLF?" in: CLAREMONT ESSAYS. 203-227.
New York: Harcourt, Brace & World, 1964; London: Secker &
Warburg, 1965.

350. Heissenbüttel, Helmut. "Mary McCarthy: Versuch eines
Portrats." DER MONAT 16, no.189 (1964): 54-67. German.
Analyzes McCarthy's work in detail, focusing in particular
on a comparison of THE COMPANY SHE KEEPS and THE
GROUP. Looks at McCarthy's sociological, political and
historical concerns and identifies self-expression and individual
experience within the parameters of societal conventions as her
primary areas of interest.

351. Mander, Gertrud. "Die überschatzte McCarthy [Mary McCarthy:
DIE CLIQUE]." NEUE DEUTSCHE HEFTE. BEITRAGE
ZUR EUROPAISCHEN GEGENWART. GUTERSLOH 102
(1964): 111-115. German.
Contends that McCarthy is an intelligent writer with insight,
wit, and stylistic verve. Disagrees with the opinion that she is to
be counted among the very important writers of the twentieth
century. Calls McCarthy a feminist, sociologist, chronicler and

critic of upper middle-class lifestyles, but not a noteworthy
literary figure.

352. Schlueter, Paul. "The Dissections of Mary McCarthy." In
CONTEMPORARY AMERICAN NOVELISTS, edited by Harry
T. Moore, 54-64. Carbondale: Southern Illinois Univ. Press,
1964.
    Argues that McCarthy's technique is to dissect her characters
and expose their flaws. Claims that her interest is not in human
beings per se, but in people as objects she can use for her own
purposes. Concludes that despite all the intellectualism, her
books seem to lack a "moral foundation, on which great art must
be based."

    Also published in: CONTEMPORARY AMERICAN
NOVELISTS. revised ed. New York: Arcturus Books, 1966.

353. Craig Faxon, Alicia. "Letters to the Editor." VASSAR
ALUMNAE MAGAZINE (February 1964): 32.
    Contends that, unlike McCarthy, she finds Vassar superior to
Radcliffe both in intellectual stimulation and accomplishment.
Writes that although the wit and fine writing of THE GROUP
are enjoyable, its lack of depth and compassion make the book
more "a piece of excellent journalism; an interim report rather
than a novel." See also McCarthy's article (item no. 48) and
Dauler Wilson's reply to this letter (item no. 368).

354. Lamberton, Gretchen L. "Letter to the Editor." VASSAR
ALUMNAE MAGAZINE (February 1964): 32.
    Calls THE GROUP "a pornographic and dreary peep-hole
show [of] utterly shallow Vassar characters the likes of which
any college would be ashamed to claim" and compares this
image of the Vassar graduate with the "thoroughbred" Jacqueline
Kennedy, a real Vassar graduate.

355. Paterson, Margaret C. "Librarian Upheld [Letter to the Editor]."
EDINBURGH EVENING NEWS (February 24, 1964).
    Series of correspondence related to the censoring of

McCarthy's THE GROUP. See also letters (item nos. 356 and 358) and Paterson's response (item no. 359).

356. "THE GROUP [Letter to the Editor]." EDINBURGH EVENING NEWS (February 27, 1964).

Responds to Paterson's letter condemning THE GROUP, and suggests that prior to criticizing the book, she should at least have read the dust cover. See also Paterson's letter (item no. 355) and her reply to this anonymous letter (item no. 359).

357. "More On Eichmann." PARTISAN REVIEW 31, no.2 (Spring 1964): 251-275.

Series of responses by Syrkin, Weisberg, Howe, Lowell, Macdonald and Abel to McCarthy's article. See also McCarthy's review (item no. 198) and her reply to this letter (item no. 259).

358. England, Joan. "THE GROUP [Letter to the Editor]." EDINBURGH EVENING NEWS (March 3, 1964).

Refutes Paterson's incorrect assumption that the main theme of THE GROUP is homosexuality. See also Paterson's letter (item no. 355) and her response (item no. 359).

359. Paterson, Margaret C. "On Hearsay [Letter to the Editor]." EDINBURGH EVENING NEWS (March 3, 1964).

Responds to an anonymous letter criticizing the fact that she should have read THE GROUP before condemning it. States that after finishing the book she is even more certain that it has no place in a library. See also anonymous letter (item no. 356).

360. Adams, J. Donald. "Speaking of Books." NEW YORK TIMES BOOK REVIEW (March 22, 1964): 2.

Discusses the National Book Awards and notes with pleasure that THE GROUP did not win.

361. "Australian Ban of GROUP Will Not Be Contested." NEW YORK TIMES (March 26, 1964): 32.

Reports that the publisher of THE GROUP will not contest its banning in Victoria State, Australia.

362. Campbell McNally, Dorothy. "Letters to the Editor." VASSAR
     ALUMNAE MAGAZINE 49, no.4 (April 1964): 64.
     Argues that THE GROUP, a catalogue of "venery, a
     disgrace to the printed word," has sullied the fine reputation of
     Vassar. Proposes that McCarthy's degree should be rescinded.

363. McLean O'Grady, Mollie. "Letters to the Editor." VASSAR
     ALUMNAE MAGAZINE 49, no.4 (April 1964): 40.
     Writes a satiric spoof on THE GROUP. See also Blodgett's
     response (item no. 367).

364. Woeltz, Colby Cleveland. "Letters to the Editor." VASSAR
     ALUMNAE MAGAZINE 49, no.4 (April 1964): 40, 64.
     Comes to the defense of McCarthy and THE GROUP saying
     that she sees shades of her own classmates in McCarthy's
     characters. Notes that college graduates should be able to see the
     work objectively as fiction.

365. "THE GROUP: Australian Uproar." BOOKSELLER (April 11,
     1964): 1594-1595.
     Reports that THE GROUP was banned by police in Victoria
     State, Australia but was permitted in other parts of the country.

366. Sparrow, John. "Judges in Israel: The Case of Adolf Eichmann."
     TIMES LITERARY SUPPLEMENT, no.3244 (April 30, 1964):
     365-368.
     Responds to McCarthy's article on EICHMANN IN
     JERUSALEM. See also McCarthy's review (item no. 198) and
     her reply to this letter (item no. 260).

367. Blodgett, Julia. "Letters to the Editor." VASSAR ALUMNAE
     MAGAZINE (June 1964): 48.
     Congratulates McLean O'Grady for her letter in the April
     issue (see also item no. 363).

368. Dauler Wilson, Margaret. "Letters to the Editor." VASSAR
     ALUMNAE MAGAZINE (June 1964): 47-48.
     Writes this letter in response to Faxon's letter and comments
     on the Vassar-Radcliffe rivalry. See also Craig Faxon's letter
     (item no. 353).

369. Hunt, Margaret K. "Letters to the Editor." VASSAR
     ALUMNAE MAGAZINE (June 1964): 48-49.
     Refuses to read THE GROUP because of a review McCarthy
     wrote of Salinger's FRANNY AND ZOOEY which Hunt found
     insensitive. Comes to the defense of Vassar. See also
     McCarthy's review (item no. 195).

370. McChesney Wyman, Martha. "Letters to the Editor." VASSAR
     ALUMNAE MAGAZINE (June 1964): 47.
     Vassar graduate repudiates THE GROUP as "pornographic
     and revolting" and deplores "the dark place in a soul that would
     drive a woman to write . . . this book."

371. "New Zealand Lifts Book Ban." NEW YORK TIMES (June 25,
     1964): 30.
     Reports that New Zealand has lifted its censorship ban on
     THE GROUP.

372. Maxwell, J. C. "Judges in Israel [Letter to the Editor]." TIMES
     LITERARY SUPPLEMENT, no.3254 (July 9, 1964): 613.
     Refers to McCarthy's review of Arendt's EICHMANN IN
     JERUSALEM. See also McCarthy's review (item no. 198).

373. Schlueter, Paul. "The Amoralist: Mary McCarthy." MOTIVE 25
     (December 1964): 46-50.
     Considers the quality of morality, the single theme that ties
     McCarthy's entire literary output. Evaluates a number of her
     works from the moral point of view, emphasizing her use of
     sexual morality as the occasion for exposure of hypocrisy.
     Wonders how much of her writing is her own philosophy of life,
     and how much is fiction, but finally judges that her novels lack
     the moral foundation necessary for enduring art.

374. Steegmuller, Francis. "Speaking of Books: Emma Bovary and
     Mary McCarthy." NEW YORK TIMES BOOK REVIEW 7
     (December 20, 1964): 2.
     Reflects that writing introductions to the classics often seems
     to be a way to "possess" a work one feels a special kinship for.
     Observes in McCarthy's highly personalized introduction to
     MADAME BOVARY that she has tried to remake Flaubert in

her own image, and in so doing has taken such liberties with the facts that they border on misrepresentation.

375. Auchincloss, Louis Stanton. "Mary McCarthy." In PIONEERS & CARETAKERS: A STUDY OF NINE AMERICAN WOMEN WRITERS, 170-186. Minneapolis: Univ. of Minnesota Press; New York: Dell Pub., 1965.

Chronicles McCarthy's career. Claims that Wilson performed a valuable service to American fiction when he encouraged McCarthy to write. Compares McCarthy to Wharton saying that "as a stylist she started at the high level that she has consistently maintained." (Also briefly refers to McCarthy in the Introduction.)

376. Baumbach, Jonathan. "Introduction." In THE LANDSCAPE OF NIGHTMARE: STUDIES IN THE CONTEMPORARY AMERICAN NOVEL, 8-9. New York: New York Univ. Press, 1965.

Explores the state of the novel and the types of novels that have been written in the past. Focuses on McCarthy as an example of the "academic novelist" saying that although she has "an abrasive critical intelligence and [is] a formidably incisive prose writer . . . [she] has not written a first-rate novel." Argues that all of her characters are recreated with her satiric pen and therefore do not come across as real people with whom the reader can identify.

Also published in British edition: London: Peter Owen, 1966.

377. de Rosa, Giuseppe. "Mary McCarthy atea per capriccio?" LA CIVILTA CATTOLICA (Rome, Italy) 116, no.4 (1965): 370-374. Italian.

Disagrees with the Italian translation of MEMORIES OF A CATHOLIC GIRLHOOD which insinuates McCarthy became an atheist as a result of her Catholic education. Discusses her religious crisis as a young girl, highlighting passages from the book, and concludes that there is no loss of faith, only a brief adolescent crisis.

378. Kazin, Alfred. "1940." In STARTING OUT IN THE
     THIRTIES, 154-159. Boston: Little, Brown & Co., 1965.
     Chronicles Kazin's development as a literary radical through
     the war years. Writes about various intellectuals of the 1940s,
     including the THE PARTISAN REVIEW group which included
     McCarthy.

     Also published in: STARTING OUT IN THE THIRTIES.
     London: Secker & Warburg, 1966 and New York: Vintage
     Books, 1980.

379. Whitehorn, Katharine. "Geistig 200--gef Ühlslmässig 24.
     Begegnung mit Mary McCarthy." WELTWOCHE. ZURICH 33,
     no.1662 (1965): 41. German.
     Visits McCarthy in Paris and records casual impressions of
     her lifestyle, and her views on France. Deals with McCarthy's
     working habits, her marriage to Edmund Wilson and her
     marriage to James West. Judges her to be clear-eyed, precise and
     analytical in the use of language, yet also finds her romantic.

380. Phillips, John, Hollander, Anne. "Lillian Hellman: An
     Interview." PARIS REVIEW 9, no.33 (Winter-Spring 1965):
     62-95.
     Includes Hellman's comments on McCarthy's talents during
     the interview, and her claims that she will not defend herself
     against McCarthy's opinions of her plays.

     Also published in: Plimpton, George, ed. WOMEN WRITERS
     AT WORK: THE PARIS REVIEW INTERVIEWS, intro. by
     Margaret Atwood. 121-146. New York: Viking Penguin, 1989.

381. Crozier, Mary. "NO MEAN CITY on BBC-2." GUARDIAN
     (Manchester, G.B.) (March 29, 1965): 9.
     Reviews McCarthy's description of Paris on the BBC-2's
     program NO MEAN CITY and claims she did a better job than
     Brian Glanville did on Florence. Maintains that although she
     made some interesting observations about the city, she wasted

time reflecting on popular, preconceived notions such as "Paris is gay" or "Paris is romantic."

382. Delpech, Jeanine. "En Attendant Kinsey: Mary McCarthy." NOUVELLES LITTERAIRES 43 (April 22, 1965): 6. French.
     Bases this article on an interview McCarthy did in the United States because she refused to be interviewed in France. Uses McCarthy's comments to support her analysis of THE GROUP.

383. Tynan, Kenneth. "Missing Osborne's Point [Letter to the Editor]." OBSERVER (London, G.B.) (July 18, 1965): 26.
     Responds to McCarthy's review of Osborne's play A PATRIOT FOR ME and wonders whether her complete failure to understand it was real or feigned. Argues that the play was strongest precisely where she finds it weakest. States that her insensitivity to this play may lie in the fact that although her writing demonstrates every masculine virtue, it lacks femininity. See also McCarthy's review (item no. 246) and her reply to this letter (item no. 262).

384. Moers, Ellen. "The Creation of Women." NEW YORK TIMES BOOK REVIEW (July 25, 1965): 1, 26.
     Discusses McCarthy in a review of Louis Auchincloss' study of female novelists, PIONEERS AND CARETAKERS.

385. Whitehorn, Katharine. "Meeting Mary McCarthy." OBSERVER. WEEKLY COLOUR SUPPLEMENT (London, G.B.) (August 29, 1965): 6-9.
     Offers biographical information and some first hand impressions of McCarthy the woman, as well as the writer.

386. Kostelanetz, Richard. "The Short Story in Search of Status." TWENTIETH CENTURY (G.B.) 174, no.1027 (Autumn 1965): 65-69.
     Analyzes the development of the short story and notes that McCarthy's stories resemble those of the twenties in which "the action is greatly pruned until the story appears rather plotless."

387. Rees, David. "The Exorcism." SPECTATOR, no.7168
     (September 17, 1965): 353-354.
         Weighs McCarthy's reputation for being a brilliant and
     knowledgeable commentator of the times with her seemingly
     bitchy, heartless critique of the John Osborne play A PATRIOT
     FOR ME. Credits her wit, powers of observation and insight in
     THE GROUP, A CHARMED LIFE and THE GROVES OF
     ACADEME. Observes that THE COMPANY SHE KEEPS
     shows a compassion for humanity rarely found in McCarthy's
     work.

388. "THE GROUP Ruled not Obscene." NEW YORK TIMES
     (November 30, 1965): 38.
         Reports that in Italy THE GROUP was finally declared not
     obscenity but sociology.

389. Aldridge, John W. "Mary McCarthy: Princess Among the
     Trolls." In TIME TO MURDER AND CREATE: THE
     CONTEMPORARY NOVEL IN CRISIS, 95-132. New York:
     David McKay, 1966.
         Begins with the premise that prior to the publication of THE
     GROUP it would have been highly inappropriate to compare
     McCarthy's writing to that of John O'Hara. Proceeds to show
     how they both reduce all human emotion and problems to basic
     sexual difficulties. Explores all of McCarthy's fiction in terms of
     satiric form and suggests that much of her writing stems from an
     egotistical need to supply every detail lest she be somehow
     punished for errors or omissions.

         Also published in: TIME TO MURDER AND CREATE: THE
     CONTEMPORARY NOVEL IN CRISIS. Reprinted ed. New
     York: Books for Libraries, 1972.

390. Symons, Julian. "That Elegant Miss McCarthy." In CRITICAL
     OCCASIONS, 90-98. London: Hamish Hamilton, 1966.
         Provides an in-depth look at McCarthy's literary
     development beginning with her early theater reviews through
     THE COMPANY SHE KEEPS and A SOURCE OF
     EMBARRASSMENT. States that even though she manages the

general themes and tackles the philosophical ideas that most writers shy away from, her gifts have not as yet been fully utilized. Reflects on the unforgettable portraits and scenes presented in her memoirs, and points out this self-portrait conveys a sensitivity not evident in her earlier work.

391. Field, Andrew. "Hermann and Felix." NEW YORK TIMES BOOK REVIEW (May 15, 1966): 5, 36-37.
     Provides an in-depth review of Nabokov's DESPAIR, examining the allegation that McCarthy's essay on PALE FIRE missed the whole point. See also McCarthy's review (item no. 194) and her reply to this article (item no. 263).

392. Barry, Joseph. "Letter from Abroad: Mary McCarthy Versus Paris." McCALLS 93 (June 1966): 40, 42, 44.
     Elaborates on McCarthy's interview with Katharine Whitehorn in which she discussed her views on Paris, French writers, and European reaction to THE GROUP.

393. Field, Andrew. "Nabokov [Letter to the Editor]." NEW YORK TIMES BOOK REVIEW (July 10, 1966): 50.
     Replies to McCarthy's letter published on the same day (item no. 263). See also McCarthy's review (item no. 194).

394. Gould, Jack. "TV: Another Face of Mary McCarthy." NEW YORK TIMES (December 5, 1966): 91.
     Focuses on the graciousness and charm displayed by McCarthy in an interview with Edwin Newman. Touches on the wide range of topics covered in their comfortable ramble, concluding that this attractively modified picture of McCarthy, often termed "Queen of the stiletto," left even the interviewer somewhat perplexed.

395. Bungert, Hans. "American College Literature (Amerikanisches Hochschulwesen in literarischer Gesaltung)." JAHRBUCH FUR AMERIKASTUDIEN DEUTSCHE GESELLSCHAFT FUR AMERKASTUDIEN (WEST GERMANY) 12 (1967): 74-91. German.
     Analyzes German and American "student novels," including McCarthy's THE GROVES OF ACADEME and THE GROUP.

Suggests that United States representatives of this genre are more critical of academia in general and disillusioned with the intellectual. Notes that Americans usually choose fiction, whereas German writers on these topics prefer autobiography, which tends to romanticize and idealize university life.

396. Burgess, Anthony. THE NOVEL NOW: A GUIDE TO CONTEMPORARY FICTION. New York: W.W. Norton & Co., 1967. 224p.
      Refers to McCarthy throughout.

      Also published in: THE NOVEL NOW: A GUIDE TO CONTEMPORARY FICTION. New York: Pegasus, 1970 and THE NOVEL NOW: A STUDENT'S GUIDE TO CONTEMPORARY FICTION. London: Faber & Faber, 1967, 229p.

397. Jardin, Claudine. "Marie McCarthy juge les produits anglais." FIGARO (February 22, 1967): 25. French.
      Comments on McCarthy's article in which she sarcastically expounds on British writers in general and Compton-Burnett in particular. See also McCarthy's article (item no. 77).

398. Grumbach, Doris. "The Subject Objected." NEW YORK TIMES BOOK REVIEW (June 11, 1967): 6-7, 36-37.
      Discusses her interview with McCarthy in Paris, McCarthy's disclosures and subsequent fury over the proofs of the book. Notes McCarthy expected her to absorb details and autobiographical facts and then write a biography without making any specific points. Defends herself against McCarthy's charges, stating McCarthy expected her to be enlightened, but not informed, and discrete, when McCarthy herself had been frank.

399. Fishel, Wesley R. "Out of Limbo [Letter to the Editor]." NEW YORK REVIEW OF BOOKS 8, no.12 (June 29, 1967): 29.
      Responds to McCarthy's "Report from Vietnam: Intellectuals," claiming that in this article "she was moved more by the flow of her own rhetoric than by the need to be factual."

See also McCarthy's article (item no. 78) and her reply to this letter (item no. 264).

400. "Mary McCarthy: 'I Think Drugs Are a Total Bore'." MIAMI HERALD (September 12, 1967): D3.
Quotes McCarthy as saying, "I think drugs are a total bore."

401. Strom, Ronald. "If Throughout His Reign . . . [Letter to the Editor]." SPECTATOR 219, no.7275 (December 1, 1967): 698.
Calls attention to a misquote of McCarthy in a review by Vizinczey and reaffirms the use of the word "feign" in her statement describing Johnson's feelings of helplessness related to the war. See also Vizinczey's review (item no. 1261) and his reply to this letter (item no. 402).

402. Vizinczey, Stephen. "If Throughout His Reign . . . [Letter to the Editor]." SPECTATOR 219, no.7276 (December 8, 1967): 732.
Responds to Strom's accusation of a misquote in his review of VIETNAM. Claims that indeed he did quote McCarthy correctly. See also Vizinczey's review (item no. 1261) and Strom's letter (item no. 401).

403. Brower, Brock. "The Updating." In OTHER LOYALTIES: POLITICS OF PERSONALITY, 78-79. New York: Atheneum, 1968.
States clearly that McCarthy is at her best when writing about the American involvement in Vietnam and probably at her most banal when she wrote THE GROUP. Supports McCarthy against Trilling in their exchange over the Vietnam War.

404. Trilling, Diana. "On Withdrawing from Vietnam: An Exchange." NEW YORK REVIEW OF BOOKS 10, no.1 (January 18, 1968): 5.
Says McCarthy's proposals do not take into account what will happen to Vietnam after the United States withdraws. Notes her callous suggestions for peace negotiations overlook the moral issue of the millions of lives at stake. See also McCarthy's article "Vietnam: Solutions" (item no. 78); her response to Trilling's article (item no. 80); and letters (item nos. 405, 406 and 407).

Also published in: McCarthy, Mary. HANOI. ix-xii. New York: Harcourt,Brace & World,1968.

405. Johnson, Gerald W. "Correspondence: Miss McCarthy in Vietnam [Letter to the Editor]." NEW REPUBLIC 158, no.4 (January 27, 1968): 35.
      Discusses the McCarthy-Trilling debate on Vietnam. Sides with McCarthy but feels she does not continue her argument to its logical conclusion. See also McCarthy and Trilling's debate (item nos. 80 and 404).

406. Bell, Daniel. "Ideology and Vietnam [Letter to the Editor]." NEW YORK REVIEW OF BOOKS 10, no.4 (February 29, 1968): 33-34.
      Emphasizes that McCarthy's ignorance of economics forces her into a defensive "either/or" situation. Agrees with Trilling that McCarthy's recollections may be "foggy" and the different views she may now have do not override her responsibility to the historical record. See also McCarthy and Trilling's debate (item nos. 80 and 404).

407. Trilling, Diana. "Ideology and Vietnam [Letter to the Editor]." NEW YORK REVIEW OF BOOKS 10, no.4 (February 29, 1968): 32-33.
      Comments that McCarthy is not worried about a Communist takeover in Vietnam because she has such a low regard for its people. Expresses concern that involvement in the war does not guarantee a democratic future for the country. Defends herself against McCarthy's charge that to be anti-Stalin is to advocate the use of the atom bomb. See also McCarthy and Trilling's debate (item nos. 80 and 404).

408. "Hanoi Confident of Victory." TIMES (London, G.B.) (April 8, 1968): 4.
      Quotes McCarthy following her return from North Vietnam.

409. Trumbull, Robert. "2 Novelists Tell of Visit to Hanoi." NEW YORK TIMES (April 8, 1968): 3.
      Notes McCarthy's and Seicho Matsumoto's views on the war

following their visits to Hanoi and subsequent conversations with North Vietnamese Premier, Pham Van Dong.

410. "Tea at the War Crimes Museum." TIME 91 (May 24, 1968): 80, 83-84.
     Comments on the first and second installments of McCarthy's report on North Vietnam to be published by the NEW YORK REVIEW OF BOOKS. Notes that her "special guest status" is obvious in her report which offers little hard news or political thought. Concentrates on glimpses afforded of McCarthy herself. See also McCarthy's series of articles (item no. 81).

411. Duff, Peggy. "Skating on Very Thin Ice." TRIBUNE (London, G.B.) (July 12, 1968): 12.
     Quotes from HANOI in a discussion of the Vietnam game plan.

412. Lijeholm, Lyn. "Notables Share Portland Buffet for McCarthy." MAINE SUNDAY TELEGRAM (July 28, 1968): A10.
     Describes a party held for Senator McCarthy which Mary and many other important supporters attended.

413. Kreutz, Irving. "Mary McCarthy's 'The Unspoiled Reaction': Pejorative as Satire." DESCANT 13, no.1 (Fall 1968): 32-48.
     Explores McCarthy's satiric method which is based on language used to describe the detail of an event. Analyzes "The Unspoiled Reaction" and says the effort she makes to keep herself out of the satire fails because her very choice of words inevitably gives her away.

414. Wiggins, John R. "Returning Prodigal: Ghost of a Sequel." PHILADELPHIA INQUIRER (December 1, 1968): 7.
     Notes the return of McCarthy to the United States after a five year stay in Paris. Presents short comments by McCarthy on a number of issues including French xenophobia and the differences between American and French youths.

415. Serpell, Christopher. "Letters: Anti-American." LISTENER 80, no.2074 (December 26, 1968): 858.
	Responds to McCarthy's letter which followed Serpell's original review. See also Serpell's review (item no. 1310) and McCarthy's reply to this letter (item no. 266).

416. D'Amato, Anthony A. CALIFORNIA LAW REVIEW 57 (1969): 1055.
	Quotes from HANOI in a discussion on the bombing of Quinh Lap leprosarium in North Vietnam.

417. Guttmann, Allen. "Protest Against the War in Vietnam." ANNALS OF THE AMERICAN ACADEMY OF POLITICAL AND SOCIAL SCIENCE 382 (1969): 56-63.
	Attempts to delineate the growing protest against American policy in Vietnam by presenting the different factions and their primary positions. Includes McCarthy's views on Vietnam in a discussion of imperialism and argues that a general hostility toward American culture lies behind her comments.

418. Lowell, Robert. "'For Mary McCarthy' and 'The Immortals'." In NOTEBOOK 1967-68, 12. New York: Farrar, Straus & Giroux, 1969.
	Offers two poems dedicated to McCarthy.

	Also published in: NOTEBOOK. 3rd ed. revised & expanded 33, 204-205. New York: Farrar, Straus & Giroux, 1970 and London: Faber & Faber, 1970.

419. "Mary McCarthy." In 200 CONTEMPORARY AUTHORS: BIO-BIBLIOGRAPHIES OF SELECTED LEADING WRITERS OF TODAY, edited by Barbara Harte, and Carolyn Riley, 181-183. Detroit: Gale Research, 1969.
	Summarizes McCarthy's critical opinions and provides biographical information.

420. McKenzie, Barbara. "The Arid Plain of 'The Cicerone'." In
THE PROCESS OF FICTION: CONTEMPORARY STORIES
AND CRITICISM, edited by Barbara McKenzie, 76-83. New
York: Harcourt, Brace & World, 1969.
Introduces this volume with a description of "what a story
is," in an effort to make fiction intelligible to the reader. Offers
a critical interpretation of McCarthy's "The Cicerone,"
concluding with a series of questions suitable for discussion.

421. CURRENT BIOGRAPHY 30 (February 1969): 270-272.
Offers a brief biographical sketch and general criticism.

422. Wolk, Anthony. "The Passive Mystique: We've Been Had."
ENGLISH JOURNAL 58, no.3 (March 1969): 432-435.
Surveys the works of a number of authors, including
McCarthy, to ascertain whether or not the passive voice is used
in contemporary, expository prose.

423. Orwell, Sonia. "Appraisal: Unfair to George." NOVA (London,
G.B.) (July 1969): 18+.
Reacts, in a methodical and measured fashion, to
McCarthy's attack on Orwell, the author's late husband. Argues
that McCarthy holds both man and text up to exemplary and
largely nonexistent models which doom them to failure.
Attributes some of her "questionable" statements to honest
differences, but can find no cause for others but wilful misuse of
information. See also McCarthy's article (item no. 203).

424. Newall, Robert H. "Mary McCarthy: Controversial Author
Speaks Mind." BANGOR DAILY NEWS (Maine) 81, no.45
(August 8, 1969): 17.
Calls McCarthy a true cosmopolite in the conclusion of an
interview that touches briefly on questions of religion, theater,
and writing satire.

425. Atkins, John. SEX IN LITERATURE: THE EROTIC IMPULSE
IN LITERATURE. London: Calder & Boyars, 1970, 411p.
Refers to THE GROUP in this analysis of sex in literature.
Includes some excerpts.

Also published in French: LE SEXE DANS LA
LITTERATURE. Translated by Tony Cartano. Paris: Editions
Buchet/Chastel, 1975, 441p.

426. Widmer, Eleanor. "Finally a Lady: Mary McCarthy." In THE
     FIFTIES: FICTION, POETRY, DRAMA, edited by Warren G.
     French, 93-102. Deland, Fla.: Everett/Edwards, 1970.
     Draws a comparison between McCarthy and George Eliot,
     pointing out that Eliot kept her personal life completely out of
     her writing, while McCarthy writes about and for her circle of
     friends and yet does not hesitate to shock, violate and undercut
     them. Analyzes the conflicting qualities in McCarthy's writing.

427. Beisner, Robert L. "1898 and 1968: The Anti-Imperialists and
     the Doves." POLITICAL SCIENCE QUARTERLY 85, no.2
     (June 1970): 187-216.
     Draws parallels between the anti-imperialists of 1898 and the
     doves of 1968, comparing the two protest movements in light of
     who the protesters were, what they did and why. Notes
     McCarthy's opinions on American policy in Vietnam.

428. Glicksberg, Charles L. "The Death of Love." In THE SEXUAL
     REVOLUTION IN MODERN AMERICAN LITERATURE,
     187-196. The Hague: Martinus Nijhoff, 1971.
     Explores McCarthy's treatment of sex, focusing on THE
     COMPANY SHE KEEPS, A CHARMED LIFE and THE
     GROUP. States that McCarthy separates sex from love, and
     describes the sex act as cold, clinical, detached. Suggests that
     she is usually hostile to men and that sex is presented in a
     "ludicrous light."

429. Schweyer, Janine. "L'Oeuvre de Mary McCarthy devant la
     critique: première bibliographie des livres, articles et recensions
     parus jusqu'en 1970." RECHERCHES ANGLAISES ET
     AMERICAINES (Strasbourg, France) 4 (1971): 172-197.
     French.
     Gathers British and American articles written about
     McCarthy for the years 1935 to 1970. Includes numerous
     references to periodicals in England and the United States. States

in her introduction that she has tried to pick up absolutely
everything that could be found on this author, although many
citations are unverified.

430. "Mary McCarthy's Road to Peking." TIMES (London, G.B.)
(March 12, 1971): 12.
Reports that Burchett is in Peking trying to obtain a visa for
McCarthy.

431. Kevles, Barbara. "Anne Sexton: [An Interview]." PARIS
REVIEW 13, no.52 (Summer 1971): 158-191.
Notes Elizabeth Hardwick's comment that McCarthy has
"never been without a man for a day in her life."

Also published in: Plimpton, George, ed. WRITERS AT
WORK: THE PARIS REVIEW INTERVIEWS, introduced by
Wilfrid Sheed. 4th series. 403-429. New York: Viking Press,
1976 and in: Plimpton, George, ed. WOMEN WRITERS AT
WORK: THE PARIS REVIEW INTERVIEWS, introduced by
Margaret Atwood. 263-289. New York: Viking Penguin, 1989.

432. Gross, Harvey. "[Letter to the Editor]." NEW YORK TIMES
BOOK REVIEW (July 11, 1971): 34-35.
Responds to Revel's interview with McCarthy in which her
views on equality in BIRDS OF AMERICA were discussed. See
also Revel's interview with McCarthy (item no. 282).

433. Tyler, Parker. "[Letter to the Editor]." NEW YORK TIMES
BOOK REVIEW (July 11, 1971): 34.
Praises Vendler's critical review of BIRDS OF AMERICA
and remarks that rarely does a "little reviewer" have the nerve to
put down a "big author." See also Vendler's review (item no.
1382).

434. Clarity, James F. "She's Not One of the Group Yet." NEW
YORK TIMES (October 30, 1971): 32.
Describes McCarthy's return to the centennial activities at
Vassar. Claims that she agreed to attend "in a moment of

generosity" but that Vassar has not really forgiven her, nor she the institution.

435. Gillen, Francis. "The Failure of Ritual in 'The Unspoiled Reaction'." RENASCENCE: ESSAYS ON VALUE IN LITERATURE (Milwaukee, Wis.) 24 (1972): 155-158.
     Discusses the themes of "The Unspoiled Reaction" focusing on the idea of theater as ritual. Shows how the puppet theater as depicted by McCarthy is similar to medieval drama.

436. Robinson, Lillian S. "Who's Afraid of a Room of One's Own?" In THE POLITICS OF LITERATURE: DISSENTING ESSAYS ON THE TEACHING OF ENGLISH, edited by Louis Kampf and Paul Lauter, 375, 387, 390. New York: Pantheon Books, 1972.
     Links McCarthy's thoughts on fiction to Woolf's theory that the novel is a uniquely feminine genre. Compares McCarthy's clinical and detached depiction of sexual scenes with that of Lessing.

     Also published in: THE POLITICS OF LITERATURE: DISSENTING ESSAYS ON THE TEACHING OF ENGLISH. reprinted ed. New York: Vintage Books, 1973.

437. Tugusheva, M. "The Empress' New Clothes." In SOVIET CRITICISM OF AMERICAN LITERATURE IN THE SIXTIES: AN ANTHOLOGY, edited & translated by Carl R. Proffer, 15-18. Ann Arbor, Mich.: Ardis, 1972.
     Focuses on the political analyses in McCarthy's works, especially THE GROUP. Concludes that it was McCarthy's mission to cut humanity off from hope.

438. "Mary McCarthy, Jean-François Revel et la jeunesse Américaine." FIGARO (June 1, 1972): 4. French.
     Notes the forthcoming interview with Jean-François Revel entitled "Je ne vois pas comment on en sortira . . ." published in FIGARO (June 3, 1972). (This interview was originally published in English, see item no. 283.)

439. Deimer, Günther. "Mary McCarthy." In AMERIKANISCHE
LITERATUR DER GEGENWART, edited by Martin
Christadler, 299-325. Stuttgart: Alfred Kroner Verlag, 1973.
German.
Scrutinizes McCarthy's work and includes a short biography
and bibliography. Refers to other literature on McCarthy and
discusses her role within the literary world. Mentions Mailer's
critique of THE GROUP as being "female tittle-tattle and
gossip." Records differences between her autobiographical,
political and cultural writings and accuses her of being
opinionated, caring little for facts or plausibility and relying on
mere intuition. See also Mailer's review (item no. 1129).

440. Kazin, Alfred. "Cassandras: Porter to Oates." In BRIGHT
BOOK OF LIFE: AMERICAN NOVELISTS AND
STORYTELLERS FROM HEMINGWAY TO MAILER,
188-189. Boston: Little, Brown & Co.; New York: Dell Pub.,
1973.
Touches on McCarthy's fiction in this critical analysis of
women writers. Maintains that the one common theme which
runs throughout her work is "none of these awful people is going
to catch me." Notes that her heroines are always distinctively
right.

Also published: London: Secker & Warburg, 1974 and London:
Univ. of Notre Dame Press, 1980.

441. "Mary McCarthy." In CONTEMPORARY LITERARY
CRITICISM, edited by Carolyn Riley, 204-207. Vol. 1. Detroit:
Gale Research Co., 1973.
Offers a bibliographic essay on McCarthy's work to date.

442. Voss, Arthur. "The Short Story Since 1940." In THE
AMERICAN SHORT STORY: A CRITICAL SURVEY,
308-312. Norman, Okla.: Univ. of Oklahoma Press, c1973.
Argues that McCarthy's short stories are distinguished by
their intellectual and analytical qualities. Says that McCarthy
strips her characters bare to reveal them as fallible and less
admirable than might be expected. Notes that McCarthy is

concerned with states of mind and "ambiguities of human
relationships" in all her work.

Also published in Spanish as LA NOVELA CORTA
AMERICANA: ORIGEN, DESARROLLO Y PERSPECTIVAS.
Translated by Emma González de Galván. 249-252. Mexico:
Editores Asociados, 1976.

443. Stannard, Una. "Women Reading Women: An Exchange."
     COLUMBIA UNIVERSITY FORUM 2, no.1 (Winter 1973):
     51-52.
         Discusses how women writers are influenced by writers of
     both sexes. Criticizes Moers' "Women's Lit" for isolating
     women writers by only comparing them with other women.

444. Leonard, John. "The Conspiracy Theory of Book Reviewing."
     NEW YORK TIMES BOOK REVIEW (February 11, 1973): 35.
         Discusses the publishing world's paranoia over book
     reviewers who, they say, dredge up "ancient grudges" when
     reviewing certain writers. Examines McCarthy's attack on
     Halberstam's BEST AND THE BRIGHTEST, in defense of book
     reviewers, denying that there is "conspiracy." Posits that if
     McCarthy had reviewed the book for them, they would probably
     have been accused of having it in for Halberstam. See also
     McCarthy's review (item no. 206).

445. "Mary McCarthy." In THE READER'S ADVISER: A
     LAYMAN'S GUIDE TO LITERATURE. 12th ed., edited by
     Sarah L. Prakken, 608-609. Vol. 1. New York: R.R. Bowker,
     1974.
         Includes McCarthy in this volume of "the best in American
     and British fiction, poetry, essays, literary biography,
     bibliography and reference." Presents a brief catalogue of her
     works, complete with descriptive notes and occasional critical
     comment.

446. Miles, Rosalind. THE FICTION OF SEX: THEMES AND FUNCTIONS OF SEX DIFFERENCE IN THE MODERN NOVEL. Barnes & Noble Critical Studies. New York: Barnes & Noble, 1974. 208p.
Refers to various scenes from THE GROUP in this discussion of sex differences in the modern novel.

Also published in: Vision Critical Studies. London: Vision Press, 1974.

447. Blanch, Andrea. "Problem of Feminine Masochism: An Approach Through Theory and Literature." CORNELL JOURNAL OF SOCIAL RELATIONS 9, no.1 (Spring 1974): 1-15.
Explores the relationship between masochism and feminine identity. Follows a fairly extensive review of the theoretical work on the subject, with an examination of the way in which four female authors deal with feminine masochism in their work. Presents several incidents from MEMORIES OF A CATHOLIC GIRLHOOD and THE COMPANY SHE KEEPS which, seemingly masochistic, could alternatively be viewed as rebellion through submission, or evidence of superiority.

448. "Objection [Letter to the Editor]." NEW YORK TIMES (March 17, 1974): 43.
Response by Howe, Kazin, Phillips, Rosenberg and Trilling to McCarthy's memorial to Rahv. See also McCarthy's article (item no. 93).

449. Fallows, James. "Mary McCarthy--The Blinders She Wears." WASHINGTON MONTHLY 6, no.3 (May 1974): 5-17.
Responds to McCarthy's article which commented on Risner's book and her meeting with him while he was a P.O.W. in Vietnam. Allows McCarthy latitude in mistakes or misperceptions she might have had, but argues forcefully that there are ugly implications in the extent of her attack. Concludes that her political writing demonstrates a profound lack of objectivity, oversimplification and a carelessness with the truth.

See also McCarthy's review (item no. 207) and Rosenberg's response to this article (item no. 1470).

450. Grumbach, Doris. "Fine Print: Women's Work." NEW REPUBLIC 170, no.21 (May 25, 1974): 32-33.
    Reacts with irritation to the tone of the introduction which detracts from some otherwise good reportage. Suggests that McCarthy is too loud, too certain, and too full of herself.

451. Davis, Judith. "Do Men Need Women's Liberation?" PSYCHIATRY 37 (November 1974): 387-400.
    Theorizes that men as well as women have been the victims of a sexist society. Uses a number of literary works to illustrate her thesis, including THE COMPANY SHE KEEPS. Calls the stories portrayals of both sexes trapped in repression, driven by myths of differentiation and inequality.

452. Yavenditti, Michael J. "John Hersey and the American Conscience: The Reception of 'Hiroshima'." PACIFIC HISTORICAL REVIEW 43, no.4 (November 1974): 24-49.
    Examines Hersey's HIROSHIMA, its reception and significance in an attempt to shed light on the wider implications of the atomic bombing for the American conscience. Notes McCarthy's Letter to the Editor criticizing Hersey's apparent moral objectivity. (See also item no. 256).

453. "Mary McCarthy." In CONTEMPORARY LITERARY CRITICISM, 326-328. Vol. 3. Detroit: Gale Research Co., 1975.
    Offers a bibliographic essay on McCarthy's work to date.

454. Taylor, Gordon O. "Cast a Cold 'I': Mary McCarthy on Vietnam." JOURNAL OF AMERICAN STUDIES (Norwich, G.B.) 9, no.1 (April 1975): 103-114.
    Traces the psychological as well as geographical changes in McCarthy. Likens her to an archeologist who, excavating ever deeper, finds the substance of self increasingly seeping into immediate reality. Provides an in-depth analysis of how her personality shapes, energizes and unites the essays.

455. Norman, Liane Ellison. "The Whale in the Rice Paddy."
BULLETIN OF CONCERNED ASIAN SCHOLARS 7
(October-December 1975): 17-27.
Provides an excerpt from THE ILIAD OR THE POEM OF
FORCE in a discussion of American participation in the Vietnam
War.

456. Bird, David. "Hannah Arendt's Funeral Held: Many Moving
Tributes Paid." NEW YORK TIMES (December 9, 1975): 44.
Notes that nearly 300 people, including McCarthy, gathered
to pay tribute to and mourn the passing of Arendt.

457. "Mary McCarthy." In CONTEMPORARY LITERARY
CRITICISM, 275-277. Vol. 5. Detroit: Gale Research Co.,
1976.
Offers a bibliographic essay on McCarthy's work to date.

458. "Mary McCarthy." In WHO'S WHO IN TWENTIETH
CENTURY LITERATURE, edited by Martin Seymour-Smith,
237-238. New York: Holt, Rinehart & Winston; London:
Weidenfeld & Nicolson, 1976.
Designates McCarthy's true category as "the very 'highest'
(but not heavy) middlebrow author." Comments briefly but never
subtly on her virtues (and as often the lack of them) as novelist,
travel-writer and critic.

Also published in: WHO'S WHO IN TWENTIETH CENTURY
LITERATURE. Reprinted ed. NEW YORK: McGraw-Hill,
1977.

459. Spacks, Patricia Meyer. "Mary McCarthy: Society's Demands."
In THE FEMALE IMAGINATION, 254-260. New York: Alfred
A. Knopf, 1975; London: George Allen & Unwin, 1976.
Analyzes the role of society in THE COMPANY SHE
KEEPS, and suggests that McCarthy uses the theory of
"imaginative vision," often found in Wharton's novels.
Concludes that McCarthy demonstrates how "imaginative vision
even operating in a context of severe moral disorder, can assert
at least limited meaning."

Also published in: Spacks, Patricia Meyer. CONTEMPORARY
WOMEN NOVELISTS: A COLLECTION OF CRITICAL
ESSAYS. 85-91. Englewood Cliffs, N.J.: Prentice-Hall, 1977.
(Spacks refers to McCarthy in the Introduction.)

460. Sirkin, Elliott. FILM COMMENT 12, no.1 (January-February
1976): 32.
    Discusses McCarthy's review of various war movies
    claiming that even though McCarthy has an aversion to movies,
    she brought her "standard dazzle" to this "insightful" piece.

    Also published as "A Filmy Version of the War" in: TOWN
    AND COUNTRY (April 1944): 72, 112.

461. Bondy, François. "Ich suche die Wahrheit mit dem Ohr. Mary
    McCarthy zwischen engagierter Zeugenschaft und satirischem
    Sittenbild. Ein nicht nur literarisches Porträt." SCHWEIZER
    MONATSHEFTE 55, no.11 (April 1975-March 1976): 880-886.
    German.
    Analyzes McCarthy's tendency towards caricature and satire,
    a style she calls "contes philosophiques." Remarks that her
    essays and novels are complementary and calls her an author of
    ideas in the French or Russian tradition. Touches on her political
    activities, particularly her opposition to the Vietnam war.

462. Mansell, Darrel. "Unsettling the Colonel's Hash: 'Fact' in
    Autobiography." MODERN LANGUAGE QUARTERLY 37,
    no.2 (June 1976): 115-132.
    Examines in some depth the critical distinction between fact
    and fiction in literature, with particular reference to
    autobiography. Uses "Artists in Uniform" and McCarthy's
    follow-up essay, "Settling the Colonel's Hash", to focus the
    discussion.

463. Borkland, Elmer. "Mary McCarthy." In CONTEMPORARY
    LITERARY CRITICS. New York: St. Martin's Press, 1977.
    Provides biographical information and a brief critical
    overview of her works to date.

Also published in: CONTEMPORARY LITERARY CRITICS.
2nd ed. 400-405. New York: Macmillan, 1982.

464. Howard, Maureen. "Introduction." In SEVEN AMERICAN
WOMEN WRITERS OF THE TWENTIETH CENTURY: AN
INTRODUCTION, edited by Maureen Howard, 23-27.
Minnesota: Univ. of Minnesota Press, 1977.
Draws attention to MEMORIES OF A CATHOLIC
GIRLHOOD and urges students of women's literature to pay
attention to the women characters and the image of the female.
Goes on to discuss McCarthy's quest for an "honest appraisal of
her self" through the characters she creates, in particular,
Margaret in THE COMPANY SHE KEEPS.

465. Spacks, Patricia Meyer. "Introduction." In CONTEMPORARY
WOMEN NOVELISTS: A COLLECTION OF CRITICAL
ESSAYS, edited by Patricia Meyer Spacks, 1-17. Englewood
Cliffs, N.J.: Prentice-Hall, 1977.
Questions whether women novelists are a special breed or
whether they are treated differently by critics. Examines the
influence of the critic's point of view on critical evaluation.
Offers many examples, one which compares her own critique of
THE COMPANY SHE KEEPS with Mailer's analysis of THE
GROUP. See also Spack's essay (item no. 459) and Mailer's
review (item no. 1129).

466. Cornwell, Ethel F. "Virginia Woolf, Nathalie Sarraute, and
Mary McCarthy: Three Approaches to Character in Modern
Fiction." INTERNATIONAL FICTION REVIEW (Fredericton,
New Brunswick) 4, no.1 (January 1977): 3-10.
Traces the shift in approach to character in fiction through
the works of Woolf, Sarraute and McCarthy. Examines Woolf's
focus on the "inner reality" and Sarraute's belief that character is
neither essential nor desirable, stressing the limitations inherent
in each. Finds McCarthy exemplifies the return to fact and the
objectively identifiable character, a viewpoint that Cornwell
states is integral to the survival of the novel as an art form.

467. Myers, Mitzi. "You Can't Catch Me: Mary McCarthy's Evasive Comedy." REGIONALISM AND THE FEMALE IMAGINATION (Penn. State Univ., University Park) 3, no.ii-iii (Fall-Winter 1977-78): 58-69.

    Begins with the premise that female humor is usually self-deprecating and that when a woman dares to look beyond herself for objects of satire and ridicule she is usually chastized. Argues that such is the case with McCarthy who has cast her net wide and written in a biting, satirical way about many things and many people. Suggests that McCarthy's humor is a "thinking woman's comedy."

468. Mitgang, Herbert. "Publishing: Ideas and Hannah Arendt." NEW YORK TIMES (December 9, 1977): C24.

    Notes as forthcoming, Arendt's philosophical trilogy, THE LIFE OF THE MIND, the manuscript which McCarthy, along with a number of friends and editors, helped to prepare.

469. Martin, Wendy. "The Satire and Moral Vision of Mary McCarthy." In COMIC RELIEF: HUMOR IN CONTEMPORARY AMERICAN LITERATURE, edited by Sarah Blacher Cohen, 187-206. Urbana, Illinois: Univ. of Illinois Press, 1978.

    Discusses McCarthy's use of satire to expose the banalities and moral dilemmas her characters face. Compares her to Austen, saying that she judges as well as "chronicles a complex social and economic reality, exposing the pretensions of men and the illusions of women in a patriarchal society." (Also refers to McCarthy in the Introduction.)

470. Munroe, Gretchen Himmele. "Mary McCarthy." In AMERICAN NOVELISTS SINCE WORLD WAR II, edited by Jeffrey Helterman and Richard Layman, 310-317. Dictionary of Literary Biography, Vol. 2. Detroit: Gale Research, 1978.

    Provides biographical information and brief notes on McCarthy's work to date.

471. Nagy, Peter. "Mary McCarthy." ACTA LITTERARIA
     ACADEMIAE SCIENTIARUM HUNGARICAE (Budapest,
     Hungary) 20 (1978): 137-40.
     Proposes somewhat reluctantly that sufficient parallels exist
     to call McCarthy the American De Beauvoir. Notes, however, a
     fundamental difference in attitude--De Beauvoir's is rooted in
     existentialism, McCarthy's in pragmatism. Declares a special
     sense of the comic in life McCarthy's most distinctive trait, but
     believes the popularity of THE GROUP is also due to the
     relatively new phenomenon of a woman writing about women in
     all their authenticity.

472. Stock, Irvin. "Mary McCarthy." In AMERICAN NOVELISTS
     SINCE WORLD WAR II, edited by Jeffrey Helterman and
     Richard Layman, 310-317. Dictionary of American Literary
     Biography, Vol. 2. Detroit: Gale Research, 1978.
     Offers a bio-critical essay on McCarthy. Catalogues her
     various publications and personal events.

473. Adams, Timothy Dow. "The Contemporary American
     Mock-Autobiography." CLIO 8, no.3 (1979): 417-428.
     Traces the growth of a new hybrid form of autobiography
     which deliberately blurs fact and fiction, using a number of
     American authors as examples. Observes that other literary
     genres have also been affected by this crossing of general
     boundaries, amongst them short stories, the novel, and new
     journalism.

474. Scott, Bonnie Kime. "Women's Perspectives in Irish-American
     Fiction from Betty Smith to Mary McCarthy." In
     IRISH-AMERICAN FICTION: ESSAYS IN CRITICISM, edited
     by Daniel J. Casey and Robert E. Rhodes, 87-103. New York:
     AMS, 1979.
     Compares McCarthy's writing to Mary Doyle Curran's and
     Betty Smith's. Points out that McCarthy is fascinated by the lives
     of women and draws careful descriptions of her grandmothers,
     her mother and the Prefect at the Catholic school she attended.

475. Horowitz, Irving Louis. "Open Societies and Free Minds: The Last Testament of Hannah Arendt." CONTEMPORARY SOCIOLOGY 8, no.1 (January 1979): 15-19.

    Describes McCarthy's postface in Arendt's THE LIFE OF THE MIND as "entirely professional and pellucid." Credits both the publisher and McCarthy with having exhibited good judgment in their contribution to this philosophical work.

476. Robertson, Nan. "Mary McCarthy Mellows as an Expatriate in Paris." NEW YORK TIMES (July 31, 1979): C5.

    Quotes McCarthy as saying that she is "utterly out of touch with America." Provides a brief biographical sketch and concludes with the finding that McCarthy, happily esconced in Paris since 1962, seems to have mellowed, or at least become more polite with age.

    Also published in: NEW YORK TIMES BIOGRAPHICAL SERVICE 10 (July 1979): 947-948.

477. Thompson, Howard. "Going Out Guide: Write On." NEW YORK TIMES (October 15, 1979): C14.

    Notes McCarthy will be making a rare public appearance, reading from CANNIBALS AND MISSIONARIES.

478. "International Support for Polish 'Flying University'." TIMES (London, G.B.) (November 27, 1979): 7.

    Mentions McCarthy is a supporter of the "Flying University" which organizes lectures on aspects of Polish history and culture that have been distorted or censored by the official educational system.

479. Eslin, J. C. "Une amitié Hannah Arendt et Mary McCarthy." ESPRIT, no.6 (1980): 39-40. French.

    Discloses that Arendt and McCarthy first met at a party during which they fought over McCarthy's comments on Hitler's motives. Notes that much later, after appearing together on several panels and finding that they were frequently in agreement on issues, they decided to be friends.

480. "Mary McCarthy." In CONTEMPORARY LITERARY
     CRITICISM, edited by Dedria Bryfonski and Laurie Lanzen
     Harris, 357-364. Vol. 14. Detroit: Gale Research, 1980.
         Presents a bibliographic essay on McCarthy's work to date.
     Includes an excerpt from McCarthy's interview with Miriam
     Gross. See also Gross' interview (item no. 286).

481. Stock, Irvin. "The Novels of Mary McCarthy." In FICTION AS
     WISDOM FROM GOETHE TO BELLOW, 156-189. University
     Park: Pennsylvania State Univ. Press, 1980.
         Discusses McCarthy's novels in chronological order.
     Explores the moral and ethical issues that are the substance of
     each novel and notes the ongoing autobiographical thread. Points
     out that while McCarthy writes in a satiric tone, the satire is the
     result of her intent to portray life as it really is.

482. Mitgang, Herbert. "Miss Hellman Suing a Critic for 2.25
     Million." NEW YORK TIMES (February 16, 1980): 12.
         Announces the filing of Hellman's lawsuit against McCarthy.
     Notes that in an interview with Dick Cavett, McCarthy called
     Hellman a dishonest writer, and when asked to elaborate, made
     the now famous statement, "I once said in an interview that
     every word she writes is a lie, including 'and' and 'the'!"

483. Slade, Margot, and Tom Ferrell. "Ideas and Trends: Literary
     Quarrel Turns Litigious." NEW YORK TIMES [Sunday Ed.]
     129 (February 17, 1980): E7.
         Notes Hellman's $2.25 million suit for damages as a direct
     result of McCarthy's statements made in a recent Dick Cavett
     interview. States that many, including Hellman herself, believe
     McCarthy's animosity stems from opposing political stands taken
     back in the 1930s.

484. Kakutani, Michiko. "Hellman-McCarthy Libel Suit Stirs Old
     Antagonisms." NEW YORK TIMES 129 (March 19, 1980):
     C21.
         Proposes that these two grandes dames of literature represent
     hostile traditions within the intellectual left. States that the
     opposing viewpoints held by McCarthy and Hellman on several
     fundamental issues contained moral as well as political

dimensions. Presents a wide and interesting array of commentary on behalf of both parties, but believes political, esthetic and personal differences are far too tangled to make a public judgment possible.

485. Maddocks, Melvin. "Literature and Litigation [column]." CHRISTIAN SCIENCE MONITOR 72, no.106 (April 24, 1980): 22.
    Presents a number of recent court cases, including the McCarthy/Hellman feud, that focus on confrontation between literature (both fiction and non-fiction) and freedom of expression. Worries about the repercussions this apparent trend might have on serious writers and publishers.

486. Mailer, Norman. "An Appeal to Lillian Hellman and Mary McCarthy." NEW YORK TIMES BOOK REVIEW 85 (May 11, 1980): 3, 33.
    Expresses no surprise that two writers with such profoundly different views of reality should detest each other, but points out that such a lawsuit could have disastrous consequences. Maintains that no writer worthy of serious attention is ever truly and consistently honest.

487. Simon, John. "Gotham: Literary Lionesses." NATIONAL REVIEW 32, no.10 (May 16, 1980): 614-616.
    Acknowledges the major political differences between McCarthy and Hellman, but contends that their major source of conflict is a difference in "brows"--McCarthy highbrow and elitist, Hellman middlebrow and populist. Places himself clearly in McCarthy's corner, calling her remarks on the Dick Cavett Show witty, memorable and meant to be taken literarily not literally.

488. Lewis, Flora. "Sartre Tradition: Role of the Master and the Void He Left." NEW YORK TIMES (June 14, 1980): 5.
    Presents the views of a number of intellectuals who met in Paris shortly after the death of Sartre, to discuss his role and his legacy. Argues that most believe a return to tolerance of differing views has nullified the tradition of "master thinker," and that the change is for the better.

489. Poirier, Richard. "Hellman--McCarthy [Letter to the Editor]."
NEW YORK TIMES BOOK REVIEW (June 15, 1980): 33-34.
Contends that Mailer's appeal to Hellman and McCarthy is
misguided at best,and as a former editor of THE PARTISAN
REVIEW and friend of Hellman, Poirier disagrees vigorously
with Mailer's notions that censorship is a likely consequence of
the lawsuit, that writers with dissimilar world views necessarily
detest each other, and that writers are naturally dishonest. See
also Mailer's article (item no. 486).

490. Weatherby, W. J. "How the Smiles Turned to Snarls."
GUARDIAN (G.B.) (July 1, 1980): 8.
Reviews the scenario to date of McCarthy versus Hellman.
Notes interventions of members of the literary establishment and
the formation of rival camps. Seems to view the confrontation as
self-indulgent and somewhat unreal.

491. Trouard, Dawn. "Mary McCarthy's Dilemma: The Double Bind
of Satiric Elitism." PERSPECTIVES ON CONTEMPORARY
LITERATURE 7 (1981): 98-109.
Contends that McCarthy's genuine search for and approval
of excellence creates the illusion that she applies unreal standards
in order to condemn. Maintains that her apparent elitism serves
as defense against uncertainties both in her personal values and
her fictional loyalties.

492. Walker, Nancy. "Do Feminists Ever Laugh? Women's Humor
and Women's Rights." INTERNATIONAL JOURNAL OF
WOMEN'S STUDIES 4, no.1 (January-February 1981): 1-9.
Looks at the use of humor in the feminist movement from
the late nineteenth century work of Marietta Holley to the essays
of Nora Ephron in the 1970s. Provides an excerpt from
McCarthy's "Up the Ladder from CHARM to VOGUE" to
illustrate how women's magazines attempt to impose uniformity
on the female population.

493. Lifson, Martha R. "Allegory of the Secret: Mary McCarthy."
BIOGRAPHY: AN INTERDISCIPLINARY QUARTERLY
(Honolulu, Hawaii) 4, no.3 (Summer 1981): 249-267.
Traces the quest for the essential self in autobiographical

writing, focusing primarily on MEMORIES OF A CATHOLIC
GIRLHOOD. Discusses the childhood fall from paradise, the
fragmentation this produces, and the attempt to recover
coherence and authenticity.

494. Medwick, Cathleen. "Mary McCarthy: An American Classic."
     VOGUE 171 (November 1981): 283+.
     Offers a popular biographic sketch of McCarthy based on a
     visit to her Maine home. Sees McCarthy as mellowed but as
     exacting, forthright and scrupulous as ever.

495. "Symposium: I Would Like to Have Written . . ." NEW YORK
     TIMES BOOK REVIEW (December 6, 1981): 7, 68-69.
     Discusses the question put to a number of writers: which
     literary work would you like to have written and why? Notes
     McCarthy responded with the name of Elizabeth Bishop, based
     not on her works, but her way of seeing.

496. McDowell, Edwin. "Drinking Habits." NEW YORK TIMES
     BOOK REVIEW 86 (December 27, 1981): 16.
     Offers his thoughts on literary symbolism from McCarthy
     and Spillane, both of whom felt the search for meanings in
     literature is often forced.

497. Barrett, William. THE TRUANTS: ADVENTURES AMONG
     THE INTELLECTUALS. Garden City, N.Y.: Anchor Press,
     1982. 270p.
     Writes a reminiscence of Rahv and comments on McCarthy's
     warm tribute to her former friend, colleague, and editor. See
     also McCarthy's article (item no. 93).

498. Flora, Joseph M. "Mary McCarthy." In DICTIONARY OF
     LITERARY BIOGRAPHY YEARBOOK 1981, edited by Karen
     L. Rood, Jean W. Ross, and Richard Ziegfeld, 104-109. New
     York: Gale Research, 1982.
     Focuses on CANNIBALS AND MISSIONARIES, IDEAS
     AND THE NOVEL, and THE HOUNDS OF SUMMER and
     provides a biographical update.

499. Hewitt, Rosalie. "A 'Home Address for the Self': Mary McCarthy's Autobiographical Journey." JOURNAL OF NARRATIVE TECHNIQUE 12, no.2 (1982): 95-104.

Discusses the concepts of "fact in fiction" and "fictions in fact" in her exploration of a literary form that is neither clearly fiction nor autobiography but an amalgam of the two. Uses THE COMPANY SHE KEEPS, CAST A COLD EYE and MEMORIES OF A CATHOLIC GIRLHOOD as the basis for her analysis; works that have not only a similar autobiographical foundation, but are also similar in format. Argues that in order to understand the author's intentions and the reader's response, one must take its publishing and reading history into consideration, as well as the text itself.

500. Dunbar, Rosalie E. "Goals and Insights of Nine Women Artists Show Individual Styles." CHRISTIAN SCIENCE MONITOR [Eastern Ed.] 74, no.28 (January 6, 1982): 19.

Reviews Kufrin's UNCOMMON WOMEN which profiles nine women artists including McCarthy.

501. Kramer, Hilton. "Partisan Culture, Partisan Politics." NEW YORK TIMES BOOK REVIEW (February 7, 1982): 1, 32-33.

Offers a vivid memoir and political analysis of the leading personalities and governing ideas of THE PARTISAN REVIEW circle before and after World War II. Notes that McCarthy is not one of the dominant characters in the book, but as a member of this intellectual group, is sharply glimpsed throughout.

502. Krebs, Albin, Robert McG., Thomas, Jr. "Notes on People: A Vassar '33 Returns." NEW YORK TIMES (February 8, 1982): B6.

Notes McCarthy is to be honored by Vassar as the first member of their distinguished visitor program.

503. "Mary McCarthy and Vassar Hit It Off." NEW YORK TIMES (February 13, 1982): 52.

Reports on McCarthy's visit to Vassar as the first President's Distinguished Visitor. Notes in particular how McCarthy surprised audiences with the statement that although she felt the

women's movement had added to the awareness of economic
exploitation, she herself was not a feminist.

504. Annan, Gabriele. "Her Thirties Values Now Seem as
     Ready-Made as Any Other." LISTENER 108, no.2271 (July 29,
     1982): 24.
     Reviews De Beauvoir's WHEN THINGS OF THE SPIRIT
     COME FIRST and compares her with McCarthy. Suggests De
     Beauvoir lacks McCarthy's humor and questions her motives in
     "digging" these stories up after so many years.

505. "Mary McCarthy." In CONTEMPORARY LITERARY
     CRITICISM, 341-350. Vol. 24. Detroit: Gale Research, 1983.
     Collects excerpts from important critical views on various
     works by McCarthy. Offers biographical information.

506. Taylor, Gordon O. "The Word for Mirror: Mary McCarthy." In
     CHAPTERS OF EXPERIENCE: STUDIES ON 20th
     CENTURY AMERICAN AUTOBIOGRAPHY. 79-100. New
     York: St. Martin's, 1983.
     Explores McCarthy's recollections of her own memoirs and
     examines the persona that she adopts in some of her works.
     Documents and discusses her use of personal pronouns, and in
     particular, I/me. Focuses on MEMORIES OF A CATHOLIC
     GIRLHOOD and the Vietnam books.

507. Kaus, Robert M. "The Plaintiff's Hour." HARPER'S
     MAGAZINE 266, no.1594 (March 1983): 14-16, 18.
     Discusses the issue of free speech and the law in the context
     of Hellman's libel suit against McCarthy. Acknowledges
     McCarthy's comments as inflammatory, but is decidedly uneasy
     about Hellman's resorting to the law as punishment. See also
     article in response to this (item no. 509).

508. Goodman, Walter. "Literary Invective." NEW YORK TIMES
     BOOK REVIEW 88 (June 19, 1983): 35.
     Follows on the yet unresolved libel suit brought by Hellman
     against McCarthy some three years previous. Considers
     McCarthy's comments well within the bounds of literary insult,

particularly when compared to the name calling that other writers have resorted to over the years.

509. "Libel Loophole." WORKING WOMAN 8 (July 1983): 102-103.

Outlines Kaus's article in HARPER'S on the McCarthy/Hellman libel suit, focusing on financial aspects and discussion of what constitutes a public figure. See also Kaus's article (item no. 507).

510. Hitchens, Christopher. "American Notes." TIMES LITERARY SUPPLEMENT, no.4189 (July 15, 1983): 752.

Discusses some of the issues raised in the McCarthy/Hellman feud and suggests that few people will be cheering, regardless of the outcome.

511. Spender, Stephen. "Lillian Hellman [Letter to the Editor]." TIMES LITERARY SUPPLEMENT (August 12, 1983): 859.

Refutes Hitchen's statement that Spender "bore a message from Hellman" and claims that he hasn't seen the woman in years. Wishes Hitchens had checked his facts before writing the article. See also Hitchens' letter (item no. 510) and McCarthy's letter (item no. 267).

512. Horowitz, Irving Louis. WINNERS AND LOSERS AND POLITICAL POLARITIES IN AMERICA. Durham, N.C.: Duke Univ. Press, 1984, 328p.

Examines twenty-four essays in relation to good and evil, the individual and the system, and winning and losing. Discusses Arendt's THE LIFE OF THE MIND, volume one, edited by McCarthy.

513. Yardley, Jonathan. "Politics of the Pen." WASHINGTON POST (January 2, 1984): C1, C8.

Takes exception to McCarthy's statement that "Americans . . . tend to get their political education through fiction . . ." Argues that, at best, only four and one half percent of the population read and only one percent read the kind of intellectual works McCarthy mentions. Suggests that she is dreaming if she

thinks American political policy is shaped by any of the left of
center writers like Doctorow or Bellow.

514. "Mary McCarthy Wins Prize." NEW YORK TIMES (April 10,
1984): C19.
    Announces McCarthy's receipt of the 1984 National Medal
for Literature, an award based on a distinguished past and
continuing contribution to American letters.

515. "Mary McCarthy Wins Medal for Literature." PUBLISHERS
WEEKLY 225, no.16 (April 20, 1984): 21.
    Observes that McCarthy has been named recipient of the
National Medal for Literature.

516. Chambers, Marcia. "Lillian Hellman Wins Round in Suit." NEW
YORK TIMES (May 11, 1984): C3.
    Notes that McCarthy's motion to dismiss, in the Hellman
lawsuit, has been denied. Explains that McCarthy sought
dismissal contending she had merely been expressing an opinion
about a public figure. Reports that action against Dick Cavett has
been dropped and appeals are expected from McCarthy's
lawyers.

517. "Hellman a Legend, but Not a Public Figure, Judge Rules."
ATLANTA JOURNAL (May 11, 1984): A3.
    Reports that the judge in the Hellman versus McCarthy libel
suit has ruled that in a legal sense Hellman is not considered a
public figure.

518. Romano, Lois. "Ruling Backs Hellman; Writer Not Public
Figure, Judge Says in Libel." WASHINGTON POST (May 12,
1984): C1, C8.
    Reports a procedural win for Hellman with the judge's ruling
that she is not a public figure for purposes of her libel suit
against McCarthy.

519. McPherson, William. "Hellman vs. McCarthy--in the Matter of
'Truth'." WASHINGTON POST (May 15, 1984): A15.
    Provides some examples of well-known literary insults
leading to a discussion of the resemblance or lack thereof of "fair

comment" to "literal truth." Grants writers sometimes exceed the boundaries of good taste or even decency, but believes they must be allowed special latitude. Says Hellman should drop the suit.

520. "Hellman Wins Round in McCarthy Suit." PUBLISHERS WEEKLY 225, no.21 (May 25, 1984): 28.
Notes McCarthy's motion to dismiss is denied by the judge who finds that as a matter of law. Hellman is not a public figure.

521. McCracken, Samuel. "'Julia' & Other Fictions by Lillian Hellman." COMMENTARY 77, no.6 (June 1984): 35-43.
Raises the question of Hellman's overall veracity and credibility in light of her libel suit against McCarthy. Examines her memoirs in detail, finding innumerable inaccuracies, inconsistencies and improbabilities. Concludes that in setting herself up as an ethical example, Hellman has manipulated millions.

522. "New England Portrait: Mary McCarthy." BOSTON MAGAZINE (June 1984): 248.
Refers to McCarthy's attacks on various establishments in THE GROUP, THE GROVES OF ACADEME, THE OASIS and A CHARMED LIFE.

523. Hitchens, Christopher. "American Notes." TIMES LITERARY SUPPLEMENT, no.4240 (July 6, 1984): 754.
Refers to an article by Samuel McCracken which stated that many of the ingredients in Hellman's PENTIMENTO were false. Argues that McCracken's article offers one more reason Hellman's suit should be dropped. See also McCracken's article (item no. 521).

524. Freedman, Samuel G. "McCarthy is Recipient of MacDowell Medal." NEW YORK TIMES 133 (August 27, 1984): C14.
Observes that the literary lioness still has sharp claws. Notes McCarthy remains absolutely unregenerate. Remarks that McCarthy, combative as ever, expressed regret about declining literary standards, and believes, on the whole, she had been given "a raw deal."

525. Higgins, Richard. "Author Mary McCarthy Awarded McDowell Medal." WASHINGTON POST (August 27, 1984): C8.
     Report on McCarthy's receipt of the Edward McDowell Medal for "outstanding contribution to literature."

526. Eakin, Paul John. "Fiction in Autobiography: Ask Mary McCarthy No Questions." In FICTIONS IN AUTOBIOGRAPHY: STUDIES IN THE ART OF SELF INVENTION, 3-55. Princeton, N.J.: Princeton Univ. Press, 1985.
     Discusses the interplay of truth and fiction in autobiographies. Focuses on McCarthy's memoirs and her own declaration that they may not always be accurate. Attempts to examine the function of autobiography as self-revelation and self-validation.

527. Wald, Alan M. "The Politics of Culture: The New York Intellectuals in Fiction." CENTENNIAL REVIEW 29, no.3 (1985): 353-369.
     Argues that the 1940s were pivotal in the transformation and deradicalization of the New York intellectuals. Believes that study of the imaginative literature produced by and about them is crucial to an understanding of their ideological transition. Focuses on five works of fiction written during that period, among them McCarthy's THE OASIS, and discusses their thematic and structural continuity in terms of ideological implications.

528. Gross, John. "Books of the Times." NEW YORK TIMES (February 12, 1985): C17.
     Reviews KING OF CATS and notes McCarthy's admirable introduction.

529. Carmody, Deirdre. "Mary McCarthy, Class of '33, Sends Papers to Vassar." NEW YORK TIMES (May 1, 1985): B1, B8.
     Discusses the purchase of McCarthy's literary and personal papers by Vassar College. Provides excerpts from correspondence written during her stormy marriage to Wilson, which details their physical and mental anguish.

530. "On the Record: The McCarthy Papers [Editorial]." NEW YORK TIMES (May 2, 1985): A26.
    Notes Vassar's acquisition of the McCarthy papers, and points out that writers' packrat instincts prove invaluable for scholarly insight and juicy gossip.

531. Mitgang, Herbert. "Autobiography in Progress." NEW YORK TIMES BOOK REVIEW 90 (May 5, 1985): 15.
    Reveals that McCarthy has been working on an intellectual autobiography for some time. Relays her statement that because one's powers of social observation decline after a certain age, she would no longer be writing novels.

532. White, Hayden. "From Faith to Fatalism." NEW YORK TIMES BOOK REVIEW (September 22, 1985): 7.
    Reviews PARADOX OF HISTORY, Chiaromonte's reflections on the fundamental notions of individual relations to major historical events. Notes McCarthy's friendship with Chiaromonte and the fact that she supplied the postface to the book.

533. Shinn, Thelma J. Wardrop. "A Strategic Retreat: Fiction of the 50's." In RADIANT DAUGHTERS: FICTIONAL AMERICAN WOMEN, 90-98, 132-133. Contributions in Women's Studies, No. 66. Westport, Conn.: Greenwood Press, 1986.
    Argues that because McCarthy was deprived of her parents and thus of normal strong male and female role models, her female characters tend to be weak women looking for male protectors and her male characters are either shallow and one dimensional or comic actors.

534. Low, Virginia. "Could It Happen Here? [Letter to the Editor]." NEW YORK TIMES BOOK REVIEW (March 9, 1986): 35.
    Takes issue with McCarthy's stinging review of Atwood's book. Declares that while McCarthy may not be taking certain trends in our society seriously, many others do, and are frightened by the prospect. See also McCarthy's review (item no. 212).

535. Kermode, Frank. "'A Herd of Independent Minds'." NEW
     YORK TIMES BOOK REVIEW (April 27, 1986): 12.
         Discusses Bloom's dissertation on the progression to
     eminence of the New York intellectuals of the 1930s. Includes an
     illustration of McCarthy, with no other mention.

536. Wald, Alan M. In THE NEW YORK INTELLECTUALS; THE
     RISE AND DECLINE OF THE ANTI-STALINIST LEFT: THE
     1930s TO THE 1980s. Chapel Hill, N.C.: Univ. of N.C. Press,
     1987.
         Explores the political and cultural implications of the rise
     and decline of anti-Stalinist Marxism among New York
     intellectuals over a fifty year period. Theorizes that a major
     obstacle in trying to reconstruct the era lies in the politics of
     memory, a complex cultural/political amnesia. States clearly that
     his sympathies lie with Marxist commitment and his purpose in
     writing the book is to help abate deradicalization. As a member
     of the group under discussion, which he defines as those who
     were occupationally involved in the production and dissemination
     of ideas, McCarthy is referred to throughout, but only fleetingly.

537. Kakutani, Michiko. "Our Woman of Letters." NEW YORK
     TIMES BIOGRAPHICAL SERVICE 18, no.3 (March 29,
     1987): 277-280.
         Chronicles McCarthy's life and work as novelist, critic,
     journalist and cultural historian. Assesses her writing to have
     been consistent throughout: a moral point of view, feminine
     angle of vision, and cool and logical tone. Notes the idea of
     justice imbues all of McCarthy's work and that betterment of self
     has been one of her central imperatives.

         Also published in: NEW YORK TIMES MAGAZINE (March
     29, 1987): 60-61, 70.

538. Robertson, Nan. "Writer's Memories Sting and Entertain." NEW
     YORK TIMES (September 23, 1987): C9.
         Reports that McCarthy came onto the stage looking like
     someone's "dear old grandmother" and proceeded to "cheerfully
     throw poisoned darts" at a variety of people. Says she kept the

overflowing house entertained with readings from her unpublished sequel to HOW I GREW and her essay "My Confession," focusing on her experiences in the 1930s, her marriage to Johnsrud and her relationship with Cowley.

539. Berman, Paul. "THE GROUP At the Y." VILLAGE VOICE 32, no.40 (October 6, 1987): 34.
     Reports on McCarthy's reading from the in-progress second volume of her intellectual autobiography. Notes that unlike many other writers, McCarthy on stage has the same effect as she does on the page.

540. Eakin, Paul John. "Reference and the Representation in American Autobiography: Mary McCarthy and Lillian Hellman." In Accardo, Anna Lucia, and Maria Ornella Marotti, eds. IDENTITA E SCRITTURA: STUDI SULL' AUTOGRAFIA NORD-AMERICANA. 21-47. Rome: Bulzoni, 1988. (Not seen)

541. Krechel, Ursula. "Autobiographien vor dem Leben." DIE HOREN: ZEITSCHRIFT FUR LITERATUR, KUNST UND KRITIK (Hanover, Germany) 4, no.33 (1988): 21-28. German.
     Distinguishes between autobiography as autobiography and autobiography disguised as fiction. Looks at two cases in particular, McCarthy's MEMORIES OF A CATHOLIC GIRLHOOD and Natalia Ginzburg's FAMILY LEXICON. Judges the two women to be unrepresentative of the genre, because while they do not ignore their respective families, they don't see themselves just as the sum-expression of their forebearers lives.

542. O'Mahoney, Ingrid. "Scoring Points [Letter to the Editor]." TIMES (London, G.B.) (May 16, 1988): 15.
     Refers to the sexual encounter in McCarthy's "The Man in the Brooks Brothers Shirt."

543. Atkinson, Mary Lou, and Carol Gelderman. "Story Behind Story of Mary McCarthy." TIMES-PICAYUNE (New Orleans, La.) (May 29, 1988): F3.
     Interviews Carol Gelderman, author of MARY

McCARTHY: A LIFE, who recounts her first meeting with
McCarthy and the ups and downs of their working relationship.

544. McDowell, Edwin. "Book Notes: THE GROUP Plus 25." NEW
YORK TIMES (October 5, 1988): C26.
Reports that six hundred Vassar students and faculty gathered
to hear McCarthy read from THE GROUP 25 years after its
publication. Notes that it was considered highly controversial and
banned in several countries at the time, but has since been
translated into seventeen languages.

545. "Three New Members for Arts and Letters Academy." NEW
YORK TIMES (December 3, 1988): 13.
Notes that McCarthy is one of three artists honored with
election to the prestigious American Academy of Arts and
Letters.

Also published in: NEW YORK TIMES (December 4, 1988):
90.

546. Atwood, Margaret. "Introduction." In WOMEN WRITERS AT
WORK: THE PARIS REVIEW INTERVIEWS, edited by
George Plimpton, xi-xviii. New York: Viking Penguin, 1989.
Includes McCarthy's answer to the question: "what do you
think of women writers?" in a synopsis of fifteen interviews,
selected from WRITERS AT WORK, series 1-8.

547. Davis, Barbara Kerr. READ ALL YOUR LIFE: A SUBJECT
GUIDE TO FICTION. 22, 147. Jefferson, N.C.: McFarland &
Co., 1989.
Provides two quotes from McCarthy's works: the first, from
MEMORIES OF A CATHOLIC GIRLHOOD begins a chapter
which looks at the role of heroines in female adolescent novels;
the second, from THE GROVES OF ACADEME is included in
a chapter that views academic life in a variety of educational
systems.

548. Gelderman, Carol. "The Lure and the Lore of Trying to Write a Serious Book That Makes a Fortune." CHRONICLE OF HIGHER EDUCATION 35, no.31 (April 12, 1989): B2.

     Reflects upon her pursuit of the serious best seller. Describes with amusement the happenstance that turned her proposed book on the portrayal of alcoholism in American literature into a biography of Henry Ford. Describes meeting and corresponding with McCarthy during the preparation of MARY MCCARTHY: A LIFE.

549. Adams, Timothy Dow. "Lillian Hellman: 'Are You Now or Were You Ever?'." In TELLING LIES IN MODERN AMERICAN AUTOBIOGRAPHY, 121-166. Chapel Hill, N.C.: Univ. of North Carolina Press, 1990.

     Introduces a discussion of Hellman's autobiographical personality with a synopsis of the McCarthy/Hellman feud. Compares them in terms of their own perceptions of honesty and identity and describes McCarthy's method of self-presentation as "identity continually refined in each revision," while Hellman's method is termed "refraction." Analyzes Hellman's four autobiographical works.

550. Adams, Timothy Dow. "Mary McCarthy: 'I Do Believe Her Though I Know She Lies'." In TELLING LIES IN MODERN AMERICAN AUTOBIOGRAPHY, 85-120. Chapel Hill, N.C.: Univ. of North Carolina Press, 1990.

     Attempts to understand McCarthy's autobiographical stance through a detailed analysis of MEMORIES OF A CATHOLIC GIRLHOOD and HOW I GREW. Focuses on her ongoing endeavor to reconcile her adult identity with her memories of childhood. Believes McCarthy is caught in a very Catholic confessional bind, a need to reveal and a need to conceal, which results in work marked by both scrupulous honesty and constant lying.

551. Chalon, Jean. "Livre de la semaine: Jeux interdits." FIGARO LITTERAIRE (January 22, 1990): 1. French.

     Suggests that McCarthy and De Beauvoir have a taste for commitment and autobiography in common. Comments that the long anticipated HOW I GREW is not nearly as interesting as it might have been.

552. Rose, Barbara. "I'll Tell You No Lies: Mary McCarthy's MEMORIES OF A CATHOLIC GIRLHOOD and the Fictions of Authority." TULSA STUDIES IN WOMEN'S LITERATURE (Okla.) 9, no.1 (Spring 1990): 107-126.

Theorizes that women biographers have no choice but to lie because autobiography is male oriented. Provides an in-depth analysis of MEMORIES OF A CATHOLIC GIRLHOOD tracing "the lies that she exposes in patriarchal myths, the urge she experiences, nonetheless, for her own authority, and the lies she is forced back into by her fathers." Claims the truth lies in the relationship between the maternal and paternal aspects of the narrative--the autobiographical chapters and McCarthy's questioning commentaries.

Book Reviews

THE COMPANY SHE KEEPS

553. Perry, Katherine. PSYCHIATRY 5 (1942): 294.
     Believes the book is of more than average interest as a
contribution to pathology. Praises McCarthy's clever handling of
the psychological implications but suggests that her treatment of
psychoanalysis in the final story is rather stereotypical in the
underrating of its value.

554. Abrahams, William. "This Year's Girl by Mary McCarthy."
     BOSTON GLOBE [Sunday Ed.] (May 13, 1942): 19.
     Calls this the book of the year written by a young woman
who looks like a glamour girl but writes like a worldly-wise
man. Suggests that the novel is the epitome of the American
1940s, successful because McCarthy is the consummate novelist
who knows exactly what she is about.

555. Fadiman, Clifton. "Books: Three Novels." NEW YORKER 18
     (May 16, 1942): 72-73.
     Regards the book as sharp rather than witty and malicious
rather than cynical. Says it reminds him of early Huxley, when
he was "still a lost soul and rather enjoying it." Attacks
McCarthy for being a gossip whose only talent is "dissecting
people and leaving a nasty mess on the table."

556. "New Writers: Mary McCarthy." PUBLISHERS WEEKLY 141 (May 16, 1942): 1837.
     Offers a brief biographical sketch of McCarthy and a synopsis of the book.

557. De Toledano, Ralph. "Personal Distillate." NEW LEADER (May 23, 1942): 2.
     Proposes that although the stories make excellent reading, the book itself can be described only as "promising." Blames the shoddy structure, maintaining that McCarthy never decided whether to write about Margaret or six other people. Comments that in trying to justify her heroine, she merely describes the people around her semi-apologetically.

558. Feld, Rose. "Novels and Short Stories on Many Themes." NEW YORK HERALD TRIBUNE BOOKS (May 24, 1942): 8.
     Finds that there is very little to unify the stories and suggests that it is not even important to read them consecutively. Praises McCarthy for her biting wit and ability to "turn a precious phrase with the skill of a brilliant fencer," but concludes that on the whole the book is "very much like a performance by a highly gifted child who is deliberately and self-consciously trying to shock his elders."

559. Walton, Edith H. "THE COMPANY SHE KEEPS and Other Works of Fiction." NEW YORK TIMES BOOK REVIEW (May 24, 1942): 7.
     Believes that the reflection of McCarthy's own experiences in the character of Margaret gives the book its liveliness and authenticity. Suggests the book will create a minor furor because of the original and sensational portrait McCarthy paints of her heroine and more particularly of the cruel way she portrays the exact talk and temper of certain circles in New York. Says that despite the definite merits the overall value of the book remains suspect.

560. Cowley, Malcolm. "Bad Company." NEW REPUBLIC 106, no.21 (May 25, 1942): 737.
     Suggests that the book, although clever and wicked, is not wickedly clever. Says that it is only the scrupulous honesty of

Margaret in the last story, "Ghostly Father, I Confess," that redeems her character as well as the book itself. Concludes this book has an unusual quality of having been lived even though it is not very likeable or well put together.

561. Laughlin, James. ACCENT 2, no.4 (Summer 1942): 236.
      Praises McCarthy for being on the right track. Compares her to Fitzgerald and hopes she will remain serious and keep company with his austere ghost.

562. CATHOLIC WORLD 155 (June 1942): 380.
      Says that despite glimpses of excellence in characterization and style, McCarthy fails in her attempt to be sophisticated and bawdy at the same time.

563. "From the Bottom of the Kennel." TIME 39, no.22 (June 1, 1942): 82-83.
      Notes that the book sets the standard for "bilish sharpness" and is arousing furious reaction among McCarthy's friends and victims. Claims McCarthy's socio-psychological criticism proceeds in part from a lack of what theologians call clarity, and that nowhere in the book do any of the characters exhibit a hint of selflessness.

564. Wade, Mason. "Books of the Week." COMMONWEAL 36, no.9 (June 19, 1942): 208-210.
      Calls the book brilliant, written with a sometimes malicious accuracy as it details the life of one social group in the "disordered 1930s."

565. Isherwood, Christopher. "Her Name Is Legion." NATION 154, no.20 (June 20, 1942): 714.
      Claims McCarthy and her publishers misrepresent the book. Suggests that if McCarthy's real aim was to develop a multi-layered character with striking contrasts and apparent contradictions, she has made a bad job of it. Maintains that Margaret is a rather colorless minor character who serves as a stooge for the well developed and much more interesting principal characters. Commends McCarthy for her warmth,

charity and insight and says she is too talented to need a pompous introduction.

566. Eastman, Max. "The Library." AMERICAN MERCURY 55, no.223 (July 1942): 118-122.
Evaluates the book within its guise as a "new kind of novel." Compares the voice of Margaret with the voice of McCarthy and concludes that both employ perception and mordantly intelligent prose.

567. Gay, Robert M. ATLANTIC MONTHLY 170 (August 1942): 109.
Criticizes the book for a lack of cumulative effect and continuity.

568. Warren, Robert Penn. "Button, Button." PARTISAN REVIEW 9, no.6 (November-December 1942): 537-540.
Questions McCarthy's contradictory messages in the introduction and in the novel itself. Poses questions about McCarthy's premise for satire and her seemingly ambiguous presentation of Margaret, a Humpty Dumpty character who may or may not offer the reader any sense of how, or if, she can put her pieces back together again. Suggests the ambiguity may be quite purposeful, and McCarthy's way of drawing a parallel to the ambiguous resolution of the book.

569. Southard, W. P. "Lady Flat on Her Back." KENYON REVIEW 5, no.1 (Winter 1943): 140-142.
Offers a brief synopsis of each story. Suggests McCarthy's arrangement of abstract experience engulfs her heroine and turns her into an abstract experience herself. Compares McCarthy to Margaret and concludes that they both have the same fault--"being aware of everything and not being able to give it form."

570. "Other New Novels: Pantomime Village." TIMES LITERARY SUPPLEMENT, no.2184 (December 11, 1943): 599.
Views this as a clever essay in fiction. Observes that McCarthy is amusing, sophisticated and always on the edge of something more interesting than mere self-consciousness.

571. Kavan, Anna. "Selected Notes." HORIZON 9, no.50 (February 1944): 138-141.

Compares the book to a photographic montage that presents an entertaining yet malicious picture of American life and society. Says there is a suggestion of smart slickness about the writing but praises McCarthy for her humor.

572. Rago, Henry. "Books." COMMONWEAL 50, no.22 (September 9, 1949): 536-537.

Claims that what distinguishes McCarthy as a brilliant journalist and essayist--her gift for epithet--is precisely what keeps her from being a novelist. Says her characters in both THE COMPANY SHE KEEPS and THE OASIS are tagged and paralyzed by her preconceived estimation of them, leaving no room for a change of pace to the narrative.

573. Wallace, Warren. "A Place Out of the Sun." TRUTH (London, G.B.) 157, no.4213 (June 21, 1957): 717.

Admonishes McCarthy for failing to give the book credibility. Calls her an exceedingly witty and perceptive woman whose malice may be edging out insight. Suggests that the book's greatest flaw is the fact that ultimately all things depend on Margaret for their validity, yet in the first five stories McCarthy does everything she can to divert interest from her. Argues that if Margaret is the final "reflector" then she and McCarthy both stand between the reader and the book obscuring its virtues.

574. Wyndham, Francis. "New Novels." SPECTATOR, no.6730 (June 21, 1957): 820.

Applauds the reissuing of the book. Calls it McCarthy's best, wherein her intelligence can be seen working in every line and her "deadly mockery grows stronger and stronger until it is almost directed at itself." Maintains she has become the official social historian of the radical 1930s New York intelligentsia.

575. Fraser, G. S. "New Novels." NEW STATESMAN AND NATION 53, no.1371 (June 22, 1957): 816.

Calls McCarthy the most notable wit-novelist of the generation. Considers her wit in the light of Freudian theory which proposes that its function is to give a paradoxically condensed expression to painful feelings. Suggests that great novelists try immersing themselves in that pain rather than merely standing back to observe it; that ordinary novelists want to avoid implausibility and thinness; and that great wit-novelists use the implausibility of human behavior and the thinness of human substance to make a point.

576. Urquhart, Fred. "New Novels." TIME AND TIDE (London, G.B.) 38, no.26 (June 29, 1957).
  Commends McCarthy for turning an unusual pattern for a novel into a complete success. Praises her for dissecting her characters with "glee, gusto and astringent wit" and for her penetrating knowledge of New York's literary, political and bohemian jungle.

577. "London Bookman: New Edition." BOOKS OF THE MONTH (London, G.B.) 72, no.7 (July 1957): 5-6, 29.
  Recommends this book very briefly as a worthwhile addition to any library. Mentions that McCarthy also wrote (mistakenly) NINETEENTH CENTURY CHILDHOOD.

578. Macdonald, Dwight. "Fictioneers." ENCOUNTER 9, no.3 (September 1957): 76-79.
  Credits the book for being lean, full of wisecracks and "right" for the period and declares a preference for this writing over some of McCarthy's later, more elaborate prose.

579. Glanville, Brian. "Sensibility Girls Are Given a Lesson." REYNOLDS NEWS (London, G.B.) (December 8, 1957): 4.
  Believes McCarthy stands as a lesson and a reproach to Britain's women novelists. Says that Europeans regard American women as domineering, neurotic and male oriented, but contends that there is a major compensation factor if the woman becomes a writer. Credits McCarthy with a rare and devastating blend of masculine intelligence and feminine sensibility, a combination that accounts largely for the different position of women in America. Observes that one must not be too hard on British women novelists when in truth there are very few men who are capable of writing as well as McCarthy.

580. Kanters, Robert. "Américains insolites: Mary McCarthy."
FIGARO LITTÉRAIRE (September 7, 1963): 2. French.
Writes that McCarthy is a brilliant star on the literary scene
and deplores the fact that it has taken over twenty years for THE
COMPANY SHE KEEPS to be translated into French. Regrets
the delay partly because the New York bohemian life that
McCarthy described is now dated, but suggests that this gives the
reader the luxury of hindsight. Believes, however, that
McCarthy's writings are both American and universal in their
reference to cosmopolitan intelligentsia.

581. CHRISTIAN CENTURY (May 31, 1967): 724.
Dismisses the book as a "gossipy names-naming biography."

582. Peden, William. "Metropolis, Village, and Suburbia: The Short
Fiction of Manners." In THE AMERICAN SHORT STORY:
CONTINUITY AND CHANGE, 1940-1975. 2d ed., rev. &
enl., 61-62. Boston: Houghton Mifflin, 1975.
Includes McCarthy in a discussion of the revival of the story
of manners. Agrees her fiction is cold, but reflects that her
unsparing view of herself, as well as her fellow mortals, add
dimension and depth to her admittedly autobiographical "short
stories." Finds their major weakness is McCarthy's tendency
towards overdiscursiveness.

(Also refers to McCarthy in: Peden, William. AMERICAN
SHORT STORY: FRONT LINE IN THE NATIONAL
DEFENSE OF LITERATURE. 1st ed. 33, 83-85. Boston:
Houghton Mifflin, 1964.)

583. "New in Paperback [column]." BOOK WORLD
(WASHINGTON POST) 11, no.28 (July 12, 1981): 12.
Presents a brief synopsis and calls the book a timeless biting
social satire.

584. Morton, Brian. "Islands in a Pattern of Failures." TIMES
(London, G.B.) (January 13, 1990): 40-41.
Writes that some readers may miss the underlying structure
of THE COMPANY SHE KEEPS--a collection of essays in
which the characters never seem to grow up.

585. Schine, Cathleen. "WOMEN AND MEN." VOGUE 180 (August 1990): 222, 224.
    Reviews WOMEN AND MEN, Home Box Office's successful adaptation of Hemingway's "Hills Like White Elephants," Parker's "Dusk Before Fireworks" and McCarthy's "The Man in the Brooks Brothers Shirt." Enjoys Elizabeth McGovern's sarcastic and seductive performance, against Beau Bridges' "perfectly ordinary businessman." Welcomes future adaptations of classic short stories and states they represent a whole new vein for television.

586. Elson, John. "WOMEN AND MEN: STORIES OF SEDUCTION." TIME 136 (August 20, 1990): 64.
    Briefly reviews three of Home Box Office's ninety minute video anthologies, including McCarthy's "The Man in the Brooks Brothers Shirt" which was directed by Frederic Raphael with lead roles played by Beau Bridges and Elizabeth McGovern. Enjoys Bridges portrayal of the crass business executive but finds McGovern miscast in her role as the radical journalist.

THE OASIS

587. Connolly, Cyril. "Introduction to THE OASIS." HORIZON 19, no.110 (February 1949): 74.
    Congratulates McCarthy for winning the Horizon Prize, noting she is exactly the type of writer the publication hopes to attract--primarily a short story writer and drama critic who should be encouraged towards longer projects. Introduces the story with a quote from McCarthy: "THE OASIS in short, is an imaginary clash between real ideologies, a roman philosophique which gradually unfolds and obscures the reader like a genial electric blanket."

588. Strachey, Julia. "New Novels." NEW STATESMAN AND NATION 37, no.938 (February 26, 1949): 211-212.
    Reports McCarthy "plunges gallantly into the thick" of complicated ideas and problems, illustrating a tendency towards

violence that is both exhilarating and amusing. Applauds her "masculine" range, her ability to see people in terms of civic and personal morality and her particular gift for epigram.

589. Strong, L. A. G. "Fiction." SPECTATOR 182 (March 4, 1949): 302.
    Comments that McCarthy's insights and the texture of her writing make this a brilliant, if somewhat chilly, book.

590. "Ways of Living." TIMES LITERARY SUPPLEMENT, no.2458 (March 19, 1949): 181.
    Reports that British readers will find the story difficult to follow because the political and social types represented are drawn from American sources.

591. KIRKUS REVIEWS 17 (June 1, 1949): 282.
    Notes briefly that THE OASIS is a satire intellectualized almost to the point of sterility.

592. Willis, Katherine Tappert. LIBRARY JOURNAL 74, no.13 (July 1949): 1024.
    Comments very briefly that this prize winning story is food for thought.

593. Medow, Florence. "Two New Novels That Examine Weaknesses in the Attitudes of Some of Today's Liberals." CHICAGO SUN TIMES 2, no.45 (August 7, 1949): 8.
    Declares the book is an oasis of polished writing, intelligence and wit in a desert of undisciplined modern fiction.

594. Barr, Donald. "Failure in Utopia." NEW YORK TIMES BOOK REVIEW (August 14, 1949): 5, 15.
    States there are two kinds of satire: the preferred, which attacks common conceit by analyzing the general nature of people and their institutions; and the other type, employed in THE OASIS, which attacks individuals, stimulating the reader's curiosity about the characters' real-life counterparts. Concludes that the lack of pity, the coldness of McCarthy's portraiture and her failure to provide a story leave the reader befuddled and harassed.

595. Barry, Iris. "Utopians, Opaque and Unheroic." NEW YORK
     HERALD TRIBUNE. WEEKLY BOOK REVIEW (August 14,
     1949): 3.
         Notes McCarthy is too perceptive to have been merely trying
     to portray a group of pitiful, hateful people. Concludes the book
     may best be described as a lengthy philosophical account with
     fictional trimmings.

596. "Quite High on a Mountain Top." TIME 54, no.7 (August 15,
     1949): 84, 86.
         Criticizes the book for sharing the same fatal flaw as the
     utopia it describes--the fact that it is built with disembodied ideas
     and peopled with puppets.

597. Gill, Brendan. "The O'Hara Report and the Wit of Miss
     McCarthy." NEW YORKER 25 (August 20, 1949): 64-66.
         Observes the book is an "unmitigated triumph" of wit and
     writing skill.

598. Munson, Gorham. "Parlor Pinks Playing Utopia." SATURDAY
     REVIEW OF LITERATURE 32, no.34 (August 20, 1949):
     12-13.
         Remarks that part of the fun of reading THE OASIS is
     trying to guess the characters' counterparts. Defends McCarthy's
     use of real models claiming it cannot be viewed as "inartistic"
     when she has "screened" them for suitability, freed them from
     their biographies, and placed them into special circumstances and
     an amusing story. Observes the faction McCarthy has
     transplanted to fiction has previously been exposed by the
     magazines THE PARTISAN REVIEW and POLITICS, and is
     composed mainly of those intellectuals who are critical of
     Stalinism and still under the spell of Marx and Engels. Believes
     she is too close to her material for it to be labelled satire,
     concluding that it is a comedy for the "civilized minority."

599. Sutcliffe, Denham. "Many Words: Small Reward." CHRISTIAN
     SCIENCE MONITOR [Eastern Ed.] (August 23, 1949): 14.
         Emphasizes that pathos and humor are not enough of a
     reward to get the reader to overlook the excessive talk, the lack
     of incident and the limited interest.

600. Jackson, Joseph Henry. "The Idea of Utopia." SAN
FRANCISCO CHRONICLE (August 30, 1949): 14.
Reports that the book will have unquestionable success with
those whose lives are on the level of ideas and those who
recognize, or think they recognize, the characters' real-life
counterparts; however, suggests others will find the book a cold,
philosophical dialogue loosely fitted into a fiction format.

* Rago, Henry. "Books." COMMONWEAL 50, no.22 (September
9, 1949): 536-537.
See item no. 572.

601. Marshall, Margaret. "Notes by the Way." NATION 169, no.12
(September 17, 1949): 281-282.
Proposes THE OASIS fails as a both a story and a satire
because its action is inconsequential and frivolous and it is
missing the two elements which are necessary for good satire:
the hatred of evil, and the love of the good and intelligent.

602. Clarke, Clorinda. "Shorter Notices." CATHOLIC WORLD 170
(November 1949): 157-161.
Notes briefly that McCarthy has written a stylish book which
is sometimes witty, but never very strong in narrative or
character portrayal.

603. Klein, Alexander. "Satirist's Utopia." NEW REPUBLIC 121
(December 5, 1949): 19-20.
Calls THE OASIS a series of vignettes forced into the
framework of a contrived moral crisis. Says the characters suffer
from intrinsic shallowness and a chronic lack of direction, and
suggests this is McCarthy's not too subtle attempt to illustrate
that their real-life counterparts are equally lacking in direction.
Concludes that McCarthy, consumed with being forever clever
and tough, succeeds on one level, but pays the price for "aiming
at the moon, by landing in a fishpond."

604. Kapp, Isa. "The 'Liberal' in the Novel." COMMENTARY 9 (January 1950): 100-102.

    Emphasizes that because McCarthy criticizes the anti-Communist left from within, implying her own participation in its failures, she cannot be compassionate. Notes the lack of "flesh and blood" characters, a general uneveness in the substance of the book and a tendency on McCarthy's part to be needlessly sarcastic.

605. OBSERVER (London, G.B.) (June 18, 1950).

    Notes briefly that A SOURCE OF EMBARRASSMENT may require some effort on the part of the British reader, but the effort is worth making. (Citation not verified.)

606. Ottaway, Robert. "It's Cruel But It's Fun." GRAPHIC (London, G.B.) [Sunday Ed.] (June 18, 1950).

    Mentions, very briefly, that THE OASIS deserves the title change to A SOURCE OF EMBARRASSMENT, and the permanence of a "stiff cover." (Citation not verified.)

607. NEWS CHRONICLE (London, G.B.) (June 19, 1950).

    Reports that even though the story is not overdone and the characters' conduct is probable, McCarthy should have worked out her theory more precisely. (Citation not verified.)

608. EVENING STANDARD (London, G.B.) (June 20, 1950).

    Warns the book should be kept way from "cranks." Notes briefly that it is a "hilarious hunting on the lunatic fringes of the left." (Citation not verified.)

609. Symons, Julian. MANCHESTER EVENING NEWS (G.B.) (June 21, 1950).

    Points out that the value of A SOURCE OF EMBARRASSMENT lies in the fact that it remains focused on the characters as true idealists. (Citation not verified.)

610. YORKSHIRE OBSERVER (G.B.) (June 22, 1950).

    Says that a rereading of the story brings its weaknesses and strengths into focus. (Citation not verified.)

611. SPECTATOR (June 23, 1950).
Says McCarthy writes a deliberately "bloodless" satire with implications that are not in the least disquieting. (Citation not verified.)

612. Watson, Colin. "Has Laughter Gone Out of Print?" NEWCASTLE JOURNAL (G.B.) (June 27, 1950).
Compares A SOURCE OF EMBARRASSMENT to Mackenzie's BUTTERCUPS AND DAISIES. Says the book fails to be "funny" because the British lack an appreciation for McCarthy's American humor. (Citation not verified.)

613. Price, R. G. G. "Booking Office: Flexible Fiction." PUNCH 218, no.5719 (June 28, 1950): 724.
Considers, on a second reading, that A SOURCE OF EMBARRASSMENT is a fiendishly precise description, successful at providing a glimpse at the future by illuminating the course of contemporary man.

614. ARGUS (G.B.) (October 14, 1950).
Praises McCarthy for delivering clear-cut thoughts on the United States while other American writers are producing historical novels about covered wagons in an attempt to glorify their country's rise from its small beginnings. (Citation not verified.)

615. Goodman, Paul. FURIOSO 5, no.1 (Winter 1950): 77-78.
Brands this a weak, toothless satire which doesn't even merit being a book.

616. Aldridge, John W. "Capote and Buechner." In AFTER THE LOST GENERATION: A CRITICAL STUDY OF THE WRITERS OF TWO WARS, 196-197. New York: McGraw-Hill, 1951.
Examines a small group of prose purists who have abandoned social manners and managed to escape the problem of giving significance to evil and guilt within the context of a valueless society. Says that several writers have gone one step further by expanding significance beyond itself and illuminating the universal issues of life. Notes McCarthy's idea of ideal

morality is weakened by the pettiness of the problems she depicts. (Refers to McCarthy in the Preface to the 1st edition, pg. xii.)

Also published: Reprinted ed. New York: Books for Libraries, 1971; New York: Arbor House, 1985; paperback ed. New York: Noonday Press, 1958 and British ed. London: Vision Press, 1959.

617. Meyer, Frank. "Pleasantly Catty." FREEMAN 2 (1951-52): 851.
     Finds McCarthy draws her characters with acid skill but contends she should restrict herself to short sketches and stories. Accuses her of "throwing her net too wide" with THE OASIS and concludes THE GROVES OF ACADEME suffers from the effort to sustain a plot.

618. Poore, Charles. "Books of The Times." NEW YORK TIMES (February 21, 1952): L5.
     Writes that McCarthy's vantage point, half-way between Tess Slesinger and Voltaire, invites criticism from those who say there are no "sunbeams among her penetrating lances." Contends that anyone who can find subjects for amiable compassion among her characters probably wouldn't write about them at all. Compares the book briefly to THE OASIS and concludes that her art almost accomplishes man's frequently stated wish that he said what he would like to have said.

619. Greenberg, Martin. "Books in Short." AMERICAN MERCURY 74, no.341 (May 1952): 110-111.
     Assesses the book's satirical merit and finds McCarthy guilty of the same kind of sentimentality for "fools" as in THE OASIS. Decides she is too sharp with her disapproval, too unself-critical, and plays too many favorites to be considered a true satirist.

620. Gottfried, Alex, and Sue Davidson. "Utopia's Children: An Interpretation of Three Political Novels." WESTERN POLITICAL QUARTERLY 15, no.1 (March 15, 1962): 17-32.
     Discusses three novels to illustrate how valuable literature could be to political scientists who might want to explore

hypotheses and develop an understanding of the emotional concept of political phenomena. Notes the three authors, Hawthorne, Orwell, and McCarthy, are interested in the people who see the vision, and not political theorists who are presenting a vision of an ideal society. Examines THE OASIS in relation to political ideals, ideal societies, and specific societal roles.

621. "Briefing: Where and When." OBSERVER (London, G.B.) (October 31, 1965): 22.
     Remarks very briefly that these two books are witty exercises in group satire.

622. Zand, Nicole. "Mary et Mavis, deux Parisiennes d'Amerique." LE MONDE (May 13, 1988). French.
     Says that while McCarthy lives in Paris she does not consider herself either an expatriot or an exile, an attitude reflected in her writing.

623. Baredette, Gilles. "McCarthy: l'esprit des mots." L'EXPRESS, no.1924 (May 27, 1988): 68. French.
     Argues that McCarthy has never supported the anti-intellectual spirit of the Anglo-American tradition, or the opposition between the literature of ideas and romantic literature, seeing all the great novels as novels of ideas.

CAST A COLD EYE

624. Miller, Nolan. "The Short Story As 'Young Art'." ANTIOCH REVIEW 10, no.4 (1950): 543-546.
     Observes that a number of current short story collections are, on the whole, concerned more and more with less and less. Concedes that McCarthy has vitality, but criticizes her self-assuredness and tendency to label. Finds she presents types rather then individuals resulting in the emotional distancing of the reader.

625. Barker, Shirley. "New Books Appraised." LIBRARY JOURNAL 75, no.16 (September 15, 1950): 1507.
     Predicts that these stories, written in a clear and direct style, are sure to be popular.

626. Poore, Charles. "Books of the Times." NEW YORK TIMES (September 21, 1950): L29.
     Expresses some reservations about McCarthy's characteristic use of types rather than individuals, but concludes that this rather remorseless collection contains brilliant sketches by a brilliant writer.

627. Fitts, Dudley. "Portraits Cut in Acid." NEW YORK TIMES BOOK REVIEW 105 (September 24, 1950): 9.
     Admires McCarthy's power as a satirist, focusing on her use of language and the almost surgical sharpness of her eye.

628. Pruette, Lorine. "Stories Told in Cold Fury and Disciplined Hatred." NEW YORK HERALD TRIBUNE BOOK REVIEW 27, no.6 (September 24, 1950): 8.
     Notes that each of the stories bears the stamp of an original Mary McCarthy, intellectually satisfying, with a compelling style and characterized by cold fury and disciplined hatred.

629. "Mary's Little Lambs." NEWSWEEK 36 (September 25, 1950): 97-98.
     Places McCarthy squarely within contemporary American intellectual circles in which all things are analyzed in political terms. Concedes that her prose is witty and beautifully polished, but says the juxtaposition of dialectical materialism with people, gardens and parties is confusing.

630. Scott, Winfield Townley. "Mary McCarthy's X-Ray Vision." PROVIDENCE JOURNAL [Sunday Ed.] (September 29, 1950): sect. 6, 8.
     Sees the stories as spare, clean writing working in conjunction with a memorable, uncompromised vision.

631. Crane, Milton. "Short Stories Written with a Rare Skill."
CHICAGO TRIBUNE. MAGAZINE OF BOOKS [Sunday Ed.]
(October 1, 1950): 4.
Grants McCarthy a place in the front ranks of contemporary
satirists based on her earlier works THE COMPANY SHE
KEEPS and THE OASIS. Admires her clear and dispassionate
style.

632. "Say Ah-h-h!" TIME 56 (October 2, 1950): 80-81.
Expresses disappointment that McCarthy's sharp satirical
skills are largely absent. Likens her characters to puppets
inhabiting a very intellectual, elegant void.

633. Miles, George. COMMONWEAL 52, no.26 (October 6, 1950):
634-635.
Finds this collection of previously published stories
interesting, well written and touched with a deep sadness. Praises
both her psychological insights and her verbal ability.

634. Halsband, Robert. "Jaundiced Eye." SATURDAY REVIEW 33
(October 7, 1950): 23.
Acknowledges McCarthy's brilliance as a satirist and
storyteller. Refutes her critics' notion that she remains detached,
believing that her jaundiced eye is trained no less on herself than
on her characters. Concludes that her bittersweet work reveals a
savage honesty as well as pitiless humility.

635. Sandrock, Mary. CATHOLIC WORLD 172 (November 1950):
152.
Contends McCarthy is ignorant of mankind, both its inherent
dignity and possible depravity. Finds her characterizations
brilliant but one-dimensional, resulting in distortion and
disappointment for the reader.

636. Bogan, Louise. "Ecstasy and Order." NEW REPUBLIC 123,
no.22 (November 27, 1950): 18-19.
Shows great admiration for a style obviously grounded in
classical education. Finds, however, that as a satirist, McCarthy
is not relentless enough, veering off before the telling blow.

Implies that were it not for her detachment and lack of emotion, McCarthy might well become a modern day Austen.

637. Poster, William. "Fractional Fiction." NEW LEADER (December 11, 1950): 24, 26.
    Contends that the book's most striking aspect is the vast gulf between subject matter and style. Focuses on "The Weeds" and "The Cicerone" as examples of McCarthy's brilliant writing but disparages her inadequate narrative invention, formulaic characters and absence of emotion. Concedes that she possesses a great natural literary and intellectual ability, however feels her apparent need for codified experience seriously impedes the realization of her potential.

638. Scott, Winfield Townley. "The Literary Summing Up." SATURDAY REVIEW (December 30, 1950): 6-8, 28-29.
    Details an admittedly personal judgment on the best books of 1950, referring briefly to the "deadly devastations" of McCarthy's entry.

639. Dahlberg, Edward. "Stalemated People." FREEMAN 1 (1950-51): 93.
    Finds the prose stale, the characters tired and bored. Sums up the book as just one more example of "chic mademoiselle pornography" masquerading as Marxism and moral realism.

640. E., C. Y. BOOKLIST 47 (September 1950-August 1951): 62.
    Calls this collection of satirical short stories one of the best of its kind.

641. Brossard, Chandler. "Noble Hawks and Neurotic Women." NEW AMERICAN MERCURY 72, no.326 (February 4, 1951): 230-234.
    Perceives McCarthy's primary concern is urban sensibility and the relationship between "thinking" people. Suggests that her often critical and contemptuous attitude toward her characters comes from a deeply disappointed moralism.

642. Fiedler, Leslie A. "Style and Antistyle in the Short Story."
KENYON REVIEW 13, no.1 (Winter 1951): 155-172.
Reflects on the growing number of short story collections
being published and the changes in the genre since its inception.
Wonders if McCarthy, with her Oscar Wildish wit and total lack
of invention, has turned to the short story because the essay has
lost its status.

643. Krim, Seymour. "Short Stories by Six." HUDSON REVIEW 3,
no.4 (Winter 1951): 626-633.
Praises McCarthy's articulate writing and keen perception
which, as in her earlier book THE COMPANY SHE KEEPS, is
"an almost masculine intelligence at work roasting the game that
a female sensibility has trapped." Admires her critical faculty,
but finds her narrative invention weak. Concludes that her
self-conscious and highly intellectualized writing, a style
promoted by THE PARTISAN REVIEW, remains rather tedious
and pedantic.

644. MacAuley, Robie. FURIOSO 6, no.1 (1952): 70-72.
Likens this collection of "pseudo-fiction" to a series of stage
sets designed to illustrate the author's theories and educate the
reader. Recognizes McCarthy's ability to argue in an ingenious
and expert manner, however concludes her unremitting focus on
the varieties of human failure is sour and nihilistic.

645. "18s. Is the Top Price Here." DAILY EXPRESS (London,
G.B.) (January 12, 1952): 4.
Calls McCarthy's dissection of human relationships brilliant.

646. Ottaway, Robert. "Twice-Bitten." GRAPHIC (London, G.B.)
[Sunday Ed.] (January 13, 1952): 9.
Observes that McCarthy's stories are worth savoring.
Reflects that "short in heart and strong in mind," they are the
reverse of customary feminine accomplishments.

647. Snow, C. P. "A Visit to Turkey." TIMES (London, G.B.)
[Sunday Ed.] (January 13, 1952): 3.
Assesses McCarthy's assured style as reminiscent of James
but without the compassion. Detects in her writing a conscious

toughness and emotional restraint currently in vogue among serious American writers.

648. Taggart, Joseph. "Mr. Onions and His Jester." STAR (G.B.) (January 14, 1952): 8.
     Recommends the collection as a fine example of lean modern writing.

649. Sheldon, G. A. "New Novels." BIRMINGHAM POST (G.B.) (January 15, 1952).
     Concedes her stories are clever, but feels her disparaging view of humanity leaves a disagreeable aftertaste.

650. "Panorama of Short Stories." BIRMINGHAM MAIL (G.B.) (January 16, 1952).
     Calls the book rewarding for readers who value chilly psychoanalytical cleverness.

651. Shanks, Edward. "Edward Shanks Reviews the New Books." DAILY GRAPHIC AND DAILY SKETCH (London, G.B.) (January 16, 1952): 5.
     Observes that while McCarthy has a considerable and implacable skill with words, his reaction is a "desire to fold up and die quietly and get it all over."

652. Betjeman, John. "New Fiction." DAILY TELEGRAPH AND MORNING POST (London and Manchester, G.B.) (January 18, 1952): 6.
     Believes that British readers will feel an immediate affinity to the American McCarthy. Calls her stories subtle and penetrating character studies.

653. Laski, Marghanita. "Fiction." SPECTATOR (January 18, 1952): 88.
     Notes her surprise at finding a number of these bitterly penetrating stories not only excellent, but also funny and extremely touching.

654. Laws, Frederick. "Funny, but Film Should Be Funnier." NEWS CHRONICLE (London, G.B.) (January 18, 1952): 4.
Expresses enormous admiration for these brilliantly written stories by the sharp-eyed and even sharper tongued McCarthy.

655. LIVERPOOL EVENING EXPRESS (January 18, 1952).
Considers these "typically American" stories by a commanding author well worth reading. (Citation not verified.)

656. Nicholson, Nigel. "Human Appeal." DAILY DISPATCH (G.B.) (January 18, 1952): 2.
Elicits a visceral "good, good, good" from Nicholson, who, in a very brief review, calls the collection un-American in style, very American in atmosphere.

657. MacRae, Alistair. "Books." EVENING CITIZEN. SATURDAY MAGAZINE (G.B.) (January 19, 1952): 1.
States briefly how impressive he finds McCarthy's in-depth portrayal of her characters in CATCH A COLD EYE [sic].

658. K., E. "American Short Stories." EXPRESS AND STAR (G.B.) (January 21, 1952): 6.
Describes these short stories as masterpieces of their kind.

659. Bloomfield, Paul. "New Fiction." MANCHESTER GUARDIAN (G.B.) (January 25, 1952): 4.
Finds the stories penetrating and thoroughly cold, both in observation and attitude.

660. GUARDIAN (Manchester, G.B.) (January 25, 1952).
Categorizes this collection as an "exemplary cosmopolitan standard," acute but cold. (Citation not verified.)

661. Parrish, Philip. "New Novels." TRIBUNE (London, G.B.) (January 25, 1952): 14.
Maintains that these excitingly chilly stories are worthy of the reader's perseverance.

662. Price, R. G. G. "Through a Glass Darkly." PUNCH 222, no.5806 (January 30, 1952): 184.
     Views the stories as social comedy, amusing and/or terrifying depending on the reader's "sophistication."

663. NATIONAL AND ENGLISH REVIEW (G.B.) (February 1952).
     Concedes that her style is flawless, but terms these stories "animated cartoons" meant only for readers who focus on verbal technique. (Citation not verified.)

664. NEW STATESMAN (February 3, 1952).
     Reflects on McCarthy's addiction to intellectual metaphor which this reviewer finds occasionally compelling but often ineffective. Believes the dynamism of her writing is a result of her view of the universe as a jungle, her sense of the worst lurking in even the best of us. (Citation not verified.)

665. Toynbee, Philip. "Bludgeon and Rapier." OBSERVER (London, G.B.) (February 3, 1952): 3.
     Calls her a very clever writer, while simultaneously reminding the reader of the word's perjorative overtones. Describes her work alternately as brilliant, absurd and distasteful.

666. H., H. G. CAMBRIDGE DAILY NEWS (G.B.) (February 7, 1952).
     Prefaces this short but querulous review with the opinion that British short story writers need not feel inferior to those in the United States. Calls McCarthy's style brittle and built on a foundation of pseudo-psychology. (Citation not verified.)

667. "New Novels: The Background First." GLASGOW HERALD (G.B.) (February 7, 1952).
     Wonders whether her ruthless analysis may not be something of a pose.

668. Raymond, John. "Limited View." TIMES LITERARY SUPPLEMENT, no.2610 (February 8, 1952): 105.
     Credits her with witty and expressive writing, but assesses the "cocksureness" of her work as a failing.

669. "For Your Bookshelf." QUEEN (London, G.B.) (February 13, 1952): 46.
     Observes that these acute essays display an understanding of the human condition but show little sympathy.

670. LADY (G.B.) (February 14, 1952).
     Describes the book as characteristic of McCarthy's clear vision, balanced judgment and sensible style. (Citation not verified.)

671. Urquhart, Fred. TIME AND TIDE (London, G.B.) (February 16, 1952): 163.
     Describes the stories as entertaining reading full of quotable passages.

672. "Bookshelf." MANCHESTER EVENING NEWS (G.B.) (February 20, 1952).
     Calls McCarthy a clever writer with a sharply focused style. (Citation not verified.)

673. Ferris, Paul. "CAST A COLD EYE on Life, on Death." SOUTH WALES EVENING POST (G.B.) (March 8, 1952).
     Spends a good part of the review musing on the notion that writers are products of their times but can never really assess them. Faults McCarthy for limited vision and at times an icy competence, but overall calls her brilliant.

674. "Reviews in Brief." LIVERPOOL DAILY POST (March 11, 1952): 3.
     Recommends this collection of McCarthy's own chosen favorites.

675. M., K. "New Novels." IRISH PRESS (Ireland) (April 8, 1952): 4.
     Considers the pieces in this collection to be as much reflective essays as they are stories. Agrees partly with Cyril Connolly's enthusiastic comparisons of McCarthy to Woolf, Bowen, Constant and Congreve.

676. S., B. J. SOUTH WALES ARGUS (G.B.) (April 21, 1952).
     Feels McCarthy's blend of fact and fiction produces a
     refreshing style. Makes the rather unusual observation that she
     writes with "a delicate touch." (Citation not verified.)

677. Bannon, Barbara A. "Forecast of Paperbacks." INSIDE BOOKS
     (PUBLISHERS WEEKLY) 2 (September 16-21, 1963).
     Observes that these stories are written in McCarthy's
     habitual dispassionate and ironic style.

  * Peden, William. "Metropolis, Village and Suburbia: The Short
     Fiction of Manners." In THE AMERICAN SHORT STORY:
     CONTINUITY AND CHANGE, 1940-1975, 61-62. Boston:
     Houghton Mifflin, 1975.
     See item no. 582.

678. Walker, Jeffrey. "1945-1956: Post World War II Manners and
     Mores." In THE AMERICAN SHORT STORY 1945-1980: A
     CRITICAL HISTORY, edited by Gordon Weaver, 7-8. Boston:
     Twayne, 1983.
     Refers to "Cruel and Barbarous Treatment" as well as
     various stories from CAST A COLD EYE in a discussion on
     short stories written after World War II. Notes that the stories
     typically depict a society in which McCarthy women roam,
     "always anticipating some excitement, and oblivious to the
     danger of hurting anyone in the process, sometimes even
     themselves."

THE GROVES OF ACADEME

  * Meyer, Frank. "Pleasantly Catty." FREEMAN 2 (1951-52): 851.
     See item no. 617.

679. Young, Vernon. NEW MEXICO QUARTERLY 22, no.1
     (1952): [322].
     Calls THE GROVES OF ACADEME a spiteful comedy that

falls short of being a classic parody because McCarthy fails to keep the necessary disinterested interpretation from becoming a sermon. Says she is highly readable if one is in the proper mood.

680. "125 Leading Campaigns of the Spring Season." PUBLISHERS WEEKLY (January 26, 1952): 427.
Announces McCarthy's forthcoming book and reports that it is said to be sophisticated, tough and bitter.

681. KIRKUS REVIEWS 20 (February 1, 1952): 84.
Notes that THE GROVES OF ACADEME is written in the same scalpel style as THE COMPANY SHE KEEPS, THE OASIS and CAST A COLD EYE. Calls it an incisive intellectual exercise but finds some of McCarthy's personal and ideological foibles have become overly monotonous.

682. Cahoon, Herbert. LIBRARY JOURNAL 77 (February 15, 1952): 361.
Praises the intellectual, sophisticated and often accurate depiction of a college administration and its personalities.

* Poore, Charles. "Books of the Times." NEW YORK TIMES (February 21, 1952): L5.
See item no. 618.

683. Gill, Brendan. "Too High, Too Low." NEW YORKER 28, no.1 (February 23, 1952): 106-108.
Emphasizes the book's big advance in scale and completeness over THE OASIS which trailed off into silence just as it promised to become interesting. Suggests she might be a greater artist if she would only take things less seriously.

684. Krutch, Joseph Wood. "Mary McCarthy on a 'Liberal' Campus." NEW YORK HERALD TRIBUNE BOOK REVIEW 28, no.28 (February 24, 1952): 4.
Praises McCarthy for not writing a banal attack on what everyone else is attacking. Credits her essayist style for making the story consistently alive, sharp and amusing.

685. Mizener, Arthur. "Immensely Entertaining If Not McCarthy's Best." COURIER-JOURNAL (Louisville, Ky.) 195, no.55 (February 24, 1952): 11.

    Assesses the book as a witty, entertaining portrayal of certain types in a small experimental college, sharpened by McCarthy's own teaching experiences at Bard and Sarah Lawrence. Says despite the fact she is observant and intelligent, her characters essentially remain "ants on an anthill" lacking any sense of existence. Decides the book should not be missed even if it is second-rate McCarthy.

686. Morris, Alice S. "When Suspicion Fell on The Impossible Mulcahy." NEW YORK TIMES BOOK REVIEW 101, no.34364 (February 24, 1952): 7.

    Calls this a mortally entertaining book by a flawless writer who has made her mark chiefly as an analyst of the cerebral fringe. Observes McCarthy bases her satire on stunning accuracy and not on exaggeration.

687. "Progressive Witch Hunt." NEWSWEEK 39, no.8 (February 25, 1952): 106-107.

    Compares McCarthy's style to Supreme Court opinions which deliver impartial injustice. Declares that in order to be understood at all, the topical allusions in the book will soon require the same professional examination given to FINNEGAN'S WAKE.

688. Wales, Ruth. "Galaxy of Varied and Engaging Current Fiction." CHRISTIAN SCIENCE MONITOR [Eastern Ed.] (February 28, 1952): 11.

    Says McCarthy exhibits a tight and urbane prose style. Believes the book may be different for anyone not familiar with the academic world, however, contends that as provocative satire it has few peers.

689. Gannett, Lewis. "Books and Things." NEW YORK HERALD TRIBUNE (February 29, 1952): 15.

    Suggests McCarthy's seriousness sometimes gets in the way of her wit. Summarizes the book and concludes that all the characters are knaves, hypocrites or fools.

690. UNITED STATES QUARTERLY BOOK REVIEW 8, no.1
(March 1952): 138-139.
Considers McCarthy to be wickedly funny with an acute eye
for the absurd. Suggests she might consider paying a little less
attention to wit and a little more to exercising greater humanity.

691. Joyce, John F. "Pal Joey of a Progressive College."
PROVIDENCE JOURNAL (R.I.) [Sunday Ed.] (March 2,
1952).
Contends that not since Dickens, has anyone created such a
roundly repulsive character as Mulcahy. Notes anyone who
expects Mulcahy to get his come-uppance in the end will be
disappointed and says McCarthy is to be admired for her courage
in sacrificing artistic integrities to stern realities. Applauds her
for reminding us that too many Mulcahys exist both within and
without academic cloisters.

692. Laycock, Edward A. "Cronin Returns to Religion." BOSTON
GLOBE [Sunday Ed.] (March 2, 1952): A19.
Observes that McCarthy has done a brilliant job of
presenting a different angle to the witch-hunt theme. Commends
her for writing a book which will excite academics.

693. Halsband, Robert. "Academic Mazes." SATURDAY REVIEW
35 (March 8, 1952): 13-14.
Praises McCarthy for writing something fresh, new and as
brilliant as the early novels of Huxley.

694. Sullivan, Richard. CHICAGO TRIBUNE. MAGAZINE OF
BOOKS [Sunday Ed.] (March 9, 1952): 4.
Likens the slyly and brightly exposed world in McCarthy's
book to a child's idea of China "with everything upside down."
Declares that for all the confusion, self-seeking, miserable, mean
and funny characters, the book possesses some kind of dark
dignity and grace.

695. Nelson, Jim. "Eagle Eye on Books." WICHITA EAGLE
(Wichita, Kans.) (March 12, 1952).
Praises McCarthy for developing a novel plot with
admirable, clearly drawn and unstereotyped characters.

696. Hayes, Richard. "Books." COMMONWEAL 55, no.23 (March 14, 1952): 570.
      Says McCarthy visualizes the world in political terms, and leads her characters on perilous ideological journeys weighed down with excessive liberal,intellectual baggage. Discusses the book in relation to her uncompromising standards and suggests it is devoid of sentiment or compassion because to dull McCarthy's analytic arrow would be fatal to her vision. Concludes the book not only illuminates the state of American culture, but also the state of American consciences.

697. Simkins, Virginia B. "Literature Instructor at Large." NEWS AND OBSERVER (Raleigh, N.C.) (March 16, 1952): sec. 4, 5.
      Describes the book as typical of many modern novels that are well written but sometimes make depressing and repulsive reading.

698. Doughty, Howard, Jr. "The Peacock Vein." NATION 174 (March 22, 1952): 280-281.
      Sees the book as a satire with a more public range of targets than McCarthy presented in THE OASIS.

699. O'Leary, Theodore M. "Satirizes a Progressive College." KANSAS CITY STAR (Kans.) (March 22, 1952): 16.
      Credits McCarthy as being one of the most accomplished satirists in America. Discusses how unorthodox institutions and ideas can become just as rigid as conservative institutions and ideas. Observes her apparent confusion of motives and suggests she is more interested in ideas, human behavior and the perfect phrase than she is in story telling. Concludes the generally cold, cruel tone of the book gets some comic relief from the poetry conference which is so well done that it belongs in any anthology of American satirical writing.

700. "Recent and Readable [As Recommended by Tribune Readers]." CHICAGO TRIBUNE. MAGAZINE OF BOOKS [Sunday Ed.] 111, no.12 (March 23, 1952): 2.
      Provides a very brief recommendation of the book.

701. Hicks, Granville. "A Chronicle of Current Fiction." NEW
LEADER 35, no.2 (March 24, 1952): 20-21.
Says that within the range McCarthy operates are infinite and
fascinating subtleties but no mysteries. Declares this is the best
book about college life he has ever read and suggests
McCarthy's account of Jocelyn's past and present in chapter four
is so insightful it should be included in all progressive education
anthologies.

702. Cole, Thomas L. "Progressive Education." CHATTANOOGA
TIMES (Tenn.) (March 30, 1952): 20.
Calls this a devastatingly accurate account of academics.
Says the book may not have wide appeal but those who do read
it with discernment will carry it around so they can read it to
anyone who they can get to listen.

703. Rosenfeld, Isaac. "Among Friends." NEW REPUBLIC 126
(March 31, 1952): 21.
Attacks McCarthy for always directing her satire at her
friends and suggests her familiarity with the things she writes
about imposes limitations on her work. Applauds her sometimes
witty and brilliant characterization but concludes her satire fails
because it is too dependent on the object of its own ridicule.

704. BOOKMARK 11 (April 1952): 159.
Outlines the book very briefly and calls it a sharply worded
satire.

705. Gauss Jackson, Katherine. "Books in Brief." HARPER'S
MAGAZINE 204, no.1223 (April 1952): 107-108.
Comments that the book is an excellent satire devoid of
heart, with witty, thought-packed dialogue.

706. Hughes, Riley. CATHOLIC WORLD 175 (April 1952): 73.
Reflects on McCarthy's dissection of the academic world and
the brilliant movement of ideas in action.

707. Rolo, Charles J. "Reader's Choice: Potpourri." ATLANTIC
     189, no.4 (April 1952): 86.
        Criticizes the absence of McCarthy's usual talent for
     corrosive satire.

708. McNiff, Mary Stack. AMERICA 87, no.2 (April 12, 1952):
     48-49.
        Admires McCarthy's handling of the dilemma of a liberal
     college situation choosing to concentrate on ideas rather than
     marital aberrations and departmental politics. Notes that
     McCarthy's disinterested compassion makes for a book in which
     the characters and their problems are treated fairly from all
     possible angles.

709. James, Rowena. "A Witch Hunt in Reverse." DES MOINES
     REGISTER (Iowa) [Sunday Ed.] (April 20, 1952): A9.
        Notes that the book has some richly satiric intellectualizing
     and commends McCarthy for sharply portraying schools of
     thought and pointing out a danger true liberalism must avoid.

710. Fiedler, Leslie A. "The Higher Unfairness." COMMENTARY
     13, no.5 (May 1952): 503-505.
        Suggests McCarthy has lost some of the troublesome
     spiritual qualities which made her earlier stories and reviews so
     powerfully attractive. Notes there are two types of satire: the
     kind which attacks eccentricity and is rooted in conservative
     optimism; and the kind which finds the human condition
     ridiculous and tends toward a religious point of view. Expresses
     disappointment that McCarthy's wit has not grown into a type of
     Christian-Swiftian satire.

 *   Greenberg, Martin. "Books in Print." AMERICAN MERCURY
     74, no.341 (May 1952): 110-111.
        See item no. 619.

711. Rodell, Katherine. "Recent Fiction." PROGRESSIVE (Madison,
     Wis.) (May 1952): 40-41.
        Considers this a must-read book, surgically so devasting that
     every once in a while the reader has to come up for air.

712. Schwartz, Delmore. "Fiction Chronicle: The Wrongs of Innocence and Experience." PARTISAN REVIEW 19, no.3 (May-June 1952): 354-359.

    Discusses the need for modern fiction to present the reader with a hero or heroine and a point of view which makes involvement possible. Criticizes McCarthy for writing about ridiculous, stupid, vicious characters who divert the reader's attention from the book's real purpose.

713. "Brief Comments." AMERICAN SCHOLAR 21, no.3 (Summer 1952): 382.

    Credits McCarthy's clear insight into current academic pitfalls but maintains the book lacks the sustained tone and careful structuring which might have made it a compelling lesson.

714. Yaffe, James. "Outstanding Novels." YALE REVIEW 41, no.4 (Summer 1952): x.

    Observes the book is not funny because McCarthy wastes her satirical style on the superficial rather than focusing on ideas and characters. Argues that she overloads sentences with superfluous clauses and always uses a long word when a short one would do.

715. "Recent Publications." SCHOOL & SOCIETY 75, no.1956 (June 14, 1952): 383.

    States the gist of the book.

716. Poore, Charles. "Books of the Times." NEW YORK TIMES (July 1, 1952): L21.

    Discusses the vintage books of 1952. Reports this is McCarthy's best and that she is America's wittiest and most unsparing lampooner of the southpaw intellectual.

717. Guerard, Albert Joseph. "Some Recent Novels." PERSPECTIVES USA, no.1 (Fall 1952): 168-172.

    Reflects on McCarthy's lack of dramatic sympathy for the fool and the scoundrel, a quality the best corrosive satirists have. Theorizes that she fails at an attempt to illustrate Dostoyevskyan intrigue because the background of the book is too palpably local and the time setting too contemporary.

718. Rudikoff, Sonya. "The Root of the Matter." HUDSON REVIEW
     5, no.3 (Autumn 1952): 453-459.
         Ponders the James' theory that writers cannot properly
     present a life which is unknown to them. Stresses that McCarthy
     does not provide a real world in which her characters can exist
     and does not give any of the characters, except Mulcahy,
     significant force or interest. Says that her excessive detailing of
     the ideological history of the college and educational practices
     takes away from the life of the novel. Concludes she is too
     interested in the absurd to see anything else.

719. "Intellect and Sentiment." TIMES (London, G.B.) (March 11,
     1953): 10.
         Observes that this is an immensely clever, psychologically
     fine-textured book that never quite frees itself from stifling
     intellectualization.

720. Price, R. G. G. "Intelligent Company." PUNCH 224, no.5867
     (March 18, 1953): 361.
         Praises McCarthy for being an exhilarating novelist who
     "deposits her novels with sharp thuds on the graves of her
     illusions." Credits her for writing a sparkling multi-layered book.

721. "Intellectual Exercise." TIMES LITERARY SUPPLEMENT,
     no.2668 (March 20, 1953): 181.
         Stresses that although McCarthy's writing is marked by a
     rigid withholding of sympathy, the book is frequently witty,
     ironic and perceptive. Suggests the book may be considered from
     four angles: as an exercise in wit; as an attempt to combine wit
     and in-depth character studies; as a satire of a progressive
     college; as an examination of the effect of current political witch
     hunts on American academic lives and standards.

722. Lean, Tangye. "Fiction." SPECTATOR, no.6510 (April 3,
     1953): 430.
         Theorizes that McCarthy is demanding to read because she
     insists on portraying difficult people. Suggests that her readiness
     to admit her readers into the lives of her characters, on equal
     terms, may at first be flattering, but notes that in retrospect, the
     book's highbrow discussions highlight the reader's intellectual

shortcomings. Observes the characters do not win the affection of either McCarthy or the reader and are, perhaps, not even worth the effort.

723. EVENING EXPRESS (Liverpool, G.B.) (May 18, 1953).
    Says that McCarthy weaves a fascinating story in her usual penetrating style.

724. Thompson, Laurence. "The Real America?" TRIBUNE (London, G.B.) (May 22, 1953): 7.
    Discusses McCarthy and Hobson in light of an America too colored by Faulkner and overdosed on "Babbitt." Observes McCarthy writes "without padding," draws Mulcahy beautifully and makes a poetry convention funny without "ever raising her gentle voice."

725. "An Intellectual Stimulant." CAMBRIDGE DAILY NEWS (G.B.) (July 20, 1953).
    Points out that satirical writing was designed to expose and remedy social ills. Notes the American fear of and struggle against communism is food for McCarthy's stimulating novel about freedom of thought in an unworthy setting.

726. Earnest, Ernest. "Catty School of Writing." SATURDAY REVIEW 40 (June 29, 1957): 7-9, 27-28.
    Discusses a branch of the modern novel concerned with showing or showing up characters in a social situation in which they appear at a disadvantage. Elaborates that this "catty" writing appears, in varying degrees, in several writers including McCarthy. Evaluates McCarthy's "cattiness" and quotes extensively from THE GROVES OF ACADEME to illustrate a number of typical devices: trivial but damaging detail; guilt by association; moments of vanity; soda-shop references; and carefully chosen spiteful phrases.

727. Latham, Earl. "The Managerialization of the Campus." PUBLIC ADMINISTRATION REVIEW 19, no.1 (Winter 1959): 48-57.
    Evaluates the state of the growing "managerialization" of the college campus in America. Quotes from THE GROVES OF

ACADEME and five other books to illustrate points of
discussion.

728. Tyler, Robert. "The I.W.W. and the West." AMERICAN
QUARTERLY 12, no.2 (Summer 1960): 175-187.
Notes the appearance of a member of the Industrial Workers
of the World union in the book.

729. Lyons, John O. "The Novel on Academic Freedom." In THE
COLLEGE NOVEL IN AMERICA, 169-74; 177-178.
Carbondale: Southern Illinois Univ. Press, 1962.
Singles out THE GROVES OF ACADEME as one of the
most important novels about academic freedom because it
examines the complexities of good and evil and displays
knowledge and insight into modern educational theory. Says the
plot is closer to the usual "academic cause célèbre," because
McCarthy effectively focuses on psychological and legal
motivations.

730. Chamberlain, John Rensselaer. "The Conservative Miss
McCarthy." NATIONAL REVIEW 15, no.16 (October 22,
1963): 353-355.
Discusses McCarthy's failure as a satirist in THE GROVES
OF ACADEME and THE GROUP. Compares her to Waugh
saying "McCarthy's fiction, unlike that of her English opposite
number...never achieves its force or meaning from her professed
political orientation."

731. Millgate, Michael. "Institutions in Fiction: The Academy." In
AMERICAN SOCIAL FICTION: JAMES TO COZZENS,
166-168. London: Oliver and Boyd, 1964.
Examines the new wave of academic novels written by
teachers and administrators and proposes that other satirical
novels owe their success to THE GROVES OF ACADEME.
Considers the differences and similarities in American and
British academic novels and concludes that what distinguishes
one from the other is the American extreme self-consciousness
about the nature of an academic society and the persistent
questioning of its aims, values and achievements.

Also published: AMERICAN SOCIAL FICTION: JAMES TO
COZZENS. New York: Barnes and Noble, 1967.

732. Fiedler, Leslie A. "The War Against the Academy."
WISCONSIN STUDIES IN CONTEMPORARY LITERATURE
5, no.1 (Winter-Spring 1964): 5-17.
   Explores the world of "college novels" and notes that most
are lacking in substance and scope and have either politics or sex
as their theme. Says that THE GROVES OF ACADEME offers
a new twist with the inefficient professor who saves his job by
claiming to be a Communist. Notes that the satiric impact of the
book depends upon the reader's knowledge of the academic
system.

Also published with revisions in Fiedler, Leslie A. WAITING
FOR THE END. New York: Stein & Day, 1964.

 *   "Briefing: Where and When." OBSERVER (London, G.B.)
(October 31, 1965): 22.
       See item no. 621.

733. Walcutt, Charles Child. "In and Out of College with Mary
McCarthy." In MAN'S CHANGING MASK: MODES AND
METHODS OF CHARACTERIZATION IN FICTION,
292-294. Minneapolis: Univ. of Minnesota Press, 1966.
   Reports that THE GROVES OF ACADEME is one of the
cleverest academic novels of the time because it penetrates to the
essence of the academic situation. Observes that McCarthy goes
beyond the standard subject matter of such novels: the ignoble
struggle for power, the dramatic interactions between male
professors and female students, and the issues generated by a
central dilemma. Notes that although THE GROUP illustrates a
rich tangle of sex, politics, art and intellectual aspirations, its
decided lack of a central idea rendered through action reduces it
to a "yeasty" collection of observations and vignettes.

734. Raymond, John. "High and Unconsortable." FINANCIAL
     TIMES (April 25, 1968).
     Refers to the book in a review of Curran's JAMES JOYCE
     REMEMBERED.

735. Carter, Angela. "The McCarthy Period." GUARDIAN AND
     GUARDIAN WEEKLY (G.B.) 122 (February 24, 1980): 22.
     Evaluates THE GROVES OF ACADEME and ON THE
     CONTRARY and calls McCarthy a good woman who prefers to
     swim with her rational conscience as a lifebelt. Emphasizes that
     she is contrary only in pitting reason against a prevalent
     irrationality.

736. McNeil, Helen. "What Would Tolstoi Say?" NEW
     STATESMAN 99, no.2563 (May 2, 1980): 678-679.
     Posits that, for a contemporary satirist, McCarthy "is too
     Horatian, too much attached to the middle ground, too clear
     about her old-fashioned values . . . ." Observes how she may not
     be vicious enough, as she "carefully distances herself from the
     everpresent likelihood of failure and self betrayal, which she
     gives over to those discarded marks of the self--her heroines."

737. "New in Paperback [column]." BOOK WORLD
     (WASHINGTON POST) 11, no.14 (April 5, 1981): 12.
     Views this as a wicked, bitterly funny book about colleges.

738. Barasch, Frank K. "Faculty Images in Recent American
     Fiction." COLLEGE LITERATURE 10 (Winter 1983): 28-37.
     Discusses the image of faculty in contemporary novels.
     Reports that in the 1950s academics were generally depicted as
     having greater interest in the issues of political freedom and job
     security and, because they were supporting a leftist's right to
     work, were often shown as losing their battles. Points out the
     book was an exception in which political roles were actually
     reversed--Mulcahy pretends to be a Communist to "save" his
     job. Theorizes that McCarthy, a Marxist and staunch
     anti-Stalinist after the war, uses the campus as a microcosm of
     the larger political picture and suggests that Hoar is a liberal
     president acting out America's give-away of East Europe to
     Stalin's government. Examine several other relevant novels.

A CHARMED LIFE

739. Adams, Robert Martin. "Fiction Chronicle." HUDSON
REVIEW 8, no.4 (1955): 627-632.
Says McCarthy has achieved the enviable position of the girl
"nice children don't play with." Claims A CHARMED LIFE
will confirm that her unusual talents are being cramped by an
inflexible point of view and failure of control. Discusses the
initial promise of the characters, however, decides that she
ultimately fumbles when they are "ripped open for a diagnosis."

740. Moynahan, Julian. PRINCETON ALUMNI WEEKLY. GOOD
READING (Supplement) (February 1955).
Evaluates the book as a lucidly written, disturbing novel.
Observes that it exemplifies the moral problems of even those
who live placid lives in less picturesque communities.

741. KIRKUS REVIEWS 23 (September 1, 1955): 672-673.
Proposes that the total impact of the book is less than the
brilliance of its parts. Finds the plot, sensational as it seems,
relatively unimportant and contrived when compared to the study
of various Bohemians and intellectuals.

742. AMERICAN NEWS OF BOOKS (October 1955): 2.
Notes McCarthy's characters are hardly endearing despite
her ability to handle them with seeming familiarity.

743. AMERICAN NEWS OF BOOKS (October 1955): 16.
Provides a brief synopsis of this "veddy s'phisticated" book.

744. RETAIL BOOKSELLER 58, no.725 (October 1955): 75.
Offers a very brief synopsis.

745. Walbridge, Earle F. "Fiction." LIBRARY JOURNAL 80, no.18
(October 15, 1955): 2237-2238.
Observes that every line in this tragi-comedy is infused with
McCarthy's keen intelligence and her own brand of wit and
irony.

746. MADEMOISELLE (November 1955).
    Says that McCarthy draws gallons of blood--at times even
    her own.

747. Poore, Charles. "Books of the Times." NEW YORK TIMES
    (November 3, 1955): 29.
    Compares A CHARMED LIFE with Coward's PRIVATE
    LIVES and finds both to be epigrammatic moralities that warn of
    the perilous effects of first husbands on second marriages.
    Observes that a McCarthy heroine always hates what she wants
    when she gets it, yet still manages to convey the sense of a
    "Renaissance" woman. Concludes McCarthy has never before
    provided such a congenial forum for the exploitation of her
    "sunny savage indignation."

748. Donnelly, Tom. "Bitters on the Rocks." WASHINGTON
    DAILY NEWS (November 4, 1955): 47.
    Says McCarthy renders a chillingly accurate story. Notes,
    however, that the book may have been more satisfying had she
    applied her satiric craft as incidental trimmings to a major
    creative work, or infused it with a touch of compassion.

749. Little, Carl Victor. "New Books." HOUSTON PRESS
    (November 4, 1955): 12.
    Wonders if McCarthy's "so logical" characters appear
    without makeup too often for her own good. Says that the
    intelligentsia will gladly buy tickets to her funeral after someone
    poisons her for writing this witty and entertaining book.

750. Holden, Theodore L. "Emotions Run Rampant in A CHARMED
    LIFE." HARTFORD TIMES (Conn.) (November 5, 1955): 18.
    Says McCarthy delights in human weakness and mixes her
    ingredients for a foregone effect. Finds the characters arty and
    intellectual not artistic and intelligent. Believes that while the
    logic of the characters seems unassailable, their emotional
    immaturity is not taken into account.

751. Kelly, James. "New Faces and New Leeds." SATURDAY
    REVIEW 38 (November 5, 1955): 17.
    Wonders if the book was written by a suave poltergeist who

enjoys making people trip over their own pretensions, an annoyed biologist who dissects but never really believes there is anything secret to be uncovered, or a sophisticated librarian who is cataloguing modern intellectual foibles to relieve monotony. Writes about the pretenses of second rate people and intellectual poses, resulting in a profusion of manner with a decided lack of content. Believes the first 100 pages will delight readers, however, continued enjoyment will depend on how much "bitter candy" the reader can digest and whether or not he or she is a fan no matter what.

752. PUBLISHERS WEEKLY (November 5, 1955): 2031.
     Offers a very brief synopsis.

753. "Author Bares a Seacoast of Bohemia." MIAMI HERALD [Sunday Ed.] (November 6, 1955): F4.
     Admires McCarthy's corrosive style and her ability to take apart her characters "leaf by leaf as though they were artichokes." Observes that A CHARMED LIFE is not a proper novel but a succession of sketches, some of which have previously appeared in the NEW YORKER.

754. Bloom, Eleanor M. "Tale of a Town Tells of Crippled Lives." MINNEAPOLIS TRIBUNE (Minn.) [Sunday Ed.] (November 6, 1955): 12.
     Details the book and notes that if McCarthy's lost souls are not particularly pleasant or even unique, they are still among her best creations--each in his own peculiarly repulsive existentialist fashion, completely fascinating. Concludes McCarthy never fails to evoke understanding of her characters, but, is as always, devoid of love or pity for them.

755. Comans, Grace P. "Dipped in Acid." HARTFORD COURANT. MAGAZINE (Conn.) (November 6, 1955): 15.
     Declares that McCarthy's characters are weak, often frustrated people who deserve better treatment than they receive from their creator.

756. Dowedeit, Glendy. "An Emptiness in Upper Bohemia."
WASHINGTON POST AND TIMES HERALD (November 6,
1955): E6.
Compares A CHARMED LIFE to Spectorsky's THE
EXURBANITES and concludes McCarthy's photographic
memory is more merciless than Spectorsky's statistics. Maintains
that readers who travel in her circles will recognize everyone and
everything. Decides that her "acid and tonic" story-telling has a
deceptively pleasant taste with an aftertaste "sweetened by a
backwash of admiration for a mocking talent."

757. Fields, Beverly. "Merciless Portrayal of Intellectuals Headed for
Disaster." CHICAGO SUN TIMES (November 6, 1955).
Explains that McCarthy meticulously constructs the story to
demonstrate that without a fixed order of universals, individual
moral action is powerless to avert disaster. Praises the
painstaking mental process with which her characters justify
themselves, her keen eye and the skill with which she unites
form and content.

758. H., J. "Strange Community Light Touch." BOSTON POST
[Sunday Ed.] (November 6, 1955): 6.
Says McCarthy has created believable, if somewhat awesome
characters, who will not interest readers of "westerns."

759. L., E. A. "Is It Wellfleet?" BOSTON GLOBE [Sunday Ed.]
(November 6, 1955): C6.
Declares the ordinary person will not read this book unless
s/he is morbidly interested in intellectuals.

760. Milne, Dick. "Balancing the Books: Mary McCarthy Lays Bare
an 'Arty' Town." FORT LAUDERDALE SUNDAY NEWS
(Fla.) (November 6, 1955).
Credits McCarthy for writing a sparkling exposé of the
hollowness of the "arty" inhabitants of New Leeds, who "insist
on conforming to nonconformity." Provides a synopsis of the
book.

761. Morris, Alice S. "The Coveted Escape." NEW YORK TIMES
     BOOK REVIEW 60 (November 6, 1955): 5.
     Comments that McCarthy shows a rare measure of
     compassion, warmth and understanding. Singles out the play
     reading chapter as the only interminably tedious part of an
     otherwise lively, thoughtful commentary.

762. Rogers, W. G. "A Fine Writer's Super-Sharp Eye."
     BRIDGEPORT POST (Conn.) (November 6, 1955).
     Feels that McCarthy's own slight faults are nothing
     compared to the faults she finds in her characters. Emphasizes
     that her ability to pounce on weakness and failure, self-deceit,
     pretense and shifting moods will delight her fans.

     Also published in PHOENIX GAZETTE (November 3, 1955):
     18; HAMMOND TIMES (November 6, 1955); MIAMI DAILY
     NEWS (November 6, 1955): E9; POST-STANDARD (Syracuse,
     N.Y.) (November 6, 1955): 6; POST-STAR (Glens Falls, N.Y.)
     (November 12, 1955): 4; NEW HAVEN REGISTER (Conn.)
     (November 13, 1955): 8 and CLEVELAND PLAIN DEALER
     (Ohio) (November 13, 1955): D56-57.

763. Scott, Winfield Townley. "A Drama of Deceptions."
     PROVIDENCE JOURNAL (R.I.) [Sunday Ed.] (November 6,
     1955): sec. 6, 10.
     Notes that the reader will admire McCarthy's brilliant
     observations and sharp-eyed, sharp-tongued gossip, but will
     remain as uninvolved as McCarthy with the characters in the
     book.

764. Yeiser, Frederick. "Some Recent Fiction." CINCINNATI
     ENQUIRER (Ohio) (November 6, 1955): 61.
     Wonders if McCarthy intended the denizens of New Leeds to
     be regarded as types or individuals considering she has fashioned
     them as both typical artists and writers and as closely defined
     individuals. Emphasizes that she treats both views with
     good-natured affection even when causing the characters to
     behave outrageously. Notes that within the framework of New
     Leeds, outrageous is normal, even rational, yet the one time

Martha fails to reason, she is led to her fatal end. Believes this is
the most winning of all McCarthy's novels.

765. Hicks, Granville. "Everyone Analyzes Everyone in Mary
     McCarthy's A CHARMED LIFE." NEW LEADER 38, no.44
     (November 7, 1955): 22.
       Questions if McCarthy might be happier and have a greater
     reputation if literary convention allowed her to write about
     "characters"--individuals who are also types. Argues that she has
     never written a sound, well-organized novel and has produced
     only a few satisfying short stories. Notes the similarity between
     Martha and McCarthy herself, calling each irritating in their air
     of superiority yet admirable in honesty and insight. Cites
     McCarthy's wit, perception and splendid comic effects which
     permit the reader to overlook the episodic structure, desultory
     movement from character to character and contrived ending.

766. "Low Temperature." NEWSWEEK 46, no.18 (November 7,
     1955): 121-122.
       Likens reading McCarthy to listening to the most "surgical
     gossip--not malicious but fully aware that one of the great studies
     of mankind is mankind's frailty." Says the reader's sympathy for
     the characters stems from McCarthy's own repugnance toward
     them.

767. Kirsch, Robert K. "The Book Report." LOS ANGELES TIMES
     (November 8, 1955): sec. 2, 5.
       Cites A CHARMED LIFE as a perfect example of fiction
     dealing with the fashionable migration of a certain class of New
     York City urbanites searching for the simple pleasures of life.

768. McKnight, Bob. "Story of Bohemians Fetching, but at Times
     Snobbish." CLEVELAND PRESS (Ohio) (November 8, 1955):
     42.
       Emphasizes that the best thing about A CHARMED LIFE is
     that it is welcome relief from Mailer's DEER PARK. Argues
     that McCarthy is guilty of intellectual snobbery and suggests
     readers arm themselves with French, Latin and English
     dictionaries.

769. O'Leary, Theodore M. "They Grope for Life's Meaning."
KANSAS CITY STAR (Kans.) (November 12, 1955): 18.
    Discusses the theory that McCarthy's characters seek the
certainties of life others seek in religion, however their failure
should not be measured by their methods, but rather the
difficulty of the search. Notes this is the first time McCarthy
shows any pity at all for her characters, and suggests that if she
ever finds the capacity for genuine compassion, she might lose
some of her ice blue coldness but gain a chance at supremacy
among American women novelists.

770. Holzhauer, Robert. "The Respectable Bohemians."
MILWAUKEE JOURNAL (Wis.) (November 13, 1955): sec. 5,
5.
    Focuses on the fact that McCarthy's curiously unpleasant,
chic and pathological characters are transfixed in fatalism,
divorcing themselves from the more blatantly arty crowd by
simulating devotion to married life and serious thought. Stresses
that for all their modern, ever-changing views and contemporary
intellectualism, they snobbishly refuse to focus on personal
integration. Believes McCarthy brilliantly portrays the conflict
between one's ability to give to another and the pleasure one
perversely derives from withholding and deceiving. Concludes
she is one of the American women writers whose core of writing
is a "dry intrepid assumption of the negativity of modern
society."

771. Hoyt, Elizabeth N. "Decaying Intellectuals." CEDAR RAPIDS
GAZETTE (Iowa) (November 13, 1955): sec. 3, 2.
    Outlines the book and says McCarthy is able to dig beneath
the surface of human behavior and write about it honestly, even
if it is unpleasant.

772. McG., M. "In the Wake of a Social Whirlwind." EVENING
STAR (Washington, D.C.) [Sunday Ed.] (November 13, 1955):
E9.
    Views McCarthy as a waspish governess whose satire is the
curled-lip rather than tongue-in-cheek variety. Attributes the
extremely neat account of social chaos to her vibrant prose style
and superb dialogue.

773. Peterson, Virgilia. "Down-at-the-Heels Highbrows on Parade."
NEW YORK HERALD TRIBUNE BOOK REVIEW 32, no.14
(November 13, 1955): 4.
Declares that McCarthy's cold eye pins down and stretches
out her specimens with the precision of a lepidopterist. Maintains
that the existence of the characters consists of watching
themselves live with the same coldly absorbed scientific
awareness which distinguishes McCarthy's writing and that even
her good intentions pave the way to hell. Concludes the book
will leave most readers unmoved.

774. BOOKLIST 52, no.6 (November 15, 1955): 125-126.
Summarizes the book as a comic tragedy with McCarthy at
her brilliant best, that examines man's dilemma of fluctuating
between belief and unbelief, courage and despair. Provides a
brief synopsis.

775. Hogan, William. "A Sardonic Analysis of Life Beyond Exurbia."
SAN FRANCISCO CHRONICLE (November 15, 1955): 21.
Suggests McCarthy examines a segment of modern America
that goes beyond the new Americanism created by Spectorsky in
THE EXURBANITES. Notes she observes her characters with
psychoanalytic power and devastating wit.

776. Kiniery, Paul. BEST SELLERS 15, no.16 (November 15, 1955):
223-224.
Observes that the book is well written and full of clever
conversation and suspense; however, does not recommend it to
any library patronized by young people primarily because of the
absence of Christian principles.

777. Rainer, Dachine. "Books." VILLAGE VOICE (November 16,
1955): 8.
Believes A CHARMED LIFE fails as a novel because
McCarthy is not motivated by love for someone or something.
Declares it's ruthless illumination of the characters is nonetheless
prodigiously entertaining. Suggests that the emergence of
articulate women writers and the way in which they view
themselves as women largely determines the quality of their
work. Cites Woolf's A ROOM OF ONE'S OWN as an example

of a novel shrilly and propagandistically conceived out of an emerging feminist movement. Notes that McCarthy has no need to insist on her femininity because there is nothing feminine about her work; her writing is an act of vengeance, precise and devoid of feeling.

778. Holzhauer, Jean. "Diamond-Hard." COMMONWEAL 63 (November 18, 1955): 171.

Stresses that McCarthy's detachment from her characters serves to remove her stories from complete conviction, leading the reader to see everything through her dark, uncommitted eye. Contends that even though her characters are not entirely compelling, her writing is detailed and meticulous. Concludes that the overall effect is of thought rather than sentiment, with McCarthy delivering a successful expression of artistic integrity in terms appropriately linear and pallid.

779. "Author of the Week." BRISTOL PRESS (Conn.) (November 19, 1955): 8.

Offers a brief biographical sketch of McCarthy.

780. Rathwell, Bruce. "Charmed." EGYPTIAN MAIL (November 19, 1955): 2.

Remarks that this brittle story has provoked one reviewer to describe it as the "glittering tragedy Noel Coward might have made out of his glittering comedy PRIVATE LIVES." Supplies a brief biographical sketch of McCarthy.

781. "Books and the Arts." SAN BERNARDINO SUN TELEGRAM (Calif.) (November 20, 1955).

Supplies a very brief biographical sketch.

782. M., W. M. "The Browsers' Box." DALLAS TIMES HERALD (November 20, 1955): sec. 8, 6.

Explains that the book bares an ugliness of existence wherein substitutes and second-raters are accepted as genuine and true. Maintains McCarthy's bizarre imagination and acid tongue startle the reader into believing that she herself has badly missed the mark.

783. Schoener, Jane C. "Frustrated Community." NEWARK NEWS
     (N.J.) (November 20, 1955): E2.
     Comments that McCarthy stirs a piquant brew, sweetening
     her bitter thesis with spiced humor. Outlines the book.

784. Seward, William W., Jr. "A Paradoxical Woman, An Unhappy
     Homecoming--Theme of Mary McCarthy Novel." VIRGINIAN
     PILOT AND PORTSMOUTH STAR (Norfolk, Va.) (November
     20, 1955): C6.
     Remarks this is a sometimes nasty, occasionally boring series
     of related scenes that relies on telling rather than showing, and
     leaves the reader unmoved.

     Also published as "Mary McCarthy: New England Summer
     Artist-Colony" in: CONTRASTS IN MODERN WRITERS:
     SOME ASPECTS OF BRITISH AND AMERICAN FICTION
     SINCE MID-CENTURY. 112-114. New York: Frederick Fell,
     1963.

785. Herbst, Josephine. "Who Is Martha?" NATION 181, no.22
     (November 26, 1955): 463-464.
     Examines the character of Martha and concludes she is a
     supreme egoist incapable of love, so confined within her shell
     that she is beyond any truly illuminating criticism. Faults
     McCarthy for the contrived coincidence at the end of the book
     that allows Martha to bypass genuine experience, leaving both
     the character and the reader nowhere.

786. Braden, Josephine. "A Witty, Effective, and Unpleasant Novel."
     COURIER-JOURNAL (Louisville, Ky.) (November 27, 1955):
     15.
     Says the book has all the elements of a slick drawing room
     comedy: an exaggerated setting, a neatly contrived plot and a
     general flavor of witty malice. Contends, however, that
     McCarthy is not content with being "merely amusing," and that
     her need to discuss and dissect in terms of her own intellectual
     standards causes an imbalance between treatment and subject
     matter. Concludes that her "instruments of destruction" are so

formidable that to use them against her lightweight characters is like using an atomic bomb when embroidery scissors would do.

787. Harris, Arthur S., Jr. "Her Satire is Energetic." TELEGRAM (Worcester, Mass.) (November 27, 1955): D1.
     Applauds McCarthy for masterfully exposing her characters. Concludes they emerge as sympathetic, believable characters because she sees them as people caught in a predicament and not as arrogant pretenders.

788. MacDonald, George. "Escape." OMAHA WORLD-HERALD. SUNDAY WORLD HERALD MAGAZINE (Nebr.) (November 27, 1955): G27.
     Describes the book as an acquired taste.

789. CINCINNATI TIMES STAR (Ohio) (November 29, 1955).
     Says this is another witty McCarthy penetration.

790. Nichols, Luther. "The Species Intellectual." SAN FRANCISCO EXAMINER (November 29, 1955): sec. 2, 3.
     Reports that it has become very fashionable to use the poor intellectual as a target, and that no one does a better inside job of illustrating the paradoxes of the intellectual than McCarthy. Declares there is more clever talk in her novels than one would find anywhere "this side of Huxley."

791. "Late Fall Fiction." CHICAGO DAILY NEWS (November 30, 1955): 18.
     Reports briefly that this is a fascinating yarn from a pen dripping with acid.

792. Rolo, Charles J. ATLANTIC 196, no.6 (December 1955): 96-97.
     Declares McCarthy is a polished writer with an uncanny sense for detail that has an electric impact on the reader. Emphasizes that A CHARMED LIFE does not suffer from the same hyperacidity as her other books.

793. "'ANDERSONVILLE' Tops 1955 Fiction List."
     MINNEAPOLIS TRIBUNE (Minn.) [Sunday Ed.] (December 4,
     1955): H6.
        Notes that this is icy, witty, superior McCarthy, not
     recommended for grandma.

794. Chaffee, Norman. "Community Capering." TULSA DAILY
     WORLD (Okla.) (December 4, 1955): 25.
        Applauds the plot and dialogue but is somewhat perplexed by
     the characters.

795. K., C. "A Brilliant Novel." COUNCIL BLUFFS IOWA
     NONPAREIL (December 4, 1955): A5.
        Says McCarthy first peels away the characters' skin,
     exposing the nerves, and then cross connects them to affect a
     quivering nervous situation for both the reader and the characters
     themselves. Contends one would have to look far and wide to
     find a more revealing segment of the present social order.

796. "Titles Selected from the Current Fiction List." ST. LOUIS
     POST-DISPATCH (Mo.) (December 4, 1955): J6.
        Mentions the book very briefly.

797. Cass, Cashenden. "Puppets in the High Bohemia." NEW
     REPUBLIC 133, no.23 (December 5, 1955): 18-19.
        Says McCarthy's charm lies in her depiction of the "grubby"
     life, and characters who are ridiculous because the grub inside
     them has an appetite for creativity, honor and mystery. Claims
     that left with slightly soiled, slightly intellectual, slightly sinning
     lives, McCarthy's puppets live according to their own logic, the
     only trouble being that their emotions are motivated solely by the
     need to have something happen so they can analyze it. Suggests
     McCarthy almost succeeds in attaining the inverted humility
     necessary to true satire, but fails to produce the requisite savage
     insurrection.

798. Massey, Linton. "Gaiety, Wit, Charm: Story of Half and Half,
     Love and Hate, for Adults." RICHMOND NEWS LEADER
     (Va.) (December 7, 1955): 13.
        Examines McCarthy's detached observations, the caustic,

incisive and pitiless treatment of her characters, and her keen reportorial ear. Concludes she is much too intelligent to ever command a wide audience.

799. Hall Brooks, Katharine. "Disturbing Picture of Sophisticates." NASHVILLE BANNER (Tenn.) (December 9, 1955): 38.

Reports that McCarthy draws a vivid, compassionate and frightening picture of the intelligenstia drifting rudderless because they question former standards of good taste and morality. Notes McCarthy's gift for discerning description makes A CHARMED LIFE a rare, thought-provoking book.

800. Schroetter, Hilda Noel. "Scenes Vary Greatly in Fiction Works." RICHMOND TIMES-DISPATCH (Va.) (December 11, 1955): F5.

Sees A CHARMED LIFE as a gruesome "bloodcurdling" warning to anyone who is in danger of mistaking talent for genius and a disorganized life for artistic freedom.

801. Mannes, Marya. "The Cat and the Mice." REPORTER 13 (December 15, 1955): 40-41.

Implies McCarthy plays cat and mouse with truth, alternating between chewing her characters to ribbons and comforting them with gentle strokes. Declares, however, that she fails to sustain that killer instinct, allowing Miles a certain degree of gallantry and Martha a sort of honesty. Reflects she has masterfully manipulated the book from a satire about disintegration among lesser intellectuals into a wry admission of their state. Concludes that she has performed an expert vivisection of her own truth; unable to completely destroy contemporary intellectual society because, in fact, her readers and she herself are a part of it.

802. Longenbauch, Dee. "Satirical Talent." DENVER POST. ROUNDUP [Sunday Ed.] (December 18, 1955): 20.

Contends that the book seems to be written by a tragedian only after one has finished reading and has had time to reflect upon the pitifulness of the story. Declares McCarthy's satirical talent brings out the complexities of her characters, making this a novel to be owned and read time after time.

803. Chamberlain, John Rensselaer. "Heavy Artillery." NATIONAL
     REVIEW 1, no.5 (December 21, 1955): 27-28.
         Declares that the book follows the standard McCarthy
     "Beauty and the Beast" formula intended to make a judgment
     with her masterfully controlling the spite she has for her
     characters. Praises her clinical coolness in dealing with the
     various disloyalties, but finds her treatment of Martha's sudden
     loyalty somewhat arbitrary. Suggests either McCarthy was
     unable to find any other way to orchestrate the fatal automobile
     accident or that the reviewer is simply unable to read the
     feminine heart. Applauds the shrewd, unblinkered writing but
     faults McCarthy for wasting her extraordinary sensibility and
     "ten inch gun" on gnats.

804. Dolbier, Maurice. "The Summing-Up in Books for 1955."
     SATURDAY REVIEW 38 (December 24, 1955): 11-12, 30.
         Lists A CHARMED LIFE among the best books of 1955.

805. "The Summing Up for '55--Books by the Pound . . ."
     NEWSWEEK 46, no.25 (December 26, 1955): 68.
         Sums up the literary successes of 1955, briefly noting that
     McCarthy scored high with her disagreeable satirical novel.

806. Svendsen, Kester. "Ideas and Mildew Batter This Family."
     DAILY OKLAHOMAN [Sunday Ed.] (January 1956): E15.
         Declares the book is a satirical novel of ideas, modern
     attitudes toward love, marriage, art and human personality.
     Contends McCarthy is psychological without being clinical,
     delivering an ironic but passionate acceptance of life.

807. Schiddel, Edmund. "Book Review: Outer Exurbia." NEW HOPE
     GAZETTE (Pa.) (February 2, 1956): 8.
         Remarks this is a bitterly Jamesian and clinical novel with
     boring characters whose saving grace is their dazzling
     presentation. Applauds McCarthy for being a true satirist,
     matchless when castigating an ideology rather than the people at
     the mercy of that ideology.

808. Podhoretz, Norman. "Gibbsville and New Leeds: The America of John O'Hara and Mary McCarthy." COMMENTARY 21, no.3 (March 1956): 269-273.

Criticizes McCarthy for creating flabby secondary characters and suggests that her intent was to expand a longish story into a novel. Purports that as possibly the best satirist in America, McCarthy creates her own heaven and hell with characters willing to face the truth about themselves with the desire and ability to be critical of their own motives. Stresses that she dramatizes one of the cornerstones of Christian thought, the hostility between "reason" and "impulse," and focuses on the assimilation of Freud's belief that one cannot control one's own character much less one's destiny. Concludes the residents of Gibbsville and New Leeds must continually justify their space, and that despite the difference in looks, Gibbsville and New Leeds are neighboring communities.

An expanded version of this article was published in: DOINGS AND UNDOINGS: THE FIFTIES AND AFTER IN AMERICAN WRITING. 76-93. New York: Noonday Press, 1964 (item no. 820).

809. Van Ghent, Dorothy. "Missing Persons: Some Recent Novels." YALE REVIEW 45, no.3 (March 1956): 460-467.

Finds that despite vivid characterization, wit, acute observation, knowledgeable technical conception and the courage to hang a tragedy on a contraceptive, A CHARMED LIFE fails to convince the reader of its seriousness and universality. Comments that the damned world McCarthy creates does not permit her characters to have dimension beyond the intellectually ruminative.

810. George, Daniel. "New Novels." SPECTATOR (April 21, 1956): 592-593.

Comments that several popular American novelists have rallied under the slogan, "come let us make lust ludicrous." Adds that they have made sex look silly and cruelty trivial, in language once unprintable and still unspeakable. Suggests that A CHARMED LIFE is one of several novels that satirizes what has too often been satirized before, slithering from the absurd to the tedious. Remarks that although the writing is often slack and loaded with cliché, it can be occasionally amusing if not taken seriously.

811. "New Fiction." TIMES (London, G.B.) (April 26, 1956): 13.
Comments that McCarthy devotes her acute intelligence less to the task of satire than to "pillorying" an attitude of mind.

812. "Waste-Lands of the Spirit." TIMES LITERARY SUPPLEMENT, no.2827 (May 4, 1956): 265.
Points out that McCarthy is inclined to be pretentious and verbose, too often conjuring up a scene merely to air her views on topics ranging from Shakespeare and Racine to modern art. Applaudes her for confining herself to a comparatively small cast and still skillfully satirizing the individuality of some very curious characters.

813. Carter, Thomas H. "Recent Fiction." SHENANDOAH 7, no.3 (Summer 1956): 52-60.
Notes that although she is perceptive, tough and witty, McCarthy fails to engage her characters in any meaningful action.

814. Maclaren-Ross, J. "American Intellectuals." PUNCH 230, no.6042 (June 20, 1956): 746-747.
Calls McCarthy a transatlantic feminine equivalent of Wilson, preoccupied with similar material but able to handle it in a much clearer, sharper, less ambivalent way. Notes that no character is spared in her acute analysis of a high-brow predicament.

815. Corke, Hilary. "Lack of Confidence." ENCOUNTER 7 (July 1956): 75-78.
Asserts that the modern writer's ideal of detachment has extended into a sort of obligation to fail to judge. Declares there is a strong sense of this perverse suspension of proper judgment in A CHARMED LIFE,where the characters seem to lack the central core of belief and standards which would make them

human beings, above and beyond merely men and women.
Concludes the book is sordid and truthless.

816. Wyndham, Francis. LONDON MAGAZINE 3, no.7 (July
     1956): 81-83.
     Reports both McCarthy and Wilson are cold-eyed satirists
     who have steadily exposed intellectual attitudes and pretensions.
     Believes McCarthy probes the depth of self-deception in her
     characters more gently and with a decided absence of fantasy,
     whereas Wilson is a caricaturist with a wider target and less
     accurate aim who records every superficial absurdity. Says A
     CHARMED LIFE is McCarthy writing at her objective best with
     pinpoint accuracy that makes her satire more deadly than
     Wilson's.

817. MacAuley, Robie. "A McCarthy Inquiry." KENYON REVIEW
     18, no.1 (Winter 1956): 155-157.
     Observes that A CHARMED LIFE is almost pure sarcasm
     wherein the characters are not "morally damned or ludicrous or
     dogged by fate; they are simply skinned alive." Applauds
     McCarthy for her slow, steady and merciless wit.

818. Mizener, Arthur. "Fiction Chronicle." PARTISAN REVIEW 23,
     no.1 (Winter 1956): 97-103.
     Contends that McCarthy commits herself to a full display of
     her talents as a Jamesian novelist, a decision that forces her to
     underplay her gift for brilliant commentaries on life and focus on
     its direct representation in alternating scenes and the meditations
     of the characters. Claims that the result is somewhat synthetic
     because the characters' attitudes are elaborated in speech, as they
     might be in an essay, rather than in dramatic portrayal moving
     from one felt attitude to another. Concludes the book has all the
     deadly charm of McCarthy's intelligence, but hardly ever comes
     to life.

819. Hartman, Carl. "Mr. Morris and Some Others." WESTERN
     REVIEW 21, no.4 (Summer 1957): 307-319.
     Reports the book is dull because it is too consistently
     sophisticated and expert. Comments that although places like
     New Leeds do exist and McCarthy has probably portrayed her

characters accurately, it is nonetheless not enough, unless one is
willing to see the book as pure sociology and not as a novel.
Finds McCarthy's irony so obscure and lacking in direction that
he wonders if it exists at all beyond the level of generalized,
sophisticated wit. Expresses disappointment that McCarthy did
not apply her undeniable talents more directly to the human
beings she is writing about.

820. Podhoretz, Norman. "John O'Hara and Mary McCarthy." In
DOINGS AND UNDOINGS: THE FIFTIES AND AFTER IN
AMERICAN WRITING, 76-93. New York: Noonday Press,
1964.
  Compares O'Hara's TEN NORTH FREDERICK's
Gibbsville to New Leeds and concludes that despite outward
differences, these are two neighboring American communities.
Discusses the lifestyles of the Vassar graduates in the thirties as
presented in THE GROUP and attempts to pinpoint exactly what
McCarthy was trying to communicate in her portraiture of these
foolish and peripheral girls. Argues THE GROUP is a lady
writer's trivial novel that scarcely bears a trace of the wit,
sharpness and vivacity found in McCarthy's earlier works.

The first half of this article was originally published in item no.
808.

821. "Mary McCarthy et les intéllectuels." FIGARO (January 18,
1968): 20. French.
  Says that McCarthy has been more successful in satirizing
East Coast small town intellectuals than Bellow, Mailer or
Albee.

SIGHTS AND SPECTACLES 1937-1956

822. KIRKUS REVIEWS 24 (April 15, 1956): 291.
     Calls these pieces occasionally corrosive, often astute and always entertaining.

823. Hogan, William. "Miss McCarthy Presents a Critical Waxworks." SAN FRANCISCO CHRONICLE (May 24, 1956): 21.
     Focuses on the "blatantly obtrusive 'splinter group' communist ideas" contained in the collection and ponders how following any party line can corrupt even a brilliant critic. Comments that he is pleased that the early pieces in particular remain intact, viewing them now almost as satire on the critical thought of the mid-1930s.

824. Krutch, Joseph Wood. "The Long Claw of Contempt." SATURDAY REVIEW 39, no.21 (May 26, 1956): 20.
     Describes McCarthy as a hatchet woman with extraordinary insight into others' weaknesses. States that her all-encompassing contempt for what she does not like conceals her own lack of belief, commitment and courage.

825. Magid, Nora. "Theater Criticism of Mary McCarthy." REPORTER 14, no.12 (June 14, 1956): 44-45.
     Finds McCarthy's prose style brilliant and devastatingly clever, however, deems her judgments are limited and often contradictory.

826. BOOKLIST 52 (June 15, 1956): 426-427.
     Finds her exacting observations on American theater and the society that shaped it, both witty and wise.

827. Rolo, Charles J. "Reader's Choice." ATLANTIC 198 (July 1956): 84-86.
     States that McCarthy yet again displays her dazzling wit, intellect and insight. Points out that her commentary is limited by

her contrariness, but if one agrees with her views, this same characteristic can prove a delight.

828. Nichols, Lewis. "Amid the Boos, Some Small Applause." NEW YORK TIMES BOOK REVIEW (July 1, 1956): 3.

Declares that McCarthy's theater reviews, as provocative and valid today as when originally written, should be read.

829. Beckett, Roger. "Seat on the Aisle with Mary McCarthy." NEW YORK HERALD TRIBUNE BOOK REVIEW 33, no.1 (August 12, 1956): 7.

Acknowledges that the collection is lively and the author knowledgeable and clever. Finds, nonetheless, that her focus on ideas and ideas alone and her obliviousness to the techniques of stage production make McCarthy and theater reviewing a mismatch.

830. Hayes, Richard. "On Mary McCarthy's Advance to Farther Frontiers." COMMONWEAL 64, no.25 (September 21, 1956): 615-616.

Traces the evolution of McCarthy's theater criticism over the twenty year period covered by the collection. Perceives a bleak and remote indifference in McCarthy's reaction to her own early persona, and returns again and again to her characteristic coldness. Finds her ultimately incomprehensible in conventional terms, the extreme reaches of her intelligence and perception alienating her from the natural human world of sympathy and compassion.

831. Gassner, John. "Report to a Minority." THEATRE ARTS 40, no.11 (November 1956): 8.

Maintains that one-sided or wrongheaded though McCarthy can be, her writing is stimulating, and often brilliantly perceptive. Feels that those involved in theater should be grateful to her for irritating them into thought.

832. R., R. TWENTIETH CENTURY (G.B.) 166, no.992 (1959): 317.

Includes the very singular statement that McCarthy is at her best when she is most appreciative.

833. Small, Christopher. "Miss McCarthy Drips Acid from Balcony."
GLASGOW HERALD (G.B.) (February 27, 1959): 5.
    Appears encouraged by McCarthy's views that the American
theater scene is no better than the British. Finds her criticism
ruthless but intelligent, and calls her one of the most
clear-sighted practitioners of the trade.

834. Glanville, Brian. "Un-American Intellectual." BOOKS AND
BOOKMEN (March 1959): 13.
    Contends that the essentially writer's essays which comprise
SIGHTS AND SPECTACLES make it an exception to most
collections of transient theatrical journalism. Calls McCarthy
extremely talented and stimulating, praising her in particular for
what he terms her combination of masculine intellect with
feminine sensitivity. Discusses a number of her other books,
judging THE COMPANY SHE KEEPS still her best.

835. Priestley, J. B. "J.B. Priestley Attacks Critics Who Kick the
Theatre." REYNOLDS NEWS (London, G.B.) (March 1, 1959):
6.
    Assumes a dual persona: as a twenty year veteran of the
theater Priestley condemns destructive criticism, stressing the
difficulties in theatrical production and the importance of the
audience; as a reader he feels that McCarthy's prose is
intelligent, perceptive and a pleasure to read.

836. Mavor, Ronald. "A Critic on the Mat." SCOTSMAN (G.B.)
(March 2, 1959).
    Questions the purpose of much of her early criticism,
marked by a signature "brittle wittiness and general
disparagement." Accepts McCarthy's confessions of youthful
excesses as disarming and sees the book in its entirety as a
warning to the young critic. Notes that her intelligence and
analytical gifts have emerged far more clearly through the years.
(Citation not verified.)

837. R., A. "Broadway Threnody." SOUTH WALES EVENING
     POST (G.B.) (March 7, 1959).
     Writes that these resurrected reviews, full of rash first
     impressions, present a vital picture of twenty years of American
     life.

838. Goldey, David. "Well Preserved Criticism." CHERWELL
     OXFORD (G.B.) (March 11, 1959): 7.
     Stresses the fierce intellectualism of both McCarthy and THE
     PARTISAN REVIEW. Argues that her passionate interest in
     ideas results in pieces which read more like book notices than
     theater reviews, but finds her assessment of dramatists accurate,
     unkind and refreshing.

839. Miller, Karl. "Outside the Theatre." SPECTATOR 202 (March
     13, 1959): 379.
     Considers her exacting tone and adherence to left wing
     theory weaknesses of the book. Accepts her criticisms as valid
     and disturbing despite the fact that McCarthy is a very literary
     writer with no special interest in the theater. Takes seriously
     McCarthy's stance that plays are part of literature, and as such
     should not be allowed special and seemingly less stringent
     standards.

840. Lambert, J. W. "Quite Contrary." TIMES (London, G.B.)
     [Sunday Ed.] (March 15, 1959).
     Contends that this collection is far more illuminating of
     McCarthy herself than of the theater it purports to criticize.
     Credits her with skill and enviable intelligence but focuses on
     what Lambert sees as her overriding determination to be
     accepted as one of THE PARTISAN REVIEW circle, a desire
     that led to the donning of intellectual blinkers which at times
     seem "positively painful." (Citation not verified.)

841. F., G. "Pretty and Witty." GUARDIAN (G.B.) (March 20,
     1959): 10.
     Begins, condescendingly, with the comment that McCarthy is
     prettier than most theater critics. Allows that she is also witty
     and, for the most part, rather sensible, although the reviewer

devotes the greater part of the review to a discussion of "a rather silly passage."

842. Pratt, Desmond. "A Critic Looks at Herself." YORKSHIRE POST (Leeds, G.B.) (March 25, 1959): 4.
Praises the "splendid honesty" McCarthy reveals in speaking of her early reviews. Calls her more mature criticism, firm but fair.

843. NORTHERN ECHO (G.B.) (March 26, 1959).
Notes that the free reign given to McCarthy in her early pieces by THE PARTISAN REVIEW, in particular, allowed for a marked tendency towards arrogance and disdain. Finds, nonetheless, that she displays a cool intelligence in her writing on world drama. (Citation not verified.)

844. "Writing for the Stage." TIMES LITERARY SUPPLEMENT, no.2978 (March 27, 1959): 172.
Finds the book highly stimulating. Believes its greatest merit lies in compelling readers to re-examine their own feelings and attitudes toward the theater.

845. Kennedy, Maurice. "McCarthyism." IRISH TIMES (Ireland) (March 28, 1959): 6.
Declares these reviews to be the most lucidly perverse since Shaw. Advises caution with regard to some of the statements contained in the volume, however, clearly finds the book brilliant and delightful, and the author a torment and a treasure.

846. Bennett, Richard. "Recommended for Your Bookshelf." BOOKS OF THE MONTH (London, G.B.) 74, no.4 (April 1959): 21-24.
Notes that this collection contains good, intelligent writing.

847. Gillet, Eric. "Charm of Kenya." NATIONAL AND ENGLISH REVIEW (G.B.) 152, no.914 (April 1959): 150-152.
Calls the book admirable and McCarthy one of the best theatrical critics of the day.

848. Hutten, Kenneth A. "Theatre." WHAT'S ON (G.B.) (April 1959).
     Differentiates between true drama criticism and the writing of reviews, defining criticism as scholarly deliberation detached from the commercial aspects of theater. Believes McCarthy to be one of its few real practitioners and warmly recommends this collection for discriminating readers. (Citation not verified.)

849. Darlington, W. A. "Prejudice--For and Against." DAILY TELEGRAPH (London, G.B.) (April 6, 1959).
     Contends that an occasional prejudice can enliven criticism, but only if the critic knows of and acknowledges such prejudgments. Believes McCarthy is often unaware of her own prejudices, seeing and hearing what she wants to see and hear. Concludes that she is a literary person who has accidently strayed into the realm of theater.

850. Williams, W. H. "Mr. Williams Again." BIRMINGHAM MAIL (G.B.) (May 1, 1959): 10.
     Calls this a readable, sometimes brilliant collection.

851. O'Brien, Conor. "From a Seat in the Gods." TABLET 213, no.6207 (May 9, 1959): 448.
     Notes that in her attempt to avoid personal reaction, McCarthy's cold style removes the aura of pleasure attached to theater going. Concludes that most of her austere reviews befitted the Trotskyite PARTISAN REVIEW and made "an infuriating brilliant book."

852. Tynan, Kenneth. "Above the Crowd." OBSERVER (May 10, 1959): 21.
     Acknowledges the dazzling analytical powers that are displayed throughout this hypnotic collection, but expresses a discomforting inability to picture McCarthy herself in a theater. Finds her omniscient style, antiseptic intelligence, and frequent failures of sympathy at odds with the very nature of theater, an art that addresses itself to the multitudes.

853. Osborne, Charles. "The Irony That Opposes." TIME AND TIDE (London, G.B.) (May 16, 1959).

   Places McCarthy in the category of critics whose primary concern is with drama as literature rather than performance. Concedes that she writes well, however, believes she neither truly likes nor understands the theater and would be better off in some other kind of criticism. (Citation not verified.)

854. Wilson, Angus. "The Intellectual on the Aisle." ENCOUNTER 12, no.6 (June 12, 1959): 68-70.

   Examines the changing world of criticism, noting the growing "alien intrusions" of non-theater people. Discusses McCarthy's strengths and weaknesses in some detail, and proposes that few critics have shown such utter disregard for the theatrical standpoint. Sees, however, that her strength as a critic lies precisely in the fact that her term of reference is modern society and not theatrical convention.

855. Barker, Frank Granville. "Sitting in Judgment." PLAYS AND PLAYERS (G.B.) (July 1959).

   Finds little to praise in this collection. Concludes with the observation that eccentric though McCarthy's opinions may be, credit may be given for their originality. (Citation not verified.)

856. Vidal, Gore. "Love, Love, Love." PARTISAN REVIEW 26, no.4 (Fall 1959): 613-623.

   Argues that the American theater has been undone by the cult of feeling. Notes, in this extended essay that takes on various aspects of "the general corruption of aesthetic and intellectual values" of our age, that McCarthy ranks first among contemporary American writers who have written about the theater.

   Also published in: Vidal, Gore. ROCKING THE BOAT. 73-87. Boston: Little, Brown & Co., 1962; London: Heinemann, 1963.

857. Cheshire, David. In THEATRE: HISTORY, CRITICISM AND
     REFERENCE, edited by K. C. Harrison, 70. Readers Guide
     Series. London: Clive Bingley, 1967.
         Comments that McCarthy's style, which focuses on the plays
     and their writers, virtually ignoring the performance aspect, puts
     her at odds with most other critics. Notes her belief that modern
     theater failed to interest her primary audience, the readers of
     THE PARTISAN REVIEW.

VENICE OBSERVED: COMMENTS ON VENETIAN CIVILIZATION

858. Hutchens, John K. "Book Review." NEW YORK HERALD
     TRIBUNE (November 15, 1956): 27.
         Stresses that McCarthy orchestrates the splendid plates,
     Chastel's commentary and her own original style into a
     magnificent book. Emphasizes that she captures the tone and
     temperament of Venice where unreality is reality and not subject
     to moral indignation.

859. Sitwell, Sacheverell. "A Caustic Letter to Venice and the
     Venetians." NEW YORK TIMES BOOK REVIEW (November
     18, 1956): 7.
         Contends the book is a first-rate piece of reporting that will
     have people wondering what Venice did to annoy McCarthy.

860. Taylor, Francis Henry. "Venice Most Splendidly Recaptured."
     NEW YORK HERALD TRIBUNE BOOK REVIEW 33, no.15
     (November 18, 1956): 5.
         Suggests McCarthy's witty, probing and sensitive book was
     motivated by her inability to forgive the laxity and inconstancy of
     Venetian life. Says her commentary on the illustrations is equal
     to a professional in the visual arts and emphasizes the book
     should be required reading.

861. Hogan, William. "Venice Presented by Miss McCarthy & Co."
   SAN FRANCISCO CHRONICLE (November 19, 1956): 27.
      Credits the people who produced the book.

862. "The Floating City." TIME 68, no.22 (November 26, 1956):
   110, 112.
      Observes that McCarthy is not an ordinary tourist who
   accepts the commonplace without question, but a writer whose
   reflections heighten perception and provide a "sense of place
   without sentimentality usurping the place of sense."

863. Poore, Charles. "Books of the Times." NEW YORK TIMES
   (November 27, 1956): 35.
      Wonders where the publishers of this series will find another
   author of McCarthy's caliber to deliver such a spirited portrait.
   Contends that her opinions on art may not be well received,
   however, notes her candid and unsparing eye makes this more
   than just another collection of expert "patterned patter."

864. Adlow, Dorothy. "Painting and Sculpting." CHRISTIAN
   SCIENCE MONITOR [Eastern Ed.] (November 29, 1956): 14.
      Says McCarthy's graceful prose and witty critical judgment
   is equal in excellence to what she is describing.

865. Adlow, Dorothy. "Books for Christmas." OPEN SHELF
   (CLEVELAND PUBLIC LIBRARY), no.7-12 (December 1956):
   2.
      Notes that this is a wise and penetrating look at Venice.

866. Rolo, Charles J. "Reader's Choice." ATLANTIC 198, no.6
   (December 1956): 92-100.
      Comments that the poor quality of the color plates prevents
   the book from achieving the highest standard. Finds her narrative
   commendable in view of the fact that there is nothing more that
   can be said about Venice.

867. Phelps, Robert. "The Worth of Venice." NATIONAL REVIEW
   2, no.29 (December 8, 1956): 20.
      Reflects that Venice offered an ideally various, contained
   subject to an author whose most conspicuous gift has always

been a tireless, agile capacity to generalize. Provides a synopsis of the book.

868. Genauer, Emily. "Critic as Shopping Guide to Some New Art Book." NEW YORK HERALD TRIBUNE (December 16, 1956): 11.
    Praises the book as the first choice in art books, written by a witty, gifted novelist whose fresh perception of the relationship between Venetian art and Venetian life and character will be welcomed by those who might be intimidated by experts.

869. Powell, Dawn. "The Sack of Venice." NATION 183, no.25 (December 22, 1956): 543.
    Proposes that this synthetic spectacular was produced in December merely to accommodate the Christmas gift-book season. Notes the fresh and lucid comments by Chastel are relegated to the appendix while McCarthy is given solitary cover credit. Applauds Venice for allowing itself to once again be "trounced, scolded, kissed and forgiven" by a writer who "plunders its legends, berates its commercialism and pins goodboy badges" on the likes of Tintoretto and Giorgione.

870. "And Then Away to Venice." TIMES LITERARY SUPPLEMENT (January 11, 1957): 26.
    Contends the only people who my be disappointed with the book are those who romanticize Venice. Notes McCarthy's skillful blend of history, personal impressions, art history and art criticism provide a useful, intelligent appraisal of the city.

871. Haskell, Francis. "Approaches to Italy." LISTENER (January 17, 1957): 123-124.
    Says McCarthy interprets the past through her impressions of the present most successfully when dealing with the fifteenth and sixteenth centuries. Observes that the common-to-travel-books "comic landlady" makes an appearance but notes she is so well recorded that she adds a new and dignified aspect to the city's history. Concludes that the book provides the final word on Venice.

872. "Shorter Notices." TIMES (London, G.B.) (January 24, 1957): 11.

Writes that it is half a pity that McCarthy's gifted prose is buried in the splendor of the illustrations.

873. Spender, Stephen. "Two Witty Women." ENCOUNTER 8, no.2 (February 1957): 77-79.

Notes that men may discover that part of the McCarthy-Macaulay charm lies in the fact that they both write from the fringe of the "guilt-ridden promiscuous cafe and pub-crawling world of men." Says the book is sometimes brilliant but nonetheless disappointing because McCarthy allows the moral shock of Venice to come between herself and the object she is observing.

874. Baxter, James E. "Slightly Adrift in Venice." REPORTER 16 (February 7, 1957): 47-48.

Theorizes that McCarthy may have been inspired by West's BLACK LAMB AND GREY FALCON which assesses the political and cultural significance of Yugoslavia. Says McCarthy rivals West for the position of the cleverest woman writer in the English-speaking world, however, points out that McCarthy's narrative reveals a lack of humility and her otherwise brilliant fiction compliments only herself and not the painters or paintings.

875. Scott, Margaret. "Venice." SPECTATOR, no.6725 (May 17, 1957): 659.

Notes McCarthy's unsentimental easy style pleasantly reproduces the color pageantry of Venice.

876. Lambert, R. T. CANADIAN FORUM 37 (June 1957): 67.

Remarks that McCarthy magnificently fuses the old with the new in a book ideal for art lovers, travellers and bibliophiles.

877. Hutton, Edward. "Venetian Spyglass." TABLET 215, no.6343 (December 16, 1961): 1209-1210.

Evaluates the book as an acute, witty account that somehow misses the illusionary Venice. Concludes that the best pages are devoted to the painters Giorgione, Tintoretto and Titian.

878. ABERDEEN EVENING EXPRESS (G.B.) (December 23, 1961).
     Notes that the book is an impeccably written, informative historical guide. (Citation not verified.)

879. BOOKS OF THE MONTH (London, G.B.) (January 1962).
     Remarks briefly that VENICE OBSERVED is written with superb tact and style. (Citation not verified.)

880. B., D. M. "Pen-Picture of a Subtle City." WEST HAMPTON EXPRESS STAR (G.B.) (January 13, 1962).
     Says McCarthy's perception could make the "stones of a mundane street in Wigan seem interesting and evocative." (Citation not verified.)

881. Tyler, Froom. "They Invented Income Tax." SOUTH WALES EVENING POST (G.B.) (February 24, 1962).
     Says McCarthy writes about Venice with unsentimental love. (Citation not verified.)

882. "Quick Guide to Europe." TIMES (London, G.B.) (June 29, 1972): 11.
     Reviews the joint publication of VENICE OBSERVED and THE STONES OF FLORENCE and claims it is a "splendid coupling of two seductive essays."

883. BOOKS AND BOOKMEN 17, no.11 (August 1972): xvi.
     Notes the publication of McCarthy's two travelogues VENICE OBSERVED and THE STONES OF FLORENCE.

884. "Holiday Reading." OBSERVER (July 15, 1979): 37.
     Notes briefly these are two witty and exciting essays which capture the essence of the cities and their histories.

885. Vanni Orestano, Francesca. "Italy in Mary McCarthy's Writings: VENICE OBSERVED and THE STONES OF FLORENCE." RIVISTA DI STUDI ANGLO-AMERICANA 4-5, no.3 (1984-85): 171-179.
     Provides quotes from a number of reviews of McCarthy's two travelogues. Finds that THE STONES OF FLORENCE is

more "scholarly" and "passionate" due to McCarthy's deeper
knowledge of the city. Notes her statement that she was able to
say what she believed in THE STONES OF FLORENCE,
whereas in VENICE OBSERVED she was more concerned with
originality.

886. "Travel Shortlist." PUNCH 289 (September 25, 1985): 61.
     Enjoys both VENICE OBSERVED and THE STONES OF
FLORENCE and states that, with the exception of James
Morris's book on Venice, there has been no better account of
contemporary Venice.

MEMORIES OF A CATHOLIC GIRLHOOD

887. KIRKUS REVIEWS 25, no.7 (April 1, 1957): 297.
     Remarks that the "warmth" and "gamine charm" of
MEMORIES OF A CATHOLIC GIRLHOOD, qualities so often
missing from McCarthy's fiction, may attract readers beyond the
anticipated audience.

888. Kitching, Jessie. "PW Forecast for Booksellers." PUBLISHERS
     WEEKLY (April 15, 1957): 40.
     Maintains that the reminiscences would be grim if not for the
humor in McCarthy's writing.

889. Hutchens, John K. "Book Review." NEW YORK HERALD
     TRIBUNE (May 16, 1957): 23.
     Examines the dark characters from McCarthy's past and
maintains that wicked Uncle Myers is straight from Dickens'
lower depths. Wonders if McCarthy would have been the "sharp,
inquiring, satiric writer" she is had she not experienced such a
harsh upbringing.

890. Poore, Charles. "Books of the Times." NEW YORK TIMES
     (May 18, 1957): 17.
     Describes "Yonder Peasant, Who Is He?" as one of the most

"stinging, brilliant and disturbing memoirs ever written by an American." Contends McCarthy's experiences are set forth with remarkable candor and praises her for being able to revise the contents without making the reader wish she had altered the original.

891. NEW YORK POST (May 19, 1957): M11.
     Notes the publication of the book and supplies a photograph of McCarthy.

892. Baker, Carlos. "Members of the Family." NEW YORK TIMES BOOK REVIEW 7 (May 19, 1957): 3.
     Recommends this readable family album and summarizes the events and characters portrayed. Maintains that the few pages which contain some religious controversy are the least important aspects of the book.

893. Bloom, Eleanor M. "City Childhood Molds a Writer: She Reveals Reason for Lack of Warmth." MINNEAPOLIS TRIBUNE (Minn.) [Sunday Ed.] (May 19, 1957): E6.
     Notes that McCarthy's writings have lacked warmth and humanity in the past; one understands why after reading this account of her childhood.

894. Lyon, William. "Girlhood Remembered by a Brilliant Observer." VIRGINIAN PILOT AND PORTSMOUTH STAR (Norfolk, Va.) (May 19, 1957): C6.
     Provides a synopsis and proposes that the religiously orthodox may be shocked (or even influenced) by various passages within the book. Claims the last essay, "Ask Me No Questions," contains McCarthy's most sensitive and mature writing.

895. "One Girl's Journey." NEWSWEEK 49, no.20 (May 20, 1957): 122-123.
     Recommends this "ardently coloured and fascinating" memoir and describes it as a penetrating account of girlhood.

896. "Poor Roy's Child." TIME 69 (May 20, 1957): 138-139.
     Gives a brief overview of the book, and describes the death

of McCarthy's parents as "the wound for which a life of writing must compensate." Concludes that McCarthy's sharp sense of reality is not colored by either utopian sentimentality or cynicism.

897. Hanscom, Leslie. "Mary McCarthy's Catholic Childhood." NEW YORK WORLD-TELEGRAM AND SUN [Brooklyn Ed.] (May 21, 1957): D27.
    Claims this is one of the few books that exposes McCarthy's "emotional marrow." Reflects on the fact that even though some Catholics were offended by the book, others recognized the deep pain and offered sympathy.

898. Reid, Margaret W. "Background of an Artist. Eight Episodes in Orphan's Life." WICHITA FALLS TIMES (Wichita Falls, Tex.) [Sunday Ed.] (May 26, 1957): D3.
    States that these essays are a contribution to American social history and present a forthright portrait of a talented artist.

899. Scott, Winfield Townley. "«They Were Ordinary People Who Behaved Quite Oddly»." NEW YORK HERALD TRIBUNE. BOOK REVIEW 33, no.42 (May 26, 1957): 3.
    Maintains that the commentaries and photographs add a great deal to this publication, and suggests that it is an example of McCarthy's finest work.

900. Sullivan, Richard. "A Moving Work of Recollection." CHICAGO TRIBUNE. MAGAZINE OF BOOKS [Sunday Ed.] (May 26, 1957): 5.
    Praises McCarthy's remarkably vivid autobiographical study, describing it as "a moving work of recollection."

901. Washburn, Beatrice. "Able Novelist Tells of Bitter Childhood." MIAMI HERALD (May 26, 1957): G4.
    Describes McCarthy's account of her childhood, and those who were part of it, as cruel and declares that it is fortunate most of McCarthy's characters are no longer alive. Wonders whether McCarthy lost not only her faith in religion, but in people as well.

902. Hogan, William. "Bittersweet Memoir by Mary McCarthy."
     SAN FRANCISCO CHRONICLE (May 29, 1957): 19.
          Posits that although the book will be controversial, McCarthy
     has succeeded in explaining herself and her art.

903. Sweeney, Anne. "Superbly Done Stories of Unhappy
     Childhood." NASHVILLE BANNER (May 31, 1957): 24.
          Writes that the title of the book is a misnomer because
     McCarthy reveals that she was never really much of a Catholic
     except by birth. Believes the book may draw strong reaction
     from Catholic readers.

904. Fowlie, Wallace. "Two American Autobiographies." ACCENT
     17, no.3 (Summer 1957): 188-192.
          Praises McCarthy for a classic, autobiographical series of
     essays which trace the shaping of her mind and character through
     her feelings about Catholicism. Suggests that McCarthy achieves
     an acceptance of self in the final essay "Ask Me No Questions."

905. Barrett, Marylin, and Mary Ellin. "Mary McCarthy's
     Memories." GOOD HOUSEKEEPING 144 (June 1957): 235.
          Declares that this work finally gives the reader a sense of
     what really makes McCarthy tick. Posits that her early loss of
     religious faith, and discovery of the lack of compassion and
     coherence in human behavior may explain her talent for cool and
     precise observation.

906. Pickrel, Paul. "New Books." HARPER'S MAGAZINE 214,
     no.1285 (June 1957): 79-80.
          Contends that many of the best passages in the book are
     explorations of the differing interpretations of the individuals and
     events in her childhood. Concludes that the commentaries
     following each essay reflect a generous and forgiving spirit.

907. Rolo, Charles J. "Remembrance of Things Past." ATLANTIC
     199, no.6 (June 1957): 90-91.
          Describes the autobiography as "a classic fairy tale drama
     filtered through a highly sophisticated mind."

908. Smith, Eleanor T. LIBRARY JOURNAL 82, no.11 (June 1, 1957): 1532.

    Argues that although McCarthy possesses remarkable creative power and human understanding, this book lacks "faith, hope and charity."

909. McGinley, Phyllis. "Mary Was an Orphan." SATURDAY REVIEW 40 (June 8, 1957): 31.

    Provides a synopsis of the book and contends that everything McCarthy has to say is "breathlessly interesting and entirely believable." See also Bradford Aresty's letter (item no. 307) and McGinley's response (item no. 308).

910. BOOKLIST 53, no.20 (June 15, 1957): 523.

    States that these brilliant autobiographical essays are rich in re-creations of personalities, places and the fluctuating emotions of youth.

911. BOOKMARK 16 (June 16, 1957): 211.

    Refers to McCarthy's autobiographical essays, claiming they "wittily" detail the writer's religious background.

912. Lange, Victor. "The Women and the Orphan Child." NEW REPUBLIC 136, no.25 (June 24, 1957): 18-19.

    Demonstrates how these essays are really studies in detection with McCarthy probing the characters of the individuals involved in her upbringing. Maintains that the last essay, "Ask Me No Questions," represents the subtle resolution of the book.

913. Hoskins, Katherine. "Give a Life to Live." NATION 185 (July 6, 1957): 16-17.

    Expresses pleasurable surprise at the gentleness of the essays, given the cold, brutal environment of McCarthy's childhood. Claims the commentaries serve as vantage points from which McCarthy reviews the "myth in the light of the actuality." Proposes that although they prove to be the most interesting parts of the book, they ultimately fail because McCarthy does not possess the kind of "ruminative, speculative mind" necessary "to wander fruitfully in the areas of myth."

914. Simons, John W. "An Author of a Few Pieties and Few
     Illusions." COMMONWEAL 66, no.15 (July 12, 1957):
     379-380.
           Proposes that the Catholic reader may question why the word
     "Catholic" appears in the book's title since there are few
     recollections which have to do with Catholicism. Doubts the
     authenticity of the clashes with the priests and maintains that
     McCarthy cannot exorcize the memory of her religious
     upbringing.

915. MacPherson, Jessie. "Books Reviewed." CANADIAN FORUM
     37 (September 1957): 138-139.
           Contends McCarthy has exploited the reader's interest in her
     ancestry and early experiences. Claims her recollections are
     marred by substandard writing, the reflections following each
     essay create a structural hodge-podge and various ruthless
     character portraits leave the impression of unresolved hostility.

916. Mullen, Barbara Dorr. "Mary, Mary." AMERICA 98, no.2
     (October 12, 1957): 38-40.
           Compares her own Catholic upbringing with McCarthy's.
     Believes they both inappropriately equated the difficulties in
     childhood to religion.

917. "New Books at City Library." WICHITA EAGLE. WICHITA
     EAGLE MAGAZINE (Wichita, Kans.) [Sunday Ed.] (October
     13, 1957): 4.
           Describes the book as a document in the complex social
     history of America.

918. Logal, Nelson W. CATHOLIC WORLD 186 (November 1957):
     157-158.
           Awards this book the Pulitzer Prize for being the "Number 1
     Cry-Baby-Book of the year." Attacks McCarthy for failing to
     find joy and affection in anything or anyone.

919. Stockwood, Jane. "The London Scene." HARPER'S BAZAAR
     [British Ed.] (November 1957): 76, 132.
           Mentions that some of McCarthy's relatives did not agree

with her recollections, raising an interesting point as to the relativity of vision and memory.

920. Connolly, Cyril. "Not Quite Contrary Enough." TIMES (London, G.B.) [Sunday Ed.] (November 17, 1957): 7.
Describes McCarthy as an "intellectual woman writer who has neither sacrificed nor abused her femininity, nor played down her masculine mind." Maintains that although this is a brilliant and passionate book, it would have been better if the spirit of the epilogues penetrated the essays.

921. Pitman, Robert. "The Little Girl Won a Prize..." DAILY EXPRESS (London, G.B.) [Sunday Ed.] (November 17, 1957): 6.
Refers to MEMORIES OF A CATHOLIC GIRLHOOD as an "enthralling" story of McCarthy's childhood.

922. Toynbee, Philip. "The Tight-Rope Walker." OBSERVER (London, G.B.) (November 17, 1957).
Theorizes that there are two reasons for writing an autobiography: either one is a talented writer who can make a dull ordinary life glow; or one's life is so extraordinary that even an unskilled account would be interesting. Suggests that McCarthy walks a tightrope, using her brilliance as a writer to make her boring childhood seem extraordinary.

923. Thomson, George Malcolm. "The Girl Who Wanted the Limelight ..." EVENING STANDARD (London, G.B.) (November 19, 1957): 12.
Recalls some of the main episodes in the book, which he describes as immensely accomplished, although somewhat uneven. Posits that McCarthy has grown up into a brilliant woman and formidable writer.

924. "Convent School Rebel." TIMES (London, G.B.) (November 21, 1957): 13.
Questions the reprinting of these chapters from periodicals and the addition of commentaries to examine their accuracy. Suggests McCarthy had three reasons for doing this: the chapters originally provoked discussion and she wanted them to be

preserved; the commentaries allow her to offer after-the-fact
opinions about Catholicism; the commentaries may not come any
nearer the truth than the original stories did.

925. Betjeman, John. "A Defenceless Childhood." DAILY
TELEGRAPH (London, G.B.) (November 22, 1957):
   Warns those expecting a book of edifying piety will be
disappointed; the Catholicism of McCarthy's childhood requiring
only a small "c." Provides a brief outline and notes that when
the memoirs first appeared in America in a magazine, McCarthy
received menacing letters about her criticism of certain aspects of
her Roman Catholic upbringing.

926. Glanville, Brian. "Dickens in Minneapolis." TRUTH (London,
G.B.) 157, no.4235 (November 22, 1957): 328.
   Observes that the novella form best suits McCarthy's
combination of feminine sensibility, sharp and sustained
masculine intelligence, and discipline. Applauds her ability to
stand back and put her observations into perspective. Compares
her to several celebrated British women novelists and says her
range of activity transcends their confined upper-middle class
domesticity.

927. Nicholson, Geoffrey. "Writing It Out." SPECTATOR, no.6752
(November 22, 1957): 710.
   Admires McCarthy's attempt to arrive at the truth by means
of critical examination following each essay. Suggests this
literary style suits her analytical talents and provides an
opportunity for the reader to see the way she works.

928. Taggart, Joseph. "Briefly Recommended." STAR (G.B.)
(November 22, 1957): 8.
   Recommends this sensitive, moving and brilliant book.

929. Bridgman, David. "Tale of a Mixed-Up Kid." SOUTH WALES
EVENING POST (G.B.) (November 23, 1957).
   Admires McCarthy's ability to scrutinize her past without
relying on "rose coloured spectacles of nostalgia" so often used
in autobiographical writing. (Citation not verified.)

930. Harrington, Eugene C. "Venom Preserved." TABLET 210, no.6131 (November 23, 1957): 462-463.

Examines McCarthy's critical thoughts on Catholicism. Suggests that although anti-Catholicism is present in this book, it is not overt but tends to seep through her highly polished and clever writing.

931. Orwell, Sonia. "Growing Up as a Writer." NEWS CHRONICLE AND DAILY DISPATCH (London, G.B.) (November 27, 1957): 8.

Admires McCarthy's desire to arrive at the truth, and admits it is remarkable to witness an intelligent child grapple with the three streams of Western thought. Notes that although the title may be misleading, it is not inappropriate as the singularity of a Catholic education adds a dimension to McCarthy's puritan upbringing.

932. "No Primrose Path of Childhood." TIMES LITERARY SUPPLEMENT, no.2909 (November 29, 1957): 725.

Maintains that only the shameless can successfully write about their childhoods without self-consciousness or guilt. Contends that McCarthy is not one of the shameless and that the book is overlaid with adult sensibility. Questions the addition of the postscripts to previously published chapters and suggests that in her pursuit of a literal truth, she damages a fabulous one. Concludes that despite some unforgettable portraits, the book is not up to McCarthy's standards.

933. Thomas, Elizabeth. "From America's Backwoods." TRIBUNE (London, G.B.) (November 29, 1957): 14.

Credits McCarthy with writing a satisfying story. Offers a synopsis of the book and applauds her honest, unusual and disarming postscripts.

934. Brooke-Rose, Christine. "Family Album." TIME AND TIDE (London, G.B.) 38, no.48 (November 30, 1957): 1501.

Offers only praise for these reminiscences. Recounts the two best stories: the first where Mary loses her faith and the second in which she becomes a woman. Maintains that although some

have questioned the truthfulness of various episodes the reviewer
was "completely convinced and captivated."

935. White, Antonia. "Withered on the Stalk." NEW STATESMAN
54, no.1394 (November 30, 1957): 740.
   Writes that this book makes fascinating reading; each essay
is "vivid and lively, occasionally slick, but more often sharply
perceptive."

936. BOOKS AND BOOKMEN 3, no.3 (December 1957): 21.
   Suggests this brilliantly written book sheds some light on the
psychological background of a very interesting writer.

937. Rovere, Richard H. "Best Nonfiction of 1957." ESQUIRE
(London, G.B.) (December 1957): 68+.
   Credits THE SANCTITY OF LIFE AND THE CRIMINAL
LAW, THE NUDE; A STUDY IN IDEAL FORM and
MEMORIES OF A CATHOLIC GIRLHOOD with exhibiting the
highest order of literacy. Comments on the fact that none of the
three works were originally written as books; McCarthy's was a
series of magazine articles, while the other two were lectures.
Contends that because magazine articles and the lecture circuit
are more profitable than writing books, it is possible to have a
first-class talent who may never write a single sustained work.

938. Lehmann, Rosamond. "Highly Natural." LISTENER 58
(December 5, 1957): 946-947.
   Praises these autobiographical essays for their humor and
total absence of self-indulgence or self-pity. Credits McCarthy's
thoughts on religion--"religion, Catholic particularly, is only
good for good people"--as clever, maybe even wise.

939. Conlay, Iris. "Communion Day Tragedy." CATHOLIC
HERALD (G.B.) (December 6, 1957): 5.
   Questions the accuracy of the story about McCarthy losing
her faith and the subsequent events. Suggests instead that
McCarthy could not have lost a faith she had never really had in
the first place. Describes the essays as partly exasperating and
partly pathetic, but always intriguing.

940. Hoult, Norah. "From Rough to Smooth." IRISH TIMES
(Ireland) (December 7, 1957): 4.
Praises this "remarkable" autobiography, and suggests
McCarthy's portraits of her Jewish grandmother and her Scottish
schoolteacher are likely to remain in the reader's memory.

* Glanville, Brian. "Sensibility Girls are Given a Lesson."
REYNOLDS NEWS (London, G.B.) (December 8, 1957): 4.
See item no. 579.

941. Maclaren-Ross, J. "Remembrance." PUNCH 233 (December 11,
1957): 706-707.
Describes these recollections as being "affectionately
amusing and objective."

942. Rans, Geoffrey. "An American Childhood." YORKSHIRE POST
AND LEEDS MERCURY (G.B.) (December 12, 1957): 4.
Recalls that in the past, although he admired McCarthy,
Rans felt estranged by her lack of feeling and generosity.
Maintains, however, that the portraits in these essays are filled
with warmth and unsentimental understanding. Concludes that
there is no better prose writer at present than McCarthy and
looks forward to a second volume of memoirs.

943. Edmonds, Richard. "Volstead Veterans in America." SPHERE
(London, G.B.) 231, no.3011 (December 14, 1957): 444.
Includes the book in a summary of recommended reading.
Describes it as a "witty, polished and creatively intelligent"
account of her childhood.

944. QUEEN (London, G.B.) (December 24, 1957).
Feels that in McCarthy's desire for self-assertion, the candid
voice of truth is lost. Claims this is an autobiography of an
"Angry Young Woman." (Citation not verified.)

945. Bridgman, David. "Ring Out the Old. Books of 1957." SOUTH
WALES EVENING POST (G.B.) (December 28, 1957): 4.
Selects McCarthy's book as his favorite American,
nonfictional work for 1957 and describes it as a unique portrait
of an artist as a young woman. Notes McCarthy's ability to

exercise a cold, unemotional detachment without sacrificing any
warmth and affection.

946. Thomas, Gilbert. "Round the Shelves." BIRMINGHAM POST
     & GAZETTE (G.B.) (December 31, 1957).
        Claims McCarthy's experiences as an orphan are relayed in a
     crisply mordant style, while her reactions to Catholicism are
     registered with characteristic candor.

947. Gillet, Eric. "War Over London." NATIONAL AND ENGLISH
     REVIEW (G.B.) (January 1958): 28-33.
        Describes McCarthy as being "one of the most interesting
     and exciting of contemporary American writers." Recommends
     this book even though it tends to hover between autobiography
     and fiction.

948. Gordon, James. "A Book's Good Company." GOOD
     HOUSEKEEPING (G.B.) 73, no.1 (January 1958): 10.
        Recommends the book, suggesting its precision will delight
     the discriminating reader. Allows that the essay on McCarthy's
     loss of faith, while amusing for the agnostic, may displease the
     Catholic reader.

949. "Vogue's Book Bag." VOGUE [British Ed.] 114, no.1 (January
     1958): 105.
        States that this is a lucid, elating exploration, which, in
     testimony to McCarthy's masculine sensibility and winning
     malice, will not bore or madden.

950. W., M. CATHOLIC NOTES (January 1958).
        Blames the lack of depth of this "intensively readable"
     memoir on the fact that McCarthy never had the opportunity to
     grow into a mature Catholic. (Citation not verified.)

951. Weightman, John G. "The Month: A Personal Diary."
     TWENTIETH CENTURY (G.B.) 163, no.971 (January 1958):
     70-77.
        Attributes the book's air of eternity to McCarthy's firm
     grasp on her personality and the material. Contemplates his own
     role as a critic and suggests that evil is the subject of all

literature and critics are defined by their ability to contemplate evil and appreciate its different qualities. Declares McCarthy is so uniquely good because her vitality and sense of evil are equally matched.

952. Kinloch, Mary. "Question of Faith--and Happiness." SCOTSMAN (G.B.) (January 4, 1958).

Writes that the diverse strands in McCarthy's Catholic inheritance are partly responsible for her brilliance. Argues, however, that although McCarthy was brilliant she was also an egoist. Maintains that egoism is the hardest of all barriers to break down and that it is not only an artistic flaw but also a moral one. (Citation not verified.)

953. J., C. "Its Looks and Title Can Belie." WEST HAMPTON EXPRESS STAR (G.B.) (January 10, 1958).

Argues that the unusual structure of the book helps to recreate the emotional experiences of McCarthy's strange childhood in such a way that the reader also experiences them. (Citation not verified.)

954. "Express Book Reviews." EVENING EXPRESS (Liverpool, G.B.) (January 31, 1958).

States that this well written book is composed mainly of vivid pen portraits of the prominent people in McCarthy's childhood.

955. LIVERPOOL EVENING EXPRESS (G.B.) (January 31, 1958).

Writes that McCarthy's "desire for prominence" helps to explain a great deal in this well written chronicle of a strange and abnormal upbringing. (Citation not verified.)

956. Hough, Graham. "New Novels." ENCOUNTER 10, no.2 (February 1958): 84-86.

Reviews MEMORIES OF A CATHOLIC GIRLHOOD together with a number of new novels maintaining that once a book is altered for artistic effect, it becomes fiction. Judges the book according to the highest standards and concludes that it fails. Questions the authenticity of McCarthy's judgment, arguing that her scale of values seems curiously incomplete.

957. Caru Alho, R. N. "A Mixed Upbringing: Educating an Orphan."
     JEWISH CHRONICLE (London, G.B.) (February 7, 1958): 24.
         Asserts that although this is a witty and informative book, it
     fails because it mocks everything and everyone. Concludes that
     one is left with the feeling "that too many decent dead people
     have been heartlessly libelled."

958. H., F. CAMBRIDGE REVIEW (G.B.) (February 15, 1958):
     341.
         Maintains these moving, often funny stories give the reader a
     glimpse of the frightening, lonely world which helped to shape
     McCarthy's brilliance and wit.

959. Wyndham-Lewis, D. B. CATHOLIC TRUTH (G.B.) (Spring
     1958).
         Writes that if only McCarthy's literary gifts had a touch of
     humility, her earlier memories would have made for better
     reading. (Citation not verified.)

960. THE MONTH (G.B.) (April 1958).
         Renames the book MEMORIES OF AN AMERICAN
     CHILDHOOD since the experiences are typically American and
     there is little evidence of Catholicism. Describes McCarthy's
     final pages in her Introduction as "incredibly superficial."
     (Citation not verified.)

961. Wyndham, Francis. "Book Reviews." LONDON MAGAZINE
     5, no.4 (April 1958): 55-59.
         Compares and contrasts the memoirs of Patrick Anderson,
     Philip O'Connor and Mary McCarthy. Proposes that there is
     very little beneath the surface of McCarthy's work, however
     even the surface contains such truth and wisdom as other writers
     may only suggest. Believes this is a function of the clarity of
     McCarthy's writing.

962. "Pointed Paragraphs: Pride's Way." LIGUORIAN (Liguori,
     Mo.) 46, no.5 (May 1958): 51-52.
         Confronts McCarthy's open rebellion against God, and
     describes her aspiring to perfect equality with the Creator as "the
     last stage of arrogance and pride." Finds that she is too

intelligent not to feel uneasy in the "arid and bitter climate of her pride."

963. Jardin, Claudine. "Les Memoires d'une petite menteuse." FIGARO (May 20, 1966): 31. French.

Comments that McCarthy has, by her own admission, fabricated many facts in her autobiography, however, believes it is more important to have a good imagination than to tell the absolute truth.

964. Bürke, Georg. "Eine Katholische Kindheit." ORIENTIERUNG. KATHOLISCHE BLÄTTER FÜR WELTANSCHAULICHE INFORMATION (Zurich) 31, no.13-14 (1967): 158-160. German.

Admits to McCarthy's great skills of observation and description, but finds the book marred by tendentiousness, exhibitionism, and calculated shock effects.

965. Saal, Rollene W. "Pick of the Paperbacks." SATURDAY REVIEW 55 (April 29, 1972): 74.

Provides brief reviews of some of the better paperbacks published in 1972. Refers to McCarthy's autobiography as a "classic recollection of convent youth."

966. Whittier, Gayle. "Nature as Birthright and Birthloss: Mary McCarthy and Colette." PERSPECTIVES ON CONTEMPORARY LITERATURE 5 (1979): 42-54.

Compares memoirs of McCarthy and Sidonie-Gabrielle Colette and traces the role of nature in each. Suggests that for each writer the authentic self is an attainment of adulthood and that it is the child's intimacy with, or estrangment from nature which determines the path of the self.

967. Chalon, Jean. "Les Malheurs de Mary Mac Carthy." FIGARO (July 29, 1986): 23. French.

Suggests that readers acquaint themselves with McCarthy by first reading MEMORIES OF A CATHOLIC GIRLHOOD. Praises McCarthy's wit and claims it has been a long time since he laughed as much as he did reading A CHARMED LIFE.

968. "Adult Nonfiction." BOOKLIST 83, no.13 (March 1, 1987): 949.
      Suggests HOW I GREW is more relaxed and controversial than MEMORIES OF A CATHOLIC GIRLHOOD. Views it as fascinating and as self-disclosing as any good autobiography if only because of the wit, intelligence and lack of complacency of the author.

969. Bloom, Lynn Z. "Mary McCarthy Remembers, Settles Old Scores." ST. LOUIS POST-DISPATCH (Mo.) (March 29, 1987): F5.
      Links the classic MEMORIES OF A CATHOLIC GIRLHOOD to the "comic bildungsroman" of HOW I GREW. Notes that the book falls short of brilliant because of McCarthy's dyspeptic lack of compassion and discursive attempts to pinpoint exact dates, characters and motives.

970. Tyler, Anne. "The Sentimental Education of Mary McCarthy." BOOK WORLD (WASHINGTON POST) 17, no.14 (April 5, 1987): 7.
      Notes that HOW I GREW often reads like a compendium of lists, with McCarthy presupposing that the reader will be interested in every detail of her most trivial experience. States that it is much more tentative and disjointed than MEMORIES OF A CATHOLIC GIRLHOOD. Concludes that although an occasional glimmer of McCarthy's sharp-tongued style shines through, MEMORIES OF A CATHOLIC GIRLHOOD explains what she is all about.

971. Goldstein, Richard. "Visitation Rites: The Elusive Tradition of Plague Lit." VILLAGE VOICE LITERARY SUPPLEMENT (October 1987): 6-9.
      Compares Poe's treatment of the influenza epidemic in MASQUE OF RED DEATH with McCarthy's description which opens MEMORIES OF A CATHOLIC GIRLHOOD.

972. M., J. "Books Encountered." ENCOUNTER 69, no.4 (November 1987): 63.
      States briefly that this is a frank, slightly rambling

Proustian-teaser which stands in modern contrast to a better, more artful, MEMORIES OF A CATHOLIC GIRLHOOD.

973. Honigmann, David. "Paperbacks." LISTENER 122, no.3128 (August 31, 1989): 28.

Contends that McCarthy arouses admiration and affection in equal measure, offering more clear-sightedness and candor than she did in MEMORIES OF A CATHOLIC GIRLHOOD. Notes HOW I GREW is vintage McCarthy, its ruthless honesty saved from pedantry by its utter charm.

THE STONES OF FLORENCE

974. "Mary McCarthy Turns to Stone." SAN FRANCISCO CHRONICLE. THIS WORLD [Sunday Ed.] (October 11, 1959): 27.

Describes this as a brilliant profile of Florence. Refers to McCarthy's earlier work, VENICE OBSERVED, incorrectly as THE STONES OF VENICE.

975. KIRKUS REVIEWS 27 (October 15, 1959): 810.

States although THE STONES OF FLORENCE lacks the passion that Florentines feel about their city, it is "an exceptional achievement in the field" and declares this book is a must for any serious traveller.

976. Poore, Charles. "Books of the Times." NEW YORK TIMES (October 22, 1959): 35.

Admires McCarthy's "fierce partisanship" and "measured detachment" and posits that few visitors will get the full range of splendid views presented in this book.

977. Beuf, Carlo. ". . . And Here Machiavelli Was at Home." NEW YORK TIMES BOOK REVIEW 64, no.43 (October 25, 1959): 7.

Views this as one of the better works on Florence and

suggests that McCarthy's style is tailor-made for depicting the
"brilliant, mercurial and skeptical" Florentines.

978. C., G. "'Stones' Stir Eloquent Pen." WASHINGTON POST
AND TIMES HERALD (October 25, 1959): E6.
Suggests THE STONES OF FLORENCE mixes history, art
criticism, travel lore and personal anecdotes "in a casserole for
gourmets."

979. Fielden, Lionel. "Labour of Love." OBSERVER (London, G.B.)
(October 25, 1959).
Wonders who this book was written for; it is "too astringent
a book for the now non-travelling 'nouveaux pauvres' and too
un-scholarly for the serious student." Observes that if McCarthy
had applied the brilliant technique of her first chapter throughout,
this book would have been a masterpiece. Says in its present
form, THE STONES OF FLORENCE is simply a beautiful
volume for those who can still afford such splendors.

980. "Fabled City." NEWSWEEK 54, no.17 (October 26, 1959):
130.
Asserts that the historic theme of THE STONES OF
FLORENCE is developed with virtuosity and that McCarthy
brings the bustle of modern Florence to life. Argues that
contrary to McCarthy's prose, Hofer's photographs focus on few
living figures, although she was able to catch the city's great
contours in its stark architectural displays.

981. "The Fifth Element." TIME 74, no.17 (October 26, 1959): 108.
Notes that once the itemized disadvantages of this city are
out of the way, McCarthy begins a solid tribute to former glories
and calamities. Finds that she combines a meticulous observation
of the past and the art which has outlived it, with some of the
year's most readable prose.

982. Hutchens, John K. "Book Review." NEW YORK HERALD
TRIBUNE (October 27, 1959): 27.
Observes McCarthy's point--that everyone has his/her own
Florence and notes McCarthy's is "turbulent, tough-minded and
argumentative." Writes that her love for Venice was evident in

VENICE OBSERVED, and her admiration for Florence is seen clearly in this "handsome" book.

983. Newton, Eric. "Enrichment Among the Dust." GUARDIAN (Manchester, G.B.) (October 30, 1959): 8.

Describes THE STONES OF FLORENCE as an "intelligent essay" on the Florentines, and an equally intelligent, though less penetrating essay on Florentine art and architecture. Concludes this book scores unusually high marks in the gift book category.

984. "Renaissance Centre." SCOTSMAN (October 31, 1959).

Suggests that not only is the work distinguished by its scholarliness and individuality, but also by McCarthy's ability to selectively convey the many faceted themes of Florentine history. (Citation not verified.)

985. Forcey, Charles. "The Soul of a City." ARCHITECTURAL RECORD 126 (November 1959): 382.

Explores various reasons for the "irritating" style of this book. States that even though the book is beautifully made--written impressionistically and accompanied by superb photographs--such evocative artistry is ultimately unsuccessful. Dislikes the typical bitterness of McCarthy's tone that results in "a cruel description of a cruel but beautiful city that cruelly languished."

986. Haskell, Francis. "Virility of Florence." SPECTATOR 203 (November 6, 1959): 640-641.

Enjoys the book primarily because one is able to see the greatest achievements of Florentine art revealed through McCarthy's vivid prose and Hofer's magnificent photographs. Finds that reading such "committed views" on subjects usually left to historians and writers on aesthetics is refreshing.

987. Russell, John. "The Inquisitive City." TIMES (London, G.B.) [Sunday Ed.] (November 8, 1959).

Asserts that so much of what McCarthy says is "apt and amusing" and ranks the book much more than an illustrated guide. (Citation not verified.)

988. Rogers, W. G. HATTIESBURG AMERICAN (Miss.)
     (November 11, 1959).
        Notes the contradiction of Florence, considered a dead city
     with a dull past, and yet home to "the most civilized people in
     Italy." Admires the superb photographs and McCarthy's ability
     to unearth secrets no one else has discovered.

        Also published in: BRISTOL HERALD COURIER (Va.)
     [Sunday Ed.] (December 20, 1959): A5; HAMMOND TIMES
     (Ind.) (November 22, 1959); WILKES-BARRE RECORD (Pa.)
     (December 22, 1959): 16; and WICHITA FALLS TIMES
     (Tex.). FEATURES MAGAZINE (January 10, 1060): 5.

989. "Feeling One's Way in Florence." TIMES LITERARY
     SUPPLEMENT, no.3011 (November 13, 1959): 662.
        Suggests the photographs save this "pretentious" book. Notes
     they reveal the enduring Florence and not the old-fashioned
     cliché--"moustachioed men in mackintoshes hanging about on the
     curb" or the modern Florence of McCarthy's colorful first
     chapter.

990. Ziman, H. D. "Where the Renaissance Was Cradled." DAILY
     TELEGRAPH (London, G.B.) (November 13, 1959).
        States this is a better book than VENICE OBSERVED,
     mostly because of Hofer's excellent photographs.(Citation not
     verified.)

991. Rankin, J. T. "Regional Pictorial Studies." LIBRARY
     JOURNAL 84, no.20 (November 15, 1959): 3561.
        Suggests that even though McCarthy adopts a very definite
     position with THE STONES OF FLORENCE, it is with many
     interesting perspectives. Praises the quality of the photographs
     and notes their arrangement is exceedingly well matched to the
     text.

992. H., J. G. "Italy's Artistic Heritage." CHRISTIAN SCIENCE
     MONITOR [Eastern Ed.] (November 19, 1959): 19.
        States McCarthy's perceptive and often original interpretation

will contribute to the reader's appreciation and knowledge of this remarkable city.

993. Phelps, Robert. "Mind's Eye View of a City." NATIONAL REVIEW 7, no.32 (November 21, 1959): 490-491.
Suggests that unlike VENICE OBSERVED whose experiences seem to be distilled through body and soul as well as intellect, McCarthy's wholly intellectual approach cannot breathe warmth into THE STONES OF FLORENCE.

994. "Reader's Guide." YALE REVIEW 49, no.2 (December 1959): xviii+.
Describes the book as a kaleidoscopic arrangement of details, some dull and worn, others piercing and original. Claims few great figures or single works are treated satisfactorily, except the offbeat artists. Concludes this is not only a collection of sweet essays but a testy and personal essay--a "moving evocation of Florence."

995. Render, John Mary. CRITIC 18, no.3 (December 1959): 36-37.
Writes the excellence of the prose style equals the quality of the photographs leaving the reader with the feeling of having toured the city in a most satisfying way.

996. Rolo, Charles J. "The Spirit of a City." ATLANTIC 204 (December 1959): 168-170.
Praises the "individuality, adventurous seriousness and literary brio" of the book. Claims McCarthy gives the impression that she has "ransacked the past and its works...in search for clues that lead her beyond accepted ideas."

997. YORKSHIRE POST (Leeds, G.B.) (December 3, 1959).
Argues that despite McCarthy's occasional bouts of distasteful humor when describing some of the noblest works of art, this book is a "great treasure." (Citation not verified.)

998. Sutton, Horace. "Cameras Click, Are You Packing?" SATURDAY REVIEW 42 (December 5, 1959): 40-41.
Asserts that THE STONES OF FLORENCE is a singular example of great intelligence without the dullness of traditional

travel writing. Admires McCarthy's ability to observe the present, and delve painlessly into Florentine history leaving the reader with a clear understanding of the art, relics, and the people.

999. T., W. "Portraits of Italy." IRISH TIMES (Ireland) (December 5, 1959): 7.

Wonders if McCarthy, perhaps anxious to write a text to match Hofer's vivid and "technically excellent" pictures, didn't occasionally lapse into over emphasis and overly dramatic commentary. Notes her obvious enjoyment of this city.

1000. Kirstein, Lincoln. "Arts and Monuments." NATION 189, no.20 (December 12, 1959): 450.

Claims the book contains some of the best architectural photographs of Florence and admires McCarthy's ability to reveal cities as coherent personalities.

1001. Hunter, Anna C. "Sacred Cows of Renaissance Scrutinized by Rare Critic." SAVANNAH MORNING NEWS. MAGAZINE (Savannah, Ga.) 109, no.361 (December 27, 1959): 12.

Declares that instead of reinforcing the belief that Florence is a shrine of the past, McCarthy reveals the city as endearingly brave, solid and enterprising. Remarks that in tearing down false idols, McCarthy builds new and glowing idols in the Florentine productions of architecture, art, literature and craft. States the book will delight realists, shock traditionalists and illuminate the subject for students of art.

1002. Smith, William S. "Miss McCarthy and the Medici." NEW REPUBLIC 141, no.26 (December 28, 1959): 17-18.

Writes that the peculiar merit of THE STONES OF FLORENCE is that it forces the reader to take a close look at the history of Florence. Describes McCarthy as a restorer who strips everything down in an attempt to get to the original which results in a magnification of the insignificant. Says that although Hofer's photographs are magnificent, they exude an unreal and incongruous silence giving the impression that the streets have been vacuumed of litter and people.

1003. Temko, Allan. "The City of the Lily in Evocative Pictures and Provocative Text." NEW YORK HERALD TRIBUNE BOOK REVIEW 36, no.22 (January 3, 1960): 6.

Notes various inconsistencies and inaccuracies in McCarthy's observations on Florentine art and architecture. Contends her appreciation of the city is essentially two dimensional and because her imagination is a literary one, her critiques are based on pictorial considerations. Concludes that THE STONES OF FLORENCE lacks the accuracy and depth of feeling necessary to be a success.

1004. Alexander, Sidney. "Mary McCarthy Quite Contrary." REPORTER (January 21, 1960): 44-45.

Criticizes McCarthy for a lack of research into her subject resulting in misinformation being presented as truth. Maintains that if a witness is unreliable in so many of her details, one cannot have much faith in her larger assertions. Notes the superb quality of the photographs but deplores the absence of people, stating that without people you don't have Florence.

1005. "Getting Away from It All." JOHN O'LONDON (G.B.) (January 28, 1960): 87.

Praises the abilities of both Hofer and McCarthy and hopes that they will go wandering together again.

1006. W., J. A.I.A. JOURNAL OF THE AMERICAN INSTITUTE OF ARCHITECTS (February 1960): 75.

Considers this scholarly evaluation is art history and criticism, as well as social and political history. States that McCarthy's tough sizing-up of the good and bad of Florence and its people has resulted in a lively appreciation of one of the prime fountainheads of our culture.

1007. BOOKLIST 56, no.11 (February 1, 1960): 322.

Describes this interpretation as "stimulating, forthright and original."

1008. Garrigue, Jean. "Books." ARTS 34, no.6 (March 1960): 14-15.

Discusses the details that differentiate THE STONES OF FLORENCE from the rest of the literature on Florence. Claims that whereas previous books typically were written in a spirit of submission to Florence's enchanting powers, McCarthy remains detached. Concludes the brilliant assemblage of anecdotes and observations bring fresh insight and unexpected interpretation to the city.

1009. Shapley, John. AMERICAN SCHOLAR 29, no.2 (Spring 1960): 256, 258.
    Maintains that even though McCarthy has not hesitated to mix fact with fiction, and her sporadic lapses into art criticism may be amateurish, the book represents a fascinating vista of European culture.

1010. Chiaromonte, Nicola. "In Praise of Florence." PARTISAN REVIEW 27, no.3 (Summer 1960): 558-560.
    Proposes that McCarthy's realistic description of modern Florence at the beginning of the book was meant to establish a safe distance between the Florence of contemporary mass tourism and the one she discovered.

1011. Levi, Peter. "Bootlegging." SPECTATOR (July 5, 1963): 26.
    Writes that THE STONES OF FLORENCE "is a perfectly decent introduction to Florence and yet it irritates." Feels that after all the illuminating sentences and amusing anecdotes, this work doesn't bring the social history of the architecture or the physical quality of the Renaissance to life. Asserts that he will recommend the book to acquaintances, but not to close friends.

1012. Wright, David. "The Mirror of Italy." LISTENER (January 9, 1964): 80.
    Reviews a number of travelogues on Italy including McCarthy's "deservedly celebrated" THE STONES OF FLORENCE.

   *   "Quick Guide to Europe." TIMES (London, G.B.) (June 29, 1972): 11.
    See item no. 882.

   *   BOOKS AND BOOKMEN 17, no.11 (August 1972): xvi.
    See item no. 883.

* "Holiday Reading." OBSERVER (London, G.B.) (July 15, 1979): 37.
See item no. 884.

1013. Wickers, David. "Ways and Means." TIMES EDUCATIONAL SUPPLEMENT, no.3474 (January 28, 1983): 37.
Reflects on his weekend visit to Florence and refers to THE STONES OF FLORENCE as one of the better books on the city.

* Vanni Orestano, Francesca. "Italy in Mary McCarthy's Writings: VENICE OBSERVED and THE STONES OF FLORENCE." RIVISTA DI STUDI ANGLO-AMERICANA 4-5, no.3 (1984-85): 171-179.
See item no. 885.

* "Travel Shortlist." PUNCH 289 (September 25, 1985): 61.
See item no. 886.

1014. Wyckoff, Peter C. "Florence Seduces with Stones." HOUSTON POST (October 4, 1987): F13.
Contends that the reader is able to peer into the soul of the city through McCarthy's "wry, warm, and incredulous" social and historical commentary.

ON THE CONTRARY: ARTICLES OF BELIEF

1015. KIRKUS REVIEWS 29 (July 1, 1961): 588.
Provides a brief synopsis and notes the book's characteristically "liberal" or "humanist" concerns.

1016. Jordan, Robert P. "The Magazine Rack." WASHINGTON POST AND TIMES HERALD (July 9, 1961): E5.
Refers to McCarthy's opinions on American playwrights (as portrayed in the essay "American Realist Playwrites") in a brief article on loudmouths.

1017. Eckberg, Carol A. LIBRARY JOURNAL 86 (August 1961): 2666.
      Includes this work in a list of recommended books. Credits McCarthy's ability to recognize her own limitations with a characteristic concern for truthful definition.

1018. T., W. TAMARACK REVIEW, no.21 (Autumn 1961): 89.
      Stresses that even though the majority of the essays are uncreative and tend to be more journalism than anything else--they are journalism of a high order.

1019. Hansford-Johnson, Pamela. "Between Glances in the Mirror, a Bright Pouncing Mind." NEW YORK TIMES BOOK REVIEW 66, no.39 (September 24, 1961): 6, 46.
      Remarks that some of the essays are annoyingly overstated and long. Praises the clarity and precision of McCarthy's critical views and her ability to offer opinions others believe, but are unable to express.

1020. Peterson, Virgilia. "A Score of Essays That Brightly Score." NEW YORK HERALD TRIBUNE BOOKS 38, no.8 (September 24, 1961): 7.
      Praises the entire collection, but believes the form, content and bite of "An Artist in Uniform" make it the best essay in the book.

1021. Poore, Charles. "Books of the Times." NEW YORK TIMES (September 26, 1961): 37.
      Declares that McCarthy's opinions are delivered in a brilliant and forceful style and her wide range of concerns makes this an especially interesting book.

1022. Buckmaster, Henrietta. "Miss McCarthy's 'Articles of Belief'." CHRISTIAN SCIENCE MONITOR [Eastern Ed.] 53, no.258 (September 28, 1961): 11.
      Attributes the "American" flavor of the essays to the fact that McCarthy's insights and conclusions were influenced by the American society, which has educated and shaped her. Praises her views on materialism, the political environment during the McCarthy era, and the sexual lives of American women.

Criticizes her assumption that we live "in a secular society that no longer believes in God" and suggests this results in a lack of warmth and power.

1023. Hogan, William. "Norman Mailer--The Cry Baby." SAN FRANCISCO CHRONICLE (September 28, 1961): 39.
    Refers to the publication of the book describing it as a "highly refined, if sardonic collection."

1024. Kirsch, Robert K. "Contrary Mary Wins Another Fan." LOS ANGELES TIMES,   Pt. 2 (September 29, 1961): 4.
    Reflects on his prior "allergic reaction" to McCarthy but admits that this book has won him over because of her sense of moral outrage and brilliant discernment for what is real over what is apparent.

1025. Rolo, Charles J. "Dissent." ATLANTIC 208, no.4 (October 1961): 125-126.
    Contends that all McCarthy's well-known qualities are present, but she occasionally gets carried away by contrariness.

1026. "Classified Books." BOOKLIST 58, no.3 (October 1, 1961): 79.
    Refers to ON THE CONTRARY in a list of recently published books.

1027. Jelliffe, R. A. "A Constant Concern for Underlying Truth." CHICAGO TRIBUNE. MAGAZINE OF BOOKS [Sunday Ed.] (October 1, 1961): 4.
    Admires McCarthy's ability to write with conviction, uncommon sense and epigrammatic sharpness. Credits her with being able to differentiate between superficial facts and the truth that lies beneath. Provides quotes from the collection in an attempt to show how the writing forces the reader to reconsider various topics of interest.

1028. "A New Aura." NEWSWEEK 58, no.14 (October 2, 1961): 90-91.
    Expresses disappointment that McCarthy's efforts at wit and hauteur don't quite make the grade in some of these essays. Claims she is a "yea-sayer" in others.

1029. Tucci, Niccolo. "An Observer Observed." SATURDAY
REVIEW 154 (October 7, 1961): 44.
        Provides a brief analysis of each of the essays and states that
the first and third sections are the most worthwhile.

1030. Schlesinger, Arthur, Jr. "Mary McCarthy's Vision of Reality."
NEW REPUBLIC 145, no.2449 (October 9, 1961): 23-24.
        Outlines how the book deals with reality and the fashionable
images portrayed in books, politics, plays and magazines.
Maintains the "moral quality" of the book is such that even if the
reader doesn't accept McCarthy's answers, there are benefits in
considerng her questions.

1031. "Books: Survival of the Fittest." NEW YORKER 37 (October
14, 1961): 222.
        Refers to this book in a list of recommended non-fiction.
Praises McCarthy's ability to examine a subject with such wit
and style that readers are unaware their opinions have been
challenged.

1032. Van den Haag, E. "Books in Brief." NATIONAL REVIEW 11,
no.20 (November 18, 1961): 350.
        Questions why De Beauvoir is more renowned than
McCarthy. Wonders if the French are more supportive of
intellectuals or if McCarthy is just too sophisticated.

1033. "Mary McCarthy's New Book Examines U.S. Scene."
SEATTLE TIMES. SEATTLE TIMES MAGAZINE [Sunday
Ed.] (November 19, 1961): 23.
        Describes McCarthy as uninhibited and witty and believes
there is truly "solid meat in what she says."

1034. Brooks, Rae. BOOK OF THE MONTH CLUB NEWS
(December 1961): 7.
        Praises McCarthy for her originality, conviction and brilliant
writing. Notes that when reading various passages from this
collection the reviewer found herself asking, "why couldn't I
have seen that as clearly?"

1035. Finn, James. "Critics' Choice for Christmas." COMMONWEAL 75, no.11 (December 8, 1961): 290.
    Includes this book in a list of recommended works and offers a brief review.

1036. Holzhauer, Jean. "Written in Protest." COMMONWEAL 75, no.15 (January 5, 1962): 392-393.
    Maintains that the literary essays are the best part of this book. Contends that many of McCarthy's other subjects have been treated elsewhere and that her arguments appear tired.

1037. Den, Petr. BOOKS ABROAD (Spring 1962): 212.
    Says that although McCarthy has been considered possibly the "cleverest writer the United States has ever produced," her essay on communism overlooked many important elements of the movement.

1038. Wilson, Angus. "Mary, Quite Contrary." ENCOUNTER 18, no.6 (June 12, 1962): 71-72.
    Believes McCarthy's novels are usually not very good, her attempt at journalism is often dull, and that she can be silly in the paradoxes she produces. States, however, that the book represents a process of self-discovery and praises its achievement. See also Enright's response (item no. 1044).

1039. Heppenstall, Rayner. "Mary, Mary, So Contrary." DAILY TELEGRAPH (London, G.B.) [Sunday Ed.] (July 22, 1962): 6.
    Offers a brief outline of various essays. Considers McCarthy to be "a critic, a feminist, and a deeply committed anti-politician." Observes that the book makes for exhilarating reading, although it may leave the reader with a "dull anger."

1040. Mitchell, Julian. "The Incisive Miss McCarthy." TIMES (London, G.B.) [Sunday Ed.] (July 22, 1962): 20.
    Comments that this collection of essays by McCarthy is "never more than fair or less than just."

1041. Toynbee, Philip. "An Amazon of the Intellect." OBSERVER (London, G.B.) (July 22, 1962): 19.
    Compares McCarthy with Trevelyan and says that even

though they are both liberal minded, educated writers, they belong to different species. Enjoys ON THE CONTRARY and describes McCarthy as rational, independent, practical and humane.

1042. "Partisan Pieces." TIMES (London, G.B.) (July 26, 1962): 15.
Maintains that McCarthy is not really contrary; she thinks for herself and the essays were not designed to shock or irritate. Notes that what is seen as provocative will vary from reader to reader.

1043. Cunliffe, Marcus. "Mary, Mary . . ." GUARDIAN (Manchester, G.B.) (July 27, 1962): 6.
Explores several trivial faults in the book noting they do not diminish the brilliant reflections on the problem of the self in literature. Says the dilemmas she identifies are genuine, and rendered even more so, because of her intense personal involvement with the subject matter.

1044. Enright, Dennis Joseph. "Contrary Wise." NEW STATESMAN 64, no.1637 (July 27, 1962): 115-116.
Responds to Wilson's review that stated McCarthy's novels are "not very good," conversely, describing them as superior. Proposes that McCarthy is saved by her sense of humor and praises her gift for evoking the physical presence of objects and events. Credits her with being a true listener and observer. See also Wilson's review (item no. 1038).

Also published with revisions as "Contrary Wise: The Writings of Mary McCarthy" in: CONSPIRATORS AND POETS. 127-133. Chester Springs, Pa.: Dufour; London: Chatto & Windus, 1966.

1045. Holloway, David. "Critical Americans." DAILY TELEGRAPH (London, G.B.) (July 27, 1962).
Summarizes this book and Miller's AIR CONDITIONED NIGHTMARE, comparing their views on America.

1046. Moore, Brian. "Books: Double-Headed Aquiline." SPECTATOR 209, no.6996 (July 27, 1962): 119-120.
    Traces many of the ideas in the book, focusing on McCarthy's controversial essays on literature. Believes that she approaches the level of Forster and Muir in her discussion of the novel. See also Paden's letter in response (item no. 334).

1047. De Vere White, Terence. "If She Be Proud." IRISH TIMES (Ireland) (July 28, 1962): 8.
    Provides numerous excerpts from the book and suggests that the merit of her writing lies in its clarity and comprehensiveness. Praises the book, but declares the essays in the section "Women and Literature" weren't worth reprinting.

1048. N., R. "A Bomb of a Book." WESTERN MAIL (THE NATIONAL NEWSPAPER OF WALES) [South Wales Ed.] (July 28, 1962): 6.
    Describes McCarthy's quarrel with the world as a "lover's quarrel" and maintains there isn't "one damp squib amongst all her intellectual fireworks."

1049. Harvey, Elizabeth. "Leading Blue-Nylon of Our Time." BIRMINGHAM POST (G.B.) (July 31, 1962): 4.
    Praises McCarthy's wilful, wayward flow of ideas and is impressed with her grasp of an argument. Notes, however, those who expect to meet a savage beast with teeth and claws bared will be disappointed.

1050. Hugh-Jones, Siriol. "The Snow Queen Speaks." TATLER & BYSTANDER (G.B.) (August 1, 1962): 250.
    States that everything McCarthy writes is clever and brilliant, but theorizes that all "extra clever ladies" must be careful to avoid that waspish buzz which can creep into their tone of voice.

1051. Church, Richard. "New Books: Fragrant Memories of Childhood." COUNTRY LIFE (London, G.B.) (August 2, 1962): 275-276.
    Contends that these essays reflect McCarthy's shrewd

comprehension of her experiences in the world of letters, politics and sociology.

1052. "High Priestess of the Intellect." TIMES LITERARY SUPPLEMENT (August 3, 1962): 558.
Views McCarthy as "the symbol of the critical spirit . . . shocked by nothing."

1053. L., S. "Honest Critic." IRISH INDEPENDENT (Ireland) (August 4, 1962): 10.
Comments that McCarthy reveals herself to be a typical American humanist intellectual, but what is less typical is the combination of honesty, toughness of mind, and the clarity of her writing.

1054. Nye, Robert. "Down with the Second Rate." SCOTSMAN. WEEK-END MAGAZINE (August 11, 1962): 2.
Provides a glowing review and suggests that all these brilliant essays are worth reading, particularly the two on literature. Comments that McCarthy's statement, "we know that the real world exists, but we can no longer imagine it," is the cleverest diagnosis of the failure of the modern prose imagination.

1055. O'Brien, E. D. "A Literary Lounger." ILLUSTRATED LONDON NEWS (G.B.) (August 18, 1962): 264.
Contrasts the book with Eleanor Roosevelt's autobiography, and states that, although Roosevelt has probably travelled more, it is McCarthy's views that are wider and less limiting. Criticizes Roosevelt's superficial account of her political life and finds her domineering, aggressive style unappealing. Prefers instead McCarthy's witty, conversational and highly amusing style.

1056. House, Jack. "A Quill-wielding Porcupine." EVENING TIMES (G.B.) (August 24, 1962): 15.
Writes that even though he has only spent five weeks in the United States, he can appreciate what McCarthy means when she says "we are a nation of 20,000 bathrooms with a humanist in every tub."

1057. Quigly, Isabel. "The Cutting Edge." TABLET 216, no.6379 (August 25, 1962): 786-787.

Says the collection is formidable, even hypnotic. Reports that the section on politics seemed to be the most valuable because McCarthy's honesty has the most scope and effect.

1058. Gransden, K. W. "The Listener's Book Chronicle." LISTENER (August 30, 1962): 325-326.

Argues that McCarthy is superior to De Beauvoir in the handling of concrete impressions and her essays on politics and ideas are among the most forceful written by a literary person since the death of Orwell. Admires her ability for communicating without preaching or lecturing and concludes this work will add to McCarthy's reputation for clear thinking and honest writing.

1059. Conacher, D. J. "Turning New Leaves (2)." CANADIAN FORUM 42 (September 1962): 133-134.

Examines two essays, "Settling the Colonel's Hash" and "The Fact in Fiction," to portray how McCarthy is guilty of overstating the obvious. Admires her "personal style" which pinpoints the middle ground between fiction and personal experience, urging the reader to read on.

1060. J., A. BOOKS AND BOOKMEN 7, no.12 (September 1962): 48.

Praises this collection of essays, particularly those on literature and the arts. Maintains that although few people will agree with McCarthy on everything, her realistic criticism is imbued with a rare combination of intelligence, wit, honesty and common sense.

1061. Swanson, Roy Arthur. "Recent Criticism: A Mélange." MINNESOTA REVIEW 3, no.1 (Fall 1962): 108-110.

Includes ON THE CONTRARY in a critical review of various contemporary novels. Describes the essays on literature as "brilliant analyses" and notes that McCarthy's conclusions on American playwrights "are just too good to be false."

1062. Kermode, Frank. "Anti-Cant." PARTISAN REVIEW 29, no.1
      (Winter 1962): 122-127.
      Provides an in-depth look at McCarthy's constant search for
      truth as portrayed in such essays as "Mlle. Gulliver en
      Amérique," "Humanist in the Bathtub," and "Settling the
      Colonel's Hash." Describes the two essays on literature as
      classical performances. Concludes that to disagree with
      McCarthy is to be aware that one cannot compare with her
      honesty and brilliance. See also Hamilton's response to this
      review (item no. 1332).

1063. VIRGINIA QUARTERLY REVIEW 38, no.1 (Winter 1962):
      xxvi.
      Includes the book in a list of recommended books, and
      describes it as further proof that McCarthy "is one of our finest
      essayists."

1064. Mauriac, Claude. "Mary McCarthy: A CONTRE-COURANT."
      FIGARO (June 23, 1965): 24. French.
      Writes that these essays, simultaneously instructive and
      disturbing, demonstrate McCarthy's intelligence, good nature and
      sense of humor. Focuses on McCarthy's attack on De Beauvoir
      and stands up in De Beauvoir's defence. Comments on "Artiste
      en uniforme" in which McCarthy insists that there are no
      symbols, and on "Ma confession," McCarthy's discussion of her
      split with the Communist party and her support of the
      Trotskyites.

1065. Revel, Jean-François. "Mary McCarthy à contre-courant."
      FIGARO LITTÉRAIRE (August 19-25, 1965): 4. French.
      Argues that McCarthy is a polemicist as evidenced in her
      various critical works and her public debates.

1066. Johnson, Paul. "Shock Troops." SPECTATOR 244, no.7909
      (February 9, 1980): 17-18.
      Reviews Podhoretz's BREAKING THE RANKS: A
      POLITICAL MEMOIR and briefly refers to ON THE
      CONTRARY. Says that Podhoretz and McCarthy have much in
      common--a clear-sighted devotion to liberal values, and a shared
      assessment of what is good and bad about America.

1067. Ryan, A. "Discovering." LISTENER 103, no.2649 (February 14, 1980): 220.
    Recounts McCarthy's views on symbolism portrayed in "Artists in Uniform." Suggests that the main theme of the book may be the richness and surprise of discovering who and what we are.

 * Carter, Angela. "The McCarthy Period." GUARDIAN AND GUARDIAN WEEKLY (G.B.) 122 (February 24, 1980): 22.
    See item 735.

THE GROUP

1068. KIRKUS REVIEWS 31, no.13 (July 1, 1963): 615.
    Declares McCarthy is "an exceptional social satirist" with the ability "not only to impale but move."

1069. Nyren, Dorothy. LIBRARY JOURNAL 88 (August 1963): 2928.
    Says this long awaited novel is disappointing, but it will be a best seller because of its sensationalism and the author's reputation.

1070. Sherman, Thomas B. "The Tribulations of Eight U.S. Girls." ST. LOUIS POST-DISPATCH (Mo.) (August 11, 1963): B4.
    Claims that the tone set by the incongruous wedding at the beginning and the expectations it arouses are never fulfilled. Notes that most of the episodes, including Dottie's seduction, border on the trivial and concludes that McCarthy has written a series of vignettes rather than a novel. Believes that she could have written a better book with the material at hand.

1071. Stallings, Sylvia. "The Heartless New World: And Eight Girls Who Graduated from Vassar in June of '33." HOUSTON POST [Sunday Ed.] (August 18, 1963): sec.3, 7.
    Believes McCarthy's great talent as a writer is not evident in this book.

1072. "Upper Middle-class Satirized Superbly." INDEPENDENT
JOURNAL (San Rafael, Calif.) (August 24, 1963): M14.
Proposes that this book is a satire, and that one of the things
best satirized is an O'Hara love scene.

1073. Beau-Seigneur, Jay. "Mary McCarthy's World of Women."
PENINSULA LIVING (Burlingame, Ca.) (August 25, 1963).
Says that McCarthy knows her subject--women--and treats it
with "unwavering accuracy." Confirms that she is an
"impressively talented and searching writer, an erudite and
articulate spokesman for her sex."

1074. Bergamo, Ralph. "Conjuring: THE GROUP Exhibits
Virtuosity." ATLANTA JOURNAL-CONSTITUTION [Sunday
Ed.] (August 25, 1963): D9.
Calls the novel a "social record of big city fun." Focuses on
McCarthy's technical ability, her style and the pace of the novel.

1075. Chester, Alfred. "Masterfully Dissecting the Thirties: Mary
McCarthy's Surgical Intelligence Focuses on Vassar's Crop of
'33." NEW YORK HERALD TRIBUNE BOOKS 40, no.4
(August 25, 1963): 1, 11.
Says the novel depicts the thirties "masterfully." Declares
that McCarthy's prose is "strong, direct and clean" and
concludes that the book is really about what goes on between the
sexes.

1076. Lawrence, Wes. "Mary McCarthy's Classmates Discover What
Life is Like." CLEVELAND PLAIN DEALER (Ohio) (August
25, 1963): G6.
Focuses on McCarthy's concern with sex. Suggests the book
is witty and satirical; gossipy but truthful rather than cruel.

1077. Martin, Jean. "Middlebrow Failure." CHICAGO SUN-TIMES.
SHOWCASE (August 25, 1963): 2.
Criticizes McCarthy for the lack of depth in her characters
and overabundance of detail. Comments that "a well-written
catalog of the furniture of her memory does not add up to a
novel." Believes, however, that despite its many shortcomings,

the book will be widely read, if only for the clinical account of Dottie's defloration.

1078. Mizener, Arthur. "Out of Vassar and the Town." NEW YORK TIMES BOOK REVIEW 7 (August 25, 1963): 1, 44.

Focuses on the "voice" the author uses, noting that McCarthy has maintained an objective distance from her characters. Claims that this objectivity has allowed her to probe the "particulars of people's lives."

1079. Powers, Dennis. "Mary McCarthy Critic and Novelist." OAKLAND TRIBUNE. EL DORADO (Calif.) (August 25, 1963): EL1-2.

Argues that the book is never "anything less than deft." Explores the structure and comments on the appeal of each member of the group. Sees the humor in the novel and notes that the comedy is "not superficial." Concludes that this "is one of this year's real delights."

1080. Rhodes, Richard. "Vassar May Confuse Them, But it Can't Defeat Them." KANSAS CITY STAR (Kans.) (August 25, 1963): E10.

Focuses on the effects that a Vassar education may have had on the eight women, noting Norine's comment, "I've been crippled for life." Suggests that they will all survive the experience.

1081. Smith, Miles A. "Mary Causes Shudders at Vassar." GARY POST TRIBUNE. PANORAMA (Gary, Ind.) [Sunday Ed.] (August 25, 1963): F13, F15.

Compares THE GROUP to a "hen party." Focuses on the marital status of the eight Vassar graduates and pronounces the book a bit long-winded for male readers though "women folk will find it as engrossing as one of those old party-line telephone circuits."

Also published in: PHILADELPHIA INQUIRER (September 8, 1963): D9.

1082. Wilson, Emerson W. "8 Girls, 7 Years." MORNING NEWS
(Wilmington, Del.) (August 26, 1963).
    Focuses on Dottie's curiosity about sex and how that
curiosity is satisfied. Says that the novel is "highly readable
although the blurb's description of it as a 'major novel of our
time' seems to be going much too far."

1083. Fuller, Edmund. "Reading for Pleasure: Eight Women Go
Forth." WALL STREET JOURNAL (August 28, 1963): 12.
    Argues that this is a novel without a single heroine because
all eight women form a composite protagonist. Claims that a
woman's perspective shapes both the writing and the descriptions
of sex. Concludes that THE GROUP offers no answers.

1084. Hutchens, John K. "Vassar, '33--A Gritty Oyster." NEW YORK
HERALD TRIBUNE (August 28, 1963): 21.
    Claims that it is difficult to say just what McCarthy is about
in this novel. Finds fault with its episodic nature but says that
McCarthy's wit, intelligence and her "hard, good style" shine
through. Expresses disappointment in the book because so much
was expected of it.

1085. Murray, James G. "Woman's World in Writing." LONG
ISLAND CATHOLIC (N.Y.) (August 29, 1963): 17.
    Argues that McCarthy's vision of the Vassar group is cruel,
malicious and "just plain cockeyed."

1086. N., R. "Miss McCarthy: So Cold and Cerebral." CHRISTIAN
SCIENCE MONITOR [Eastern Ed.] (August 29, 1963): 11.
    Accuses McCarthy of dealing with her characters in the same
condescending way they deal with those who are not Vassar
graduates. Concludes that the book is not as sophisticated as
McCarthy would suggest, but rather unsavory gossip that would
have been better left unwritten.

1087. Poore, Charles. "Mary McCarthy's Lives of the Vassari." NEW
YORK TIMES (August 29, 1963): 27.
    Writes that the book is built around three essential elements:
politics, art and love; and that these elements connect the main
characters.

1088. Rogers, W. G. "Vassar '33 Girls Face the World." NEW YORK WORLD TELEGRAM AND THE SUN (August 29, 1963): 21.
    Argues that this is a "remarkable novel ... rich with life and full of people you will not forget. It is a salute to the searching and independent mind, and a savage assault on all that is purposeless, routine and trite."

1089. Cournos, John. "Eight from Vassar." BULLETIN (Philadelphia, Pa.) [Evening Ed.] (August 30, 1963): 14.
    Suggests that the book is not about what women do with their higher education, but what they do with their sexual desires.

1090. Price, Emerson. "Eight Girls Are in THE GROUP." CLEVELAND PRESS. SHOW TIME (Ohio) (August 30, 1963): 13.
    Notes that McCarthy has undertaken a difficult task and achieved her aims.

1091. Burton, Hal. "Eight Portraits Etched in Acid." NEWSDAY (Long Island, N.Y.) 23, no.306 (August 31, 1963): 37.
    Declares that this is a book of disillusionment and that McCarthy "has missed the boat."

1092. Hicks, Granville. "What to Be After Poughkeepsie." SATURDAY REVIEW 46, no.35 (August 31, 1963): 19, 30.
    Writes that this is McCarthy's best book and that it will be remembered as social history. Notes the compassion with which she writes about the eight Vassar graduates, sympathizing with them rather than ridiculing their mean lives. See also Hicks' second review (item no. 1158).

1093. Hinson, Elizabeth. "Expanded Picture Is Lacking Here." CHARLOTTE NEWS (N.C.) (August 31, 1963): A6.
    Criticizes the novel for its lack of focus and purpose. Sees few redeeming features, finding even the technical devices which hold the book together "mechanical." Claims that THE GROUP is little more than a "shallow-play of manners and morality."

1094. Kauffmann, Stanley. "Miss McCarthy's Era." NEW REPUBLIC 149, no.9-10 (August 31, 1963): 25-28.
    Does not see the book as an evaluation of the decline of progress but rather a "surface reproduction" of the thirties.

1095. Mathewson, Ruth Murray. "The Vassar Joke." COLUMBIA UNIVERSITY FORUM 6, no.4 (Fall 1963): 10-16.
    Discusses the novel in terms of Bergson's theory of comedy. Finds all the characters comic figures and proposes that the joke of the book lies in McCarthy's understated description of Kay's death. Notes the central question of the book is the ability to learn. See also Hicks' review (item no. 1158).

1096. Barrett, William. "Reader's Choice." ATLANTIC MONTHLY 212, no.3 (September 1963): 120-121.
    States that McCarthy writes with the "understanding and compassion" that were often missing in her earlier works. Proposes that her characters finally come alive and into their own. See also Mailer's review (item no. 1129).

1097. Fadiman, Clifton. "Reading I've Liked." HOLIDAY 34, no.3 (September 1963): 17.
    Declares that if McCarthy were a man, her "bitchiness" would be considered "satirical power" and her descriptions of the seduction scene would be attributed to "candor" and "honesty." Suggests that this is a "feminist novel," McCarthy "implying that in our world the cards are stacked against intelligent, well-bred women."

1098. Highet, Gilbert. BOOK OF THE MONTH CLUB NEWS (N.Y.) (September 1963): 7.
    Suggests that the book focuses on the ridiculous and pathetic jokes that nature plays on women. Feels that McCarthy handles it with "a skillful blend of clinical realism and sadly smiling sympathy." Calls attention to her superb technical skill.

1099. Peterson, Virgilia. "When a Girl Graduates." COSMOPOLITAN 155 (September 1963): 24.
    Focuses on McCarthy's preoccupation with sex and her description of how the characters in the book deal with sexual

relations. Describes the book as a social history of the American middle and upper middle class.

1100. BOOKLIST 60, no.1 (September 1, 1963): 31.
Refers to the novel as "strangely humorless" and overloaded with details.

1101. Bunke, Joan. "Miss McCarthy's New Novel is Satirical and Abrasive." DES MOINES REGISTER (Iowa) [Sunday Ed.] (September 1, 1963): 5-F.
Presents THE GROUP as a social history of a particular era. States that McCarthy offers a myriad of details about a world of leftist politics, psychoanalysis and sex. Seems to be uncomfortable with a woman writer who writes so candidly about sex, but concludes that her sheer ability as a novelist ought to make her male counterparts "a bit uneasy."

1102. Cannon, Cordelia Penn. "Mary McCarthy's 'Examined Lives Not Worth Living'." GREENSBORO DAILY NEWS (N.C.) (September 1, 1963): D3.
Refers to McCarthy's essay "Characters in Fiction" and suggests that she proves her own point in THE GROUP, "sex annihilates identity." Concludes that it is sad to see McCarthy delve into "voyeurism" and a "clinical exploration of intimate and personnel incidents," observing that if this is a "major novel of our times," for which a Guggenheim Fellowship was granted, as the jacket states, we have indeed reached a "cultural old age."

1103. Corddry, Mary. "Eight Girls Depict an Era." SUN (Baltimore, Md.) [Sunday Ed.] (September 1, 1963): A5.
Comments that "the author provides objective, penetrating, readable observations of an era as seen through the experience of eight specific individuals." Notes that while all eight girls have ambitious plans for the future, they all rely on the security of their established backgrounds and social positions.

1104. Culligan, Glendy. "The Girls Faced Life in a Brave New World." WASHINGTON POST (September 1, 1963): G6.
Discusses McCarthy's attention to detail in her descriptions of the girls and their love affairs. Notes the novel's solid

historical basis and praises McCarthy as "a social historian
without peer." Remarks, however, that McCarthy lacks
sensitivity and for a novel of sensibility one must "turn to
another author."

1105. Erickson, Shirley. "8 Vassar Girls at Large." DETROIT FREE
PRESS (September 1, 1963): B5.
Comments that McCarthy has presented an accurate and
compelling picture of the New Deal era.

1106. McAleer, John J. BEST SELLERS 23, no.11 (September 1,
1963): 180.
Compares the structure of THE GROUP to Dreiser's THE
BULWARK stating that both novels begin with a marriage and
end with a death. Suggests that given the unsure and morally
questionable age which forms the setting for the characters, it is
no surprise that the eight Vassar graduates cannot succeed. Notes
that McCarthy really is a moralist who relishes telling the
readers about sin and never fails to pass moral judgment.

1107. McIntosh, Joan. "Vassar '33." SOUTH BEND TRIBUNE (Ind.)
(September 1, 1963): 10.
Discusses the real life Vassar experience and comments on
McCarthy's exploration of the lives of the eight women and their
progress from university to a life beyond.

1108. McKenna, J.H., Jr. "Mary McCarthy Turns Clinical Eye on
Vassar Fledglings Out in the World." SAVANNAH NEWS.
MAGAZINE (Savannah, Ga.) (September 1, 1963): 8.
Suggests that the episodic quality of the novel is the main
flaw. Explains that this technique does not permit any one
character to emerge as the heroine and therefore does not permit
the reader to identify with the character. Concludes that although
this is not a "great" novel, it is a "good" one.

1109. Newquist, Roy. "THE GROUP: Intimate, Powerful." CHICAGO
HEIGHTS STAR (September 1, 1963): 6.
Praises McCarthy for her clever portrayal of a slice of
American society. Comments that the eight women are not meant
to be representative, but rather individuals, each carefully drawn

and possessing a particular point of view. Claims that the quality of McCarthy's writing, always excellent, gains a new level of perfection in this novel--a book that will not easily be forgotten.

1110. Radmilovich, Walt. "Another Triumph for Mary McCarthy." DAILY OKLAHOMAN [Sunday Ed.] (September 1, 1963): D9.
   Proposes that the heroine of the novel is not one character, but a composite of all eight Vassar graduates. Argues that McCarthy's novels "are reviews of other lives in the world of half truths between fiction and reality" and as such, THE GROUP is a probing analysis of life at the time. Concludes, however, that this is not McCarthy's best novel and doubts that she can be completely satisfied with it.

1111. Thomas, Lucy. "McCarthy Novel Highly Interesting." SOUTHWEST TIMES-RECORD (Fort Smith, Ark.) (September 1, 1963): D2.
   Suggests that the eight girls are the collective heroine of the story but that Kay, around whom the story is woven, is the most completely presented and perhaps the most pitiable. Concludes that their journey to maturity is "highly interesting and brilliantly presented."

1112. Warrington, Margaret. "Eight Women Make Tedious Heroines." MIAMI NEWS (September 1, 1963): B6.
   Criticizes the book saying that McCarthy's writing lacks style, "wit and brilliance." Says that she has failed to depict the reality of women emerging into the political and economic life of America.

1113. Wellejus, Ed. "Ed Wellejus' Bookshelf." ERIE TIMES NEWS. MAGAZINE 7, no.34 (September 1, 1963): 5.
   Cautions that "the romantic lives" of the eight girls are outlined with "brutal clarity" which may offend some readers.

1114. Wilkins, Margaret. "Propriety Was Not for Them." VIRGINIAN PILOT (Norfolk, Va.) (September 1, 1963).
   Focuses on the socio-historical aspects of the novel and criticizes McCarthy for not giving her heroines sufficient space.

Says "McCarthy seems to create her characters merely to score a point. This accomplished, they are caused to vanish."

1115. "Eight to Beware." TIME 82, no.10 (September 6, 1963): 86-88.

    Sees the main theme as the war between the sexes. Claims that THE GROUP is a female dominated book in which the males come off badly. Suggests that this is probably because no male can quite measure up to the sisterhood.

1116. Sullivan, Richard. "Mary McCarthy Gives Some Vassar Alumnae 'F' As Human Beings." CHICAGO TRIBUNE. MAGAZINE OF BOOKS [Sunday Ed.] (September 15, 1963): 4.

    Argues that THE GROUP is cluttered with annoying details and appears to be a collection of short stories rather than a novel with a central theme or purpose. Refers to THE GROUP as "sophisticated" in the most pejorative sense of the term.

1117. Hyman, Stanley Edgar. "The Girls of Slender Talents." NEW LEADER 46 (September 16, 1963): 17-18.

    Compares THE GROUP with two other "synthetic novels": MISS BANNISTER'S GIRLS by Louise Tanner and THE GIRLS OF SLENDER MEANS by Muriel Spark. Declares that McCarthy has "neither a fictive imagination nor any sense of novelistic form."

1118. Gardiner, Harold C. AMERICA 109 (September 21, 1963): 317-319.

    Labels the book "feminine gossip" and claims that it shows none of McCarthy's former brilliance. Proposes that she has written a compassionless story about corrupt, "moral cretins."

1119. Kiely, Robert. "The New Wayfarers." NATION 197, no.8 (September 21, 1963): 163-165.

    Explains that the novel focuses on the opposite characters of Kay and Polly, however, neither one is the main character, that role being reserved for "the group." Comments that the "voice" the author uses to describe each character tends to reflect the character's personality.

1120. "On Mary McCarthy: In the End, Vassar's Like Anywhere Else." MACLEAN'S MAGAZINE 76, no.18 (September 21, 1963): 65-66.

Proposes that McCarthy has produced a detailed critique of the ideals of the time and shown that the eight women are just like many others despite their Vassar education. Concludes that this is an important and fascinating book.

1121. Ohmann, Carol B., and Richard M. Ohmann. "Class Notes from Vassar." COMMONWEAL 79 (September 27, 1963): 12-15.

Argues that as a realist, McCarthy's aim is to make the reader see society the way it is. Notes, however, that her characters never develop; they do not grow older or wiser but are constantly surprised and caught off guard by life. Concludes that while she will never be another Tolstoy, the "connection" is there.

1122. "Books." PLAYBOY 10, no.10 (October 1963): 42.

Claims that the novel is merely "pretty good" because the themes are predictable and their treatment superficial, there is no biting wit and no real characterization. Concludes that "a book that combines the sociopolitical grasp of a Koestler with the precise bite of a Waugh, a marriage of extraordinary intellect and humanity--that novel it isn't."

1123. DeMott, Benjamin. "Poets, Presidents and Preceptors." HARPER'S MAGAZINE 227, no.1361 (October 1963): 98 + .

Contends that McCarthy is an "objective moralist" and the reader always knows "where he is in moral terms." Suggests that the unwritten sin of most of the characters is that of obliviousness; they are unaware of the real problems of the world around them, focusing their attention on trivial ones.

1124. Lowrey Ross, Mary. "The Vassar Version of the American Way." SATURDAY NIGHT 78, no.9 (October 1963): 34.

Offers a portrait of "the Vassar graduate" and claims that as a Vassar graduate herself, McCarthy can well understand and depict her fellow alumnae.

1125. Podhoretz, Norman. "Mary McCarthy and the Leopard's Spots."
      SHOW 3 (October 1963): 52, 54-55.
          Focuses on the trivialities that make up the book and
      proposes that the joke is really on McCarthy herself for creating
      such shallow characters and insignificant situations. See also
      reviews by Mailer (item no. 1129) and Aldridge (item no. 1205).

1126. Holzhauer, Jean. CRITIC 22, no.2 (October-November 1963):
      73-74.
          Argues that this is a tough-minded book that shows eight
      Vassar graduates grappling with the problems of modern society.
      Calls it comic, in a Chaplinesque way.

1127. Knapp, William. "Should College Girls Go to College?"
      REPORTER 29, no.6 (October 10, 1963): 60-63.
          Dissects THE GROUP referring to food recipes McCarthy
      lists in the book. Says she "stirs into her prose, like Sun Maid
      Raisins or Baker's Chocolate Chips, clichés that would jolt even
      an editor of a woman's magazine." See also Hartt's and Hunt's
      letters (item no. 345).

1128. "Mary, Mary, Quite Contrary Grows Her Garden Nicely."
      TIMES (London, G.B.) [Sunday Ed.] (October 13, 1963): 31.
          Provides some first-hand biographical information about
      McCarthy gained during an interview. Offers McCarthy's notion
      of what the book is about--a period in America from the
      inauguration of Roosevelt. Suggests that the controlled clarity
      and wit of the novel will be overshadowed by the "sexy" bits.

1129. Mailer, Norman. "The Mary McCarthy Case." NEW YORK
      REVIEW OF BOOKS 1, no.4 (October 17, 1963): 1-3.
          Debates whether or not McCarthy has succeeded in writing a
      great novel. Quotes from two opposing critics, Norman
      Podhoretz and William Barrett, and proceeds to pass judgment
      on the novel. Proposes that given the characters and situation,
      the odds are "a hundred-to-one or a thousand- to-one against
      bringing off the book" and that McCarthy "came just far enough
      to irritate the life out of us." Argues that the book fails, by being
      good but not good enough, that it is great sociology but not great
      literature. Concludes that one day she might get tough enough

"to go it with the boys." See also reviews by Barrett (item no. 1096); Podhoretz (item no. 1125); Hicks (item no. 1158); and Meyer Spack's article (item no. 465).

Also published in:
Mailer, Norman. CANNIBALS AND CHRISTIANS. 133-140. New York: Dial Press, 1966; London: André Deutsch, 1967; New York: Dell Pub., 1967; London: Spere Books, 1969; New York: Dell Pub., 1970; and New York: Pinnacle Books, 1981.

Spacks, Patricia Meyer, ed. CONTEMPORARY WOMEN NOVELISTS: A COLLECTION OF CRITICAL ESSAYS. 75-84. Englewood Cliffs, N.J.: Prentice-Hall, 1977. (Spacks also refers to McCarthy in the Introduction.)

* Chamberlain, John Renssealer. "The Conservative Miss McCarthy." NATIONAL REVIEW 15, no.16 (October 22, 1963): 353-355.
See item no. 730.

1130. Rowland, Stanley J., Jr. "Like Having the Measles." CHRISTIAN CENTURY 80 (October 23, 1963): 1309.
Says that McCarthy has written a novel in which the characters are so superfluous they are meaningless. Reduces the novel to the level of dirty laundry and personal issues better left untold.

1131. Adams, Robert Martin. "Books." ESQUIRE 60 (November 1963): 39-40, 47.
Reduces the eight Vassar girls to their basic components and suggests that the female characters are shallow and spiritless. Finds a real absence of male characters and notes the few that do appear are less than ideal. Argues that the book ends neither like a comedy nor a tragedy but like an Ibsen problem "with a joyful, permanent, divorce."

1132. Johnson, Lucy. "McCarthy and Grass." PROGRESSIVE
(Madison, Wis.) 27, no.11 (November 1963): 49-51.
Argues that although structure has never been McCarthy's
strong point, the ability to capture a period and a mood is, and
with these aspects she has succeeded.

1133. Connolly, Cyril. "A Woman's World in Flower." TIMES
(London, G.B.) [Sunday Ed.] (November 3, 1963): 36.
Argues that McCarthy owes the inspiration for the book to
Emile Zola. Believes that the novel was conceived as a
sociological document, McCarthy viewing her characters in
historical perspective. Concludes that the book is "extremely
funny and totally adult--by far her best book."

Also published in: Connolly, Cyril. THE EVENING
COLONNADE. 296-299. New York: Harcourt Brace
Jovanovich, 1975.

1134. Quinton, Anthony. "When Girls Grow Up." DAILY
TELEGRAPH (London, G.B.) [Sunday Ed.] (November 3,
1963): 17.
Discusses McCarthy's exposure of human frailty. Notes the
weaknesses of the various characters and the graphic
psychological details offered to the reader in this "a fine old
traditional novel."

1135. Wyndham, Francis. "Eight Smart Girls." OBSERVER.
WEEKEND REVIEW (London, G.B.) (November 3, 1963):
Begins by focusing on the detached way in which McCarthy
depicts sexual encounters. Argues that her book is totally
objective to the extent that one element,"sympathy, subjectivity,
poetry, mystery--there is no exact word for it," is missing. Says
that McCarthy loses control over the book's construction and,
contrary to opinion, believes the last chapter is a mistake.

1136. Brooke, Jocelyn. LISTENER 70 (November 7, 1963): 764.
Suggests that McCarthy's purpose is not "primarily satirical"
and that "THE GROUP seems to be the American equivalent of
LES MANDARINS, with Sartre left out."

1137. "New Fiction." TIMES (London, G.B.) (November 7, 1963): 15.

Argues that this novel is concerned with the paradox of the progressive woman and concludes that because it is "in some ways the most outrageously distorted of her novels, it is also perhaps the most enjoyable."

Also published as "Paradox of the Progressive Woman" in: TIMES WEEKLY REVIEW (November 14, 1963): 13.

1138. "The Vassar Girls." TIMES LITERARY SUPPLEMENT, no.3219 (November 7, 1963): 901.

Focuses on the style of the novel and the idea that the girls are all identical except for Lakey, who is a lesbian. Argues that like Lessing's and De Beauvoir's heroines, McCarthy's are "women of courage, intelligence and class but with a fatal streak." Claims that McCarthy gets too bogged down in details to give us anything more.

1139. Shrapnel, Norman. "Reunion." GUARDIAN (G.B.) (November 8, 1963): 9.

Argues that although McCarthy has the talent to make it appear that she is giving all the details, in reality all she offers is a surface view--"skin deep, shadow deep."

1140. Gross, John. "Class of '33." NEW STATESMAN 66, no.1705 (November 15, 1963): 702-703.

Writes that "we are presented not with a neatly contrived artificial pattern, but with the loose ends and ragged edges of life itself." Emphasizes McCarthy's comments in the PARIS REVIEW interview and concludes with a comment on what Jane Austen might have thought of McCarthy. See also interview (item no. 273).

1141. Hickey, William. "Hits and Misses in the World of Books." DAILY EXPRESS (London, G.B.) (November 15, 1963): 3.

Notes that while the British publisher Rupert Hart-Davis turned this book down, Weidenfeld and Nicholson published it and are reaping many benefits.

1142. Mitchell, Julian. "Nothing But the Facts, Ma'am." SPECTATOR (November 15, 1963): 633.

Suggests that anyone who writes a novel should really begin by wondering if the story would not be better told in some other medium. Argues that both the group itself and the novel lack any real "centre" and that the book is just a collection of unconnected episodes that leave the reader with the sense that something has been left out.

1143. Hill, W. B. AMERICA 109 (November 23, 1963): 683.

Notes that the novel is "neatly woven" but the writing is "undistinguished" and the girls "eminently forgettable."

1144. L., S. L. ATLANTIC ADVOCATE 54, no.4 (December 1963): 68.

Suggests that the novel is about "the recline and pall" of eight fictitious Vassar graduates. Notes that it is "less gloomy" than McCarthy's other books and a best seller probably because of its "snob appeal."

1145. Rogers, Thomas. "A Survey of Recent Fiction." COMMENTARY 36, no.6 (December 1963): 488-489.

Questions why McCarthy is often referred to as "brilliant." Claims that she has the style "of a writer on whom nothing is lost and for whom everything figures." Suggests that in all her works she writes a "drama of the sexes" but always skimps on the attention paid to her male characters.

1146. Whitehorn, Katharine. "Three Women." ENCOUNTER 21, no.6 (December 1963): 78-82.

Compares McCarthy's, Spark's and Murdoch's new novels and says that the Spark and McCarthy would "have had the publishers sending out for champagne after the first chapter," but Murdoch "would probably never have got published at all." Focuses on McCarthy's sense of history and her creation of characters, arguing that she might have written a better book had she focused on the four main portraits.

1147. Pollock, Venetia. "New Fiction." PUNCH 245 (December 4, 1963): 828.

    States that THE GROUP is "tremendous fun" and praises McCarthy for depicting women so well. Says that THE GROUP "comes over as very real and endearing," indeed its only fault lies in the fact that McCarthy got too involved in some of the characters and upset the balance of the book.

1148. Igoe, W. J. "Eight Little Maids from Vassar." TABLET 217, no.6447 (December 14, 1963): 1360.

    Suggests that this novel is a series of portraits in which each girl is made to appear "defenseless before the unselfconsciously predatory males she encounters." Believes that "the agony of women and the quite diabolical egotism of the men . . . is something inseparable from society."

1149. "The Year That Was: Books." NEWSWEEK 62, no.26 (December 23, 1963): B76, B78.

    Refers to THE GROUP as the year's "supreme best-selling novel." Claims that McCarthy has crammed "every deficiency" into the book and has managed to lament the lives of several Vassar alumnae.

1150. Cargill, Oscar. KEY REPORTER (Washington, D.C.) (Winter 1963-1964): 5.

    Says this is McCarthy's best novel--a variation on THE GRAND HOTEL.

1151. Lalley, J. M. "Bovaryism: East Coast." MODERN AGE 8 (Winter 1963-1964): 94-98.

    Provides some information on the founding of Vassar and the philosophy of the institution, and argues that McCarthy and her characters are not typical Vassar graduates. Declares that "as an artistic effort, the novel must be accounted an almost total failure . . . [but that as] a social document . . . and as an index to the prevailing literary climate, the book has much interest and importance."

1152. Sale, Roger. "The Newness of the Novel." HUDSON REVIEW
16, no.4 (Winter 1963-1964): 601-609.
Provides an overview of the novels published in 1963.
Discusses THE GROUP and Spark's THE GIRLS OF
SLENDER MEANS, suggesting a "kind of double
ventriloquism" that makes two books by two different authors
seem the same. Refers to McCarthy and Spark as "middle-aged"
ladies who write in a "bored, detached tone."

1153. Blöcker, Günter. "Abschied vom Amerikanischen Traum."
MERKUR 18 (1964): 1078-1080. German.
Praises McCarthy's freshness of vision, humor and critical
intelligence which result in a congruency of reality and her
literary vision. Traces this to McCarthy's own experience of life
at Vassar College and her background as an essayist and literary
critic.

1154. "Novels of 1963: THE GROUP." In T.L.S.: ESSAYS &
REVIEWS FROM THE TIMES LITERARY SUPPLEMENT:
1963, 105-107. Vol.2. London: Oxford Univ. Press, 1964. Not
seen.

  *   Podhoretz, Norman. "John O'Hara and Mary McCarthy." In
DOINGS AND UNDOINGS: THE FIFTIES AND AFTER IN
AMERICAN WRITING, 76-93. New York: Noonday Press,
1964.
See item no. 820.

1155. Maclaren-Ross, J. "Miss McCarthy and the Class of '33."
LONDON MAGAZINE 3 (January 1964): 98-101.
Suggests that McCarthy's "bland, impersonal" description of
sex sets her apart from most female novelists who usually overly
romanticize the act.

1156. Lyons, Leonard. "The Lyons Den." NEW YORK POST
(January 17, 1964): 41.
Predicts that THE GROUP will be the number one favorite
to win the 1964 National Book Award.

1157. Cook, Eleanor. "Group Dynamics." CANADIAN FORUM 43 (February 1964): 260.

Proposes that the book is about progress and progressive ideas. Suggests that it might have been wise to make Lakey the main figure in the novel and let her serve as the focal point for the others because she is the most intelligent.

1158. Hicks, Granville. "THE GROUP on Second Meeting." SATURDAY REVIEW 47, no.8 (February 22, 1964): 51-52.

Rescinds his former position on THE GROUP as a result of reading Mathewson's and Mailer's analyses. Believes the joke is on him and that his previous review in which he saw the book as a social history was entirely wrong. Argues now that McCarthy felt her subjects "too obviously ridiculous to be worthy of satiric treatment." See also reviews by Mathewson (item no. 1095); Mailer (item no. 1129) and Hicks (item no. 1092).

1159. Darrell, Margery. "Mary McCarthy and THE GROUP." LOOK 28, no.4 (February 25, 1964): 106-110.

Describes McCarthy's return to Vassar and conversations with former graduates. Notes the parallels between McCarthy's life and that of her fictional character Kay.

1160. Fruchter, Norman. "A Realist Perspective." STUDIES ON THE LEFT (Madison, Wis.) 4, no.2 (Spring 1964): 110-134.

Offers first an analysis of Lukas' studies on the novel and then examines four books, concentrating on "form". Argues that the characters in THE GROUP all have notions about society which are slowly but systematically destroyed during the course of the book, and finds McCarthy's inability to create characters a major flaw. Suggests that her listing of objects makes the style "heavily naturalistic." Concludes that instead of the humor inherent in the situation we are only left with McCarthy's "dry chuckle."

1161. Howes, Barbara. "Three Women Writers." MASSACHUSETTS REVIEW 5, no.3 (Spring 1964): 583-586.

Says McCarthy "has seriously failed us" with this "interminable documentary of the cliché."

1162. Kuehn, Robert E. "Fiction Chronicle." WISCONSIN STUDIES
      IN CONTEMPORARY LITERATURE 5, no.1 (Winter-Spring
      1964): 77-82.
         Points out that this book is not a novel but a "meticulously
      researched sociology." Claims that as a sociology text it deserves
      to be placed in a time capsule, but as a novel, it is flawed
      because the characters do not come alive. Goes on to compare it
      to Spark's novel, THE GIRLS OF SLENDER MEANS, in
      which the characters are given scope and opportunity to
      experience and explore life.

1163. Patton, Frances Gray. "Mary McCarthy's Sad Comedy."
      SHENANDOAH 15, no.3 (Spring 1964): 70-71.
         Poses the question: does this novel carry a message with
      sociological implications or is it simply the story of a particular
      group of women at a particular time? Feels that McCarthy might
      have written an incomparable comedy of manners had she not set
      out to prove that she was capable of stern critical judgments.

1164. Soule, George. "Must a Novelist Be an Artist?" CARLETON
      MISCELLANY 5, no.2 (Spring 1964): 92-98.
         Discusses the novel's literary style and draws comparisons
      with Spark's THE GIRLS OF SLENDER MEANS. Suggests that
      McCarthy's use of trivial detail does not enhance the novel and
      that her attempt to portray real life often results in clichés.
      Argues that even though McCarthy is a novelist, she is definitely
      not an artist and the contrived structure of the book lessens its
      impact.

1165. Cook, Bruce. "Mary McCarthy: One of Ours?" CATHOLIC
      WORLD 199, no.1189 (April 1964): 34-42.
         Approaches the book from a Catholic point of view. Argues
      that the characters, except for Lakey and Polly, are "dreary,
      inane creatures." Says Polly is more interesting because she has
      McCarthy's own background--her Catholic girlhood. Goes on to
      discuss McCarthy's immaturity and notes that none of her
      characters get any pleasure from sexual intercourse. Concludes
      that she has been "frozen in the haughty moral posture of her
      Catholic girlhood."

1166. Bowen, Croswell. "Author Reviews GROUP Cites Misuse of VC Name." VASSAR MISCELLANY NEWS (April 29, 1964): 2, 6.

Notes, with some pleasure, that THE GROUP did not win the 1964 National Book Award. Argues that McCarthy exploits the name of Vassar in order to write a novel about sex. Cites one Vassar father who has threatened to take legal steps against any movie company making a film of this book.

1167. Kenworthy, Christopher. "Mary McCarthy Shocks the Class of '17." EVENING STANDARD (London, G.B.) (May 7, 1964): 7.

Reveals that McCarthy finished THE GROUP ten years before it was published and in fact, worried that it was not saleable. Quotes her as saying that chapter two was the most controversial but that she was determined to publish it as written, supporting her decision with the belief that the publication of LOLITA and TROPIC OF CANCER changed the way Americans look at censorship.

1168. De Bellis, Jack. "THE GROUP and John Updike." SEWANEE REVIEW (Sewanee, Tenn.) 72, no.3 (Summer 1964): 531-536.

Examines a collection of novels that are "organized to a great extent around the conflict between the desire for love and the necessity of self-knowledge." Argues, in this context, that McCarthy's style and excessive use of detail does not "permit a serious confrontation of the two worlds of value."

1169. Wood, Frederick T. "Current Literature, 1963." ENGLISH STUDIES (Amsterdam) (June 1964): 259-269.

Mentions THE GROUP as one of the best novels published in 1963. Focuses on Norine, noting that because she expected so little from life, she is the only one not disappointed and disillusioned.

1170. G., E. TEMPO PRESENTE 9, no.8 (August 1964): 73-75. Italian. Not seen.

1171. Mazzaro, Jerome L. "Where Have All the Flowers Gone?"
NORTH AMERICAN REVIEW n.s., 1, no.3 (Autumn 1964):
72-75.
Proposes that what McCarthy has written is a mock chronicle
about, and a disillusionment with, the idea of progress. Notes
that her novels are based on "natural symbols" rather than
mythic or traditionally symbolic figures and themes, but finds
that she is unsuccessful in her choice of incidents to illustrate the
failure of progress in THE GROUP. Compares McCarthy to De
Beauvoir saying that while both wrote well about childhood
experiences, they failed to write as well about adult experience.

1172. Hartung, Rudolf. "Die Kunst des Bauchredens. Über den Roman
"Die Clique" der Amerikanischen Schriftstellerin Mary
McCarthy." DIE ZEIT. WOCHENZEITUNG FUR POLITIK,
WIRTSCHAFT, HANDEL AND KULTUR. HAMBURG 19,
no.35 (September 4, 1964): 12. German.
Criticizes her previous work, especially her "flippant"
critique of Arendt's book on the Eichmann trial. Notes that
Helmut Heissenbüttel considers THE GROUP to be one of the
important works of the epoch. Disagrees with this assessment
and categorizes THE GROUP as a series of witty observations
on womens' lives which lack real depth. See also Heissenbüttel's
article (item no. 350).

1173. Abrahams, William. "After the Daisy Chain." PARTISAN
REVIEW 31, no.1 (Winter 1964): 107-110.
Refers to this as a "public novel" and discusses the
relationship of art and life as depicted by McCarthy. Notes her
attention to fact and how she mixes the fact with fiction. Notes
that the author's voice is silent throughout the novel but
concludes that this serves to remind the reader "of what has been
sacrificed to obtain the virtuoso style-that-is-no-style of THE
GROUP."

1174. Higginson, Jeannette. "The Parish, the Family and Other
Groups." MINNESOTA REVIEW 4, no.2 (Winter 1964):
253-262.
Claims that THE GROUP is a technical advancement over

McCarthy's other novels and that the interesting, satirical subject matter produces the anticipated "ill-natured enjoyment."

1175. "Notes on Current Books." VIRGINIA QUARTERLY REVIEW 40, no.1 (Winter 1964): viii.

Attributes a very sardonic viewpoint to McCarthy and claims that she has created characters who, failing miserably in the real world, "endure more agonies then any [Samuel] Richardson could have invented."

1176. Owens, Patricia. "Eight Heroines, No Hero." TAMARACK REVIEW, no.30 (Winter 1964): 93-94.

Argues that the book is neither tragedy nor satire but rather on the level of an article from LADIES HOME JOURNAL.

1177. Franck, Jacques. "Mary McCarthy: LE GROUPE." REVUE GENERALE BELGE (Brussels), no.6 (1965): 99-103. French.

Argues that the book is written with incredible feminine cruelty. Suggests that THE GROUP becomes a refuge for its members who all think and act with one voice, a very American characteristic. Proposes that the novel is really like a Bergman film; very few, if any, events of note, just the normal occurrences of day-to-day life. Concludes that she has written the most sensitive and intelligent commentary on humanity to appear in a long time.

1178. Petersen, Clarence. "Personal Choices for Personal Pleasure." CHICAGO TRIBUNE. BOOKS TODAY [Sunday Ed.] (February 28, 1965): 13.

Comments that she "nit-picked" her characters "down to the bone."

1179. Taylor, Angela. "Clothes From the 1930's Set Scene for Actresses." NEW YORK TIMES (June 28, 1965).

Comments on the authentic costumes used in the film.

Also published in: NEW YORK TIMES ENCYCLOPEDIA OF FILM. Vol. 8. New York: New York Times, 1984.

1180. Lerman, Leo. "Group on: THE GROUP." MADEMOISELLE
61 (September 1965): 166-168.
     Offers comments of the actors playing the various parts in
the movie. Notes the director's feelings that the film script is
better than the novel.

1181. "Eight Girls from College." OBSERVER. WEEKLY COLOUR
SUPPLEMENT (London, G.B.) (October 31, 1965): 41-42.
     Provides a description of each of the main characters of this
"soon to be released" film.

1182. FILMFACTS 9, no.7 (1966): 61-64.
     Offers a synopsis of the story and information about the cast.
Presents excerpts from several critiques.

   *   Walcutt, Charles Child. "In and Out of College with Mary
McCarthy." In MAN'S CHANGING MASK: MODES AND
METHODS OF CHARACTERIZATION IN FICTION,
292-294. Minneapolis: Univ. of Minnesota Press, 1966.
     See item no. 733.

1183. "Briefing: When and Where." OBSERVER (London, G.B.)
(February 6, 1966): 22.
     Comments that the novel is "honed on ruthless wit and
insight."

1184. Cluny, Claude Michel. "A Propos de Mary McCarthy."
NOUVELLE REVUE FRANÇAISE 14, no.159 (March 1966):
527-528. French.
     Proposes that although McCarthy is considered to be a great
American writer, this book lacks compassion and empathy and
her characters are merely mannequins. Argues, however, that the
ideas are well presented and that her talent must be
acknowledged.

1185. Robe. VARIETY (March 2, 1966): 6.
     Concentrates on the acting in the film and notes with regret
that while the most beautiful woman, Candice Bergen, was given
the part of Lakey, the dialogue written for her was poor.

Comments that the film will be enjoyed most by those who are not familiar with the novel.

1186. "Something for the Girls." TIME 87, no.10 (March 11, 1966): 82, 84.

Says that "although THE GROUP's McCarthyish airs are trivial as sociology, more dazzling than deep as drama, no sorority party in years has dished out so much trenchant and exhilarating tattle."

1187. Christ, Judith. "THE GROUP--Schmaltz and Candy Bars." NEW YORK HERALD TRIBUNE (March 17, 1966): 15.

Declares that the film is "hackery and stale morality." Suggests that the characters in the film version are even more shallow and have less substance than McCarthy's originals.

1188. Crowther, Bosley. "Screen: 3 Theaters Show THE GROUP." NEW YORK TIMES (March 17, 1966): 35.

Contemplates whether the fault for the failure of this movie lies with McCarthy's "formless book" or with Sidney Lumet's inept direction.

1189. Alpert, Hollis. SATURDAY REVIEW (March 26, 1966). Not seen.

1190. Wharton, Flavia. FILMS IN REVIEW 17, no.4 (April 1966): 250-251.

Finds fault with the screenplay, which makes McCarthy's characters even more unreal than she had made them; and the director, who Wharton feels is incompetent.

1191. Kael, Pauline. "Groups or Girls--Wordly and Unwordly." McCALLS (May 1966): 46, 157.

Says the book is enjoyed for its satire, parody and wit, but the movie portrays the characters much more sympathetically.

1192. Sarris, Andrew. "Films." VILLAGE VOICE 11, no.30 (May 12, 1966): 29.

Argues that the book was more "adapted" than "adopted" for the screen and that it loses much of McCarthy's satiric wit.

Suggests that the movie is more a piece of nostalgia than social criticism.

1193. Aaron, Daniel. "The Thirties, Now and Then." AMERICAN SCHOLAR 35, no.3 (Summer 1966): 490-494.
   Offers an overview of McCarthy's political and social allusions, examining 1930s America.

1194. Burgess, Jackson. FILM QUARTERLY 19, no.4 (Summer 1966): 59-60.
   Comments that THE GROUP lacks a point of view "or any other point," catalogues the failures of the eight Vassar graduates and trivializes the depression.

1195. Hanson, Curtis Lee. "Point of View." CINEMA (July 1966): 50.
   Claims that the film, THE GROUP, "is a sad and disturbing failure," and the novel is no better, going nowhere and adding up to nothing.

1196. Fenwick, J. H. SIGHT AND SOUND (London, G.B.) 35, no.4 (Autumn 1966): 200.
   Comments that this is a "nice old-fashioned movie" but that the film has not captured McCarthy's compulsion with the truth or her views on morality.

1197. Durgnat, Raymond. FILMS AND FILMING (London, G.B.) 12, no.12 (September 1966): 14-15.
   Comments that the film is bold and sympathetic. Proposes that the theme is the struggle the characters have to see reality clearly and to discover their own feelings within the context of a complex society. Compares THE GROUP to PEYTON PLACE, "a nineteenth century piece of sentimental whitewashing," and to THE CHAPMAN REPORT, a "more healthy and honest film." Suggests that THE GROUP goes further "not only in its censor-defying honesty but in its reminder that even the right ideas are subtly dehumanizing when applied in an exterior insensitive way."

1198. Thompson, Howard. "Candice of California: On an International Kick." NEW YORK TIMES (December 18, 1966A).
    Interviews Candice Bergen who talks about her role as Lakey in the film.

    Also published in: NEW YORK TIMES ENCYCLOPEDIA OF FILM, Vol. 8, 1984.

1199. Fruchter, Norman. "An Act of Comic Revenge." In THE YOUNG AMERICAN WRITERS: FICTION, POETRY, DRAMA AND CRITICISM, selected and introduced by Richard Kostelanetz, 123-127. New York: Funk & Wagnalls, 1967.
    Sees this as a comic novel that fails because McCarthy attempts to produce comedy from "the inhumanities of the ideology and the limitations of the characters."

1200. Gold, Suzanne. "A Reexamination of Mary McCarthy and THE GROUP." ROCKY MOUNTAIN REVIEW (Billings, Mont.) 4, no.1 (1967): 49-62.
    Reflects upon McCarthy's career as a writer and examines THE GROUP in particular. Suggests that because so much was expected of McCarthy in this long anticipated work, it is a disappointment. Declares that McCarthy is "a critic by choice, a novelist by inclination, but a satirist by nature."

1201. Petrie, Graham. "The Films of Sidney Lumet: Adaptation as Art." FILM QUARTERLY 21 (Winter 1967-1968): 9-18.
    Analyzes most of Lumet's films, commenting on each. Sees THE GROUP as a continuation of Lumet's critique of liberation which he began in THE PAWNBROKER and THE HILL. Proposes that the frenzied cadence of the movie pointedly articulates the frantic pace of the girls' lives and the trivialities with which they are concerned.

1202. Kael, Pauline. "The Making of THE GROUP." In KISS KISS BANG BANG, 65-100. Boston: Little, Brown & Co., 1968.
    Analyzes the making of the movie THE GROUP. Explores the motivation and plans of the director and producer and comments on the reactions of the actors to the stage directions.

Notes that McCarthy was not involved in the production and that although she was sent a copy of the script she declined comment. See also Sirkin's film review (item no. 1206).

Also published: KISS KISS BANG BANG. New York: Bantam Books, 1969, 498p. and London: Calder & Boyars, 1970.

1203. Raban, Jonathan. "Portrait of Libby MacAusland." In THE TECHNIQUE OF MODERN FICTION: ESSAYS IN PRACTICAL CRITICISM, 93-100. London: Edward Arnold; Notre Dame, Indianapolis: Univ. of Notre Dame Press, 1969.
Provides an excerpt from THE GROUP followed by an analysis of McCarthy's use of manners to portray the character of Libby.

1204. Harvey, David D. "Muddle-Browed Faction." SOUTHERN REVIEW n.s., 5 (Winter 1969): 259-272.
Touches upon several novels of the period in an attempt to explore the basis of the modern novel. Counsels that McCarthy ought to have chosen more formidable characters for her satire and argues that THE GROUP is already dated.

1205. Aldridge, John W. "Egalitarian Snobs." SATURDAY REVIEW 54, no.19 (May 8, 1971): 21-24.
Provides an in-depth look at THE GROUP and BIRDS OF AMERICA. Examines how McCarthy's preoccupation with objects, lifestyles and classification of attitudes trivializes material of potentially great significance. Agrees with Podhoretz's suggestion that McCarthy has an abiding fear of appearing ridiculous but believes a writer who is committed to the values of the material must be prepared to take such risks. Concludes each novel had the potential to be a major work, yet neither actually achieved greatness; both were within reach of McCarthy's talent, but not her courage.

Also published as "Good Housekeeping with Mary McCarthy" in: THE DEVIL IN THE FIRE: RETROSPECTIVE ESSAYS ON AMERICAN LITERATURE AND CULTURE. 217-223. New York: Harper's Magazine Press, 1972.

1206. Sirkin, Elliott. "Film Favorites." FILM COMMENT 8, no.3 (September-October 1972): 66-68.

Discusses the film THE GROUP referring to Kael's analysis in her book KISS KISS BANG BANG. Notes that the screenplay is not as flawed as Kael suggests and that Buchman captures the essence of the story. See also Kael's review (item no. 1202).

1207. Showalter, Elaine. "Killing the Angel in the House: The Autonomy of Women Writers." ANTIOCH REVIEW 32, no.2 (June 1973): 339-353.

Documents the difficulty women writers have in expressing their experiences and depicting their female characters as strong, and in control. Uses McCarthy and THE GROUP as an example of a female writer "struggling against convention to tell her own truth," despite "male critics' contempt for it, and female critics' suspicion of it."

1208. Ballorain, Rollande. "From Childhood to Womanhood (or from Fusion to Fragmentation): A Study of the Growing Up Process in XXth Century American Women's Fiction." REVUE FRANÇAISE D'ETUDES AMERICAINES 6, no.11 (1981): 97-112.

Deals with the scope of feminist writing from the early 1900s to the 1970s. Focuses on McCarthy's frank discussions about sexual relations and the need for contraception.

1209. Stimpson, Catharine R. "Zero Degree Deviancy: The Lesbian Novel in English." CRITICAL INQUIRY 8, no.2 (1981): 363-379.

Examines the "lesbian" novel noting two basic theories: "the narrative of damnation" in which the lesbian suffers as an outcast from society, and the "enabling escape" which allows the lesbian to rebel against society and succeed. Argues that Lakey belongs to the second category emboding the secure, successful individual. Notes, however, that the rest of "the group" show uneasiness in dealing with her.

MARY McCARTHY'S THEATRE CHRONICLES 1937-1962

1210. Lloyd, Eric. "Reading for Pleasure: Hurricane Mary." WALL
STREET JOURNAL (August 16, 1963): 6.
Criticizes McCarthy for her devastating reviews of plays and
playwrights.

1211. Fitzpatrick, Tom. "Scanning the Paperbacks." CHICAGO
TRIBUNE. MAGAZINE OF BOOKS [Sunday Ed.] (August 18,
1963): 7.
Notes that McCarthy the reviewer is anything but timid,
citing some of the criticisms she has directed at famous
playwrights as examples.

1212. "Lady with a Microscopic Gaze." KANSAS CITY STAR
(Kans.) (August 25, 1963): E10.
Calls her one of the most discerning drama critics, who
fulfills the primary obligation of helping others distinguish
between the valuable and the shoddy.

1213. Brien, Anne. "Acid Criticism of Recent Drama Is Couched in
Deathless Prose." CHATTANOOGA TIMES (Tenn.) (September
15, 1963): 20.
Judges McCarthy's reviews to be cruel and not ruthlessly
honest as advertised. Acknowledges McCarthy's casually
excellent style nonetheless, and almost guiltily admits that this
makes her work a joy to read.

1214. Jost, Edward F. AMERICA 109, no.19 (November 9, 1963):
594-595.
Questions the reason for publication of this volume,
consisting as it does primarily of material available in an earlier
collection. Believes the theater is not a natural environment for
McCarthy, a brilliant and caustic intellectual, whose interest lies
in social history and who treats plays as commodities.

*   Cheshire, David. In THEATRE: HISTORY, CRITICISM AND
    REFERENCE, edited by K. C. Harrison, 70. Readers Guide
    Series. London: Clive Bingley, 1967.
        See item no. 857.

VIETNAM

1215. "Mary in the Big PX." NEWSWEEK 69 (April 17, 1967):
      72-73.
          Summarizes the series of articles which appeared in the
      NEW YORK REVIEW OF BOOKS. Wonders if after having
      visited Vietnam her opinions regarding a solution for an end to
      the war have changed, and quotes from a conversation she had
      with other reporters, ". . . I realize now that we are in a very
      confused imbroglio. Simply pulling out of Vietnam will not solve
      the problem."

1216. KIRKUS REVIEWS 35 (August 1, 1967): 933.
          Outlines some of McCarthy's observations from her trip to
      Vietnam, and says the book merits wider exposure.

1217. Fleischer, Leonore. "Forecasts: Paperbacks." PUBLISHERS
      WEEKLY 192 (August 14, 1967): 52.
          Contends McCarthy's opinions are delivered strongly and
      heatedly in this exposé of the mess the Americans are making of
      Vietnam.

1218. Bixler, Paul. LIBRARY JOURNAL 92, no.15 (September 1,
      1967): 2932.
          Provides a brief review and proposes that the book is not
      really about Vietnam, it is about the American soul.

1219. Fremont-Smith, Eliot. "Report on America in Vietnam." NEW
      YORK TIMES (September 1, 1967): L29.
          Maintains this is the most provocative and disturbing
      indictment of the Vietnam War to date. Recounts McCarthy's

belief that spokesmen in Vietnam don't morally understand the horror of the war, and relays her scorn for the intellectuals who have cooperated in the Americanization of this small country. Believes that whether or not this book will be persuasive will depend on the reader's prior attitudes toward the war.

Also published in: INTERNATIONAL HERALD TRIBUNE [Paris Ed.] (September 2-3, 1967): 6; DETROIT FREE PRESS (September 10, 1967): B5; DAYTON DAILY NEWS (Ohio) (September 17, 1967): 30; SEATTLE POST-INTELLIGENCER. NORTHWEST TODAY (September 17, 1967): 4.

1220. "Pick of Pack in Paperbacks." OREGONIAN (Portland, Oreg.) [Sunday Ed.] 90, no.40 (September 3, 1967): F3.
    Refers to VIETNAM in a list of worthwhile paperbacks.

1221. Rosenfeld, Arnold. "Books: Varied Fare." HOUSTON POST. SPOTLIGHT [Sunday Ed.] (September 3, 1967): 8.
    Includes this "potent piece of anti-war reportage" in an article on recommended books.

1222. Kenney, Herbert A. "New Books: From War to Pain." BOSTON GLOBE (September 6, 1967): 43.
    Credits McCarthy for pointing out a major moral concern which has not been addressed elsewhere--that American materialism and commercialism may do more harm to Vietnam than the Viet Cong.

1223. "A Touch of Home." NEW YORK POST (September 6, 1967): 46.
    Presents an excerpt from VIETNAM in a discussion on the war.

1224. Stella, Charles. "Nothing Goes Right." CLEVELAND PRESS. SHOW TIME (Ohio) (September 8, 1967): 19.
    Describes McCarthy as a "hard-eyed observer" and states that one may not agree with her conclusions, but her insight will add to an understanding of the issues.

1225. McDonough, Richard. "Paperbacks: Thoreau, Brooke, Brown, & Berne." BOSTON HERALD TRAVELER [Sunday ed.] (September 10, 1967): A5.

   Claims McCarthy has earned her reputation for pure venomousness, exemplified by this work filled with "colour words, irrelevancies, and judgments."

1226. Prendergast, Charles. "On the Contrary." ST. LOUIS POST-DISPATCH (Mo.) (September 10, 1967): C4.

   Admires McCarthy's passionate protest against the war and perceives this work to be a deeply disturbing indictment of American policy.

1227. Smith, Miles A. "Mary McCarthy Criticizes the War." GRAND RAPIDS PRESS (Mich.) (September 10, 1967): 67.

   Argues that many of McCarthy's political and ideological viewpoints have been previously reported and observes that she makes no attempt to study the military aspects of the conduct of the war.

   Also published in: EVENING STAR (Washington, D.C.) [Sunday Ed.] (September 17, 1967): D3; NEWS & COURIER (Charleston, S.C.) (September 17, 1967): B5; TIMES. SAN MATEO TIMES & DAILY NEWS LEADER (September 23, 1967); WINOMA NEWS (Minn.) (September 24, 1967); MONROE NEWS (Mich.) (September 25, 1967); BERKELEY DAILY GAZETTE (October 19, 1967): 7; BATESVILLE GUARD (Ark.) (November 1, 1967): 11; CLARION-LEDGER JACKSON DAILY NEWS (Miss.) (November 5, 1967): C6; BRIDGEPORT POST (Conn.) (November 26, 1967): E5; SAN JOSE MERCURY (Calif.) (January 14, 1968).

1228. NATION 205, no.7 (September 11, 1967): 216.

   Includes this "perceptive" work in a list of books on Vietnam.

1229. Prescott, Peter S. ". . . and Fine Living: Books." WOMEN'S WEAR DAILY 115, no.179 (September 15, 1967): 24.

   States McCarthy's lack of authority and brief exposure to

Vietnam has resulted in "an astringent application of uncommon sense."

1230. Sanders, Nicholas. "Vietnam Study--More Wrath Than Reason." NASHVILLE BANNER (Tenn.) (September 15, 1967): 29.

Writes that the blatant bias reflected in McCarthy's opening statement: "I must confess that when I went to Vietnam early last February I was looking for material damaging to the American interest . . ." immediately causes all else to be suspect. Recalls various situations with the Germans which make the reader wonder whether McCarthy isn't more impressed with non-Americans. Criticizes the last section in which McCarthy offers no clear solutions and merely reiterates what others have said before.

1231. Sauter, Van Gordon. "Mary McCarthy on Vietnam: Fuel for Both Hawks and Doves." CHICAGO DAILY NEWS. PANORAMA (September 16, 1967): 9.

Believes that although there is little original material in VIETNAM, McCarthy's conclusions provide clear and provocative insight into a turbulent sea of propaganda.

1232. Borden, Pat. "American Policy Gets It in the Neck." GASTONIA GAZETTE (N.C.) (September 17, 1967): P4.

Provides a synopsis of the book, and describes it as a work of "political and intellectual thought."

1233. Fournier, Norman. "Mary McCarthy's VIETNAM." PORTLAND TELEGRAM (Maine) [Sunday Ed.] (September 17, 1967): 60.

Discusses McCarthy's move, with her husband James West, to Castine, Maine, after a long stay in Paris. Refers to the publication of this political and ideological work.

1234. Moczygemba, Arthur. "A Shallow View of Vietnam." EXPRESS AND NEWS (San Antonio, Tex.) [Sunday Ed.] (September 17, 1967): H3.

Disagrees with McCarthy's statement that "the worst thing that could happen to us (Americans) is to win the war."

Criticizes McCarthy's arguments and claims she gets mixed up with what is moral and what is not.

1235. C., G. "The Way to End It is Simple: Get Out." MONTREAL STAR (Montreal, Que.) (September 21, 1967): 8.

Relates how there have been numerous articles on the situation in Vietnam, and yet McCarthy's ability to cut through the camouflage and get to the heart of the problem makes this one of the more important. Claims her pleas to stop the war will leave the reader trembling in frustration and desperation.

1236. Cooke, Alistair. "Mary McCarthy in Vietnam." CHICAGO SUN TIMES. BOOK WEEK [Sunday Ed.] (September 24, 1967): 1, 15.

Provides an in-depth look at McCarthy's thoughts on the war including opinions about the American presence in Saigon and the "intellectuals" back at home. Admires her call for total defiance of the war, especially as few other critics ever went out on a limb and actually offered solutions.

1237. Reddin, John N. "Mary McCarthy's VIETNAM." MILWAUKEE JOURNAL (Wis.) [Sunday Ed.] (September 24, 1967): sec. 5, 4.

Chronicles the effects of the American presence in Saigon as presented in VIETNAM.

1238. Schlesinger, Arthur, Jr. "Mary McCarthy: The Dove Who Flies Like a Hawk." BOOK WORLD (CHICAGO TRIBUNE) (September 24, 1967): 1, 20.

Writes that this book provides an excellent look at the American presence in Vietnam and describes it as a "profoundly sad and moving evocation of an American tragedy." Believes, however, the section entitled "Solutions" contains a few holes and lacks McCarthy's usual intellectual rigor. Proposes this work will make it hard for Americans to remain self-righteous and complacent accomplices to the destruction in Vietnam.

Also published in: WASHINGTON POST. BOOK WORLD (September 24, 1967).

1239. Newquist, Roy. "Sobering View of Viet." CHICAGO HEIGHTS STAR (September 28, 1967): A12.
       Traces the reaction of both non-Americans and Americans to the United States involvement in Vietnam and earlier wars. Looks at the widespread criticism by various groups, ranging from the intellectuals to the hippies. Reflects on some of the more logical arguments about Vietnam by McCarthy and others.

1240. Hurlbert, Roy. "McCarthyism in Vietnam." PENINSULA LIVING (Burlingame, Calif.) (September 30, 1967).
       Argues that McCarthy hasn't exposed anything that hasn't previously been exposed and feels that she is rough on President Johnson and his generals.

1241. Rye, Jack A. "Mary McCarthy Hits US Vietnam Policy." SACRAMENTO BEE (Calif.) (October 1, 1967): L20.
       Recounts McCarthy's views and observations on the American presence in Saigon formulated during her trip to Vietnam.

1242. S., L. F. "Vietnam Offers No Action Plan." ROANOKE TIMES (Roanoke, Va.) (October 8, 1967): B4.
       Criticizes the admitted prejudice of the book and claims it adds nothing new to the voluminous literature on the war.

1243. Lawrence, Wes. "No Honorable Exit from Vietnam." CLEVELAND PLAIN DEALER (Ohio) (October 10, 1967): 15.
       Recounts McCarthy's argument for pulling out of Vietnam.

1244. Mottley, Robert. "Books on Vietnam Raps US Mission." ROANOKE WORLD-NEWS (Va.) (October 12, 1967): 20.
       Writes that this "cruelly probing view of the war" will distress the average American who hopes his/her country can do no wrong. Recommends this book even though it is not easy to read.

1245. Rettew, Thomas M. "McCarthy on Vietnam." MORNING NEWS (Wilmington, Del.) (October 17, 1967): 21.
       Describes this work as an incredible saga and says the last section "Solutions" is an ironic coup.

1246. "Easy Option for Soft Consciences." GUARDIAN (Manchester, G.B.) (October 26, 1967): 10.

Refutes McCarthy's claim that the United States should pull out of Vietnam absolutely, and that American policy is wholly immoral with no chance of success. Says that control has been extended in the populous areas and, in many cases, life is returning to normal there.

1247. Jay, Ivor. "Miss McCarthy is Unfair to the Marines." BIRMINGHAM EVENING MAIL (G.B.) (October 27, 1967): 14.

Disagrees with McCarthy who questions the integrity of marines who offer toys and money to Vietnamese children one day, and drop bombs on their families the next. Wishes she had tried to expose some of the fallacies of President Johnson's argument, which states that this war is necessary in order to reduce the chance of escalation to nuclear warfare.

1248. Brackman, Arnold C. "Vietnam: An End in Itself." SATURDAY REVIEW 50, no.43 (October 28, 1967): 32.

Evaluates the most recently published books about the war and states that VIETNAM was discredited by the obvious bias it reveals in McCarthy's opening sentence.

1249. De Vere White, Terence. "Mother Knows Best." IRISH TIMES (Ireland) (October 28, 1967): 10.

Comments that McCarthy's deeply committed opinions leave the reviewer with the impression that America is losing all moral influence in this "maniacal" war.

1250. Duffy, Maureen. "To Set the Statesmen Right." TIMES (London, G.B.) (October 28, 1967): 21.

Says that Americans have relinquished their political and moral responsibilities to the politicians and suggests that McCarthy's VIETNAM will make it impossible for them not to reassume those responsibilities.

1251. Gardiner, William. "Vietnam: A Case for Withdrawal." BIRMINGHAM POST (G.B.) (October 28, 1967).

Admires the American system of self-revelation and

self-criticism, however, feels McCarthy's case for the withdrawal
of American troops would have been more effective if she had
been more selective in her presentation of details. Feels
McCarthy has lost the reader's attention by the time she portrays
horrors such as the malnutrition and filth in the refugee camps.

1252. Mitchison, Lois. "Vietnam Dishonour." GLASGOW HERALD
(G.B.) (October 28, 1967): 9.
Compares VIETNAM with two other books on the war,
AUTHORS TAKE SIDES ON VIETNAM and TEN
VIETNAMESE. Analyzes McCarthy's book and comments the
other two pale in comparison. Believes VIETNAM is more
effective as a book than as a series of articles and that it will be
an influential work.

1253. BOOKLIST 64, no.5 (November 1, 1967): 313.
Provides a brief synopsis of the book.

1254. Ascherson, Neal. "The Little Cream Schoolhouse." LISTENER
78, no.2014 (November 2, 1967): 577-578.
Reviews this book along with AUTHORS TAKE SIDES ON
VIETNAM and NEW LEGIONS and states it constitutes the
"most piercing wound delivered to America's conception of itself
since the war."

1255. Roberts, Adam. "Damaging the American Interest." NEW
SOCIETY, no.266 (November 2, 1967): 640-641.
Describes VIETNAM as a brilliant, sometimes unfair, but
always perceptive plea to fellow Americans to lose the war and
pull out. Observes, however, that McCarthy has not really come
to terms with the effects of an American withdrawal on the South
Vietnamese.

1256. "Pamphleteer for Doves." TULSA DAILY WORLD (Okla.)
[Sunday Ed.] (November 5, 1967): 14.
Argues that McCarthy normally has a keen ability to satirize
every telling detail, and yet she has not brought any analytical
judgment to the situation in Vietnam, nor has she reported events
objectively. Shows how this is especially true in her final chapter

where she ignores the lessons of history and the realities of Southeast Asian politics.

1257. "It Is a Moral Issue." TIMES LITERARY SUPPLEMENT (November 9, 1967): 1051.

Describes VIETNAM and Duncan's NEW LEGIONS as compelling and forthright. Writes that many opponents of the war have fallen into the trap of offering solutions which are then easily shot down by the Pentagon. Offers high praise for McCarthy's ability to convey the moral wrongness of the war and agrees with her conclusion--while Americans must determine the morality of the war, it is up to the government to find a solution.

1258. Snowman, Daniel. "The Wrong and Filthy War." TRIBUNE (London, G.B.) (November 10, 1967): 10.

Reviews three books about the war: Bodard's QUICKSAND WAR, Duncan's NEW LEGIONS and McCarthy's VIETNAM. Credits the three with offering the reader interesting tales about the authors' personal experiences, however, wonders, in the case of VIETNAM, whether anyone has written so poignantly about the misdirected sincerity that characterizes so many Americans in Vietnam. Agrees with McCarthy's answer to the smug question "well, what would you do?"--Americans must voice their beliefs that the war is wrong.

1259. Dent, C. A. "Vietnam." NORTHERN DESPATCH (G.B.) (November 17, 1967): 12.

Says that the combination of McCarthy's intellectual discipline and deeply felt morality has resulted in a stimulating document.

1260. "Viet Nam in Print." TIME 90 (November 17, 1967): 112.

States the book is seen darkly through a bile-colored glass. Notes McCarthy's claim that she visited Vietnam to seek out what was damaging to America, and criticizes her for not looking for anything else.

1261. Vizinczey, Stephen. "If Throughout His Reign Napoleon..."
SPECTATOR 219, no.7274 (November 24, 1967): 637.
Refers to McCarthy's observation of the psychological
phenomenon of disassociation where American soldiers and
President Johnson both feign to relinquish control over the
escalating situation in Vietnam. Questions the obsession of the
American government with the War and proposes that this
obsession originates from the pursuit of the unattainable--power.
See also Strom's letter in response to this review (item no. 401)
and Vizinczey's reply (item no. 402).

1262. Mirsky, Jonathan. "The War in Vietnam." NEW YORK TIMES
BOOK REVIEW 72 (November 26, 1967): 10, 12, 14.
Assesses some of the views in Woolf's AUTHORS TAKE
SIDES ON VIETNAM in relation to the corrupting atmosphere
of McCarthy's VIETNAM. Asserts that VIETNAM recreates the
effect of the war on the military and civilians better than any
other publication about the war. Reveals how both books have
attempted to speak to Americans, urging them to confront their
government and stop the callous destruction of a backward
peasant country.

1263. Sayle, Murray. "Societies at War." TIMES (London, G.B.)
[Sunday Ed.] (November 26, 1967): 55.
Considers McCarthy's account of two events witnessed by
both Sayle and herself, and maintains that what McCarthy says is
true. Believes her description of the pulverised life in South
Vietnam reveals not only aspects of the war, but also the society
she comes from.

1264. "War--as Women See It." SOUTH WALES ECHO (G.B.)
(November 29, 1967).
Notes the differences in style between McCarthy's
VIETNAM and Dayan's A SOLDIER'S DIARY. Concludes
that, although Dayan is less opinionated and less literary,
McCarthy's indictment of the United States presence results in an
infinitely more damning report.

1265. Jelenski, A. K. "Les solutions de Mary McCarthy." PREUVES (Paris) 202 (December 1967): 85-87. French.
   Summarizes McCarthy's views on the handling of the Vietnam War by the United States government. Focuses on McCarthy's analysis of the "politics" involved and her belief that politics have replaced a conscience in most Americans.

1266. Muggeridge, Malcolm. ESQUIRE 68 (December 1967): 58, 92.
   Considers this to be a "television war with a built-in audience and all the dreariness and melancholy inseparable, therefrom" and proposes that if anyone has succeeded in portraying it's true nature, it is McCarthy.

1267. OBSERVER (London, G.B.) (December 3, 1967): 28.
   Refers to VIETNAM under "Other New Books."

1268. "Books Briefly: VIETNAM By A Novelist." WESTERN DAILY PRESS (G.B.) (December 4, 1967): 6.
   Describes VIETNAM as one of the more vivid and incisive books about the war.

1269. "Shorter Notices." SPECTATOR 219, no.7276 (December 8, 1967): 721.
   Briefly describes VIETNAM as an "accurate, often emotional," account of the atrocities of the war.

1270. Hoffmann, Wayne W. PRESBYTERIAN OUTLOOK (Richmond, Va.) 149, no.45 (December 11, 1967): 15.
   Gives a brief review of this "pop style work which is aimed at the living room reader." Argues it should be preceded by a documentary and followed with a practicum.

1271. Kirsch, Robert K. "Paperbacks Put Christmas in Your Pocket." LOS ANGELES TIMES (December 20, 1967): sec. 4, 15.
   Includes VIETNAM in a list of recently published paperbacks.

1272. Bacon, Roslyn. "Recommended to All Who Support the War in
      Vietnam." MORNING STAR (London, G.B.) (December 27,
      1967): 4.
          Recommends the book to all literary supporters of the war
      and compares it in importance to the report by the International
      War Crimes Tribunal. Admires McCarthy's disciplined behavior
      during the interviews with the "many arrogant, mindless,
      robot-like and cynical military officers" and expresses sorrow for
      the callous near-destruction of Vietnam and its people.

1273. Hardwick, Elizabeth. "Reading Around the World." TIMES
      (London, G.B.) [Sunday Ed.] (December 31, 1967): 22.
          Considers that VIETNAM is really about America; an old
      picture album in which every turn of the page cheerfully displays
      Americans in American clothes with American goods and
      American faces--"Americans on a World Tour"--against the
      dismal Asian backdrop.

1274. Washer, Jane Dennis. "A Critical Comment on Vietnam."
      RICHMOND TIMES-DISPATCH (Va.) (January 7, 1968): F5.
          Briefly summarizes this "highly critical and somewhat
      sarcastic commentary" on Vietnam.

1275. French, Philip. "American Conflicts." FINANCIAL TIMES
      (London, G.B.) (January 18, 1968): 10.
          Refers to VIETNAM as one of the most important pieces of
      reportage, despite it's open declaration of bias.

1276. "Vietnam Critic." PRESS AND JOURNAL (Aberdeen, Scotland)
      (January 20, 1968): 6.
          Notes the publication of this document of "human tragedy."

1277. "Books in Brief." STAR-BULLETIN AND ADVERTISER
      (Honolulu) [Sunday Ed.] (January 21, 1968): 23.
          Notes the publication of VIETNAM in a list of recently
      published books.

1278. L., B. "Inside Story of War in Vietnam." MORNING STAR
      (London, G.B.) (January 25, 1968): 4.
          Claims there are numerous books that have been written

about the war, however, maintains VIETNAM is invaluable for two reasons: McCarthy's "straight" presentation of the situation condemns Johnson's war practically right out of the mouths of his own generals; and the final section counters the demand from United States policy makers to produce a foolproof blueprint for obtaining peace.

1279. "Paperback Pickings." GUARDIAN (Manchester, G.B.) (January 26, 1968): 6.

Refers to VIETNAM in a column.

1280. Greenwood, Paul. "Paperbacks." WATFORD EVENING ECHO (G.B.) (January 27, 1968).

Admires McCarthy's ability to rip into the half-truths of the Saigon public relations machine, without resorting to propaganda sensationalism.

1281. "Paperback Parade." LIVERPOOL DAILY POST (January 31, 1968): 10.

Sums up VIETNAM as "a blazing indictment, full of emotion, horror and integrity, but despite the last chapter, devoid of alternatives."

1282. Woodcock, George. "Turning New Leaves: The Other War." CANADIAN FORUM 47 (February 1968): 256-257.

Agrees with McCarthy's insistence that "the ending of the war is the goal of the opponents, whereas how the war is to be ended is for the generals to determine." Maintains that McCarthy occasionally loads the scales too heavily against Americans, however, she presents a true reflection of the agony of sensitive Americans who see their country engaged in a war that negates all its greatest traditions.

1283. OXFORD TIMES (G.B.) (February 2, 1968).

Notes that when this book first appeared it had some critics crying treason.

1284. "Paperbacks of the Month." GLASGOW HERALD (G.B.)
(February 3, 1968): 9.
      Includes the "withering, polemic" VIETNAM in a list of
new paperbacks.

1285. Whitehorn, Katharine, and Gavin Lyall. "Publish and Be
Damned." OBSERVER (London, G.B.) (February 11, 1968):
30.
      Notes that despite McCarthy's lack of a political background,
she has given clear and simple answers to the many questions
posed by Vietnam.

1286. Walker, Martin. "Critic's Compendium." CHERWELL
OXFORD (G.B.) (February 14, 1968): 11.
      Believes these honest and precise essays will lead the reader
through the confused moralities of terrorism and napalm.

1287. "Paperback Short List." TIMES (London, G.B.) [Sunday Ed.]
(February 18, 1968): 51.
      Includes VIETNAM in a list of recommended paperbacks.

1288. Arblaster, Anthony. "The Meaning of 'Imperialism'." TRIBUNE
(London, G.B.) (February 23, 1968): 12.
      Provides an in-depth look at the relationship between the
American troops and the Vietnamese in VIETNAM and Harvey's
AIR WAR--VIETNAM. Recalls numerous examples of the
indiscriminate way destructive power was used by American
troops to level Vietnamese villages, scorch the land and exert
total control. Expresses dismay over the real relationship
between these two groups, and states the "sugar-coating of
'benevolence' may conceal this from observers in Washington,"
but few others.

1289. Brogan, Hugh. "The Americans: Vietnam, Vietnam."
CAMBRIDGE REVIEW (G.B.) (February 23, 1968): 305-308.
      Credits McCarthy with revealing the wickedness of the
Vietnam War and includes many of her observations in a
discussion on the moral wrongness of American participation in
Vietnam. Demonstrates how McCarthy was able to destroy the
American claim of moral superiority over the Viet Cong and

argues that without this claim, Americans cannot justify their presence in this country.

1290. Hamilton, Ian. "Vietnam: The Path to the Impasse."
ILLUSTRATED LONDON NEWS (G.B.) (March 2, 1968): 30-31.
Reviews four books about the war, focusing primarily on VIETNAM. Refutes McCarthy's solution for peace which would require the Americans to surrender to the North Vietnamese Communists and their allies of the Viet Cong. Claims McCarthy doesn't recognize the fact that the war is different from the way it was three years ago. Declares the situation is more complex than simply telling the soldiers to pack up and come home.

1291. Tomalin, Nicholas. "Tell Me Truths About Vietnam." NEW STATESMAN 75, no.1933 (March 29, 1968): 416-417.
Looks at a number of books about the war, focusing on McCarthy's VIETNAM, Duncanson's GOVERNMENT AND REVOLUTION IN VIETNAM and Schell's VILLAGE OF BEN SUE. States McCarthy's book provides the best straight forward reporting and observes ironically that even though she had preconceived attitudes, her report was more significant than the ones that claimed to be fair.

1292. CHOICE 5, no.2 (April 1968): 265.
States this undiluted attack on the American government should be included in any academic library which wants to offer a comprehensive collection on American history.

1293. INTERNATIONAL AFFAIRS (London, G.B.) (July 1968): 598.
Refers to VIETNAM in a list of books about Asia.

1294. Grimes, Paul. "North Vietnam Study Hurt By Its Pro-Hanoi Bias." PHILADELPHIA INQUIRER (December 1, 1968): 7.
Not seen.

1295. "Notes on Current Books." VIRGINIA QUARTERLY REVIEW 44, no.1 (Winter 1968): xxxviii.
Argues that the book should be read, not as a book about

Vietnam, but as a book about the United States and how
Americans are destroying the civilization in that country.

1296. "Other Books Received." PACIFIC AFFAIRS (Univ. of B.C.)
42, no.3 (1969): 422-423.
Remarks that this is a readable account of incidents and
conversations that confirm McCarthy's biases about the
inappropriate nature of the war.

HANOI

1297. PUBLISHERS WEEKLY 194, no.14 (October 7, 1968): 42.
Provides a brief background of McCarthy's visit to North
Vietnam in this announcement of the publication of HANOI.

1298. KIRKUS REVIEWS (October 15, 1968): 1196.
Proposes that McCarthy's sharp eye and keen awareness
offer little comfort to those who prefer their issues clearly black
and white.

1299. Toynbee, Philip. "Polite Guest in North Vietnam." OBSERVER
(London, G.B.) (November 10, 1968): 25.
Acknowledges that his heartfelt desire to hear good news
rather than bad is at odds with memories of how western
observers were so easily duped by Stalinism in eastern Europe.
Points out a number of instances, which cause him some unease,
but concludes that McCarthy, while certainly an advocate of the
regime, is an honest and shrewd one.

Also published as "See No Evil" in: CRITIC 27, no. 5
(April-May, 1969): 84-85.

1300. Tench, Sharon. "Books Give Readers Awareness."
PENSACOLA NEWS (Fla.) (November 13, 1968).
Calls HANOI a brilliant study in absurdity, but deems it a
failure because it offers no alternatives.

1301. Duncanson, Dennis J. "Five-Star, One-Star." SPECTATOR 221,
no.7325 (November 15, 1968): 699-700.
Suggests the reader's primary impression is triviality. Feels
that McCarthy, in her deadly earnestness, misses the real
problems.

1302. Jackson, Harold. "A Reporter Disarmed." GUARDIAN
(Manchester, G.B.) (November 15, 1968): 6.
Judges the book to be unbelievably shallow and virtually
unreviewable.

1303. Kopkind, Andrew. "Innocent Questions." NEW STATESMAN
75, no.1966 (November 15, 1968): 673-674.
Argues that the book, missing a fundamental connection
between author and subject, fails to transmit the reality of life in
North Vietnam. Expresses admiration for her descriptive and
perceptual abilities, but feels that her detached objectivity
ultimately makes her no more than a mouthpiece.

1304. Williams, Bernard D. BEST SELLERS 28, no.16 (November
15, 1968): 345.
Feels that although some readers may disagree with her
analysis, McCarthy should be admired for her determination to
increase awareness in the American public.

1305. Ambrose, Stephen E. "Mary McCarthy Quite Contrary." SUN
(Baltimore, Md.) (November 17, 1968): D5.
Describes the book as tripe; McCarthy's contribution to the
quota of silly writing engendered by every war.

1306. Just, Ward. "Fabulous North Vietnam." WASHINGTON POST
(November 21, 1968).
Startles the reader in his equating McCarthy in Hanoi with
De Beauvoir in the United States, using the damning prose of a
1952 article written by McCarthy herself. Terms McCarthy's

illogical and unfair parallelisms between communism and capitalism offensive. Summarizes the book as shrill and polemical, but as always, beautifully written.

Also published in: INTERNATIONAL HERALD TRIBUNE (November 23-24, 1968): 7 and KANSAS CITY STAR (December 15, 1968): 7.

1307. Stella, Charles. "Author Helps Explain Hanoi War Riddle." CLEVELAND PRESS. SHOW TIME (Ohio) (November 22, 1968): 21.
    Focuses on McCarthy's palpable bias. States the book is nonetheless a valuable contribution by a respected intellectual.

1308. Lillard, Richard G. "Mary McCarthy Reports from Hanoi." LOS ANGELES TIMES. CALENDAR (November 24, 1968): 47.
    Likens McCarthy's fair and balanced presentation of the North Vietnamese to Homer's humanization of the Trojans in THE ILIAD.

1309. Pfeffer, Richard M. "Two Reports from North of the DMZ." BOOK WEEK (CHICAGO SUN TIMES) (November 24, 1968).
    Views the first half of the book as a clever but undisciplined travelogue with little to justify a recommendation. Highly recommends the latter portion of the book, describing it as an incisive and poignant exploration of America, North Vietnam, western liberals and McCarthy herself.

1310. Serpell, Christopher. "Tiptoe." LISTENER 80, no.2070 (November 28, 1968): 731-732.
    Contends that his objection is not to McCarthy's basic thesis but her conscious refusal to recognize the complexity of the situation. Describes her visit to North Vietnam as a joyride, and the resulting essays nourishment for half-baked anti-Americanism. See also McCarthy's letter in response to this review (item no. 266) and Serpell's reply (item no. 415).

1311. Buckley, Tom. "On the Subject of Hanoi, a Muted Voice."
BOOK WORLD (CHICAGO TRIBUNE) (December 1, 1968):
24.
Contrasts the tone of her Vietnam articles--witty and
angry--with that found in HANOI--a voice nearly strangled by
her anger and shame. Agrees that such strong passions inhibit
her performance as a reporter. Finds her "protective, even
maternal" attitudes excessive, to say the least.

1312. "Mary McCarthy's Complaint." VARIETY (N.Y.) (December 4,
1968): 68.
Notes McCarthy's claim that HANOI is being ignored by
critics in the United States.

1313. Caldwell, Malcolm. INTERNATIONAL AFFAIRS (London,
G.B.) 45, no.3 (1969): 560-561.
Offers the reader an overview of some aspects of life in
North Vietnam which obviously impressed McCarthy. Declares
that a distancing from western style development cannot come
too soon.

1314. Bixler, Paul. LIBRARY JOURNAL 94 (January 15, 1969): 174.
Assesses the book as confusing and unimpressive. States that
this may be due to McCarthy's becoming entangled in her own
emotions as well as suffering from culture shock.

1315. "Bombs and Peace." TIMES LITERARY SUPPLEMENT
(January 16, 1969): 51-52.
Notes that HANOI is frankly polemical in this review of a
number of books about Vietnam.

1316. ANTIOCH REVIEW 29, no.1 (Spring 1969): 110.
Deems McCarthy intellectually irresponsible. Terms the
elevation of her socio-philosophical conclusions of actual events
an extreme example of the new journalism.

1317. Fitzgerald, Frances. "A Nice Place to Visit." NEW YORK
REVIEW OF BOOKS 12, no.5 (March 13, 1969): 28-31.
Contends that notwithstanding the overwhelming journalistic
attention paid to Vietnam, McCarthy and Sontag are the first to

attempt an understanding of the North Vietnamese people.
Suggests that both writers embarked on journeys of inspection
that turned into journeys of introspection.

1318. Lockwood, Lee. "Book Marks: Trips to Hanoi." NATION 208,
no.12 (March 24, 1969): 374-377.

Examines five recent books written by Americans who have
visited North Vietnam. Bases this analysis on his own experience
as a photographer and writer in Hanoi, and reflects upon the
"separate distortions" each author brings to what is essentially
the same story. Finds McCarthy's book the most descriptively
informative and most elegantly written. Notes a number of
similarities to Sontag's TRIP TO HANOI.

1319. CHOICE 6, no.3 (May 1969): 437.

Believes HANOI, as well as the earlier VIETNAM, exhibits
McCarthy's subliminal consciousness of the dilemmas of the
war. Calls its "high journalism" a way of avoiding the hard
questions; nonetheless considers it important.

1320. Shaw, Peter. "Sentimental Journeys." COMMENTARY 48 (July
1969): 84, 87-88.

Reviews books by McCarthy and Sontag, both of whom,
tired of reasoned criticism which seems to have had little effect,
felt the need for more active protest. Allows for good intentions,
but firmly believes McCarthy's application of double standards to
the United States and North Vietnam leads to obvious distortions.
Claims this in turn may lead to distrust from even sympathetic
readers and in the end prove far from beneficial to the anti-war
cause.

1321. Girling, J. L. S. PACIFIC AFFAIRS (Univ. of B.C.) 42, no.3
(Fall 1969): 421.

Calls the book lightweight, far more telling about McCarthy
than about North Vietnam.

WRITING ON THE WALL AND OTHER LITERARY ESSAYS

1322. KIRKUS REVIEWS 37 (December 1, 1969): 1302.
    Focuses on McCarthy's passion for accuracy, both in her use
    of language and need to render moral judgments. Calls her work
    masterful and often brilliant, but questions what lies beneath the
    surface.

1323. "Nonfiction Forecasts." PUBLISHERS WEEKLY 196
    (December 1, 1969): 37.
    Appears equally unimpressed by this collection and
    McCarthy's apparent affinity for the literary aristocracy.

1324. Carruth, Hayden. "Miss McCarthy and the Ephemeral."
    CHICAGO DAILY NEWS. PANORAMA (January 24-25,
    1970): 7.
    Claims McCarthy is a pragmatic, flexible critic who cleverly
    and effortlessly incorporates historical, biographical and
    psychological analyses. Finds some of the pieces successful, but
    reserves his major criticism for what he considers a
    preponderance of essays on books and authors of less than
    enduring interest.

1325. Hogan, William. "A High Styled Invitation from Mary
    McCarthy." SAN FRANCISCO EXAMINER & CHRONICLE.
    THIS WORLD [Sunday Ed.] (January 25, 1970): 43.
    Comments briefly on a number of the reprints McCarthy's
    publishers sent several critics to publicize this forthcoming
    collection.

1326. Kumin, Maxine. "Mary McCarthy's New Essays: Vivid,
    Acidulous, Sometimes Tender." BOSTON GLOBE (January 29,
    1970): 19.
    Declares that although these may be literary essays,
    McCarthy the social critic is ever present. Calls her pungent
    insights and observations a privilege to read and savor.

1327. Barkham, John. "First Lady of Letters Aims Sharp Pointer at Several Contemporaries." WAUKEGAN NEWS-SUN. WEEKEND LIFE (Ill.) (February 7, 1970): 10.
    Calls McCarthy our first lady of letters and a formidable critic. Concedes that not only is she on target more often than most, but the incisiveness of her writing makes it sometimes easier to be wrong with her than right with others.

    Originally published in SATURDAY REVIEW (not seen) and also published with revisions in BLADE (Toledo, Ohio) (February 8, 1970): I5; GARY POST TRIBUNE (Ind.) (February 8, 1970): 14; GRAND RAPIDS PRESS (Mich.) (February 8, 1970); TIMES UNION (Albany, N.Y.) [Sunday Ed.] (February 8, 1970): E7; and YOUNGSTOWN VINDICATOR (Ohio) (February 8, 1970): B16.

1328. Derrickson, Howard. "To Mary McCarthy, Macbeth is a 'Babbitt'." ST. LOUIS GLOBE DEMOCRAT (Mo.) (February 7-8, 1970): D5.
    Describes the book as an adventure in fact and fantasy. Spends the greater part of the review on McCarthy's "misreading" of MACBETH. Expresses shock that this essay has been reprinted in a school text, as well as included in an earlier collection of McCarthy's "critical effrontery."

1329. Thomas, W. H. J. "Current Reading." NEWS AND COURIER (Charleston, S.C.) [Sunday Ed.] (February 8, 1970): C16.
    Credits her with superior critical faculties in comparison to other women essayist-critics. Cites Mailer as the number one gun, and rates McCarthy a very classy welterweight in the arena of literary journalism. States that her versatility lies not in her subject matter but in her fresh approach to the familiar.

1330. Lehmann-Haupt, Christopher. "Mary McCarthy Still Loves a Good Fight." NEW YORK TIMES (February 9, 1970): 37.
    Accepts as a given, McCarthy's extraordinary writing style, her stunning intelligence and learning. Displays some reservations when he attempts to formulate a grander design for

the essays as a whole, reflecting that too often they seem to
serve no purpose other than to dazzle.

Also published in: LEDGER-STAR (Norfolk, Va.) (February
11, 1970): A7; MONTEREY PENINSULA HERALD (Calif.)
(February 14, 1970): 27 (edited); METRO-EAST JOURNAL
(St. Louis, Mo.) (February 15, 1970): M-E10 (edited);
WISCONSIN STATE JOURNAL (February 15, 1970): 3
(edited); SEATTLE POST-INTELLIGENCER. NORTHWEST
TODAY (February 22, 1970): 18; CHATTANOOGA TIMES
(Tenn.) (March 9, 1970): 9; and HARTFORD TIMES (Conn.)
[Sunday Ed.] (May 24, 1970): F4.

1331. Griffin, Lloyd W. LIBRARY JOURNAL 95, no.4 (February 15,
1970): 668.
Recommends McCarthy's latest book as waspish, fresh and
engaging as ever.

1332. Hamilton, Ian. "Two Cheers for Honest Paradoxology." BOOK
WORLD (CHICAGO TRIBUNE) 4, no.7 (February 15, 1970):
4.
Begins with the assertion that male critics have shown an
unusually propitiative attitude towards McCarthy. Declares her
critical faculty extraordinary but almost defiantly notes several
failures of sympathy which he believes stem from failures of
understanding. See also Kermode's review (item no. 1062).

1333. Wolff, G. "Umpire Broadsword, Saint." NEWSWEEK 75
(February 16, 1970): 98-100.
Considers the collection distinctively McCarthy in elegance
and intelligence, but uncharacteristic in that a greater number of
essays pay tribute rather than deal destruction.

1334. Hyland, Mary Jane. "Mary McCarthy Dissects Others'
Writings." RICHMOND NEWS LEADER (Va.) (February 18,
1970): 9.
Presents a picture of McCarthy as a steely-eyed literary
technician avidly anticipating the next dissection. Counts herself
among Orwell fans who will be alienated by McCarthy's piece.

Allows that the collection contains some lively writing and provocative ideas, but for the most part, Hyland is simply bored.

1335. Stella, Charles. "Salinger a Fake--McCarthy." CLEVELAND PRESS. SHOW TIME (Ohio) (February 20, 1970): 12.
    Recalls the silent generation's enamorment with Salinger's hero in CATCHER IN THE RYE. Acknowledges, albeit reluctantly, the validity of McCarthy's assessment. Finds her to be just as tough-minded and incisive as her former husband Wilson.

1336. Coxe, Louis. "Louis Coxe: Moral Vitamins." NEW REPUBLIC 162 (February 28, 1970): 20, 22.
    Presents McCarthy as a formidable polymath who functions best in the role of literary or political assassin. Argues that the impetus for her criticism is not really literary at all, but rather the moral fervor of a spoiled nun.

1337. Kennedy, Sister Eileen. BEST SELLERS 29, no.22 (March 1, 1970): 445-446.
    Takes issue with some of her literary evaluations, but commends her on her intellectual energy. Judges her best essays as those that combine research capacity, insights into humanity and honest judgments of value.

1338. Paul, Barbara. "Critic's Hatchet Wit Overburdens Essays." PITTSBURGH PRESS (March 1, 1970).
    States that the essays clearly illustrate McCarthy's tendencies toward destructive criticism. Grants that her writing is entertaining, but feels that too often, her preconceived standards ride roughshod over the writers' own purpose.

1339. Schipke, Eloise. "Swift Leaps." HARTFORD COURANT. SUNDAY COURANT MAGAZINE (Conn.) (March 1, 1970): 21.
    Believes that the collection, destined to have a limited general audience, will delight critical minds.

1340. Bell, Pearl K. "Writers & Writing: Two Critical Sensibilities."
NEW LEADER 53, no.5 (March 2, 1970): 16-17.
Agrees "enfant-terrible egotism" has been the hallmark of
McCarthy's reputation for over thirty years, but is pleased to
note that the collection displays her considerable intellectual and
rhetorical skills primarily in the cause of scholarship. Points out
that the book does contain some of her assassinations which the
reviewer considers tiresome, but these seem to be well
compensated by a number of essays which Bell finds
extraordinarily perceptive, lucid and memorable.

1341. Burgess, Anthony. NEW YORK TIMES BOOK REVIEW
(March 8, 1970): 4, 29.
Considers McCarthy a "brand name" that assures excellence,
not only in what she says but in her recognition of excellence in
others. Focuses on her fascination with structure and traces this
aspect of her analysis through a number of the essays. Endorses
the collection enthusiastically.

1342. Hall, Joan Joffe. "Mary McCarthy Essays: Perverse and
Passionate." COURIER-JOURNAL & TIMES (Louisville, Ky.)
[Sunday Ed.] (March 8, 1970): F5.
Acknowledges that McCarthy, alternatively perverse,
malicious or full of praise for kindred spirits, is anything but
forgettable. Judges McCarthy to be at her best when passionately
defensive because, in Hall's belief, a satirist's obligation is to
embody the moral norm.

1343. Newman, Edwin. "Linking Macbeth with Eichmann." NEWS
AND OBSERVER (Raleigh, N.C.) (March 8, 1970): 6.
Argues that the collection clearly demonstrates that good
literature need not be treated pedantically. Recognizes in
McCarthy a vibrant intellect whose work is always worth
reading.

1344. Loercher, Diana. "Fire without Destruction." CHRISTIAN
SCIENCE MONITOR [Eastern Ed.] 62, no.89 (March 12,
1970): 11.
Expresses some ambivalence toward the essays. Praises
McCarthy for her thought-provoking intelligence and wit, at the

same time, pointing out her tendency toward dogmatism and
pedantry. Nonetheless concludes that the champion of truth
triumphs over the dragoness of destruction.

1345. Hollenbeck, Ralph. "A Mixed Bag of Essays." SAN
FRANCISCO EXAMINER (March 13, 1970): 37.
    Observes that the scope of the collection attests to
McCarthy's versatility and range of interest. Calls her critiques
incisive, and her subject knowledge all-inclusive.

1346. Barnes, Robert J. "Mary McCarthy Explodes Salinger Myth in
Essay." BEAUMONT JOURNAL (Beaumont, Tex.) (March 27,
1970).
    Declares McCarthy not guilty of placing greater importance
on her own critical ingenuity than on helping the reader
understand.

1347. Meyer, Nancy. "Mary McCarthy Brilliant, Versatile Essayist."
PASADENA CALENDAR. ARTS AND BOOKS (Calif.)
(March 29, 1970).
    Notes that McCarthy adheres to no systematic theory of
criticism. Says she is a brilliant and versatile essayist who covers
a wide range of subjects.

1348. Cole, Thomas L. CHATTANOOGA TIMES. PERSPECTIVE
(Tenn.) (April 19, 1970): B2.
    Notes that reader's interest in the book will probably be
proportionate to their interest in the writers discussed.

1349. Mather, Bobby. "Two Great Ladies with Rapier and Stiletto."
DETROIT FREE PRESS (April 19, 1970): B5.
    Reviews collections by Porter and McCarthy and declares
they will appeal to die-hard admirers and English literature
majors. Concludes that both of these "ladies of the literary
aristocracy" have been cleaning out their files.

1350. BOOKLIST 66, no.17 (May 1, 1970): 1074.
    Describes her writing as intellectually vigorous and
sometimes caustically honest.

1351. Bergonzi, Bernard. "Books: Views and Reviews." NEW
SOCIETY 15, no.399 (May 21, 1970): 881.
Expresses disappointment in McCarthy as a literary critic
and proposes that his particular dissatisfaction may be traced to
her inadequate sense of audience. Allows that she is clever but
faults her for vague intellectual organization, stating the obvious
and sophomoric reflections.

1352. Tube, Henry. "Creative Critic." SPECTATOR 224, no.7404
(May 23, 1970): 683-684.
Considers her best pieces to be those elucidating complex
and demanding works, which to date, have been largely
misunderstood or ignored. Notes the limitations in her one track
approach, and her need to present the finished product tied up
with a yellow ribbon.

1353. Connolly, Cyril. "Critical Moments." TIMES (London, G.B.)
[Sunday Ed.] (May 24, 1970): 35.
Reviews a number of collections of criticism. Notes that
McCarthy, as a novelist whose reputation no longer rests
primarily on her critical writing, can afford to take risks.
Focuses on her essay on Orwell, which Connolly finds biased
and overly severe.

1354. Hamilton, Ian. "Special Pleading." OBSERVER (London. G.B.)
(May 24, 1970): 30.
Concentrates on McCarthy's "lawyer-like" attributes, finding
her at her most impressive and least trustworthy in essays on
Arendt and Orwell.

1355. King, Francis. "Mary Quite Contrary." DAILY TELEGRAPH
(London, G.B.) [Sunday Ed.] (May 24, 1970): 11.
Considers her essays on Sarraute and Compton-Burnett the
best in the collection, showing a strong sense of style and
appreciation of intellectual worth. Finds the Macbeth essay
marvelous but marred by a lack of historical sense. Concludes
that among contemporary women writing in English, only West
is McCarthy's equal in scope and intellectual brilliance.

1356. Hope, Francis. "Unfinished Arguments." NEW STATESMAN 79, no.2046 (May 29, 1970): 775-776.
    Suggests that in her remorseless desire to stimulate, McCarthy raises good questions, but fails to provide the answers. Acknowledges that she is clever, provocative and erudite, but nevertheless feels cheated.

1357. Dodsworth, Martin. "Uses of Literacy." ENCOUNTER 34, no.6 (June 1970): 75-80.
    Details the essay as a literate form of communication and examines some of its current practitioners. Finds McCarthy's work vibrant, witty and a pleasure to read, but declares that her reductionist thinking leads to serious shortcomings.

1358. Grossman, Edward. "Mary à la Mode." COMMENTARY 49, no.6 (June 1970): 81-85.
    Focuses on the "serious" essays that Grossman feels might actually have an impact on the real world. Assesses eleven of the thirteen essays as in keeping with McCarthy's usual level of excellence, while simultaneously protesting that it would be "simple-minded" to call such writing meaningless or useless. Conserves his energies for rebuttal of the Orwell and Arendt essays. Finds her attack on Orwell, a writer Grossman obviously holds in some esteem, unacceptable. Declares McCarthy's defense of Arendt totally out of her province and undeserving of serious consideration.

1359. Pritchard, William H. "Tones of Criticism." HUDSON REVIEW 23, no.2 (Summer 1970): 365-376.
    Reviews a number of diverse collections and contends that McCarthy's engagement with language makes her a true philosophical critic as well as a critic of texture not of text. Agrees that she is clever and inventive, but repudiates the notion that it is for shock value. Clearly admires her hardworking and canny mind, effortless prose, and depth of her understanding.

1360. "Making It New." TIMES LITERARY SUPPLEMENT, no.3562 (June 4, 1970): 604.
    Hypothesizes that her chief virtue and chief defect both stem from the same source, an insistence on making it new. Maintains

that the defects outweigh the virtues in this collection. Expresses discomfort with McCarthy's alleged refusal to maintain a consistent point of view, resulting in a lack of coherence.

1361. Mitchell, Julian. "What's Going On." GUARDIAN AND GUARDIAN WEEKLY (G.B.) 102 (June 6, 1970): 19.
    Observes that it is a lamentable comment on the literary scene when McCarthy's publishers recognize the need to send reputable critics copies of the books under discussion. Describes her work as explicatory rather than critical, bold and clever but often based on dubious evidence. Although he hardly ever agrees with her, Mitchell considers McCarthy a formidable intellect and admires her clarity and concern.

1362. Ricks, Christopher. "Mary and Martha." LISTENER 83, no.2150 (June 11, 1970): 791.
    Theorizes that the unifying principle in the essays is McCarthy's preoccupation with division, duality and duplicity. Unearths a number of such images scattered throughout the collection and suggests that they might mirror some of the self-divisions in her own life.

1363. Cline, Elizabeth. "McCarthy Critiques Prophetic." BIRMINGHAM NEWS (Ala.) 113 (July 5, 1970): E7.
    Finds her fresh, imaginative approach a harbinger of things to come in the field of literature.

1364. Stanford, Derek. "Mother McCarthy's Chickens." BOOKS AND BOOKMEN 15, no.11 (August 1970): 14.
    Claims that whether or not one agrees with her opinions, the singular and modish Miss McCarthy is always an entertaining performer. Takes issue with her attack on Orwell, but concedes outstanding merit to two of the essays, "On Madame Bovary" which Stanford calls the best he has ever read and "General Macbeth" which he calls the bitchiest.

1365. Kermode, Frank. "Critical List." NEW YORK REVIEW OF BOOKS 15 (August 13, 1970): 31-33.
    Contrasts the splendid continuity of Rahv's literary criticism with McCarthy's unpredictable flashes and flares. Expresses

some surprise that THE WRITING ON THE WALL, while
demonstrating the quality of McCarthy's critical sense, lacks a
base of steadfast literary and political attitudes. Finds the
Macbeth essay disastrous, the piece on Orwell full of
inexplicable rancour and her discussion of Sartre uneasily
combative and truculent.

1366. CHOICE 7, no.7 (September 1970): 843.
     Recommends the collection, assessing it to be in McCarthy's
usual vein, witty, acerbic and frequently nasty.

1367. Hardwick, Elizabeth. "Books." VOGUE 156 (September 1,
1970): 306.
     Reflects that over time McCarthy has moved beyond mere
fashionableness, discarding the need for youthful cleverness and
drama for its own sake. Sees the collection as great prose talent
at work.

1368. Muggeridge, Malcolm. "Books." ESQUIRE 74, no.4 (October
1970): 94, 239.
     Presents this collection as a characteristic blend of shrewd
and imaginative insight with occasional lapses of naivete shading
into stupidity. Confesses to a total lack of understanding of some
of her attitudes, but notes that even when he disagrees with her,
she is illuminating.

1369. Bondy, François. "Keine gute Hasserin. Ein neuer Band stellt die
Essayistin Mary McCarthy vor." DIE ZEIT.
WOCHENZEITUNG FUR POLITIK. WIRTSCHAFT.
HANDEL UND KULTUR. HAMBURG 25, no.41 (October 9,
1970): 20. German.
     Looks at McCarthy the essayist, on the occasion of the
publication of the German translation of THE WRITING ON
THE WALL. Reviews her essays on Compton-Burnett,
Nabokov, Burroughs, Arendt, Orwell and Faulkner. Questions
the suitability of some of the essays for German audiences.
Believes her to be most convincing when she avoids affectation,
and does not search for effects.

1370. Donoghue, Denis. "On the Contrary: Mary McCarthy's WRITING ON THE WALL." ART INTERNATIONAL 14, no.9 (November 1970): 17-18.

    Proposes that McCarthy chooses topics based on strong feelings of sympathy or antipathy. Further suggests that she is fascinated by fiction totally unlike her own, which does not claim a personal response. Judges her work to be perceptive, inventive and occasionally splendid, but feels her bright ideas often run away with her and become distorted for the sake of effect, eliciting the outraged response frequently voiced by reviewers.

1371. NEW YORK TIMES BOOK REVIEW (December 6, 1970): 100.

    Includes THE WRITING ON THE WALL in a list of selected books from 1970.

1372. Grumbach, Doris. "Mary McCarthy As Critic: High Intelligence, Flawless Style." NATIONAL CATHOLIC REPORTER (December 11, 1970): 12.

    Views the collection as a significant critical success. Professes that she finds some aspects of McCarthy's writing distracting: her habit of occasionally entering the work through her own personal experience; her obvious preference for the highly intricate and illusive, however, the resulting criticism is so clever and seemingly "finished" that one has no inclination to return to the original. Selects the essay on Macbeth as an illustration of McCarthy at her best.

1373. Podhoretz, Norman. "A Minor Cultural Event." COMMENTARY 53, no.4 (1972): 7-8, 10.

    Refers to McCarthy's critical review of Orwell in an article on Rahv's commentary on James.

1374. Bayley, John. PARTISAN REVIEW 39, no.3 (Summer 1972): 398-403.

    Prefaces this slightly revised piece with a lengthy discussion of his fully conscious literary prejudices. Regards McCarthy as an excellent critic but also a follower of fashion, and as a result does not believe this collection will wear well.

1375. "Literary and Criticism." BOOKS AND BOOKMEN 18, no.11
(August 1973): 139.
   Describes the book as brilliant and provocative.

1376. Jardin, Claudine. "Cette semaine chez votre libraire." FIGARO
(September 30, 1974): 28. French.
   Refers to McCarthy as the great lady of leftist American
literature. Notes that the title essay was dedicated to Nathalie
Sarraute.

1377. Le Clec'h, Guy. "De Madame Bovary á Nabokov." FIGARO
(October 26, 1974): 13. French.
   Comments that although McCarthy is living in Paris she is
not in exile from the United States and still looks critically at
American affairs and actions.

BIRDS OF AMERICA

1378. Rapoport, Janis. "Yankee Doodle Not So Dandy." TAMARACK
REVIEW, no.58 (1971): 83-87.
   Finds a major contradiction in the fact that Peter considers
himself a social, political egalitarian. Considers if these
principles were acted upon there would be less diversity in the
world, more mass production, and more harm to the
environment. Criticizes McCarthy's unsympathetic professional
coolness, the emptiness of the characters and the basic plotless
structure.

1379. Tindall, Gillian. "CANDIDE Flavour." NEW SOCIETY 18,
no.468 (1971): 526.
   Expresses disappointment that the book did not become
memorable over time and blames the numerous, essentially
superficial scenes which were hilarious set-pieces rather than
integrated events. Wonders if the ignorance of Peter was so
extreme that his usefulness as a commentator was limited. Posits

that the problem may also be the fact that McCarthy dislikes
Paris too much to write about it positively.

1380. Bannon, Barbara A. "PW Forecasts." PUBLISHERS WEEKLY
199, no.13 (March 29, 1971): 45.
    Predicts this honest love letter to a decent young American
will be a great success.

1381. Avant, John Alfred. LIBRARY JOURNAL 96, no.7 (April 1,
1971): 1290.
    Contends that tiresome characters and repetitious ideas make
this an exhausting book, although the structure is admirable and
there are some entertaining passages.

   *   Aldridge, John W. "Egalitarian Snobs." SATURDAY REVIEW
54, no.19 (May 8, 1971): 21-24.
       See item no. 1205.

1382. Vendler, Helen. "Mary McCarthy Again Her Own
Heroine--Frozen Foods a New Villain." NEW YORK TIMES
BOOK REVIEW (May 16, 1971): 1, 16, 18.
    States that McCarthy is examining her own duality: Peter as
a fantasy of what she might be if she were an adolescent in the
1970s, and Rosamund as a version of herself today. Proposes
that the moral of the book is that Peter grows beyond both his
mothers--Rosamund and Mother Nature. Writes that although
McCarthy draws from her own experiences, stereotypes take
over where knowledge leaves off. See also Tyler's letter in
response to this review (item no. 433).

1383. Murray, Michele. "Miss McCarthy Is Gentle With a Bleak
World." NATIONAL OBSERVER 10 (May 17, 1971): 19.
    Summarizes the plot and characters, tracing Peter's close
relationship with his mother. Credits McCarthy for writing a
winning tale which presents the world's foolishness with more
kindness than one would expect from her.

1384. Broyard, Anatole. "An Unfriendly Ornithologist." NEW YORK
TIMES (May 19, 1971): 45.
    Writes that part of the problem with the book is McCarthy's

treatment of Peter who becomes so loaded down with idiosyncrasies that he is no longer a boy. Refers to McCarthy's thoughts on America as verging on hysteria and observes that she isn't writing novels the way she used to. See also Halio's review (item no. 1428).

1385. Maddocks, Melvin. "Miss McCarthy's Obit to Nature." LIFE 70, no.19 (May 21, 1971): 12.

Writes this book brings together all that McCarthy has ever learned or hoped for from art and civilization. Claims it is not only about how man has fallen out of harmony with nature but also with his fellow man and himself. Concludes that because McCarthy is able to treat tragedy with such clarity and range, the book becomes a healing act for the reader.

1386. Kramer, Hilton. "Mary McCarthy's Valentine to Fanny Farmer." BOOK WORLD (WASHINGTON POST) 5 (May 23, 1971): 1, 5.

Criticizes the book's lack of substance, "undernourished, somewhat dehydrated cliché of a plot," and poor character sketches. States McCarthy cannot write a novel because she lacks the essential fictional element--the ability to "imagine" others. Compares her novels with her earlier theater reviews and observes that she does not create multi-dimensional characters but relies instead on a "review" of their ideas and actions.

1387. Fuller, Edmund. "Miss McCarthy's Likeable Hero." WALL STREET JOURNAL (May 24, 1971): 12.

Describes Peter as "immensely likeable, keenly intellectual, with a winning blend of sophistication and naiveté." Refutes the last sentence of the book--Kant's "Nature is Dead"-- and claims that the main flaw in an otherwise good book is McCarthy's lack of faith in Peter's idealism.

1388. Prescott, Peter S. "CANDIDE Without Voltaire." NEWSWEEK 77, no.21 (May 24, 1971): 103-103A.

Notes the problem with the novel is McCarthy tells the story from the point of view of Peter, a basically uninteresting character. Continues that even though McCarthy is well-qualified

to write an American CANDIDE her attempt at a sentimental
CANDIDE, emphasizing warmth, kindness and realism, fails.

1389. Duffy, Martha. "A Tale of Two Cultures." TIME 97, no.22
(May 31, 1971): 62, 64.
States that BIRDS OF AMERICA is McCarthy's "calmest,
most magnanimous, most reflective book." Examines the lifestyle
and background of this "literary vampire."

1390. Pritchett, V. S. "Ironical Aviary." NEW YORK REVIEW OF
BOOKS 16, no.10 (June 3, 1971): 13-15.
Describes BIRDS OF AMERICA as a Bildungsroman of the
young man who meets the wrong people abroad and discovers
that the modern world is polluted with questions. Recounts how
the reader waits for Peter to commit at least one rash act. States
that "in a novel Peter's character would be thin as he is, but in
the European American laboratory, he is a ready piece of Puritan
litmus."

Also published in: TALE BEARERS: LITERARY ESSAYS.
156-163. New York: Random House, 1980 and in Vintage Books
Ed. 156-163. New York: Random House, 1981.

1391. Parker, Dorothy L. "Satire for the Third Ear." CHRISTIAN
SCIENCE MONITOR [Eastern Ed.] 63 (June 10, 1971): 7.
Focuses on some of the highpoints of BIRDS OF
AMERICA. Contends that McCarthy has mellowed, except when
dealing with "birds of another stripe," predators and scavengers
like the noncombatant military officer who lives off the fat of
some other land, and the United States administrations that
perpetuated the Vietnam War.

1392. Ryan, Frank L. BEST SELLERS 31, no.6 (June 15, 1971):
134-135.
Criticizes McCarthy for substituting a series of events,
perceived by a nineteen year old, for a plot. Claims BIRDS OF
AMERICA is not a novel but rather a chance for McCarthy to
show off her erudition.

1393. Grumbach, Doris. "In BIRDS OF AMERICA 'GROUP' Author Gropes but Fails." NATIONAL CATHOLIC REPORTER. SUPPLEMENT 7 (June 18, 1971): A6.

    States that McCarthy's morally puritannical, culturally nostalgic and politically egalitarian notions have never been before presented at such length. Admires her witty, lively style but writes that it is not enough; she has become the victim of her own wistfulness for the American past and her disdain for the present.

1394. Boatwright, James. "Carnival Ducks and Acute Social Criticism." NEW REPUBLIC 164, no.25 (June 19, 1971): 25-26.

    Compares ventriloquism with writing fiction maintaining that both must have more than one voice. Says this is a problem with McCarthy's novels because her voice is so strong, clear, sure and convincingly deployed that her characters never really have a chance. Claims they are either an attenuation of her, or "plastic carnival ducks floating by, whose only purpose is to be knocked over." Concludes that the novel, along with many of McCarthy's other novels, is really a series of "razor sharp essays on manner and mores, or acute criticisms of foreign policy and domestic madness."

1395. Adams, Phoebe. "Short Reviews: Books." ATLANTIC 228, no.1 (July 1971): 103.

    Recommends BIRDS OF AMERICA because it presents McCarthy's widening view of dealing with an age group and set of experiences quite different from her own.

1396. McConathy, Dale. "Books: All Mom and Frozen Apple Pie: Mary McCarthy's Latest." VOGUE 158 (July 1971): 90.

    Argues the book ironically represents an "extraordinary exercise in the mode of fiction McCarthy has always said she most despised: 'the ladies' magazine story'." Declares that BIRDS OF AMERICA could have been a breakthrough novel but it falls short because McCarthy avoided the darker, deeper questions and may even have missed the point of what has been happening in America.

1397. Kapp, Isa. "Writers and Writing: Plumbing the Heights." NEW LEADER 54, no.14 (July 12, 1971): 17-18.

Describes BIRDS OF AMERICA as "less a novel than a tract about our modern condition, in two equally glum parts": the first claims that most of us have defied the natural world, and the second, that those elite who are gentle with plants and animals are likely to despise humans. Poses the question: "Why ... does Peter find intolerable the human traces in the bathroom and the human voices in the Sistine Chapel?" Wonders if Peter is not in fact a chip off the old block, even though he is critical of his mother for basing her ethics on style.

1398. BOOKLIST 67, no.22 (July 15, 1971): 931.

Provides a brief summary of the novel.

1399. Hayes, Carol. CRITIC 29, no.6 (July-August 1971): 70-72.

Chronicles many of the themes presented in BIRDS OF AMERICA, focusing on Peter and his struggle to survive in the world. Reveals how the reader's attitude is controlled "in a manner reminiscent of Austen or J.F. Powers." Describes the book as a perceptive and often funny novel.

1400. Whitman, Charles. "Criticism: Books and the Arts. An Eerie Premonition." CHRISTIAN CENTURY 88, no.33 (August 18, 1971): 983-984.

Thinks this book missed the boat if McCarthy's intention was to write about a boy's growing up, about what it means and how it happens. Decides that it is essentially an essay on the effect of American follies (particularly Vietnam) and on a young man just beginning to confront them.

1401. Morse, J. Mitchell. "Fiction Chronicle." HUDSON REVIEW 24, no.3 (Autumn 1971): 526-540.

Provides an in-depth look at character portrayal with particular focus on Peter. Suggests that McCarthy's characters are representations of her attitudes, values and points of view, and that Peter was intended to be the representation of an idea. Praises some scenes but describes others as "curiously lifeless."

1402. "Notes on Current Books." VIRGINIA QUARTERLY REVIEW 47, no.4 (Autumn 1971): clx.

   Maintains this warm, readable narrative is actually a parable of McCarthy's development in which her career as "sexual nonconformist, intellectual and political iconoclast, and religious orthodoxy" falls into place.

1403. Hughes, Catherine. "On the Wing." PROGRESSIVE (Madison, Wis.) 35, no.9 (September 1971): 50-51.

   States there is no flesh on Peter's bones and sees him more as a mouthpiece than anything else. Wonders why McCarthy seems considerably more interesting than the characters she creates. Concludes that her lack of passion and cool detachment make this more a fiction-essay than a novel.

1404. Hirsch, Foster. COMMONWEAL 94, no.19 (September 3, 1971): 459-460.

   Chronicles the events in Peter's life which influence his perception of the world. Parallels the themes and characters with THE COMPANY SHE KEEPS concluding that although THE COMPANY SHE KEEPS was more flamboyant, BIRDS OF AMERICA is wiser and more mellow.

1405. Wyndham, Francis. "Sliced Life." LISTENER 86 (September 16, 1971): 376.

   Traces the dilemmas which confronted Peter suggesting that the book steadily diminishes in intensity with each successive predicament. Explores the possibility that the novel's impact is reduced because McCarthy became infected by Rosamund's hysteria.

1406. Hope, Francis. "Owlish." NEW STATESMAN 82, no.2113 (September 17, 1971): 369.

   Traces the development of Peter's moral education and his search for the truth. Describes BIRDS OF AMERICA as a moral comedy, but perceives that the book doesn't work either morally or comically. Concludes that "one may admire the intellectual plummage, but not the lifeless bird."

1407. "Sobering Self-Education." TIMES LITERARY SUPPLEMENT, no.3629 (September 17, 1971): 1105.

Recognizes that many of McCarthy's admirers may find this book "too episodic, too obviously a vehicle in which the protagonist merely suffers various rituals, and in which arguments are aired but emotions never involved." Defends the book pointing out that the development of Peter's character offers some of the funniest scenes McCarthy has ever written and her description of the European cities and their inhabitants is handled with relish and great skill.

Also published in: T.L.S.: ESSAYS AND REVIEWS FROM THE T.L.S. Vol. 10. 48-51. London: Oxford Univ. Press, 1972.

1408. Waugh, Auberon. "Auberon Waugh on Mary McCarthy." SPECTATOR (September 18, 1971): 414-415.

Terms "brephomimesis" the illness of some mothers who become obsessed with the idea that the world wants to hear every word their young children utter once they have learned how to talk. Writes that the results are appalling whatever McCarthy's "brephomimesis" is--psychic or somatic, hysterical or physical. Concludes that her opinions are banal, that nothing ever happens and the book was difficult to finish.

1409. Wall, Stephen. "An American CANDIDE." OBSERVER (London, G.B.) (September 19, 1971): 32.

Chronicles Peter's year in Paris focusing on various events which helped to shape his character, and concludes he is more a series of dilemmas and a sequence of propositions, than a person in his own right. States his character is descended from the heroes of eighteenth century philosophical tales, but unfortunately the book does not share their elegance.

1410. Allum, Nancy. BOOKS AND BOOKMEN 17, no.1 (October 1971): 50.

Chronicles the plot and characters in this "charming" novel.

1411. Midwood, Barton. "Fiction." ESQUIRE 76, no.4 (October 1971): 63, 66.
      Ranks BIRDS OF AMERICA as one of the best books by an American in the last forty years. Contrasts McCarthy's treatment of Peter to Dostoyevsky's treatment of Lebedyev in THE IDIOT, their justification of the world and its inhabitants. Praises McCarthy's strategy saying that she is careful to direct attention to the flickering of kindness in even the most offensive person, thereby calming a public believed to be full of volatile prejudices and miscalculated hatreds.

1412. Thompson, John. "Words." COMMENTARY 52, no.4 (October 1971): 108-111.
      Reviews the themes and styles in various books, singling out BIRDS OF AMERICA as enjoyable because it is not simply words. Praises McCarthy's ability to "locate in the actual texture of life, in things so small and so important that we never notice them, the signs of the great drift of time," and commends her for recognizing them and assuring they are sociologically correct.

1413. Davenport, Guy. "Low Seriousness and High Comedy." NATIONAL REVIEW 23, no.39 (October 8, 1971): 1123-1124.
      Maintains that Peter's character is not very believable and wishes that McCarthy had written about a more typical American abroad.

1414. Shrapnel, Norman. "Nature and Human Nature." GUARDIAN AND GUARDIAN WEEKLY 105 (October 9, 1971): 30.
      Describes BIRDS OF AMERICA as a "satisfying comic novel, pretty deadly in its impact, a soft-nosed bullet fired at the life-denying, deep-freeze world we are building for ourselves." (See also item no. 1416.)

1415. "In Moult." ECONOMIST 241, no.6689 (November 6, 1971): vi.
      Criticizes the book for its lack of wit and cutting edge. Theorizes that middle-aged ladies should not attempt to describe the thought processes of teenage youths because "it unsexes both of them."

1416. "Top Shelf of the Year." GUARDIAN AND GUARDIAN
WEEKLY 105 (December 25, 1971): 18.
  Provides excerpts from Shrapnel's review in a summary of
recommended books for 1971. See also Shrapnel's review (item
no. 1414).

1417. Bondy, François. "Mary McCarthy und der Vietnamkrieg."
MERKUR 26 (1972): 1041-1043. German.
  Reviews two books about the Vietnam War, BIRDS OF
AMERICA and MEDINA. Argues that for McCarthy, Medina's
acquittal and the lack of public outcry mirrors the moral apathy
in BIRDS OF AMERICA. Notes that McCarthy, like Arendt,
discovers a "banality of evil" based on both the military chain of
command which relieves the individual of responsibility for his
actions, and the so-called extenuating circumstances of warfare.

1418. May, Derwent. "Amis, McCarthy, Naipaul: New Novels."
ENCOUNTER 38, no.1 (January 1972): 74-78.
  Investigates various themes and observes that even though
Peter's dilemmas and decisions rarely involve any dramatic
consequences, McCarthy is able to hold the reader's interest with
charm, humor and a passion for detail.

1419. Forrest, Alan. "B & B's Look at 1955." BOOKS AND
BOOKMEN 17, no.5 (February 1972): 27.
  Includes BIRDS OF AMERICA in a discussion of the worst
fiction of the year.

1420. Feinstein, Elaine. "Loneliness Is Cold." LONDON MAGAZINE
11, no.6 (February-March 1972): 177-180.
  Provides a synopsis, focusing on some of the more comic
and touching moments. Claims the book is less a lament for the
displaced wildlife in America than nostalgia for a New England
way of life that is quickly disappearing.

1421. Spacks, Patricia Meyer. "A Chronicle of Women." HUDSON
REVIEW 25, no.1 (Spring 1972): 157-170.
  Includes BIRDS OF AMERICA in a discussion of the female
writer's struggle for personal identity. Finds that the novel fails
because the struggling character of Peter is no more than a

fictional device for McCarthy's angry wit, and because it used
people and events for vague ideological purposes.

1422. Bannon, Barbara A. "Paperbacks." PUBLISHERS WEEKLY
201, no.13 (March 20, 1972): 70.
    Includes this work in a list of recent paperbacks, and
describes it as a beautifully written character study.

1423. "Mary McCarthy: LES OISEAUX D'AMERIQUE ont du plomb
dans l'aile." FIGARO (May 10, 1972): 30. French.
    Argues that the theme of this novel is a young man's
apprenticeship to Parisian life.

1424. Black, Steven A. WEST COAST REVIEW (Burnaby, B.C.) 7,
no.2 (October 1972): 76-77.
    Reports that there is little purpose to the book other than as a
view of some of the major events of 1964-1965 through the eyes
of a nineteen year old. Concludes that BIRDS OF AMERICA is
a gentle, entertaining novel and not a sermon on various cultural
and political issues, only because McCarthy respects her
characters and her craft.

1425. Doherty, Paul C. "The Year's Best Buys in Paperbacks."
AMERICA 127, no.20 (December 16, 1972): 526-527.
    Discusses Skinner's "literature of dignity" which places a
character in a situation where he must struggle against those who
want to diminish his personal worth. Notes that McCarthy's
interplay between American and un-American, government and
governed, provides an excellent setting for Skinner's theory.

1426. Field, J. C. "The Literary Scene: 1971." REVUE DES
LANGUES VIVANTES (Brussels) 39, no.1 (1973): 83-96.
    Includes McCarthy in a discussion of the various problems
facing contemporary writers. Theorizes that modern life often
resists fictional treatment. Observes how BIRDS OF AMERICA
is an example of one method of meeting the challenge by
portraying nostalgic evocations of a way of life now lost.
Criticizes the book for being disjointed and unconvincing and
wonders if it is because Peter's character was never clearly
defined.

1427. Inoue, Fumiko. "Nature Is Dead in Mary McCarthy's BIRDS
OF AMERICA [Collected Essays by Members of the Faculty in
Commemoration of the 20th Anniversary]." KYORITSU JOSHI
DAIGAKU (Tokyo), no.20 (1973): 98-103.
Evaluates Kantian philosophy and its influence on Peter.
Claims that Peter's passionate love of nature and art helps to
explain his affinity for Kant, whose "ethic offers...a moral
landscape." Examines Kant's dicta "God is Dead" and "Nature is
Dead" from the point of view of language.

1428. Halio, Jay L. "First and Last Things." SOUTHERN REVIEW
n.s. 9, no.1 (Spring 1973): 455-467.
Places BIRDS OF AMERICA in the not recommended
section of a discussion about suggested reading. Disagrees with
Broyard's statement that "McCarthy erred in trying to squeeze
her sensibility into a 19 year old persona." Theorizes instead that
she tried to "fit a running political, social and ecological
commentary-cum-satire into the form of a novel that cannot
sustain it." See also Broyard's review (item no. 1384).

1429. Dawson, Helen. "Paperback Round-up." OBSERVER (London,
G.B.) (June 3, 1973): 33.
Writes that this "hilarious portrait of migrant Americans in
Paris is vintage McCarthy."

1430. BOOKS AND BOOKMEN 18, no.11 (August 1973): 137.
Includes the "picturesque" and "subtle" BIRDS OF
AMERICA in a list of recommended fiction.

1431. Spender, Stephen. "American Redemption." In LOVE-HATE
RELATIONS: ENGLISH AND AMERICAN SENSIBILITIES,
126-130. New York: Random House, 1974.
Investigates McCarthy's view of the United States in BIRDS
OF AMERICA. Believes her point is that Americans are the
kindest people in the world and that even the adulterated material
values with which they have surrounded themselves have not
mechanized their feelings. Concludes that McCarthy's America is
best described as a series of close and detailed studies similar to
Audubon's wonderful colored plates of American birds.

Also published: LOVE-HATE RELATIONS: ENGLISH AND
AMERICAN SENSIBILITIES. New York: Vintage Books,
1975.

MEDINA

1432. "Paperbacks." PUBLISHERS WEEKLY 201, no.19 (May 8,
1972): 51.
    Calls this a shocking report by one of America's most
perceptive and conscientious writers.

  *   Bondy, François. "Mary McCarthy und der Vietnamkrieg."
MERKUR 26 (1972): 1041-1043. German.
    See item no. 1417.

1433. "This Week." CHRISTIAN CENTURY 89, no.25 (June 28,
1972): 722.
    Notes that while the trial may have been a bore, McCarthy's
book is not.

1434. Buck, David D. LIBRARY JOURNAL 97, no.13 (July 1972):
2421-2422.
    Views the book as a series of courtroom reports, well
written but slight.

1435. Friedman, Fredrica S. SATURDAY REVIEW 55, no.29 (July
15, 1972): 55-56.
    Sees the book as making no pretense of objectivity. Feels,
nevertheless, that books such as MEDINA, which ask basic
questions, should be written and should be read.

1436. Johnson, Keith R. "Verdict on My Lai." TIME 100, no.5 (July
31, 1972): 50-51.
    Calls this a disquieting, provocative meditation.

1437. Emerson, Gloria. "The Famous Little Sting." NEW YORK
TIMES BOOK REVIEW (August 13, 1972): 21-22.
   Stresses that while the reviewer is as staunch an opponent of
the war and the army cover-up as McCarthy, she cannot help but
criticize the seemingly smart-aleck tone and upper class contempt
that permeate the book. Declares that this account reads as if it
were written by a shrewd observer working under deadline
pressures. Declares that it will not stand the test of time.

1438. Laut, Stephen J. BEST SELLERS 32, no.10 (August 15, 1972):
234.
   Declares that MEDINA offers no answers but asks all the
right questions. Finds it typical McCarthy--witty, incisive and
infuriating.

1439. Koch, Stephen. "Crimes of the Left: Capt. Medina." NATION
215, no.7 (September 18, 1972): 220-222.
   Contends the book is not true investigative journalism.
Believes the war to be self-evidently evil and the United States
an "unregenerate international criminal," a viewpoint that would
place McCarthy only minimally left of center. Credits her with at
least trying to address ethical and political dilemmas, but feels
she does not pursue her intellectual reflections nearly far enough.

1440. Paquet, Basil T. "Is Anyone Guilty? If So, Who?" NEW YORK
REVIEW OF BOOKS 19, no.4 (September 21, 1972): 35-38.
   Begins with an exploration of the concept of war crimes.
States from personal experience as a medic in Vietnam, that
inhumane and racist treatment of Vietnamese POWs was
commonplace. Finds McCarthy's keen moral sensibility her most
impressive quality, and views the book as an attempt to force us
to recognize the nature of our involvement.

1441. BOOKLIST 69, no.3 (October 1, 1972): 113.
   Considers the book an incisive, thought-provoking adjunct to
fuller treatments of My Lai.

1442. Fuller, Roy. "Deeds and Words." LISTENER 89, no.2291
(February 22, 1973): 248.
   Considers the book brilliant and thought-provoking, a work

of art in its distillation of the essence of a tedious, anticlimactic event. Finds McCarthy's discussion of language and how it reflects the mentality behind My Lai, crucial.

1443. Paskins, Barrie. "Bloody Assize." NEW STATESMAN 85, no.2188 (February 23, 1973): 273-274.
    Agrees in essence with McCarthy's main points. Comments on some of the mistakes made regarding the trial, but finds the fact that the majority of Americans apparently failed to accept the principle of individual responsibility far more disquieting.

1444. Dworkin, Ronald. "War-Crime and Punishment." OBSERVER (London, G.B.) (February 25, 1973): 36.
    Calls the book a brilliant and witty account of small men and the moral culture that produced them. Gives some credence, unlike McCarthy, to the position that in a war which required the destruction of a culture, distinctions between military and civilian killings became untenable.

1445. TIMES (London, G.B.) [Sunday Ed.] (February 25, 1973): 31. Not seen.

1446. Cohen, Stan. "Massacre as Duty." TIMES EDUCATIONAL SUPPLEMENT, no.73 (March 9, 1973): 15.
    Contends that the courtroom often serves as a stage for society's morality plays and judges MEDINA to be a superb moral tract. Notes that McCarthy offers no conspiracy theory to account for the acquittal of Medina other than a generalized refusal by the army, the government and the public to face the larger question of war crimes.

1447. Webb, W. L. "My Lai and After." GUARDIAN AND GUARDIAN WEEKLY 108 (March 10, 1973): 25.
    Notes McCarthy's ability to recognize the vital relationship between the trials of Calley and Medina.

1448. "After My Lai." TIMES LITERARY SUPPLEMENT, no.3706 (March 16, 1973): 283.
    Believes it important that a record be kept of these events

(for which transcripts are apparently unavailable) and finds McCarthy's report clear and careful.

1449. Jardin, Claudine. "Cette semaine, chez votre libraire." FIGARO (April 16, 1973): 18. French.
    Says that McCarthy has attempted to be objective but her objectivity may be consistent with a young Viet Cong.

1450. Jannand, Claude. "Il était un capitaine ..." FIGARO (April 28, 1973): 17. French.
    Notes that although the book is a commentary on the Medina trial, its real importance lies in McCarthy's analysis of how the trial affected and divided the American people.

1451. Ray, Robert. BOOKS AND BOOKMEN 18, no.8 (May 1973): 118-119.
    Uses the greater part of this review to air his own views on the My Lai massacre and the ensuing events. States very emphatically that the system was so "rigged" that a fair assessment of the facts was virtually impossible. Mentions McCarthy's account of the trial almost as an afterthought. Finds her reporting perfect, much to his gloomy satisfaction.

1452. JOURNAL OF CONTEMPORARY ASIA (Stockholm, Sweden) 4, no.1 (1974): 111.
    Finds this account readable and perceptive.

MASK OF STATE: WATERGATE PORTRAITS

1453. Bannon, Barbara A. "PW Forecasts." PUBLISHERS WEEKLY 205, no.14 (April 8, 1974): 82.
    Calls the book a refresher course on Watergate, written with McCarthy's usual flair.

1454. KIRKUS REVIEWS 42 (April 15, 1974): 463.
    Regards McCarthy's insights on the Watergate hearings as

theater as well as politics. Feels her keen perception revives the spirit of amateur detection and civic outrage that animated the millions who viewed the televised proceedings.

1455. Emerson, Gloria. "Mary, Mary, Quite Contrary." BOOK WORLD (WASHINGTON POST) (June 2, 1974): 5.
     Introduces this review with a lengthy look at the preface to THE SEVENTEENTH DEGREE, an essay the reviewer finds very hard to swallow in light of the fact that she herself is a former Vietnam War correspondent. Declares that McCarthy is not a journalist, but rather a celebrity of sorts, who invariably has to be the center of attention always getting her own way.

1456. Ridley, Clifford A. "Two Watergate Books: Facts First." NATIONAL OBSERVER 13 (June 8, 1974): 23.
     Contends that as a source of information, McCarthy's book is almost embarrassingly inadequate, full of incoherent theorizing and pure speculation. Finds her writing, however, lively and evocative, the work of an artist rather than a reporter.

1457. Dooley, Eugene A. BEST SELLERS 34, no.6 (June 15, 1974): 136-137.
     Focuses primarily on her acidic style, acknowledging her keen eye and crisp vocabulary. Takes special note, and just a little offence, at the passing "swipe" at the Jesuits.

1458. Weigel, Jack W. "The Contemporary Scene." LIBRARY JOURNAL 99, no.12 (June 15, 1974): 1689-1690.
     Declares that since she makes no pretense of being a sober, objective reporter, this book may be of interest more as an example of McCarthy's writing than a study of Watergate.

1459. Howard, Anthony. "Morality Stories." NEW STATESMAN 87, no.2258 (June 28, 1974): 923.
     Describes this very short book as an old-fashioned morality play. Finds a number of her arguments persuasive, but is critical of her insistence that the witnesses sported not only horns but tails as well.

1460. Goodwin, Richard. "Watergate Observed." NEW YORK TIMES BOOK REVIEW (June 30, 1974): 5-6.

Reflects that journalists' insistence on reporting only the "facts," and their belief that truth is inherent in the "facts," constitute journalism's fatal flaw. Accepts McCarthy's factual accuracy but stresses that her novelist's sensibilities and synthesizing intelligence are far more important.

1461. BOOKLIST 70, no.21 (July 1, 1974): 1169-1170.

Views this series of astringent essays as outstanding reporting.

1462. Jenkins, Peter. "Routine Inquiries." GUARDIAN AND GUARDIAN WEEKLY 111 (July 6, 1974): 20.

Brief discussion that serves almost as a postscript to a review of ALL THE PRESIDENT'S MEN. Feels that while Woodward and Bernstein's book is riveting, McCarthy's collection offers greater insight.

1463. TIMES (London, G.B.) [Sunday Ed.] (July 7, 1974): 38.

Not seen.

1464. Squerciati, Maria. VILLAGE VOICE 19 (July 11, 1974): 31.

Credits McCarthy with adding another dimension to our understanding of Watergate. Enjoys her caricaturist's clarity and Jamesian sense of tone, critical only of the book's brevity.

1465. OBSERVER (London, G.B.) (July 14, 1974): 33.

Calls these reports Watergate's most penetrating analysis to date.

1466. Beedham, Brian. "Open America." LISTENER 92, no.2364 (July 18, 1974): 92-93.

Theorizes that the Watergate hearings should be viewed not as an American tragedy but as a celebration of a society in which men of power are held accountable for their actions. Concludes his review of Woodward and Bernstein's work with the statement that this is an honorable book; McCarthy's motives he finds less commendable. Says that MASK OF STATE is not a political analysis but a venting of hatred towards Nixon, his men, and even the large part of the American public who voted them into office.

1467. Adler, Larry. "Conversation." NEW SOCIETY 29, no.618 (August 8, 1974): 369.
    Praises McCarthy for interpreting Watergate in her clean and accurate style. Finds the book indispensable.

1468. Marty, Myron A. "Lessons of Watergate." CHRISTIAN CENTURY 91, no.31 (September 18, 1974): 858-859.
    Contends that the book is a superb source of information and insight, the historical value of which will only increase with time. Focuses on the vividness of her portraits and her ability to impressionistically convey the feel of the hearings.

1469. Carron, Alain-Marie. "Sur la piste du Watergate." LE MONDE (October 4, 1974): 1, 21. French.
    Reviews MASK OF STATE: WATERGATE PORTRAITS and ALL THE PRESIDENT'S MEN and argues that they are written from different perspectives. Says the Woodward/Bernstein book relates the adventure of uncovering the truth behind the Watergate affair, whereas McCarthy's essay is a polemic in which she leaves no doubt that she hates Nixon and is obsessed with American involvement in Vietnam.

1470. Rosenberg, Harold. "Up Against the News." NEW YORK REVIEW OF BOOKS 21, no.17 (October 31, 1974): 16-18.
    Contends that McCarthy was more vitally involved in Vietnam and Watergate than any other American literary personality. States that both THE SEVENTEENTH DEGREE and MASK OF STATE are clearly rhetorical in intent with no pretense at journalistic neutrality, but finds the viewpoint of writer rather than reporter in no way less viable. Devotes a large part of the review to a rebuttal of James Fallows' attack on McCarthy. See also Fallows' article (item no. 449).

1471. Moeller, Leslie G. JOURNALISM QUARTERLY 51 (Winter 1974): 746-747.
    Suggests that McCarthy's performance compares favorably with Rebecca West's outstanding reporting of the trials following

World War II. Calls McCarthy a skilled observer, penetrating thinker and superb writer.

1472. NEW YORK TIMES BOOK REVIEW (December 1, 1974): 78.
    Includes McCarthy's book in a selection of noteworthy titles from 1974.

1473. Campbell, W. R. "'Administration' and the Death of Politics." WORLDVIEW 18 (January 1975): 54-57.
    Offers a lengthy discussion of the system of beliefs that underlie American covert activities. Deems McCarthy's book, one of several being reviewed, very perceptive, although disagrees with her contention that the public reaction to Watergate was laden with guilt over Vietnam.

1474. Raskin, Marcus. "From Vietnam to Watergate." PARTISAN REVIEW 42, no.4 (Winter 1975): 625-629.
    Analyzes McCarthy's books on Vietnam and Watergate within the framework of the sixties, both personal and political. Contends her role in Vietnam was that of a committee person who happened to write, and admires both her passionate stance and powerful insights. Finds her Watergate portraits less successful. Believes anger and impatience have masked the need to ask the more fundamental question--why it all happened.

THE SEVENTEENTH DEGREE

1475. "This Week's Arrivals." CHRISTIAN CENTURY 91, no.20 (May 22, 1974): 569.
    Calls the book large for the price, full of conscious raising observations and arguments.

  * Emerson, Gloria. "Mary, Mary, Quite Contrary." BOOK WORLD (WASHINGTON POST) (June 2, 1974): 5.
     See item no. 1455.

342   *Mary McCarthy: An Annotated Bibliography*

1476. BOOKLIST 70, no.21 (July 1, 1974): 1176-1177.
Notes that the bold insight and bitter moral outrage of the book stems from the trilogy, VIETNAM, HANOI, and MEDINA.

1477. Muggeridge, Malcolm. "Books." ESQUIRE 82 (August 1974): 34, 44.
Offers a passing reference to the book as just one more addition to the equally fraudulent patriotic/antipatriotic outpouring on the war.

1478. Wright, Scott. LIBRARY JOURNAL 99, no.14 (August 1974): 1963.
Questions the republishing of this material, thoughtful and well written as it may be.

1479. CHOICE 11 (September 1974): 1024.
Assesses that its value, if somewhat dubious, lies in being representative of American anti-Vietnam War criticism.

*   Rosenberg, Harold. "Up Against the News." NEW YORK REVIEW OF BOOKS 21, no.17 (October 31, 1974): 16-18.
See item no. 1470.

1480. Capp, Al. "American Farce." SPECTATOR 234, no.7651 (February 15, 1975): 182.
Introduces her as part of a rarefied circle whose only sortie into real life came about inadvertently with the publication of THE GROUP. Compares her to Jane Fonda and Joan Baez, and finds a difference only in the fact that they have had the good sense to be embarrassed about the stand they took in the sixties. Calls her "exhibit A in the dishrag category of women's liberation" while insinuating that her husband might have been a CIA agent. Argues that the Mary McCarthys not only didn't help end the war, but by bringing Nixon to power, helped prolong it.

1481. Allman, T. D. "Versions of Vietnam." GUARDIAN AND GUARDIAN WEEKLY (G.B.) (February 22, 1975): 22.
Argues that this publication, composed primarily of reprints, is an exercise in self-indulgence. Uses her corrosive review of

Halberstam's best seller THE BEST AND THE BRIGHTEST as
a springboard to examine McCarthy's pique over what she
believes to be insufficient media attention given to her original
pamphlets. Proposes that the articles were simply "terribly
average" although her commitment to the issues was sincere.

1482. J., C. OBSERVER (London, G.B.) (March 2, 1975): 26.
States that this substantial volume is thoughtful and
interesting.

1483. Theroux, Paul. "Mother Superior." NEW STATESMAN 89,
no.2294 (March 7, 1975): 311-312.
Empathizes with the anger and sadness that infuse these
candid and thoughtful essays. Attests, from his own personal
experience, that Vietnam is a shattered and scarred country, and
the war, for the Vietnamese, has not ended. Counters allegations
that this material has outlived its usefulness by warning that
increased military spending is once again being sought;
McCarthy's book might yet move from the realm of history to
that of prophecy.

1484. West, Richard. "A Sorry Story." TIMES (London, G.B.)
[Sunday Ed.] (March 27, 1975): 14.
Credits McCarthy with being one of the few literary figures
who actually visited the battle front, but suggests that she would
have written a more valuable book if she had stayed longer.
Admires her shrewd and observant essays and describes THE
SEVENTEENTH DEGREE as "one of the few really good
books" about the tragic involvement of the United States in
Vietnam.

* Raskin, Marcus. "From Vietnam to Watergate." PARTISAN
REVIEW 42, no.4 (Winter 1975): 625-629.
See item no. 1474.

CANNIBALS AND MISSIONARIES

1485. Mitgang, Herbert. "New Mary McCarthy." NEW YORK
TIMES BOOK REVIEW 84 (June 17, 1979): 39.
    Quotes from an interview with McCarthy held just before the
publication of CANNIBALS AND MISSIONARIES. Notes that
although McCarthy does not like all of her own books, she does
like this one.

1486. Bannon, Barbara A. "PW Forecasts." PUBLISHERS WEEKLY
216, no.7 (August 13, 1979): 49.
    Comments that this "superb storyteller" spins "a tale [that is]
psychologically astute, ironic and ultimately heartbreaking."

1487. KIRKUS REVIEWS 47 (August 15, 1979): 953-954.
    Argues that true to form, McCarthy's characters are
undeveloped and the plot is arbitrary and "hardly suspenseful."
Suggests, however, that the novel does explore socio-political
issues and that McCarthy offers enough "little rewards" to make
the novel worth reading.

1488. BOOKLIST 76, no.2 (September 15, 1979): 96.
    Suggests that the book, which explores the questions of
ethics and aesthetics, is "compulsively readable" although it lacks
the "acid bite" of her earlier work.

1489. VILLAGE VOICE 24, no.38 (September 17, 1979): 45.
    Describes the novel as "Airport 75 . . . dressed up and
politicized."

1490. Gordon, Mary. "A Novel of Terrorism." NEW YORK TIMES
BOOK REVIEW 84 (September 30, 1979): 1, 33-35.
    Proposes a feminist reading of the novel, one which takes
into account McCarthy's own background and sensibilities. Sees
the book as providing a clear understanding of the psychology of
terrorism. Admires both the form and content and claims the
tone is one of "lively pessimism."

1491. Bell, Pearl K. "Elizabeth Hardwick and Mary McCarthy."
COMMENTARY 68, no.4 (October 1979): 65-67.
Compares the novel with Hardwick's SLEEPLESS NIGHTS.
Says that McCarthy's novel is a "sort of suspense thriller with
high intellectual gloss." Argues that while the book is replete
with facts, they do not often add to the story. Suggests that
McCarthy seems to have lost her lucid vision and "unslipping
indignation" and wonders whether or not she has made up her
own mind about the story's meaning.

1492. Medwick, Cathleen. "Books." VOGUE (October 1979): 36.
Argues that McCarthy, who has the talent to "make the
parochial seem universal," has failed and made "the universe a
size too small."

1493. Kempf, Andrea Caron. LIBRARY JOURNAL 104 (October 1,
1979): 2119-2120.
Proposes that this is a tragi-comedy of manners in which the
value of art, as opposed to human life, is the main theme.

1494. Sheppard, R. Z. "When Worlds Collide." TIME 114, no.14
(October 1, 1979): 89.
Suggests that even though her "olympian view" has remained
keen in her seventh novel, McCarthy has "overflown her
subject." Claims that her cast of characters is so large that she
fails to create personalities for them, substituting instead
cumbersome dossiers.

1495. Lehmann-Haupt, Christopher. "Books of the Times." NEW
YORK TIMES (October 4, 1979): C20.
Describes the book as a social satire that explores the moral
implications of a situation the author has "dreamed up." Sees the
novel as an intellectual game that asks the reader to decide who
are the cannibals and who are the missionaries.

Also published in: BOOKS OF THE TIMES 2 (October 1979):
484.

1496. Clemens, Walter. "Mortality Play in the Sky." NEWSWEEK 94 (October 8, 1979): 92, 95.

Argues that the book is a "double disappointment," lacking the thrills of a hijacking story and the malice and wit usually expected from McCarthy. Comments that her characters do not come to life and notes that it's only saving grace is the portrayal of behavior under stress.

1497. Stone, Laurie. "Cannibal Stew." VILLAGE VOICE 24, no.41 (October 15, 1979): 41-42.

Examines the form of the book and suggests that it becomes more interesting two-thirds of the way along. Explains that the method of building chapters around particular characters only works when the characters are of sufficient interest. Concludes that the book lacks passion and the end is a letdown.

1498. Sage, Lorna. "Picnic with Terror." OBSERVER (London, G.B.) (October 21, 1979): 39.

Proposes that the novel is a "tragi-comedy of liberalism," the American contingent taking on the task of going to Iran only because they have run out of noble causes at home. Concludes that McCarthy has "decided that moral understanding and action are even further divorced from each other now than they were in the 1950s."

1499. Adams, Robert Martin. "Unhappy Landings." NEW YORK REVIEW OF BOOKS 26, no.16 (October 25, 1979): 38-40.

Calls this novel a "high comedy of mixed motives, inept calculations, and personal weakness." Finds the details too tedious to be cohesive. Suggests that the novel is open to many diverse interpretations because it leaves so many of the human and intellectual equations unresolved.

1500. "Picks & Pans." PEOPLE WEEKLY (October 25, 1979): 16.

Suggests that McCarthy's "old-fashioned literary pretenses spoil most of the pleasure one might get from this book."

1501. Mortimer, Penelope. "Hold-All." NEW STATESMAN 98, no.2536 (October 26, 1979): 641-642.

States clearly that the tedium of facts and the flatness of the characters make this an uninteresting novel. Suggests that McCarthy would do well to concentrate on factual writing and leave fiction to those with some imagination.

1502. Clapperton, Jane. "Cosmo Reads the New Books." COSMOPOLITAN (November 1979): 62.

Argues that McCarthy has a knack for exploring and exposing human flaws, artfully depicting the hostages fear for their lives while they fight for bathroom privileges. Suggests that "terrorism" is the most frightening "boogyman" of our age and that no one can depict this more effectively than McCarthy.

1503. DeMott, Benjamin. ATLANTIC MONTHLY 244, no.5 (November 1979): 93-94.

Proposes that the main issue in the novel is "who are the cannibals and who are the missionaries?" Says the novel lacks focus, the potentially exciting plot never takes off, and the characters rarely come to life. Suggests that the only genuinely sympathetic character is the leader of the terrorists.

1504. Howard, Maureen. "Liberals and Libidos." ESQUIRE 92, no.5 (November 1979): 16, 18.

Criticizes, reluctantly, the novel's pace. States that McCarthy should have let the story, because it is a thriller, move forward instead of imposing her essayist's style. Points out that she does not control her minor characters well but does succeed in writing some particularly touching scenes, especially the one describing the Bishop's funeral.

1505. King, Francis. "McCarthyism." SPECTATOR 243 (November 3, 1979): 24.

Looks at the novel with a cynical eye and concludes that what it "intermittently lacks is the intensity of imagination that made her earlier novels so remarkable."

1506. Lingeman, Richard. "She Gets No Kick in a Plane." NATION 229, no.15 (November 10, 1979): 470-472.

Comments that although McCarthy is normally successful writing about people in social situations, she has picked the wrong situation and the wrong mix of characters in this case.

Suggests that one would normally expect some revealing clashes between the characters but none occur. Concludes that there is something missing; an "emptiness" which is defined as a lack of "the passionate heart and mind of the author herself."

1507. Edwards, Thomas R. "Books and Arts: CANNIBALS AND MISSIONARIES." NEW REPUBLIC 181, no.20 (November 17, 1979): 30-32.

Points out that the facts do not hang together despite McCarthy's stated intention to present a totally realistic picture. Finds the characters unconvincing and the hijackers demands totally lacking authenticity. Suggests, in fact, that no government would ever place a higher value on art than on human life. Adds that the dialogue and situation between the hijackers and the captives is, at the most basic level, unrealistic. Concludes that despite the shortcomings, McCarthy "has pleasure and instruction to give to anyone who values wit, intelligence, and seriousness of purpose."

1508. NEW YORK TIMES BOOK REVIEW (November 25, 1979): 46.

Refers to the book as "the most political, the least autobiographical" of McCarthy's novels.

1509. DeMott, Benjamin. "Tales of Two Writers." SATURDAY REVIEW 6 (December 1979): 53-55.

Compares CANNIBALS AND MISSIONARIES with Lessing's SHIKASTA and suggests the two books have a similar theme--the difficulty of learning to see oneself. Suggests that part of McCarthy's mission is to examine the resources people possess for self-clarification.

1510. Roman, David R. BEST SELLERS 39, no.9 (December 1979): 324.

Calls this a "tedious tale" and argues that McCarthy spends too much time laying the ground work and not enough developing the plot or the characters. Accuses her of not having a feel for terrorist politics and suggests that she misses the opportunity to discuss differing attitudes and ideologies at any level other than the very basic. Concludes that the book is "stimulating reading" despite its shortcomings.

1511. Miner, Valerie. "A Setting for Heroism--but ..." CHRISTIAN SCIENCE MONITOR (December 3, 1979): B19.
    Argues that while McCarthy raises many moral and philosophical questions, she provides very few answers.

1512. Binyon, T. J. "Cash and Carry." TIMES LITERARY SUPPLEMENT, no.4003 (December 7, 1979): 86.
    Proposes that the early chapters are the most satisfying in this novel of ideas.

1513. Grumbach, Doris. "All the Fictions for a Seasonal Feast." BOOK WORLD (WASHINGTON POST) 9, no.18 (December 9, 1979): 1, 8-9.
    States that this is a "successful and timely adventure-suspense story."

1514. Tennant, Emma. "On the Polder." LISTENER 102, no.2641 (December 13, 1979): 824-825.
    Argues that the "modern-ness" of the prose is the main reason for the lack of excitement in the novel. Claims that her prose style deadens the reader to the violence and the moral dilemmas of the age.

1515. Wimsatt, Margaret. "Books: Terrorists vs. Talkers." COMMONWEAL 106, no.23 (December 21, 1979): 727.
    Argues that the book is about "the philosophies of terrorism, the attitudes attendant upon ownership, and the fallacies of liberalism," and not about the current political situation in Iran. Suggests that McCarthy empathizes with the liberal committee members, draws them carefully and lets the reader know them best. Explores the argument of the relative value of art and human life, cynically suggesting that the "average reader does not feel a 'thrill of horror' at the vandalism of art, and would probably rather have saved Aldo Moro than any picture, anywhere."

1516. Hayman, Ronald. "Mary McCarthy's Terrorism." BOOKS AND BOOKMEN 25, no.4 (January 1980): 53-54.

Argues that McCarthy does not fully explore the ideas in the book. Suggests that she might have better conveyed her message by writing an essay or an article. Goes on to explore the notion that while parts of the book are indeed brilliant, the whole does not hang together; characters are created and then dropped, the plot moves slowly if all, and the ending seems contrived.

1517. Weinberger, David. "The Wrong Stuff." MACLEAN'S MAGAZINE 93, no.2 (January 14, 1980): 48-49.

States that McCarthy has written a novel reflecting an intellectual's idea of a hijacking, yet her own intellect fails her. Finds it unrealistic that the hijackers and captives have "essay-question" discussions while the events are unfolding.

1518. Cole, Diane. GEORGIA REVIEW 34, no.1 (Spring 1980): 228-231.

Argues from the point of view of a hostage. Claims that McCarthy does not represent the experience realistically, leaving many unanswered questions. Believes she has done her research but has failed to enter the minds and souls of both the hostages and the terrorists.

1519. Epstein, Joseph. "Too Much Even of Kreplach." HUDSON REVIEW 33, no.1 (Spring 1980): 97-110.

Criticizes McCarthy's writing in general, saying that the artist is constantly in conflict with the intellectual and the artist loses. Suggests that because of McCarthy's desire to espouse left-wing politics, the terrorists appear less intimidating than they might and the hostages evoke very little sympathy. Concludes that while CANNIBALS AND MISSIONARIES [is] the work of a writer of maturity and recognized accomplishments, [it] is a novel [that is] neither entertaining nor profound."

1520. West, Barbara. "At Home with Hijackers and Hostages." CHATELAINE 53 (April 1980): 10.

Summarizes the main plot of this "entertaining, but flawed book." Suggests one problem with CANNIBALS AND

MISSIONARIES is that many of the cast remain unrealized and by the final scene the reader is indifferent.

1521. Durkin, Mary. CRITIC 38 (April 1, 1980): 4-5.
Argues that this is not a typical "thriller" despite the presence of some of the standard elements. Says McCarthy portrays the shallowness of all the characters and explores their psychological interrelationships. Concludes that "the reader must decide if what went before is worth the effort of reading through to the conclusion."

1522. Young-Bruehl, Elisabeth. "A Judicious Stance." CANTO; REVIEW OF THE ARTS 3, no.2 (May 1980): 168-173.
Sees the novel in terms of the game "cannibals and missionaries" from which McCarthy borrowed the title for the book, and suggests that the question or puzzle really is, "who will live and who will die, in what order, and for what reasons." Proposes that only the journalist Sophie Weil has the strength of mind and character to ask the questions McCarthy wants asked. Concludes that the novel leaves one wondering "what would happen if?"

1523. PUBLISHERS WEEKLY 218, no.4 (July 25, 1980): 156.
Writes "McCarthy is, as always, a superb storyteller, and she builds the suspense as adroitly as if she had been writing thrillers all her life."

1524. Mano, D. Keith. "Down and Out in Holland." NATIONAL REVIEW 32, no.16 (August 8, 1980): 974.
Comments that the novel does not succeed as a thriller. Finds her examination of the value of art and morality only mildly interesting since both have been discussed by many other writers. Ridicules McCarthy for needing help with New York "social" names saying, "not only has she written a dreadful book, she needed help to write it."

1525. "Paperbacks: New and Noteworthy." NEW YORK TIMES BOOK REVIEW 85 (September 14, 1980): 43.
Includes CANNIBALS AND MISSIONARIES in a listing of recommended new paperbacks and provides a brief synopsis.

1526. Rolin, Gabrielle. "Le Prix des otages." LE MONDE (February 6, 1981). French.
    Argues that McCarthy writes like a reporter, overpowering the reader with details of plans and events. Says that this book really questions what it is that we value and forces us to gradually lower our standards as the book progresses.

1527. Kilpatrick, James J. "For a Writer, Nothing Beats a Good Lumberyard." ATLANTA JOURNAL (July 20, 1984): 12.
    Proposes that many of the images used by McCarthy in the book come from McCarthy's "lumberyard" of memories.

1528. Tremblay, Jean-Noel. "Portraits...d'une époque." L'ANALYSTE, no.15 (Autumn 1986): 76-77. French.
    Argues that McCarthy offers a clear analysis of a familiar situation. Claims that the strength of the novel is her ability to see humor even in tragedy and merge it with a biting social portrait.

1529. Gordon, Mary. "Mary McCarthy: OCCASIONAL PROSE and CANNIBALS AND MISSIONARIES." In GOOD BOYS AND DEAD GIRLS: AND OTHER ESSAYS, 57-66. New York: Viking, 1991.
    Examines McCarthy's ability to balance her devotion to excellence with a sense of justice. Says she is political, but within a world of ideas based on philosophy and not sociology. Acknowledges her superb reminiscences of Arendt, Dupee and Didion. Attributes her understanding and depiction of physical fear, communal bonding and the psychology of terrorism to her experiences in Vietnam, noting that she has once again asked the difficult question and confronted the difficult problem.

IDEAS AND THE NOVEL

1530. Mallon, Thomas. "Review: The Novel on Elba."
SHENANDOAH 31, no.4 (1980): 95-100.
Dubs IDEAS AND THE NOVEL the most stimulating book
about fiction since Forster's ASPECTS OF THE NOVEL. Notes
McCarthy expands on ideas she first examined in ON THE
CONTRARY and THE WRITING ON THE WALL with such
wit and energy that the reader feels a sense of loss and wonder at
the literary choices s/he may have made. Details her theories in
relation to Kiely, Barth and Snow, and suggests that unless
criticism bolsters its search for the "light" it will, and probably
should, "put itself out of business."

1531. KIRKUS REVIEWS 48 (September 1, 1980): 1213.
Views the lectures as insightful and a fine taking-off point
for discussion of past and present fiction, but disappointing
because they end up begging their own questions.

1532. Ott, B. BOOKLIST 77, no.4 (October 15, 1980): 299.
Agrees that McCarthy's thesis is not unjustified, however,
contends that she never seems to progress beyond a hazy notion
of rules and ideas as strange bedfellows. Recommends the book
for venues of literary criticism.

1533. Cook, Carole. SATURDAY REVIEW 7, no.15 (November
1980): 77.
Emphasizes that McCarthy's brilliant, passionate argument of
a familiar theme makes this an admirable book that may alter the
fate of the Western novel in the twenty-first century.

1534. Leonard, John. "Books of the Times." NEW YORK TIMES
(November 18, 1980): C12.
Proposes that McCarthy has been over this ground before in
ON THE CONTRARY and THE WRITING ON THE WALL,
but never with such charm and skill. Reflects that one can almost
picture her sitting in front of a fireplace with the great nineteenth
century novelists, burning texts about structuralism and

deconstructionism. Theorizes that McCarthy mourns "the modern failure of curiosity" above all, and applauds her for making serious literature matter again.

Also published in: BOOKS OF THE TIMES 4, no.1 (January 1981): 37.

1535. Alter, Robert. "McCarthy: Minding the Story." BOOK WORLD (WASHINGTON POST) 10 (November 30, 1980): 1, 6.
        Observes the book has clear, urbane prose with shrewd perceptions, but lacks the incisiveness of THE FACT IN FICTION and CHARACTERS IN FICTION. Examines the two main problems--the book reviews more than instructs and lacks the ideas of key critics such as Girard and Bakhtin. Criticizes casual manner with literary facts and her vagueness about the meaning of "idea."

1536. Vidal, Gore. "The Thinking Man's Novel." NEW YORK REVIEW OF BOOKS 27, no.19 (December 4, 1980): 10, 12.
        Discusses IDEAS AND THE NOVEL, theorizing about the notion of the artist as a martyr, the role of the publisher, the historical and political novel, the novel of ideas, what is being written and why, and what is being read and why. Examines the serious novel and concludes it is of no actual interest to anyone including the sort of people who write it.

Also published as "Thomas Love Peacock: the Novel of Ideas" in: THE SECOND AMERICAN REVOLUTION AND OTHER ESSAYS (1976-1982). 115-131. New York: Random House, 1982.

1537. Romano, John. "In Praise of Loose Baggy Monsters." NEW REPUBLIC 183, no.24 (December 13, 1980): 32.
        Questions why McCarthy's own novels are only slightly "ideé" when she is so passionate about the lost "graces of novels with ideas." Argues that despite the insightful study of the French novel in relation to her thesis, she has missed the mark in her study of Tolstoy, Eliot and Dostoyevsky.

1538. Hauptman, Robert. LIBRARY JOURNAL 106, no.1 (January 1, 1981): 57.

Reports briefly that this is a thought provoking study with sometimes distracting plot summaries and occasional serious lapses in McCarthy's dogmatic assertations.

1539. Donoghue, Denis. "Should Novels Argue?" NEW YORK TIMES BOOK REVIEW 86 (January 18, 1981): 9, 27.

Analyzes McCarthy's thesis in detail and concludes it is unconvincing. Says that James did not banish ideas from the novel; in fact his novels THE BOSTONIANS and THE PRINCESS CASAMASSIMA are not only full of ideas but he is relentless in debating them. Contends McCarthy's real aim is to defend the kind of fiction she has written and suggests the essays are only interesting seen in relation to her books, A CHARMED LIFE, THE COMPANY SHE KEEPS, and BIRDS OF AMERICA.

1540. Jordan, Francis X. BEST SELLERS 40, no.11 (February 1981): 408.

Stresses that the book is McCarthy's intelligent attempt to destroy the modern critic's attitude that the novelist must abandon ideas in order to show rather than tell. Reviews the book's critical insights into James, Lawrence and Mailer and stresses that the perceptive readings of several novels, as well as the quality of style similar to that of a skilled conversationalist, make the book a delight to read.

1541. Nolte, William H. AMERICAN SPECTATOR 14, no.2 (February 1981): 33.

Considers that McCarthy's assessment of James' achievements will "ruffle the feathers of devout Jamesians." Says that McCarthy concludes reviewers and literature teachers must be disarmed for the novel to be revitalized. Stresses McCarthy has something important to say about important books and she says it in a sharp, fresh way.

1542. CRITIC 39 (February 1, 1981): 8.

Comments on McCarthy's thesis that the modernist movement was responsible for diminishing the worth of philosophies and ideas in fiction. Reports the book will stir up the embers of the literary community.

1543. Allen, Walter. "McCarthy's Improving Books." TIMES (London, G.B.) [Sunday Ed.] (February 8, 1981): 43.
    Comments that the book is a literary "polemic" of the highest order. Discusses McCarthy's ideas and theories.

1544. Weightman, John G. "Rag-Bag Or Art Form?" OBSERVER (London, G.B.) (February 8, 1981): 33.
    Takes exception to McCarthy's theory that ideas are virtually absent from the modern art novel. Claims, however, to have enjoyed her "debanking" of James and suggests that she ought to write a full-length analysis of his work.

1545. Boston, Richard. "Contrary Mary." PUNCH 280 (February 11, 1981): 242.
    Disagrees with McCarthy's main thesis and suggests that diminishing the power of the idea by subjecting it to "real life" is in fact one of the functions of the novel. Stresses that McCarthy always has something new to say and that she says it with intelligence and confidence.

1546. Stone, Laurie. "Belting Chastity." VILLAGE VOICE 26, no.7 (February 11, 1981): 44-45.
    Criticizes McCarthy for writing a book which reads like an "angry letter banged out after a feverish night." Examines the book's inaccuracies, preposterous assertations and lack of in-depth study on the contemporary novel.

1547. Davies, Peter. TIMES (London, G.B.) (February 18, 1981): 13.
    Contends that even though the book has an abundance of good ideas, McCarthy's thesis wears thin when she discusses the English novel.

1548. Pritchard, William H. "Criticism As Literature." HUDSON REVIEW 34, no.1 (Spring 1981): 117-124.
    Notes the book's fine perceptions but says McCarthy's arguments become less convincing the more one thinks about them. Theorizes that she sat down to write about an idea she had

about ideas and by the end of it all, the idea had her. Concludes the book can be read with pleasure only after admitting that its organizing idea is full of holes.

1549. Burris, Keith. "Playing With Ideas." NATIONAL CATHOLIC REPORTER (March 6, 1981): 17.

Observes there is less of McCarthy's good sense and independent nerve in IDEAS AND THE NOVEL than in THE WRITING ON THE WALL and ON THE CONTRARY. Discusses her concern with the lack of thought in modern literature. Praises her for dealing with ideas and thinking through stories about the things that matter most.

1550. Campbell, James. "Writing in the Good Old Way." NEW STATESMAN 101, no.2607 (March 6, 1981): 20-21.

Compares the book to Nabokov's LECTURES ON LITERATURE and says McCarthy would "moan" over his central dogma that style and structure are the essence of great literature. Emphasizes the exceptions to McCarthy's thesis that the modern novelist suspects ideas are unsightly, particularly in the books of Miller, Kerouac, Golding and Malamud. Concludes the book suffers from being a series of lectures with too many loose ends, dressed up to look like a collection of essays.

1551. Grosskurth, Phyllis. "An Absence of Abstraction." TIMES LITERARY SUPPLEMENT, no.4066 (March 6, 1981): 252.

Reflects on the experience of hearing McCarthy lecture and decides that although one can savor the wit, premeditated pauses and charm of her as a speaker, the reader gains time to ponder the force and plausibility of a particular argument. Criticizes her for presenting an unclear picture of an "idea" and failing to identify what has been lost in the novel or what now stands in its place. Maintains the book is a "red herring rag-bag" of undeveloped impressions written by a good novelist who is not a good theorist.

1552. "Mary, Mary Quite Contrary." ECONOMIST 278, no.7178 (March 28-April 3, 1981): 102.

Says that while McCarthy no doubt ended her series of lectures in London to applause, her written work "begs all sorts of questions." Maintains the reader will reflect upon his or her own reading experiences and realize that McCarthy's provocative account of the course of the novel is a "travesty of alarming exclusion" and uncertainty as to what is meant by "ideas."

1553. Howard, Jane. "Books." MADEMOISELLE (April, 1981): 140.
Discusses McCarthy's thesis that ideas in a novel are now held to be unsightly and that the novelist's concern must be to save the particulars whatever the cost to the perfection of the design.

1554. "Recent Arrivals." CHRISTIAN CENTURY 98, no.12 (April 8, 1981): 395.
Observes that one must be an insider to catch all the allusions in this welcome addition to high-level cocktail conversation.

1555. Hulbert, Ann. "The Province of Art." COMMENTARY 71, no.5 (May 1981): 92-94.
Examines McCarthy's thesis in detail and proposes that her warnings about the plight of ideas in the modern novel may be exaggerated. Suggests that the aesthetics that have fostered experimentation with language and sensibility are not yet as much "the law" as McCarthy states, nor has the debate over whether fiction should offer philosophical truth or aesthetic pleasures been settled in favor of aesthetics. Concludes that what the novel needs is a complex understanding of the human spirit in plot, setting and character.

1556. WILSON QUARTERLY 5 (Summer 1981): 160-161.
Offers a synopsis of McCarthy's thesis.

1557. Bergonzi, Bernard. "The Foundling & the Bastard: Theories of Fiction." ENCOUNTER 57, no.1 (July 1981): 64-70.
Examines the theory of fiction in several books. Proposes that McCarthy's book, witty and energetic as it is, never makes a strong case and her claim that "ideas are held not to belong to the novel" depends on how the ideas work. Stresses that her argument that there were more ideas in nineteenth century fiction than in twentieth is countered by the fact that ideas, common in

Victorian fiction, tend to be religious not political. Continues that she contradicts her thesis by admitting American Jewish writers have a special license to juggle ideas in full view. Suggests she should have considered how feminist writers, particularly French, Weldon and Fairbairn, are virtually obsessive in their use of certain governing ideas.

1558. Stevick, P. "Miscellaneous." MODERN FICTION STUDIES 27, no.4 (Winter 1981-82): 748-752.
      Admires McCarthy's art, wit and infectious sense of power and adds the book encourages one to read the texts discussed. Finds that McCarthy expands on what excites her, leaves in the odd sentence which amuses her and ignores large portions of potential material. Argues that she should have had more to say about twentieth century literature, particularly Sartre, Camus, Beckett and Barth, and concludes the book is self-indulgent, thin and partial.

1559. Exner, R. WORLD LITERATURE TODAY 56 (Winter 1982): 115-116.
      Warns readers to approach the book as warily as they would any book written by a practicing novelist who deals with theoretical pronouncements on literary history and writing. Observes McCarthy offers pleasurable reading and fresh insight into the great novels, however, considers it ironic that she thinks reviewers and teachers stifle the modern author when they are exactly the ones who will be reading her book.

   * Zand, Nicole. "Mary et Mavis, deux Parisiennes d'Amerique." LE MONDE (May 13, 1988). French.
         See item no. 622.

   * Baredette, Gilles. "McCarthy: l'esprit des mots." L'EXPRESS, no.1924 (May 27, 1988): 68. French.
         See item no. 623.

HOUNDS OF SUMMER AND OTHER STORIES:
MARY McCARTHY'S SHORT FICTION

1560. Lodge, Sally A. "Fiction Originals." PUBLISHERS WEEKLY
219 (June 12, 1981): 52.
Describes the stories as cool and finely calculated, covering
a wide array of characters, settings and moods.

1561. BOOKLIST 77, no.22-23 (July-August 1981): 1434.
Notes the range of this new collection of essays, the majority
of which appeared previously in CAST A COLD EYE.

1562. "Paperbacks: New and Noteworthy." NEW YORK TIMES
BOOK REVIEW 86 (September 13, 1981): 55.
Reports on the publication of this collection composed
primarily of pieces found in CAST A COLD EYE with two
additional stories.

OCCASIONAL PROSE

1563. KIRKUS REVIEWS 53, no.6 (March 15, 1985): 271.
Calls this an offbeat collection of variously impressive
pieces, characterized by McCarthy's steely wit and lucid style.

1564. Stuttaford, Genevieve. "PW Forecasts." PUBLISHERS
WEEKLY 227, no.12 (March 22, 1985): 47.
Evaluates the collection, while not of startling impact, as
well worth reading.

1565. Simon, Linda. LIBRARY JOURNAL 110, no.6 (April 1, 1985):
144.
Considers McCarthy's comments on the intellectual life
always worth hearing.

1566. BOOKLIST 81, no.16 (April 15, 1985): 1152.
 Acknowledges the spirited individuality and intelligence that distinguishes this collection of social and literary criticism.

1567. Kanfer, Stefan. "Reflections." TIME 125, no.15 (April 15, 1985): 101-102.
 Maintains that time has validated Wilson's appraisal of McCarthy, written more than forty years previously, when he wondered, might she not be the "woman Stendahl." Quotes McCarthy extensively to illustrate the distinctive voice and cool analytic manner he obviously finds a delight.

1568. Moynahan, Julian. "You Pay Attention, You Learn Something." NEW YORK TIMES BOOK REVIEW 90 (May 5, 1985): 15.
 Notes her distinctive eye for detail and inclination to view public events as theater. Admires her ability to unravel serious texts, although comments that she "tries" to do something similar to her superb explication of twenty-five years ago. Commends her seemingly unique ability to link diverse elements of her broad base of knowledge, although he disagrees with some of her opinions. Views McCarthy's opinions, nonetheless, as invigorating and her writing distinguished and always worthy of attention.

1569. Schott, Webster. "Mary, Mary, Quite Contrary." BOOK WORLD (WASHINGTON POST) 15, no.19 (May 12, 1985): 5, 8.
 Observes that the broad spectrum of writing found in this collection clearly shows why McCarthy can almost be considered a national cultural asset. Feels much of her attraction lies in her independent mind and her "pollution-free intellect." Believes that her purpose is to redefine human experience and action, and in doing so, find meaning and order in life.

 Also published in: GUARDIAN AND GUARDIAN WEEKLY (June 23, 1985): 18.

1570. Kendall, Elaine. "McCarthy, Firm Foe of Human Folly." LOS
ANGELES TIMES (May 13, 1985): V6.
    Describes this sampler as a splendid reminder of her
versatility and range. Realizes McCarthy's commitment is as
implacable, adamant and passionate as ever despite his initial
reaction that she had appeared more mellow. Claims if there has
been a change, it has been not in the writing, but in the
response.

1571. Kuehn, Robert E. "Mixed Company: McCarthy Recycles Her
Odds and Ends." BOOK WORLD (CHICAGO TRIBUNE) (May
19, 1985): 43.
    Questions the value of reprinting a collection of dissimilar,
unconnected pieces in which there is no apparent unifying
principle, and concludes the only rationale can be "getting paid
twice for the same work." Acknowledges, however, that the
rhetorical analysis in several of the longer pieces is marvellous.
Favors "The Very Unforgettable Miss Brayton," as a detailed
and ironic portrait reminiscent of the female characters in THE
GROUP.

1572. Linkous, Robert. SAN FRANCISCO REVIEW OF BOOKS 10,
no.1 (Summer 1985): 10.
    Argues that this compilation consists largely of trivialities
with only the odd treasure. Finds, for the most part, that which
is not obscure is merely innocuous; the lectures sophomoric, the
reviews little more than jacket blurbs. Concludes, rather
heavy-handedly, that OCCASIONAL PROSE is not worth the
bother.

1573. Austin, Jacqueline. "A Sense of Occasion." VILLAGE VOICE
30, no.23 (June 4, 1985): 47.
    Contends that the title should be understood to mean
pertaining to occasions, rather than merely miscellaneous
writings. Believes McCarthy retains the quality of amateurism in
the old sense of the word, doing what she does for the love of it.
Recognizes McCarthy's knowledgeable wit and daring, but
reserves the highest praise for her ability to transform the
external into the personal, making each moment into an occasion.

1574. "And the Critics Commend." LOS ANGELES TIMES [Sunday Ed.] (June 16, 1985): B14.
   Supplies a very brief commendation.

1575. Rubin, Merle. "'Contrariety' Is McCarthy Prose Theme." CHRISTIAN SCIENCE MONITOR [Eastern Ed.] 77, no.151 (June 27, 1985): 23-24.
   Views this collection as ongoing testimony to McCarthy's keen intelligence and a style that beautifully conveys deeply felt emotions and ideas. Focuses on her history of contrariness, which Rubin sees as a direct result of her dialectical approach; a way of thinking largely attributed to McCarthy's "contrary" childhood.

1576. S., C. WEST COAST REVIEW OF BOOKS 11 (July 1985): 35.
   Calls this collection minor writings of a great essayist. Recommends them for the intellectual reader.

1577. Jackson, Marni. CHATELAINE 58, no.8 (August 1985): 4.
   Enjoys McCarthy's responsive and intelligent commentary on a wide variety of topics.

1578. Meyers, Jeffrey. "Mistress of Paradox." NATIONAL REVIEW 37, no.17 (September 6, 1985): 55-56.
   Introduces McCarthy as the American Rebecca West, since both writers address a wide range of topics with clarity, intelligence, irreverence and commitment. Feels that similar to a number of other contemporary American novelists, McCarthy's strength lies in her nonfiction. Notes the shrewd insights contained in most of the essays, but seems disappointed in what he perceives to be the mellowing of an "eminence grise."

1579. Sage, Lorna. "In Defence of Common Sense." OBSERVER (London, G.B.) (September 22, 1985): 26.
   Examines McCarthy's favored vantage point, the author imbued with "common sense," the faculty of understanding the world we all have in common. Focuses on the balancing act she must constantly practice in order to reconcile this quality with the lack of reality in the world.

1580. Wood, Michael. "Warring with Words." TIMES (London, G.B.)
[Sunday Ed.] (October 13, 1985): 45.
    Reflects on how there are few actual writers left in Britain
although some still exist in the United States. Suggests that
Sontag, Didion, and Vidal are among those capable of moving
easily from one mode of writing to another and claims that
McCarthy is one of the most distinguished in this sense. Finds
OCCASIONAL PROSE exemplary of McCarthy's talent as a
writer.

1581. Fallowell, Duncan. "A Sentimental Intellectual." SPECTATOR
255, no.8206 (October 19, 1985): 31-32.
    States at the outset that some of this is unreadable. Believes
McCarthy possesses many of the attributes necessary for a
successful essayist, but she is often merely pedestrian. Suggests
that both style and content are marred by a rigidity born of a
bureaucratic mind. Feels she allows a freshness and
sentimentality to emerge in the obituaries and in an essay on
collections of art, elevating them above the rest.

1582. Gordon, Mary. "When Beauty Is Truth, Truth Beauty."
ESQUIRE 104, no.5 (November 1985): 249, 251.
    Believes the self-assurance of McCarthy is based on intellect
and the power to attract. Admires her for clearly differentiating
between high and pop culture and for her love of excellence
which coexists with her love of justice. Feels her ability to move
back and forth between the realms of ideas and things, and the
abstract and the concrete, gives her writing an elegance and
clarity not often found in modern thought.

1583. Johnson, Diane. "American Readings." TIMES LITERARY
SUPPLEMENT (January 31, 1986): 111.
    Introduces McCarthy as a visible and influential figure of
American letters who recently received one of its most
prestigious awards, the National Medal for Literature. Points out
that this accolade has seldom been bestowed on a writer of
satire, an intellectual, or a woman. States that part of her
enjoyment of this collection stems from McCarthy's own obvious
pleasure in definition and analysis.

1584. Williams, Larry. WESTERN HUMANITIES REVIEW 40, no.2
(Summer 1986): 181-183.
    Traces his personal response to her work over the years.
Notes he was originally captivated by a younger McCarthy's
honesty and courage, but later disappointed in what he perceived
to be a misapplication of her talent in several of her novels.
Concedes that she continues to think clearly and write well but
contends that her attitudes have "congealed" into standard left
wing liberalism.

1585. Brown, John L. WORLD LITERATURE TODAY 60, no.1
(Winter 1986): 115-116.
    Finds that time has mellowed McCarthy's acid tongue and
pitiless intelligence.

HOW I GREW

1586. KIRKUS REVIEWS 55, no.255 (March 1, 1987): 355.
    Notes that this is a refreshingly candid autobiography by a
still feisty McCarthy. Says that her "alternative interpretations"
of the stories involve the reader by revealing the workings of an
original mind in the act of remembering. Concludes this is a
dazzling memoir by one of America's major talents.

   *   "Adult Nonfiction." BOOKLIST 83, no.13 (March 1, 1987):
949.
    See item no. 968.

1587. Stuttaford, Genevieve. PUBLISHERS WEEKLY 231, no.9
(March 6, 1987): 98-99.
    Claims the book depicts universal experiences and will
appeal to admirers of MEMORIES OF A CATHOLIC
GIRLHOOD.

* Bloom, Lynn Z. "Mary McCarthy Remembers, Settles Old Scores." ST. LOUIS POST-DISPATCH (Mo.) (March 29, 1987): F5.
    See item no. 969.

1588. Caldwell, Gail. "The Growing Pains of a Contrary Mary." BOSTON GLOBE [Sunday Ed.] (March 29, 1987): A11.
    Observes the book covers McCarthy's intellectual progression and not the emotional history of MEMORIES OF A CATHOLIC GIRLHOOD. Attributes her lack of "gilded resonance" to the thirty years between the two books, noting that time may have led McCarthy to a "quieter agenda." Contends the book is a brilliantly eccentric backward glance from less tempestuous times at "bluestocking" roots.

1589. Mackey, Mary. "The Budding of an Intellectual." SAN FRANCISCO CHRONICLE. REVIEW (April 5, 1987): 1, 10.
    Declares that McCarthy has been so blatantly honest about her miserable childhood, four husbands and minor passions, that she only had this longitudinal study of the unfolding of her mind left to tell. Credits her for abandoning her usual "sparse crisp style for a slow discursive mind of her own memories" and for using the style to involve the reader in her discoveries. Praises her for being too good a writer to continue unswervingly with any style which isn't working and concludes the book gets better as it goes along.

* Tyler, Anne. "The Sentimental Education of Mary McCarthy." BOOK WORLD (WASHINGTON POST) 17, no.14 (April 5, 1987): 7.
    See item no. 970.

1590. Lehmann-Haupt, Christopher. "Books of the Times." NEW YORK TIMES (April 13, 1987): C16.
    Comments that McCarthy reports facts but does little to explain anything. Maintains that the facts are often beguiling because of her "basilisk vision" and "supple symmetrical prose." Compares the book to Tolstoy's DEATH OF IVAN ILYICH in which a man is dying from a mysterious unidentified pain and

suggests that a milder form of pain overshadows HOW I GREW but McCarthy never even tries to look at it.

1591. Ives, Nancy R. LIBRARY JOURNAL 112, no.7 (April 15, 1987): 85.

Calls this a fascinating account from an important American writer.

1592. Sheed, Wilfrid. "Her Youth Observed." NEW YORK TIMES BOOK REVIEW 92 (April 19, 1987): 5-6.

Reviews the McCarthy/Hellman case and suggests that HOW I GREW is McCarthy's answer to the question that started the feud--What is Truth? Continues that McCarthy's passion for strict truth combined with her "scars" from the feud weigh too heavily on the beginning of the book. Elaborates that McCarthy's confessional writing leads her to recite as many youthful lies as she can; lies which leave an exasperating curtain between herself and what she is trying to remember. Suggests that HOW I GREW and MEMORIES OF A CATHOLIC GIRLHOOD are geniune artwork as original as any of her fiction.

Also published in NEW YORK TIMES BIOGRAPHICAL SERVICE 18 (April 1987): 340-342.

1593. Koenig, Rhoda. "Girls Will Be Girls." NEW YORK 20 (April 20, 1987): 81-82.

Argues that MEMORIES OF A CATHOLIC GIRLHOOD is superior to HOW I GREW because McCarthy told all her best stories the first time around. Adds that most of HOW I GREW is a reading list or a series of fragmentary "I wonder what happened to him" recollections. Explains the book can be seen as a winding up of McCarthy's clock of wit and suggests that in future volumes we can look forward to hearing that clock strike.

1594. Gray, Paul. "Mary, Mary." TIME 129, no.17 (April 27, 1987): 82.

Considers that despite the smugness of the title, a lack of information and the self-congratulatory veneer, the book is worth some effort because of its considerable poignancy and appeal, enlivened by McCarthy's remarkable memory for scattered detail.

1595. Medwick, Cathleen. "The Private Dancer." VOGUE 177 (May 1987): 196.
    Contends the book is a too honest memoir by an author whose intent was to come to terms with herself as a "critical spirit." Says there is little elation in the book and that, in itself, is revealing.

1596. Dudar, Helen. "Growing Pains." CHICAGO TRIBUNE [Sunday Ed.] (May 3, 1987): sec. 14, 6.
    Stresses that this is a painfully disapproving book full of insignificant details and digressions. Contends it does not live up to the graceful prose and supple discipline of MEMORIES OF A CATHOLIC GIRLHOOD. Provides an excerpt from the book.

1597. Eder, Richard. LOS ANGELES TIMES (May 10, 1987): B3-B4.
    Denies McCarthy is an autobiographer by nature. Stresses that readers are interested in the quality of a writer's remembrances not the minute particulars. Notes that although the details and anecdotes remain coldly undigested and untransformed, they are warmed somewhat by McCarthy's intelligence. Evaluates the book as something written out of a sense of duty redeemed only by the opportunity it provides to watch an endowed mind and courageous spirit at work.

1598. Wolcott, James. "Nose Jobs." NEW REPUBLIC 196, no.19 (May 11, 1987): 34-37.
    Maintains the book is a series of small punctures, petty beyond belief, written by "a hostess who masks her hauteur with a smile set in cool marble as she passes around amusing anecdotes on a snack tray." Adds that McCarthy is a bit too coy, directly addressing the reader and beginning paragraphs with "pithy comments and quaint ejaculations." Admonishes her for unsympathetic portrayals and being "too damned retroussé."

1599. Adams, Phoebe. "Brief Reviews." ATLANTIC 259, no.6 (June 1987): 82.

  Reports that this stimulating memoir "crackles with provocative opinions stated with brisk elegance."

1600. Lott, Clarinda Harriss. "Mary McCarthy's Icy Coming of Age." WASHINGTON TIMES. BOOKS MAGAZINE (June 1, 1987): M5.

  Proposes that the graphic description of how McCarthy lost her virginity has not seen a more "asphyxiatingly dull" counterpart since Plath's THE BELL JAR. States that this cold, relentlessly detailed autobiography treats intimacy clinically, making her perception appear damaged. Examines the book's shortcomings: McCarthy's questioning rather than stating her feelings; her systematic meanness towards the men and women in the book; and her "curiously masculinized" language.

1601. Lurie, Alison. "True Confessions." NEW YORK REVIEW OF BOOKS 34, no.10 (June 11, 1987): 19-20.

  Reveals McCarthy's own belief, quoted in a recent interview, that she "had not the slightest effect on the public behavior." Disagrees with McCarthy and says that not only has she altered public perception of what a woman of letters can be, she has also helped to free women from the belief that they could only grow up to be happy housewives or dignified spinsters. Continues that McCarthy's achievement was to invent herself as a "totally new type of woman who stood for both sense and sensibility; who was both coolly and professionally intellectual and frankly passionate." Stresses that the book is more discursive and rambling than MEMORIES OF A CATHOLIC GIRLHOOD.

1602. Rifkind, Donna. AMERICAN SPECTATOR 20 (July 1987): 36-37.

  Suggests that McCarthy regards her youth as a laboratory specimen--"curiously, poking at it a little, watching it ooze and then wiping her hands briskly and walking away." Decides the self-revealing writing is uncharacteristically dull, lacking the mocking humor and wit of her previous books. Believes the reader never becomes engaged in the emotional side of

McCarthy's life because she herself fails to be. Concludes that "when McCarthy is bad, she is very very good; but when she is good, she is boring."

1603. Stevens, Elisabeth. "The Way She Was." WOMEN'S REVIEW OF BOOKS 4, no.10-11 (July 1987): 29-30.
    Assesses the book as a gossipy, sometimes garrulous retelling of school days and sexual experiences. Believes McCarthy's depictions of her lovers, classmates, teachers and relations are diminished by the sense that her entire cast of characters exist only as a foil for her own experiences. Compares the book to Jewett's THE COUNTRY OF THE POINTED FIRS, pointing out that the latter exemplifies the imaginative empathy McCarthy sorely lacks.

1604. Slater, Joyce. "Mary McCarthy and How She Grew." ATLANTA JOURNAL-CONSTITUTION (July 26, 1987): J12.
    Says the book leads one to conclude that the teenaged McCarthy was a disagreeable, opinionated brat. Calls it a cold unsympathetic book by a writer who concedes that she is as impossible as we think she is.

1605. Fordham, Henrietta. "Hardback Previews." PUBLISHING NEWS (London, G.B.) (August 21, 1987): 12.
    Comments that McCarthy has enlivened an historical account with "informal essays in education, politics and literature."

1606. Carey, Daniel. "'McCarthy' an Imperfect Self-portrait." TIMES-PICAYUNE (New Orleans, La.) (August 23, 1987): F7.
    Describes the first sixty pages as approximating ONE WRITER'S BEGINNINGS without the Welty charm. Notes that as her memory begins to serve, McCarthy attaches ideas to anecdotes and challenges the reader to think. Summarizes that despite some pretension, she redeems herself by being relentlessly thoughtful and honest.

1607. Knapp, Bettina L. "Memoirs." WORLD LITERATURE TODAY, no.61 (Autumn 1987): 634.
    Declares that McCarthy's overly cerebral tone and failure or inability to question and search out her feelings mar the book.

Suggests that, had she explored the disturbing stereotypical images of Jews in more depth, she might have added more substance to her autobiography instead of sentencing it to the list of chatty Americana.

1608. "Out Now." BOOKS (September 1987): 27.
Summarizes the book.

1609. Schaffner, Perdita. "High Achiever Holds Back." NEW DIRECTIONS FOR WOMEN 16, no.5 (September-October 1987): 16.
Emphasizes that McCarthy digresses into literary and philosophical byways to escape explanations. Commends the fascinating range of the book but concludes it is distracting, unsatisfactory and lacking in lightness and spontaneity.

1610. Williams, Mary Ann. SCHOOL LIBRARY JOURNAL 34 (September 1987): 208-209.
Says the book has three qualities unusual in the genre: intellectual stimulation, wit and forgiveness. Recommends it to young adults who may be encouraged to compare their own intellectual growth with the author's.

1611. Waugh, Auberon. "No, I Tell a Lie, It Was Wednesday." INDEPENDENT (London, G.B.) (September 12, 1987).
Sees McCarthy as egotistical and self-indulgent and believes these vices stem from the acclamation bestowed upon writers in America. Claims that such acclaim turns male writers into "bores" and gives female writers "a sublime sense of their own importance." Goes so far as to suggest that McCarthy's cruel Uncle Myers was not so wrong when he beat her with a razor strop to keep her from getting stuck-up after winning an essay contest.

1612. Dinnage, Rosemary. "Casting a Cold Eye." TIMES LITERARY SUPPLEMENT, no.4407 (September 18-24, 1987): 1022.
Proposes that MEMORIES OF A CATHOLIC GIRLHOOD was a success not only because it concentrated on the dramatic events of childhood but also because the New Yorker chapters were enjoyably literary. Adds that in HOW I GREW, McCarthy

does not separate literature from commentary but deliberately plays with memory as she writes. Maintains that the book lacks the emotion required to properly portray intellectual growth.

1613. Sigal, Clancy. "A Cold Eye On Myself: Clancy Sigal on Mary McCarthy's Autobiography." GUARDIAN (G.B.) (September 18, 1987): 14.
    Expresses disappointment with this bloodless memoir given McCarthy's controlled, focused and aggressively spearlike talent. Questions her lack of feeling and emotion but maintains she is too fine a writer for this to really explain the book's disconnectedness. Suggests that her dislocated childhood has finally overwhelmed her and she is too proud to treat herself with any more mercy than she has shown her fictional characters.

    Also published in: GUARDIAN AND GUARDIAN WEEKLY 137 (October 4, 1987): 21.

1614. Lively, Penelope. "Bolshoy Mary." DAILY TELEGRAPH (London, G.B.) (September 19, 1987).
    Has nothing but praise for this "rich generous" book. Believes that McCarthy "was not so much a natural rebel as a natural questioner...."

1615. Carey, John. "The Company She Kept." TIMES (London, G.B.) [Sunday Ed.] (September 20, 1987): 57.
    Discusses the book in terms of McCarthy's ability to recall and accept her past. Concludes that although attention to detail is one of her great gifts, her memory lapses remind us all "how we invent our past."

1616. Drabble, Margaret. "Black Holes in Time." OBSERVER (London, G.B.) (September 20, 1987): 28.
    Suggests that the rehashing of stories McCarthy has already told in books and essays may be an attempt to satisfy her own "need to know" about her past. Questions whether or not her superb recollections are in fact accurate. Asserts that there is a simple indivisible truth which cannot be altered by multiple uses

and abuses; even though the truth cannot entirely be known, it does exist.

1617. Mount, Ferdinand. "Romance of an Orphan." TELEGRAPH (G.B.) [Sunday Ed.] (September 20, 1987): 16.

Traces McCarthy's life and notes how the account of her early childhood makes it clear that she understands the "dramatic potential of orphanhood" and that "being an orphan is not all it is cracked up to be."

1618. Edmonds, Richard. "Memories from Quite a Contrary Mary..." BIRMINGHAM POST (G.B.) (September 24, 1987).

Suggests that it might be interesting to reread THE GROUP after reading HOW I GREW, in order to identify the characters. Says that "we have grown to expect a lively and perceptive narrative from this gifted writer and there are no disappointments."

1619. Tucker, Eva. "Mary, Quite Contrary." LONDON EVENING STANDARD (G.B.) (September 24, 1987).

Believes that her failed marriages account for McCarthy's conviction that friendship is the essential ingredient to "the intellectual growth hormone." Notes that, like many other atheists, once McCarthy lost her faith, she became obsessed with truth.

1620. Billington, Rachel. "Seattle to Vassar." FINANCIAL TIMES (London, G.B.) (September 26, 1987).

Summarizes the book, focusing on McCarthy's descriptions of her cruel guardians, the loss of her virginity and her affair with Johnsrud. Argues that instead of a dull chronology of her life, she offers an essay in "self-discovery."

1621. Brookner, Anita. "The Making of a Member of THE GROUP." SPECTATOR (September 26, 1987): 28-29.

Emphasizes that the reader will need MEMORIES OF A CATHOLIC GIRLHOOD to make sense of this noble effort. Provides a synopsis of the book. Concludes it is somewhat lifeless and more sparse than MEMORIES OF A CATHOLIC

GIRLHOOD, but together they form a considerable addition to the archives of the times.

1622. Chisholm, Anne. "More Moisture Needed." LITERARY REVIEW (G.B.) (October 1987): 16-17.
    Says that most of McCarthy's novels have been, to some extent, autobiographical due to her interest in "the sources of fiction and the processes of memory and creativity." Concludes that the book is "full of riches, both moving and subtle," for those readers who have long appreciated her humor and consistent, fierce moral intelligence.

1623. De Vere White, Terence. "Anything Goes." IRISH TIMES (Ireland) (October 3, 1987).
    Comments that "this book read like a tape-recording of someone clearing out an old cupboard." Says that although McCarthy claims that truth is all important, there is little evidence of truth in this autobiography.

1624. Davies, Clive. "Once Upon a Times in America..." YORKSHIRE POST (Leeds, G.B.) (October 15, 1987).
    Notes that the book is an account of a woman's "intellectual and emotional development" and not a "classic autobiography."

1625. Bayley, John. "Other Selves." LONDON REVIEW OF BOOKS 9 (October 29, 1987): 19.
    Discusses how writers use themselves better in their novels and stories than they do in autobiographies. Says the book leaves the reader cold because it lacks the "zing" and energy of illusions that was so evident in McCarthy's other books. Considers she is writing for two kinds of readers: the very young who remember what it is she is talking about, and the elderly who will be thrilled to hear the "sacred monster" reminisce. Draws comparisons between HOW I GREW and Stewart's MYSELF AND MICHAEL INNES and reflects that Stewart gives the reader his view of how things grow while McCarthy brushes irony aside. Concludes HOW I GREW is a flat book, written out of habit and lacking in relish, intensity and surprise.

*   M., J. "Books Encountered." ENCOUNTER 69, no.4
(November 1987): 63.
     See item no. 972.

1626. McFadden, Grania. "Bookshelf." BELFAST TELEGRAPH
(U.K.) (November 9, 1987).
     Calls this a "lively and perceptive narrative."

1627. Mansbridge, Alison. "Lapsed Catholic." TIME OUT (London,
G.B.) (November 11, 1987).
     Notes that despite a tendency to didacticism, McCarthy's use
of the technique of new style autobiography is successful.

1628. Laski, Marghanita. "Me! Me! Me!" COUNTRY LIFE (London,
G.B.) (November 26, 1987).
     Argues that this book is insincere and full of half-truths.
Points out that McCarthy is not important enough for the minute
details of her life to be of interest.

1629. Barnes, Hugh, Jack McLean, and Christopher Small. "Critics
Choice." GLASGOW HERALD (G.B.) (November 28, 1987).
     Comments range from McLean's "it is a bitter sweet tale,
splendidly written," to Barnes' comment that "it is an unusual
and unusually honest book," to Small's note that "it offers a
pretty bleak picture."

1630. Lillie, Helen. "Mary McCarthy Looks Back in Style."
GLASGOW HERALD (G.B.) (December 16, 1987): 9.
     Suggests that McCarthy's brilliance and mental curiosity
gave her an "intellectual and social insecurity...which she
covered up...with the acidulous wit that made her, in the words
of Katherine Anne Porter: 'In some ways the worst-tempered
woman in American letters.'" Argues that in reading the
reminiscences of another's life, we recall our own and that this
factor makes such autobiographical books popular. Concludes
that although McCarthy has written about this time in her life
before, it is worth reading again.

1631. Lawson, Sarah. "Catholic Girlhood." NEW HUMANIST (G.B.) (March 1988): 34.

Argues that McCarthy's themes, time and memory, suggest immediacy and the inevitable uncertainty of one's memories which urge the reader to focus on and participate in her life. Points out some errors in the text that McCarthy may have found "galling" and concludes that this book is complementary to MEMORIES OF A CATHOLIC GIRLHOOD.

1632. Johnson, George. "New & Noteworthy." NEW YORK TIMES BOOK REVIEW 93 (June 26, 1988): 46.

Asserts that her feud with Hellman about dishonesty fuels McCarthy's intense confessional writing. Regrets the price paid is that the "laser beam never goes off."

1633. Rudikoff, Sonya. "An American Woman of Letters." HUDSON REVIEW 42, no.1 (Spring 1989): 45-55.

Reviews Gelderman's biography, MARY MCCARTHY: A LIFE and McCarthy's autobiography, HOW I GREW. Criticizes Gelderman for not putting enough distance between herself and her subject to write an objective book, and claims that she fails to explore and report McCarthy's profound influence on the literary scene. Argues that McCarthy's own book suffers greatly from the lack of an aggressive editor who would have blue-pencilled the inappropriate comments, "wilfull and silly discussions of private schools and the ignorant, inept analysis of class, culture and education..."

1634. "Paperbacks." OBSERVER (London, G.B.) (June 25, 1989): 45.
Observes the book is brilliant often enough to be worthwhile.

*   Honigmann, David. "Paperbacks." LISTENER 122, no.3128 (August 31, 1989): 28.
See item no. 973.

1635. Koning, Christina. "New Paperbacks." GUARDIAN WEEKLY (G.B.) 141, no.11 (September 17, 1989): 28.

Criticizes the book's redundancy with MEMORIES OF A CATHOLIC GIRLHOOD, but states that it is nonetheless a good story.

Theses

1636. Collins, Verna A. "Mary McCarthy: Critic with a 'Cold Eye'."
Master's thesis, Columbia University, 1965. 81 p.
Examines McCarthy's views about women in relation to the
female characters in her books. Observes that her belief that a
novel should deal with fact and reality is supported by her
frequent use of autobiographical material.

1637. Rock, Mary H. "Mary McCarthy As a Social Critic in Her
Fiction." Master's thesis, East Tennessee State University, 1965.
52 p.
Attempts to clarify McCarthy's fictional criticisms of society.
Evaluates specifically her critical views of: the teaching
profession and how teachers are forced to conform to the
educational system in THE GROVES OF ACADEME and "The
Vassar Girl"; college students and their susceptibility to influence
in THE GROVES OF ACADEME and THE GROUP; and
marital relationships in "The Weeds," THE OASIS, A
CHARMED LIFE, and THE GROUP.

1638. Schutter, Howard Nelson. "Academic Freedom and the
American College Novel of the Nineteen Fifties." Ed.D. diss.,
University of Michigan, 1966. 217 p.
Focuses on how McCarthy, Sarton, Barr and Morrison have
treated the problem of academic freedom and the effect it has
had on their novels as works of art. Examines THE GROVES
OF ACADEME on several levels: as a problem of a

377

teacher-rascal who is taking advantage of a politically liberal
college to further his own gains; as a picture of the differences in
a particular aspect of human behavior; as an illustration of
physical repulsiveness and domestic ugliness; as a satire; and as
the subtle illustration of human antagonisms and acceptances.
Concludes that McCarthy's book is cold and sophisticated but
fails to live up to the standards of a work of art.

1639. Shinn, Thelma J. Wardrop. "A Study of Women Characters in
Contemporary American Fiction 1940-1970." Ph.D. diss.,
Purdue University, 1972. Not seen.

1640. Gohlman, Susan Carol Ashley. "The Modern Bildungsroman:
Four Novels." Ph.D. diss., University of Michigan, 1973. 201p.
    Discusses the literary genre of "Bildungsroman," the process
of dealing with one's early life and development. Describes
BIRDS OF AMERICA as McCarthy's effort to use several types
of literary genres--Bildungsroman, the novel of education, the
novel of development and the novel of adventure--to portray a
time when precise social and personal values were accessible to
those who sought them. Traces the character of Peter through
these stages, quoting extensively from the book.

1641. Hoerchner, Susan Jane. "'I Have to Keep the Two Things
Separate'; Polarity in Women in the Contemporary American
Novel." Ph.D. diss., Emory University, 1973. 225 p.
    Proposes that "a major current of American thought and art
has portrayed women in terms of a sexual versus social polarity"
and that authors tend to fall into two categories depending on
whether they believe that biology or society controls women's
lives. Argues that the most interesting female characters are
those who "do not fit either stereotypical role"; notes however
that there may be conflict between roles as illustrated by Martha,
who "loses her life when she decides to terminate her
pregnancy."

1642. Adams, Timothy Dow. "Autobiographical Boundaries: The
Contemporary American Mock-Autobiography." Ph.D. diss.,
Emory University, 1979. 227 p.
    Studies five writers who have each written a hybrid type of

autobiography--mock-autobiography--which combines elements from traditional, fictional and autobiographical genres. Examines MEMORIES OF A CATHOLIC GIRLHOOD as a parody of an autobiography and discusses how McCarthy substitutes a non-heroic figure for the famous person at the center of the book.

1643. Crossley, Brian Miles. "The Last Frontier: Self-Destruction in Contemporary American Fiction. A Study of Literary Techniques." Ph.D. diss., State University of New York, 1981. 395 p.

Analyzes the literary techniques used in portraying the schizophrenic mind and a psyche obsessed with self-destruction in McCarthy's THE GROUP, Plath's THE BELL JAR, Green's I NEVER PROMISED YOU A ROSE GARDEN and Didion's PLAY IT AS IT LAYS. States the use of myth has an underlying part to play, reinforcing as the symbolic and timeless dimension of madness. Considers THE GROUP and THE BELL JAR in relation to myth, symbol and ritual journeys from innocence to experience.

1644. McDonald, Susan Sias Waugh. "Writing and Identity: Autobiographies of American Women Novelists." Ph.D diss., St. Louis University, 1981. 430 p.

Examines MEMORIES OF A CATHOLIC GIRLHOOD, and eleven other autobiographies written between 1930 and 1955, to illustrate women's expanding awareness and the scale used to analyze both the personal life and writing life of the authors. Discusses autobiography and identity, the nature of history and its relationship to identity, historical context, overall design and intent, portrayal of childhood, early maturity and old age, and the writer's own perception of life choices and literary accomplishments.

1645. Levy, Helen Fiddyment. "No Hiding Place on Earth: The Female Self in Eight Modern American Women Authors." Ph.D diss., University of Michigan, 1982. 509 p.

Examines the socio-literary background of the work of eight modern American women authors. Reports that McCarthy tests the boundaries between nonfiction and fiction, revealing an awareness that she must first gain credibility by insisting her account is based on fact. Observes her life parallels the common structure of American women's fiction and notes she breaks away from the literary pack into the role of gender-neutral reporter in THE SEVENTEENTH DEGREE, arriving at a level where she can find no way to bring her social vision to material reality.

1646. Nerney, Brian James. "Katharine S. White, NEW YORKER Editor: Her Influence on the NEW YORKER and on American Literature." Ph.D. diss., University of Minnesota, 1982. 278 p.
      Uses corroboration from McCarthy in an examination of White's influence on the American literary scene.

1647. Welch, Kathleen Ethel. "A Mirror Both Scientific and Poetic: Rhetoric and History in English and American Autobiography." Ph.D. diss., University of Iowa, 1982. 179 p.
      Uses MEMORIES OF A CATHOLIC GIRLHOOD, Mill's AUTOBIOGRAPHY and Franklin's AUTOBIOGRAPHY to examine the writing strategies of various "literary autobiographies." Credits McCarthy for being one of the most imaginative writers to use the "all revealing anecdote" and maintains her reflective commentaries bring the real but elusive relationship between autobiography and history, and autobiography and fiction into focus.

1648. Parrish, Richard Dale. "Style in Lillian Hellman's PENTIMENTO: The Rhetoric of Elusiveness." Ed.D diss., East Texas State University, 1985. 117 p.
      Identifies the modern fictional techniques that characterize Hellman's style. Considers the contradictory nature of information concerning Hellman's life and explores the controversy surrounding her lawsuit against McCarthy. Argues that Hellman creatively distorts time and place and fuses the past and the present, and that it is this attempt to create a second narrative self, and not deliberate deception, that results in the "elusiveness" of her work.

1649. Lansford, Ingrid Gimm. "Rise and Fall of the Artist Aristocrat in the American Novel." Ph.D. diss., University of Texas at Austin, 1988. 270 p.

Chronicles the role of the artist in twentieth century American fiction. Draws on a number of works from this period including McCarthy's A CHARMED LIFE, in an attempt to demonstrate a more realistic concept of the artist as "Everyman" with family and community responsibilities. Concludes that Freud's theories are responsible for most of the fictional characters in the 1940s and after.

1650. Heidt, Edward R. "Narrative Voice in Autobiographical Writing." Ph.D diss., University of Southern California, 1989.

Examines how McCarthy and other authors use autobiographical comment to express acts and states of consciousness unique to the author.

Biographies

BOOKS

MARY McCARTHY (1966)

1651. McKenzie, Barbara. MARY MCCARTHY. New York: Twayne Publishers, 1966. 191 p.

Provides a thorough examination of McCarthy's published works ending with her two travelogues, THE STONES OF FLORENCE and VENICE OBSERVED. States that this study is an attempt to "find the key that works the fiction and essays of McCarthy...[as she] is a very personal writer in a very public way."

THE COMPANY SHE KEPT

1652. Grumbach, Doris. THE COMPANY SHE KEPT. London: Bodley Head, 1967; New York: Coward-McCann, 1967. 218 p.

Expresses impatience with what has been written about McCarthy, stating that the critics have misunderstood her intent and accomplishments. Emphasizes the fresh approach she takes in this biography, which examines McCarthy's life and work to discover the common thread between fact and fiction.

1653. Jones, Frank N. LIBRARY JOURNAL 92, no.7 (April 1, 1967): 1492.

    States briefly that Grumbach's academic style may alienate some readers who have enjoyed, or have been shocked by McCarthy.

1654. McDonnell, Thomas P. AMERICA 116 (May 27, 1967): 791-792.

    Praises Grumbach's fascinating portrait of a strong minded McCarthy. Notes that she fails to examine McCarthy's religious beliefs or political conscience.

1655. Ellmann, Mary. "Mary, Mary." BOOK WEEK (CHICAGO SUN TIMES) (May 28, 1967): 3.

    Examines Grumbach's claim that one must know the facts of McCarthy's life before they can know the fiction. Claims Grumbach's evaluations are ambiguous because the characters in McCarthy's books do not always match their supposed counterparts. Finds fault with Grumbach's critical analysis.

1656. Hicks, Granville. "Orations with Figures." SATURDAY REVIEW 50 (June 3, 1967): 25-26.

    Applauds Grumbach for not beating around the bush when dealing with the subject of who is who in McCarthy's fiction. Discusses her evaluation that the female characters in McCarthy's stories are so superior that they strive to excel at everything including self-criticism. Concludes that Grumbach is an academic who has failed to recognize McCarthy as essentially a moralist and critic who aspires to the best and manages to suggest it in her work.

1657. Henahan, Donal J. "Literary Sleuthing, Artistic Detachment." PHILADELPHIA INQUIRER (June 11, 1967): 7.

    Evaluates the biography as a demonstration of McCarthy's fiction as an all but perfect parody of her career. Believes that Grumbach's graceless writing and shallowness as a critic of McCarthy's fiction undermines any lasting value the book may have had, reducing it to literary chit-chat.

1658. Moers, Ellen. "Fictions and Facts." NEW YORK TIMES BOOK REVIEW (June 11, 1967): 7.

Suggests that Grumbach's claim that there are counterparts to McCarthy's fictional characters is suspect because the husbands, artist colonies and political situations are so devoid of talent or distinction that only a powerful imagination could find any link between them and the interesting company that McCarthy actually kept. Concludes that other than offering a sympathetic reading of McCarthy's work, Grumbach fails to treat her very seriously.

1659. "The Gripe." TIME 89 (June 30, 1967): 76.

Says the galley proofs for the biography so enraged McCarthy that they were approved only after numerous deletions and revisions. Comments that McCarthy is still furious over Grumbach's contention that the characters in THE GROUP are based on people McCarthy knew at Vassar. Points out that Grumbach fails to explore McCarthy's talent or wit and concludes the biography is an overblown, not particularly clever, literary bio-critique.

1660. Maddocks, Melvin. "A Lady and Her Silk Blackjack." CHRISTIAN SCIENCE MONITOR [Eastern Ed.] (July 13, 1967): 7.

Notes that only a female critic could have done McCarthy justice because a man may have been too cowardly to take on McCarthy unarmed, or judged her "masculine" qualities of unsparing honesty, intellect and wit as ill advised. Comments that despite Grumbach's overemphasis on trivia and persistent backtracking to corroborate McCarthy's tastes and style, she is a fearless biographer and critic.

1661. BOOKLIST 63, no.21 (July 15, 1967): 1176.

Comments briefly that Grumbach may not go beyond surface probing but she does manage to stimulate the desire to read or reread McCarthy.

1662. Casey, Geneviev M. BEST SELLERS 27, no.9 (August 1, 1967): 179-180.
   Dismisses Grumbach's dissection of McCarthy's personal life to explain her fiction.

1663. VIRGINIA QUARTERLY REVIEW 43, no.4 (Autumn 1967): clxi, clxiv.
   Says Grumbach's critical approach is based on the idea that one must examine the facts behind the fiction to understand the writer. Says that her analyses of McCarthy's stories reveal "everywoman" characters who are frail and easily wounded, and not, as one might expect, strong, heartless over-intellectuals.

1664. Richler, Mordecai. "Mr. & Mrs. Wilson." GUARDIAN (Manchester, G.B.) (September 15, 1967): 5.
   Reviews this book along with A PRELUDE: LANDSCAPES, CHARACTERS AND CONVERSATIONS FROM THE EARLIER YEARS OF MY LIFE, written by McCarthy's ex-husband Wilson. Writes that the trivialities presented by Grumbach may make for juicy dinner conversation but don't really enlighten the reader as to what makes McCarthy tick.

1665. Harrington, Stephanie. COMMONWEAL 87, no.1 (October 6, 1967): 35-38.
   Discusses McCarthy's charge that Grumbach was indiscrete. Says the book is filled with clichés and might have been written by a parody of the Warren Coe character in A CHARMED LIFE. Examines THE GROUP quoting from Mailer. See also Grumbach's article (item no. 398) and Mailer's review (item no. 1129).

1666. "Brief Reviews." CRITIC 26, no.2 (October-November 1967): 88-89.
   Notes that Grumbach is guilty of a few misreadings and of overestimating the importance of her subject.

1667. Mac Namara, Desmond. "Nin et Al." NEW STATESMAN 74, no.1916 (December 1, 1967): 778-779.
   Evaluates the biography as a stimulating guide to McCarthy's

"roman à clef," likely to titillate her admirers as well as those who regret she did not graduate from a Catholic girlhood to an "enclosed convent."

1668. Martin, Augustine. "The McCarthy Phenomenon." IRISH PRESS (Ireland) (December 2, 1967): 12.

Observes that McCarthy lacks the generosity necessary to be a great writer. Criticizes Grumbach for playing "spot the prototype" by trying to identify specific characters in McCarthy's books. Calls McCarthy a superior journalist who has an "unerring sense of sociological relevance that is so easily mistaken for literary genius."

1669. "Mr. Wilson's Diaries." TIMES LITERARY SUPPLEMENT, no.3432 (December 7, 1967): 1184.

Points out that McCarthy has an instinct for creation through autobiography, drawing, as Grumbach suggests, a faint line between the people she knows and the characters in her books. Observes that Grumbach's failure to adequately explain the complex interactions necessary to such a process reduces the book to gossip.

MARY McCARTHY: A BIBLIOGRAPHY

1670. Goldman, Sherli Evens. MARY MCCARTHY: A BIBLIOGRAPHY. New York: Harcourt, Brace & Co., 1968. 80p.

Presents an exhaustive bibliography of works by McCarthy to 1968. Cites every appearance in print of McCarthy's work and provides complete descriptive cataloguing for each entry. Provides that all citations are verified and reprint information is included as required. Includes a title and name index.

1671. Bone, Larry Earl. LIBRARY JOURNAL 93, no.2 (June 15, 1968): 2468.

Remarks that this specialized bibliography would make an interesting addition to a large literary collection.

1672. AMERICAN LITERATURE 40, no.4 (January 1969): 596.
      Describes this "sturdy" bibliography very briefly.

1673. CHOICE 5, no.11 (January 1969): 1426.
      Questions the validity of a bibliography on a relatively young
      author. Recommends the book for graduate and research
      libraries.

MARY McCARTHY (1968)

1674. Stock, Irvin. MARY MCCARTHY. University of Minnesota
      Pamphlets on American Writers, no.72. Minneapolis: Univ. of
      Minnesota Press, 1968. 45 p.
      Argues that the predominant theme in all her work is "the
      search for truth, and the human defects that hinder it."

      Also published with revisions in:
      Unger, Leonard, ed. AMERICAN WRITERS: A COLLECTION
      OF LITERARY BIOGRAPHIES. Vol.2. 558-584. New York:
      Charles Scribner's Sons, 1974.

      Howard, Maureen, ed. SEVEN AMERICAN WOMEN
      WRITERS OF THE TWENTIETH CENTURY: AN
      INTRODUCTION. 214-264. Minnesota: Univ. of Minnesota
      Press, 1977.

1675. "Notes on Current Books." VIRGINIA QUARTERLY REVIEW
      45, no.1 (Winter 1969): xxii.
      Notes that Stock's critique of McCarthy focuses mainly on
      her fiction and autobiographical works.

MARY McCARTHY (1981)

1676. Hardy, Willene Schaefer. MARY MCCARTHY. New York:
      Ungar, 1981. 214 p.
      Provides an in-depth analysis of McCarthy's works including

her two travelogues, her essays on the war and American politics and her fiction. Concludes that although her novels rank among the best of our time, only two, THE GROVES OF ACADEME and THE OASIS, will be established as classics.

1677. D., D. P. BOOKLIST 78, no.5 (November 1, 1981): 365.
    Considers this to be a "nice balanced description and evaluation of McCarthy's work."

1678. McBride, Mary. LIBRARY JOURNAL 107, no.4 (February 15, 1982): 459.
    Refers to the biography as a "concise and balanced introduction" to McCarthy's work and credits Hardy with having refrained from offering a definitive opinion of McCarthy's contribution to the literary scene.

1679. Davis-Langdell, Cheri. JOURNAL OF AMERICAN STUDIES (Norwich, G.B.) 17, no.2 (August 1983): 278.
    Criticizes the fact that McCarthy's powerful political books such as THE MASK OF STATE are not dealt with effectively and that there is no mention of the flamboyant McCarthy/Hellman feud. Maintains this biography doesn't capture any of McCarthy's wit and intellectual vigor and is really for individuals who want to "taste the flavour of McCarthy's works without having to read them."

MARY McCARTHY: A LIFE

1680. Gelderman, Carol. MARY MCCARTHY: A LIFE. New York: St. Martin's Press, 1988. 430 p.
    Provides an exhaustively researched biography written with the cooperation of McCarthy herself, who consented to interviews, arranged introductions to friends and provided access to correspondence. Acknowledges the strong relationship between McCarthy's life and her work, but declares that one of her primary aims was to explore the discrepancy between the public image and the private person.

1681. R., D. H. WEST COAST REVIEW OF BOOKS 14, no.1
(1988): 43-44.
      Reflects on the oddity of writing a biography of McCarthy
while she is very much alive and still producing her own
autobiographical works. Comments, as an obvious fan of
McCarthy, that Gelderman's detailing of McCarthy's life is a
momentous achievement.

1682. PUBLISHERS WEEKLY 233, no.7 (February 19, 1988): 66.
      Points out that interviews with McCarthy and many of her
contemporaries, as well as access to previously unavailable
correspondence, makes this the first comprehensive biography of
her.

1683. Mackey, Mary. "The Bright Wild Girl from Seattle." SAN
FRANCISCO CHRONICLE. REVIEW (February 28, 1988): 1,
10.
      Offers a mixed review of this first full scale biography of
McCarthy. Acknowledges Gelderman's distinct disadvantage in
having to compete with McCarthy's autobiographical writing,
and notes she only comes into her own in the period after 1933
when McCarthy's own autobiographies stop. Finds Gelderman at
times perceptive, at others seemingly mired in lists and
documentation in lieu of analysis.

1684. KIRKUS REVIEWS 56 (March 1, 1988): 340-341.
      Concedes that Gelderman has all the facts, but argues that
the lack of analysis and failure to present any new interpretations
of McCarthy's life and work, results in a dull book.

1685. Waldron, Ann. "Plums from Mary's Cake." LOS ANGELES
TIMES (March 27, 1988): B6.
      States that much of the factual information in Gelderman's
book has been presented before, both in McCarthy's own
memoirs and the fairly recent biography by Grumbach. Believes,
nonetheless, that McCarthy's accomplishments merit further
study and calls Gelderman's well crafted, sound biography most
interesting.

1686. Drew, Bettina. LIBRARY JOURNAL 113, no.6 (April 1, 1988): 85-86.
    Says that this book, while dutifully and thoroughly documented, lacks animation and feeling.

1687. O., R. BOOKLIST 84, no.15 (April 1, 1988): 1305.
    Describes the book as friendly but critical, finding Gelderman's assessment of McCarthy's writing genuinely sound and balanced.

1688. "Random Notes." NATIONAL REVIEW 40, no.6 (April 1, 1988): 48.
    Notes that this first comprehensive biography of McCarthy is objectively written and interesting.

1689. Mitgang, Herbert. "High Tea in Maine." NEW YORK TIMES BOOK REVIEW (May 8, 1988): 46.
    Decides that Gelderman's biography is a "well-balanced and enjoyable account of a remarkable American life." Offers the inside story on how Gelderman obtained permission from McCarthy to do the biography.

1690. Towers, Robert. "The Company They Kept." NEW YORK TIMES BOOK REVIEW (May 8, 1988): 1, 46.
    Describes the book as a well researched, well balanced account of a remarkable life. Comments on its modest, low-key approach, suggesting that Gelderman's aim appears to be a retelling of McCarthy's life in straight chronological order. Notes Gelderman's avoidance of psychological analysis as well as her preference to be referee rather than critic of McCarthy's work.

1691. Simon, John. "Mary McCarthy and The Company She Kept." BOOK WORLD (WASHINGTON POST) 18, no.21 (May 22, 1988): 1, 8.
    Introduces this lively review with clear reservations both about the writing of biographies of living people in general, and the writing of this one in particular. Calls on his experience as a film and drama critic to evaluate the book as thorough but

undistinguished without the style and sophistication McCarthy merits.

1692. Bonner, Thomas, Jr. "Inside THE GROUP Mentality."
TIMES-PICAYUNE (New Orleans, La.) (May 29, 1988): E5.
Calls MARY McCARTHY: A LIFE an even-handed, often compelling account. Notes Gelderman's technique of linking incidents in McCarthy's life with her work is, for the most part, successful.

1693. Green, Laura. "Mary McCarthy Foundering in a Sea of Detail."
CHICAGO TRIBUNE. BOOKS [Sunday Ed.] (June 5, 1988): 5.
Deplores Gelderman's refusal to pass judgment and place McCarthy in a broader context as writer and critic. Calls the book a strange mixture of trivia, information and insight; a chronicle rather than a critical biography.

1694. Hildebrand, Holly. "Mary McCarthy Wasn't One to Shy Away from Telling It All." HOUSTON POST (Tex.) (June 5, 1988): 12.
Presents an overview of McCarthy's life, focusing on her absolute candor, a trait that at times hurt both others and herself. Refers to Gelderman's book as well researched and evenhanded.

1695. Crain, Jane Larkin. "What Becomes a Legend Least."
NATIONAL REVIEW 40, no.11 (June 10, 1988): 49-51.
Introduces a joint review of Rollyson's biography of Hellman and Gelderman's biography on McCarthy with a summary of their well published feud. Contends that McCarthy's literary accomplishments were overshadowed by her political stupidity, and states that Gelderman has captured McCarthy's life and work with almost novelistic amplitude and elegant critical precision.

1696. Smelstor, Marjorie. "Books." USA TODAY 117, no.2518 (July 1988): 95-96.
Calls the book a study of both McCarthy's truth-seeking intellectualism and her colorful private life. Points out that Gelderman's book emulates McCarthy's life in its honoring of the particular, while at the same time coherently synthesizing details.

1697. Rubin, Merle. "Celebrity Biographies That Balance Truthfulness and Tact." CHRISTIAN SCIENCE MONITOR [Eastern Ed.] 80, no.164 (July 20, 1988): 17-18.
Comments on some of the particular problems inherent in the writing of celebrity biographies. Reviews a biography of Hellman alongside McCarthy's, and sums up the Gelderman book as well researched and fair minded.

1698. Stuewe, Paul. "Carver Selected . . . Capote Redeemed . . . McCarthy Examined . . ." QUILL & QUIRE 54, no.8 (August 1988): 28.
Deems Gelderman's balanced portrait of McCarthy an effective treatment of an interesting literary career.

1699. Bemrose, John, Darlene James, and Michael Coren. "Salacious Peeks into Writers' Lives." MACLEAN'S MAGAZINE 101, no.37 (September 5, 1988): 65-66.
Reviews a selection of recently published literary biographies. Calls Gelderman's book a sympathetic exploration of a turbulent life that reveals the origins and cost of McCarthy's uncompromising stance.

1700. Allen, Bruce. SMITHSONIAN 19, no.9 (December 1988): 211-212.
Praises Gelderman's superb biographical style and notes the book is full of fresh material and perceptive insights. Finds Gelderman at times curiously non-judgmental and overly reticent in her portrayal of McCarthy as the "satirist and scourge."

1701. BOOKS (January 1989): 20.
Calls the book thorough and scholarly, noting that Gelderman has added a new dimension of gentleness and complexity to the usual portrayal of her controversial subject.

1702. Philips, Robert. "'There Is Properly No History; Only Biography!'" AMERICA 160, no.1 (January 7, 1989): 14, 16-19.
Discusses a number of biographical works, including MARY McCARTHY: A LIFE. Finds the book sympathetic, balanced,

and sufficiently enticing to make him want to reread and
reevaluate McCarthy.

1703. Bailey, Paula. "McCarthy Trial: Insufficient Evidence." TIMES
(London, G.B.) [Sunday Ed.] (March 26, 1989): G3.
    Questions whether McCarthy really authorized the writing of
this biography and wonders why such a graceless writer was
entrusted with writing about such a graceful writer. Believes the
best parts of Gelderman's book are written by Arendt, Wilson,
Hardwick and, most notably, McCarthy herself.

  * Rudikoff, Sonya. "An American Woman of Letters." HUDSON
REVIEW 42, no.1 (Spring 1989): 45-55.
    See item no. 1633.

1704. Spender, Stephen. "The McCarthy Era." OBSERVER (London,
G.B.) (April 2, 1989): 44.
    Summarizes Gelderman's biography, noting that McCarthy's
passion for truth shines throughout.

1705. Spalding, Frances. "Outward Mobility." LISTENER 121,
no.3108 (April 6, 1989): 31.
    Finds the McCarthy story is absorbing but notes that
Gelderman's brisk and efficient biography is disappointing
because it fails to analyze.

1706. Diski, Jenny. "The Visible Life of Mary McCarthy." NEW
STATESMAN & SOCIETY 2, no.44 (April 7, 1989): 38-39.
    Notes the dissonance between McCarthy's life and work, and
the slippage between what is said and what is done, however
finds Gelderman's analysis unengaging and unexceptional.

1707. Annan, Gabriele. "Orphan Mary Is Always in Trouble."
SPECTATOR 262, no.8387 (April 8, 1989): 31-32.
    Considers Gelderman an invaluable guide to the alignments
of the American intelligentsia and McCarthy's lifelong search for
the truth. Notes that her lively style balances her insistence on
including absolutely everything, and her obvious growing
affection for her subject hooks both herself and the reader.

1708. Blandford, Linda. "That Gleaming Young Girl." GUARDIAN WEEKLY (G.B.) 140, no.17 (April 23, 1989): 28.
    Declares that although Gelderman faithfully and exhaustively catalogues the external McCarthy, she fails to capture her spirit.

1709. Jackson, Kevin. "Smart and Sexy." PUNCH 296 (April 28, 1989): 49.
    Faults Gelderman for her lack of critical engagement as well as pure mindedness to the point of perversity. Finds her industriously researched book has managed to make McCarthy's life, a gift to any biographer, bland and bloodless.

1710. Chisholm, Anne. "Questions of Judgment." TIMES LITERARY SUPPLEMENT, no.4498 (June 16-22, 1989): 672.
    Compares reading Gelderman's biography of McCarthy to "watching a minnow in pursuit of a barracuda." Stresses Gelderman's apparent nervousness in writing about her formidable subject results in a bland, chatty account. Concludes that McCarthy deserves a more rigorous, politically astute biographer.

WRITING DANGEROUSLY: A CRITICAL BIOGRAPHY OF MARY McCARTHY

1711. Brightman, Carol. WRITING DANGEROUSLY: A CRITICAL BIOGRAPHY OF MARY McCARTHY. New York: [Crown Publishing Group], [1992].
    Expected date of publication is Fall 1992.

BIOGRAPHICAL SOURCES

1712. Candee, Marjorie Dent, ed. CURRENT BIOGRAPHY YEARBOOK 1955, 378-379. New York: H.W. Wilson, 1955.

1713. Kunitz, Stanley J., and Vineta Colby, eds. TWENTIETH
      CENTURY AUTHORS: A BIOGRAPHICAL DICTIONARY
      OF MODERN LITERATURE. 608-609. 1st. suppl. New York:
      H.W. Wilson, 1955.

1714. MODERN AMERICAN LITERATURE, compiled and edited by
      Dorothy Nyren, 303-305. New York: Frederick Ungar Pub.,
      1960.

      Also published in: Curley, Dorothy, Maurice Kramer, and
      Elaine Fialka Kramer, eds. MODERN AMERICAN
      LITERATURE. 4th enl. ed. 241-246. New York: Frederick
      Ungar Pub., 1969.

1715. Gerstenberger, Donna, and George Hendrick. AMERICAN
      NOVEL: A CHECKLIST OF TWENTIETH-CENTURY
      CRITICISM, 240-241. Vol. I: 1789-1959. Denver: Alan
      Swallow, 1961.

1716. Burke, William Jeremiah, and Will D. Howe. "Mary
      McCarthy." In AMERICAN AUTHORS AND BOOKS: 1640
      TO THE PRESENT DAY. rev. ed., rev. and augmented by
      Irving R. Weiss, 478. New York: Crown Publishers, 1962.

      Also published with updates in: Burke, W.J. & Will D. Howe.
      AMERICAN AUTHORS AND BOOKS: 1640 TO THE
      PRESENT DAY, revised by Irving R. and Anne Weiss. 3rd rev.
      ed. New York: Crown Publishers, 1972.

1717. Herzberg, Max J., ed. THE READER'S ENCYCLOPEDIA OF
      AMERICAN LITERATURE. 667-668. New York: Thomas Y.
      Crowell, 1962.

      Also published in: THE READER'S ENCYCLOPEDIA OF
      AMERICAN LITERATURE. London: Methuen, 1963 and in
      Benet, William Rose, ed. READER'S ENCYCLOPEDIA OF
      AMERICAN LITERATURE. 2d ed. 611-612. New York:
      Thomas Y. Crowell, 1965.

1718. Rigdon, Walter, ed. BIOGRAPHICAL ENCYCLOPAEDIA & WHO'S WHO OF THE AMERICAN THEATRE. 663. New York: J.H. Heineman, c1965.

1719. Walker, Warren S. TWENTIETH-CENTURY SHORT STORY EXPLICATION: INTERPRETATIONS 1900-1975 OF SHORT FICTION SINCE 1800. 2nd ed., 445. Hamden, Conn.: Shoe String Press, 1967.

Also published in: 3rd ed. 482-483. Hamden, Conn.: Shoe String Press, 1977; Supplement II to Third ed. 193. Hamden, Conn.: Shoe String Press, 1984; Supplement III to Third ed. 253. Hamden, Conn.: Shoe String Press, 1987; and Supplement IV to Third ed. 176. Hamden, Conn.: Shoe String Press, 1989.

1720. Harte, Barbara, and Carolyn Riley, eds. CONTEMPORARY AUTHORS. Vol.5-8, 1st. rev. 749-751. Detroit: Gale Research, 1969.

Also published in: CONTEMPORARY AUTHORS. New Revision series, Vol. 16. Detroit: Gale Research, 1986.

1721. Richardson, Kenneth, ed. TWENTIETH CENTURY WRITING; A READERS'S GUIDE TO CONTEMPORARY LITERATURE. 387-388. London: Newnes Books, 1969.

Also published in: TWENTIETH CENTURY WRITING; A READERS'S GUIDE TO CONTEMPORARY LITERATURE. Amer ed. Levittown, N.Y.: Transatlantic Arts, 1971.

1722. Schlueter, Paul. "Mary McCarthy." In ENCYCLOPEDIA OF WORLD LITERATURE IN 20th CENTURY, edited by Bernard Wolfgang Fleischmann, 401-402. Vol. 2. New York: F. Ungar Pub., 1969.

1723. Nevius, Blake comp. THE AMERICAN NOVEL: SINCLAIR
      LEWIS TO THE PRESENT, 71. Goldentree Bibliographies in
      Language and Literature. New York: Appleton-Century-Crofts;
      Northbrook, Ill.: AHM Pub., 1970.

1724. Moritz, Charles, ed. CURRENT BIOGRAPHY YEARBOOK
      1969. 270-272. New York: H.W. Wilson, 1970.

1725. Ward, A.C., ed. LONGMAN COMPANION TO TWENTIETH
      CENTURY LITERATURE. 331-332. Harlow, England:
      Longman, 1970.

      Also published in: LONGMAN COMPANION TO
      TWENTIETH CENTURY LITERATURE. 2nd ed. 332.
      London: Harlow, 1975 and LONGMAN COMPANION TO
      TWENTIETH CENTURY LITERATURE. 3rd ed. 331-332.
      London: Harlow, 1981.

1726. THE AUTHOR'S AND WRITER'S WHO'S WHO. 6th ed.,
      513. London: Burke's Perrage Ltd., 1971.

1727. Bradbury, Malcolm, Eric Mottram, and Jean Franco, eds. THE
      PENGUIN COMPANION TO AMERICAN LITERATURE.
      162. New York: McGraw-Hill, 1971.

1728. Adelman, Irving, and Rita Dworkin. CONTEMPORARY
      NOVEL: A CHECKLIST OF CRITICAL LITERATURE ON
      THE BRITISH AND AMERICAN NOVEL SINCE 1945,
      329-331. Metuchen, N.J.: Scarecrow Press, 1972.

1729. Moore, Harry T. "Mary McCarthy." In CONTEMPORARY
      NOVELISTS, edited by James Vinson, 932-935. New York: St.
      Martin's Press, 1972.

      Also published in: Vinson, James and D.L. Kirkpatrick, eds.
      CONTEMPORARY NOVELISTS. 2nd ed. New York: St.
      Martin's Press, 1976.

1730. Steinberg, S. H., ed. CASSELL'S ENCYCLOPAEDIA OF WORLD LITERATURE, rev. and enl. in 3 vols. by J. Buchanan-Brown, 87. New York: William Morrow & Co.; London: Cassell & Co., c1973.

1731. W., R. "Mary McCarthy." In WEBSTER'S NEW WORLD COMPANION TO ENGLISH AND AMERICAN LITERATURE, edited by Arthur Pollard, 424. New York: World Publishing, 1973.

1732. Pownall, David E. ARTICLES ON TWENTIETH CENTURY LITERATURE: AN ANNOTATED BIBLIOGRAPHY 1954-1970, 2411-2414. Vol. 5. New York: Kraus-Thomson Organization Ltd., 1976.

1733. Rosa, Alfred F., and Paul A. Eschholz. CONTEMPORARY FICTION IN AMERICA AND ENGLAND 1950-1970: A GUIDE TO INFORMATION SOURCES, 219-220. Detroit: Gale Research, 1976.

1734. A DIRECTORY OF AMERICAN FICTION WRITERS, 14. New York: Poet & Writers, 1976.

1735. Kay, Ernest, ed. INTERNATIONAL AUTHORS AND WRITERS WHO'S WHO. 7th ed. 641. Cambridge, England: Melrose Press, 1976.

Also published in: INTERNATIONAL AUTHORS AND WRITERS WHO'S WHO. 8th ed. Cambridge, England: International Biographical Centre, 1977.

1736. NOTABLE NAMES IN THE AMERICAN THEATRE. new and rev. ed., 966. Clifton, N.J.: James T. White & Co., 1976.

1737. Lichtenstein, Nelson, ed. POLITICAL PROFILES: THE JOHNSON YEARS. 372-373. Vol. 4. New York: Facts on File, 1976.

1738. THE WRITERS DIRECTORY 1976-78, 705. New York: St.
      Martin's Press, 1976.

      Also published in: WRITERS DIRECTORY 1980-82. 824. New
      York: St. Martin's Press, 1979.

1739. Seidel, Alison P., comp. In LITERARY CRITICISM AND
      AUTHORS' BIOGRAPHIES: AN ANNOTATED INDEX, 115.
      Metuchen, N.J.: Scarecrow Press, 1978.

1740. Magill, Frank N., Hanson, Stephen L., and Patricia King
      Hanson, eds. MAGILL'S BIBLIOGRAPHY OF LITERARY
      CRITICISM: SELECTED SOURCES FOR THE STUDY OF
      MORE THAN 2,500 OUTSTANDING WORKS OF WESTERN
      LITERATURE. 1247-1251. Englewood Cliffs, N.J.: Salem
      Press, 1979.

1741. Nordland, Brady. 20TH CENTURY AMERICAN
      LITERATURE, 379-381. New York: St. Martin's, 1980.

1742. Hardy, Willene Schaefer. "Mary McCarthy." In AMERICAN
      WOMEN WRITERS, edited by Lina Mainiero, 65-69. Vol. 3.
      New York: F. Ungar Pub., 1981.

1743. McNeil, Helen. "Mary McCarthy." In MAKERS OF MODERN
      CULTURE, edited by Justin Wintle, 323-324. New York: Facts
      on File; London: Routledge & Kegan Paul, 1981.

1744. Weixlman, Joe. "Mary McCarthy." In AMERICAN
      SHORT-FICTION CRITICISM & SCHOLARSHIP 1959-1977:
      A CHECKLIST, 374-375. Chicago: Swallow Press, 1982.

1745. Hart, James David. OXFORD COMPANION TO AMERICAN
      LITERATURE. 5th ed., 454-455. New York: Oxford University
      Press, 1983.

1746. THE INTERNATIONAL WHO'S WHO 1983-84. 47th ed., 845.
      London: Europa Pub., 1983.

1747. Blackwell, Earl. "Mary McCarthy." In THE CELEBRITY
REGISTER 1990, compiled by Celebrity Service International,
285. New York: Gale Research, 1990.

Obituaries

1748. Folkart, Burt A. "Mary McCarthy, 77, Novelist Noted for Feisty Style, Dies." LOS ANGELES TIMES (October 26, 1989): A3, A36.

   Observes that McCarthy battled the intellectual elite and questioned the value of history and the worth of the novel. Says she believed women should learn to think and act for themselves. Notes that in 1987, when she was asked for a self-assessment, she replied, "not favorable."

1749. Kakutani, Michiko. "Mary McCarthy, 77, Is Dead; Novelist, Memoirist and Critic." NEW YORK TIMES (October 26, 1989): A1, B10.

   Says her novels were idiosyncratic chronicles of American life as well as thinly disguised exercises in autobiography. Reports she admitted she found fiction more difficult to write than essays or reviews and confessed that each of her novels was the result of willed creation.

   Also published as "Leading U.S. Novelist Mary McCarthy Dies" in: VANCOUVER SUN (October 26, 1989): C4. (condensed)

1750. "McCarthy Wrote Novel THE GROUP." GAZETTE (Montreal, Que.) (October 26, 1989): C15.

   Traces her career and comments that McCarthy was one of America's pre-eminent literary figures.

403

1751. "Scathing, Witty Novelist McCarthy Dies at 77." WINNIPEG
      FREE PRESS (Winnipeg, Manitoba) (October 26, 1989): 53.
           Chronicles her life and literary career with quotes from
      Mailer, Merrill and Kazin

1752. "The Contrarian [Editorial]." NEW YORK TIMES (October 27,
      1989): 34.
           Says McCarthy was the most vivid presence of the New
      York literary subculture and was known in those circles as the
      "Dark Lady of American letters." Notes that she refused to be
      fazed by tradition or authority, choosing to walk her own path
      often to the dismay of classmates, friends and spouses.

1753. "Décès de la romancière Mary McCarthy." FIGARO (October
      27, 1989): 32. French.
           Announces McCarthy's death and provides a brief summary
      of her literary career.

1754. "Mary McCarthy: Lioness of the American Literary Scene."
      TIMES (London, G.B.) (October 27, 1989): 18.
           Discusses McCarthy's background and literary career. Says
      she has etched herself into the memory of the public
      consciousness.

1755. Zand, Nicole. "La mort de Mary McCarthy." LE MONDE
      (October 27, 1989): 1, B22. French.
           Recalls her as an intelligent witness of her times who
      explored politics, feminism and sexual liberty. Chronicles her
      personal life and literary career.

1756. Seymour-Smith, Martin. "A Class Chronicler." TIMES (London,
      G.B.) [Sunday Ed.] (October 29, 1989): G7.
           Remembers McCarthy as a formidable personality with a
      ferocious intelligence who was more interested in ideas than
      people. Concludes that a few of her books will be remembered if
      only for their shrewd observations.

1757. Duffy, Martha. "She Knew What She Wanted: Mary McCarthy,
      1912-1989." TIME 134 (November 6, 1989): 87.
           Says despite the fact she was incorrigibly modern, McCarthy

used a manual typewriter, avoided electric kitchen gadgets, never had a credit card, and considered herself old-fashioned. Observes she paved the way for generations of young women by ignoring the constraints of gender. Quotes from her keynote speech at the MacDowell Colony in 1984.

1758. "Mary, Mary Quite Contrary." U.S. NEWS & WORLD REPORT 107, no.18 (November 6, 1989): 16.
Reports that when Hellman was near death, two words could raise her to wide-awake fury--Mary McCarthy. Says McCarthy applied her uncompromising attitude, classic refinement and proclivity towards modernity to her own writing.

1759. McGuigan, Cathleen. "Company She Kept: Mary McCarthy 1912-1989." NEWSWEEK 114 (November 6, 1989): 91.
Says McCarthy created the persona of a moralistic biting satirist, as famous for her feuds and love affairs as she was for her intelligence and wit.

1760. Dunning, Jennifer. "In Friends' Words and Her Own, Mary McCarthy Is Remembered." NEW YORK TIMES (November 9, 1989): D27.
Reports that 200 people attended the memorial service for McCarthy at the Pierpont Morgan Library. Quotes Hardwick and Schlesinger.

1761. Wadler, Joyce. "Coolheaded but Fiercely Outspoken, Mary McCarthy Never Backed Down from a Fight." PEOPLE WEEKLY 32 (November 13, 1989): 75-76.
Remembers McCarthy as a writer who had so many battles going that she kept a file marked "controversy." Provides a summary of her personal life and literary career.

1762. "Mary McCarthy, RIP." NATIONAL REVIEW 41, no.22 (November 24, 1989): 14-15.
Contends intellectuals write better nonfiction than fiction. Suggests McCarthy's books were tellingly close to her life because she lacked the ability to relax her sense of self. Discusses her books briefly, noting that her intelligence must have taken a time out when she wrote HANOI.

1763. "Mary McCarthy." In CURRENT BIOGRAPHY YEARBOOK 1990, 657. New York: H.W. Wilson, 1990.
     Summarizes her career.

1764. Daniels, Anthony. "McCarthy and Her Friends." NATIONAL REVIEW 42 (February 5, 1990): 24, 26.
     Notes that he was in Saigon when he heard of McCarthy's death. Discusses his experiences and the differences that exist between life there now and life the way McCarthy predicted it would be in HANOI.

1765. Schlesinger, Arthur, Jr. "Mary McCarthy: 1912-1989." PARTISAN REVIEW 57, no.1 (Winter 1990): 14-15.
     Acknowledges McCarthy's generosity in offering constructive criticism of his book CRISIS OF THE OLD ORDER. Remembers her as a close personal friend who triumphed over trouble by the sheer force of her strong will, intelligence, courage and joyous instinct for life.

Author Index

The Author Index includes the names of all authors, editors, compilers and translators of all cited works. Bold faced item numbers in the index indicate that the item appears in the first section--**Works By McCarthy**.

Named Person/Title Index

The Named Person/Title Index includes major references to individuals, books, journal titles, films and plays. It should be noted that it is the actual article that has been indexed and not the abstract; therefore names and titles listed in the index, although an indicator of significance in the original article, do not necessarily appear in the abstract. Short stories have not been indexed. Bold faced item numbers in the index indicate that the item appears in the first section--**Works By McCarthy**.